Atlantis in America

Navigators of the Ancient World

Ivar Zapp & George Erikson

Adventures Unlimited Press • 1998

Design and typography by Jim Cook/Santa Barbara

Published by Adventures Unlimited Press, One Adventure Place, Kempton, Illinois 60946.

ISBN 0-932813-52-6

Acknowledgments

First of all, I thank all the authors who wrote interesting books that helped me understand the world in a more ample and profound way than I was taught during my "schooling." Many of these authors are listed in the bibliography.

Among my friends who gave me encouragement and support I would like to name Edgar Brenes Montealegre, Humberto Carro, Luis Diego Gomes, Alfonso Chase, Cristina Rojas, Sergio Salas, Ricardo Vilches, and Guadalupe Avila who has encouraged me during the last twelve years. I'd like to thank the University of Costa Rica School of Architecture in whose classrooms some of the concepts in this book were born.

I especially want to thank the Polynesian people who have saved ancient "know how" of astronomy and navigation from the ravages of time and for the benefit of mankind.

—IVAR ZAPP

San Jose, Costa Rica, January 1998

Foremost, I'd like to thank my sister, Lois Shearer, who has shepherded this work through every stage of its development; Jacque La Tourette for initiating contact between Ivar and myself; David Dahl, who has honed this work into a finished manuscript; David Hatcher Childress for fashioning it into final book form; and Noel Young, whose long-time friendship, advice and expertise have eased the pangs of its creation.

Further thanks go to: Jim Cook, James Owen, Brad Johnson, Frederick Usher, John and Susan Daniel, Richard de Mille, and the late Harriet Topsey. Special and unending thanks go to Anne Erikson for her patience and support, and to Sandra Erikson for sharing the excitement of "discovery" when we initially undertook the adventure that would result in this book.

—GEORGE ERIKSON

Santa Barbara, March 1998

I dedicate this book to the memory of my dear brother,
who shared with me all he had.

Holger Zapp

This book is dedicated to the memory of a beloved brother
who, if he had had time and health enough,
might have written this work in my stead.

Buzz Erikson (1939-1985)

Contents

Introduction

What truly is our past? "Antiquity is full of the
praises of another Antiquity still more remote."
—VOLTAIRE

What truly is our future?
"A crack in the teacup opens a lane to the land of the dead."
—W. H. AUDEN

I N 1947, when Thor Heyerdahl led an expedition aboard a primitive
balsa raft, the *Kon-Tiki*, across over 4,000 miles of the Pacific and to
successful landfall in Polynesia, science dismissed him as a lucky
adventurer. In 1970 when Heyerdahl successfully navigated the *Ra II*, a bundle-reed raft, from Africa to the Americas, archaeologists pronounced his theory of man's migration by sea as "junk science," and described his achievement as one man's bravery against incredible odds. But neither the *Kon-Tiki*
nor the *Ra* expeditions were based on man's defiance of the seas. They were
based on defiance of scientific dogma and on the concept that man was a
marine migrator, willing and able to take to the sea on sturdy rafts. One of
Heyerdahl's sea ventures began in the Americas; the other culminated there.
Both journeys, as well as hundreds of solo ventures by sailboats, rafts and virtual bathtubs that soon followed, were facilitated by the steady push of the
great ocean currents of the Atlantic and the Pacific—currents that almost
meet at the slender heart of the Americas.

In 1979 when Ivar Zapp first realized that the great stone spheres of the
Diquis Delta in southern Costa Rica were the work and the record of ancient
navigators, several compelling questions occurred to him: Who were the people that built them? Was Central America the site if not the center of an

ancient sea-faring civilization? If so, how has knowledge of this civilization been lost to known records?

Plato wrote of Atlantis as a great island-continent, a center of ancient knowledge, with a navigational base at its capital city. The Americas form a great island-continent with an ancient navigational base at its center. Plato also wrote of a Golden Age wherein myth and knowledge of the heavens were recreated in ordered city-states on a peaceful Earth. The sphere-builders constructed an orderly, even precise, depiction of the heavens. Were they descendants of Atlantis? If so, how did these people relate to the nearby Olmecs and to the ancient Maya? Unlike the Europeans that "discovered" them, the Maya were able to construct great city-states that existed for centuries *without walls*, without defensive fortifications, and with interconnecting roads and canals that beckoned visitors from other cities, and other continents. The keen vision of the Mayan priests, looking through an unpolluted atmosphere, allowed them to view the heavens in three dimensions, a wonderful event that only sailors of the mid-Pacific can now experience. Were they the keepers of the knowledge of the Golden Age—an age of peace and mutual understanding? Did the sphere-builders and the Mayan astronomers once interact with the peoples of other great megalithic sites, among them the builders of Cuzco in Peru, Stonehenge in England, and the Great Pyramids of Egypt? This work will provide an approach to answering these questions.

Who are we? What were our ancestors like? When did man achieve mastery of his environment and how did he spread his dominance throughout this world? How did he relate his recent existence to the greater cosmos? These essential questions of who we have been, and why we are what we are have long been answered by myth and by the oral traditions of many peoples of many diverse lands. By their telling, man was not insignificant—he was an essential player in the record of the universe. But since Aristotle, our Eurocentric world's tradition of categories and materialistic science has absolutely rejected any explanations or answers provided by myth, with its animism, fabulous tales, and recountings of great cataclysms. While the tales and legends that myths have provided have been discredited by our written history, that history itself is deeply flawed, stained by its repeated attempts to justify military and religious conquerors who burned libraries and usurped the real history of past empires.

Outside of questionable written records, conventional history has had only glimpses to go by—moments of insight into the long, most often lost, record of mankind. Yet, motivated by a belief in Darwinian gradualism, twentieth-century historians and archaeologists alike have, for the most part, agreed on a single model, a defining paradigm, for the emergence of "civilized" man.

This paradigm depicts man as a land migrator, a wanderer over cold, bleak, and desolate expanses, a hunter seeking game while struggling against great adversities, until, after many travails, he happened upon the fertile river valleys that provided his every want. Only then, according to this linear and simplistic model, did this fearful descendant of an aggressive ape become more than a mere survivor following a "territorial imperative." In these river valleys he discovered agriculture, which delivered bountiful food and a sedentary life.

This, in turn, encouraged division of labor and inspired a system of cooperation under which man quickly prospered. He grew in wisdom and skills, and, in short order, he founded great cities, and civilization itself. This paradigm has held sway in our leading academic institutions, been taught to the masses, and universally accepted as unquestionable fact.

Prevailing theorists have even claimed to have found the exact location for the onset of civilization in an area the Greeks called Mesopotamia, a land that lay between the Tigris and Euphrates rivers, and that geographically framed the early temple builders of Sumer. History has likewise settled on certain dates, the seventh millennium B.C. for cultivation of wheat and barley, and the fourth millennium B.C. for the full-flung rise of civilized cities. According to the current model of civilization's inception, written records, astronomy, and temple-building, all suddenly arose in this area where agriculture and stability first emerged. Kingdoms, city-states, and empires soon evolved. Ancient Egypt and the civilizations of the Minoans, Greece, and Rome all followed in stately linear progression. So we have been told.

Did it really happen that way? Just as Plato spoke of a Golden Age, legends and myth throughout the world have likewise long spoken of an era of peace and harmony, and of great discoveries by navigation and celestial observations. Our modern view has separated myth from science and history, seeing them as contradictory forces. However, in books carefully recorded by the ancient Egyptians, and in numbers devised by the ancient Maya, early man has told us a far different story. In Egypt, priests spoke of a great land to the west as both the birthplace and as the final destination of man. Even in the records of Sumer, deemed the "cradle of civilization," similar myths had placed the origin of man's great knowledge, and imposing accomplishments, at a far earlier age and in a place across a vast sea.

In the sixteenth century A.D., as if in confirmation of these myths, Spaniards encountered a civilization—carved in stone—that portrayed knowledge similar to that described by the ancients of Sumer and of Egypt. A record of temple building, hieroglyphics and astronomy, together with similar means of agriculture to those found in the river valleys of Mesopotamia and

Egypt, were all discovered to have arisen in an unexpected place—Mesoamerica.

To many minds the stories of myth were revived by these startling discoveries. Christopher Columbus even suggested that he may have discovered the original garden of Eden. The Church of Rome recoiled at the notion. State authorities and historians of the Age of Reason, who had long dismissed myth as a conduit of knowledge, similarly dismissed the Americas as a site of significant ancient civilization. But did not the discovery of so vast and sophisticated an empire at America's heart require the rational sciences to at least consider these civilizations as an important link in man's cultural history? The Catholic Church and conventional science both answered that essential question in the negative.

In the sixteenth century the Church of the Inquisition decreed that the peoples of the Americas were too primitive. Their city-states were judged more recent than Jesus Christ and the civilization of the Mediterranean that had preceded him. In the twentieth century American archaeology echoed that edict by declaring that "the ancient Maya emerged from barbarism during the first or second century of the Christian Era." They were judged too recent and too pagan to have played a significant role in the development of world-wide civilization.

In fact, the constructions of ancient American cultures not only had similar means of design in their star temples to those found in the Middle East (figs. I1, I2), they had *earlier* devised a mathematics superior to any other in the world. However, while admitting these advanced civilizations were remarkable and surely older than some cities in Europe, historians soon pronounced that their constructions were not the equal of ancient sites in Egypt or Mesopotamia. Experts assured the Eurocentric world that the American city-states had not been occasioned by a long period of development, but had somehow spontaneously sprung from a more primitive people, dubbed "inspired savages" by historians. The possibility that the advanced cultures of the "Old World" and "New World" could have been interrelated was dismissed as "impossible" and "preposterous."

Quashing all speculation that the step-pyramid builders of the Americas could have been related to the ancient Middle East, archaeologists pronounced that construction of even the crudest temples in the Americas had not begun until *after* pyramid building had ceased in Egypt, Sumer, and in Sumer's recipient cultures of Babylonia and Akkad.

These simplistic declarations have been proven false. Only in the last few decades of this century have we realized that known Maya sites are much older than previously thought, reaching back over 4,000 years at Cuello in

I.1. Reconstruction of the Temple of Marduk in Babylon, Mesopotamia, 600 B.C.

I.2. Reconstruction of the Piedras Negras site (conservatively dated 300 B.C.) on the Usumacinta River, which now forms the border between Mexico and Guatemala. The concept of zero was known to the builders of the ziggurats in Sumer and Babylon as well as to the builders of Mayan temples. But numbers in excess of a million continued to confuse western European thought until the nineteenth century.

Although the similarities of design and construction between the step-pyramids of the newly discovered American sites and the oldest known Mesopotamian sites were immediately evident to early investigators, the 16th-century Church quickly found proofs that they could not be related.

Belize, or recognized that the Olmecs were building pyramids and great stone megaliths for thousands of years before the Classic Maya built their cities. Discovery after discovery has revealed that the accepted dates for civilization in the Americas *are very wrong*. At Chan Chan, in Peru, Chavin culture, instead of sudden emergence, displays a continual line of development of a naval culture that dates back over 8,000 years. Pedra Furada, in Brazil, is now known to have supported a diverse culture over 12,000 years ago. Monte Verde, in Chile, is at least that old and may have supported a navigational culture *32,000 years ago!*

Without a doubt civilizations in the Americas go back further than established dates for Mesopotamia or Egypt. Eight thousand year old mummies in Peru predate identically embalmed Egyptian mummies by three thousand years. Residue of wholly American tobacco and cocaine recently discovered in 5,000-year-old mummies in Egypt and in the Sudan establish evidence of contact between the "Old" and "New World" thousands of years before Christ. The appearance of genetically American cotton in Asia 10,000 years ago, and evidence of coconuts, sweet potatoes, and the American parrot in the Pacific and in Asia 12,000 years ago all confirm a repeated worldwide contact of cultures that could only have been accomplished *by navigation.*

The great megalithic structures of the Americas—the spheres of Costa Rica, the great wall of Sacsahuaman in Peru, and the observatory at Kalasasaya near Tiahuanacu in Bolivia—defy the dates assigned to the "origins" of civilization by our contemporary model. By significant example the relatively new science of archaeoastronomy—an interpretation of the skies as they appeared to the builders of star temples at Giza in Egypt, at Stonehenge in England, and at the "Standing Pillars" of Kalasasaya—confirms at each site a civilization more ancient than that established at Sumer.

Newly established dates confound traditional history. Not yet established dates at the thousands of known sites not yet excavated will ridicule the current model. How large is forgotten history? What has been "forgotten" may exceed remembered history by a dimension we cannot perceive. There are now ten thousand known sites of early man in Belize alone. Only a few dozen have been excavated but the rest remain unexcavated, including the great underwater site at Cerros Maya. New evidence, which we will document, shows that the Maya of Guatemala, the Olmec of Mexico, and the sphere-builders of Costa Rica were not alone in their mathematical or navigational expertise. And they were not alone in the Americas. The evidence now emerging is that there was not one people, but many who shared the heart of the Americas: Negroid, Asians, Semitic, Aryan, Nordics, and Polynesians . . . and they were all navigators of the ancient skies and of the ancient seas (figs I3, I4).

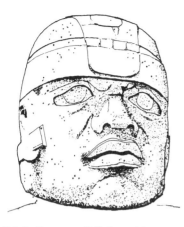 

I.3-4. OLMECS. Called pre-Mayans and proto-Mayans by archaeologists, their likenesses reveal that they weren't Mayan at all. There were many faces, many peoples in Mesoamerica long before Columbus. While most of the carved figures at Olmec sites, conservatively dated 1,000 B.C., were definitely Negroid (fig. I3. left) with kinky beards and braided hair, some were definitely Semitic (fig. I4. right), possibly Phoenicians.

The emergence of civilization in the Near East, six or seven thousand years ago is not a lie, but the story of its *exclusive* emergence there reveals a profound ignorance of what was occurring in the rest of the world, and of what had occurred in past civilizations. The academic isolation of the Americas from a past worldwide navigational culture *is* a lie, and whether it was conspired to by deliberate revision or by simple arrogance, it remains a lie—one that we will decisively prove later in this work. We will detail, throughout this work, sites of significant contact between early sea peoples well before the accepted dates of the rise of civilization in the Near East. It is our contention that world-wide intercontinental navigation was commonplace at these ancient dates—a contention, bolstered by the evidence provided herein, that is the crux for our proposal that Atlantis was indeed real, and that its site was in Mesoamerica.

It is easy to accept what science teaches us. It is hard to question authority. When we have been told that there was once a more harmonious time on Earth, a Golden Age, conventional wisdom has scoffed at the idea. Hasn't survival of the fittest always been the rule? Aren't we the inheritors of the genetic traces that have proven us the most able? Are we not now at the pinnacle of achievement? A simplistic approach would have us agree with these views. And although our current state may appear, in our material conveniences, to be unparalleled, it may prove, in the longer view, to be only a highly technological phase of an extended trough of ignorance.

We can easily see how science, without computers and without the Hubble telescope, could not understand Chaos Science or its implications for celestial collision. We can understand how it was logical to assume that the Sphinx and all the pyramids of Egypt were built in the same era. We can even assume it was logical for the early Spanish Conquistadors and missionaries to assume that the Aztecs and Incans they encountered knew both how and why the ancient star temples of the Americas were built, even though these natives almost unanimously repeated that they were "gifts" from an earlier people, and from an earlier time. What the present authors cannot understand is the historic and current lack of interest in discovering just who man *was* when he created passages in the seas and gateways to the stars.

A host of related questions confront us:

Why did the Church destroy the written records of the Maya? Why do we continue to stress the barbaric and warring aspects of the Aztecs and decadent Maya when we have come to understand that, unlike Europe and the Near East, most of their cities were built without defensive fortifications, and with great interconnecting canals and roadways, implying commerce and peaceful coexistence? Why have we ignored the true significance of their astronomy, myths, and mathematics?

Why did early twentieth-century science dictate that no dates earlier than 3,000 B.C. were possible even for primitive man in the Americas? Why in the face of the discovery of far earlier dates did science adopt an obscure and faulty Inquisition-inspired theory, Beringia, for man's migration across great ice sheets to the Americas? Why, when the site of Tikal was mistakenly dated as A.D. 100, did Archaeology and history immediately decide that this single site was the oldest in Mesoamerica, while thousands of other presumed, but unknown, sites lay unexcavated and undated? Why has startling evidence of far earlier sites, such as the stone spheres of Costa Rica, been deemed "out of context" and ignored by conventional archaeology? If a site is "out of context" should we blame the site or the context?

Why did Plato and the Egyptian priests insist on Atlantis as an *actual* place, and the Golden Age as an *actual* occurrence rather than as a theological or dialectical argument? Why have recent believers in the existence of Atlantis placed its location in the middle of the Atlantic Ocean, despite obvious evidence that no island-continent could have existed there in the space of time that man has inhabited Earth?

Why have theorists long ignored Atlantis' obvious placement at the heart of the Americas, where, in glacial times, with extremely cold, dry, and hostile conditions encircling much of the Earth, it could have flourished? Why does Plato's vision of the universe, a spiral within a spiral, resemble a DNA molecule, the building block of human biology? What knowledge did Plato have that was lost to the Eurocentric mind but was retained, and carved in stone in the Americas, for millennia before, and for several centuries after Christ?

Why have myths of flood and cataclysmic destruction been deemed "unreliable" and "impossible" by prevailing historians and archaeologists? How does the conventional version of history account for tales by Indians in the America's southwest of "a green mound of water" sweeping over the Earth—a legend remembered by a people who lived hundreds of miles from the sea in an area where local floods are always brown with mud washed down from the mountains? How does history account for Noah's flood, or for similar accounts in Sumerian and Chinese myth?

Why does the myth of the Tower of Babel, in Mesopotamia, find its exact retelling in the story of Cholula, a Mexican pyramid near Pueblo, whose base is the largest of any excavated pyramid in the world, and whose upper levels were devastated by soldiers and priests working for the Catholic Church of the Inquisition?

How do we account for the sudden disappearance of the mammoth, mastodon, dire wolf, saber-toothed tiger, and many other species of large animals in the Americas at about 12,000 B.P., a date Plato assigned to the destruction of Atlantis, and which also corresponds to recent geological evidence of a sudden melting of the icecaps and a rise in sea levels of several hundred feet in the Caribbean?

How do we account for sophisticated rock paintings in the Americas at Pedra Furada 32,000 years ago, thousands of years before the traditional dates for the invention of culture in America? Among the animals depicted in the Brazilian paintings are horses and camels, both abundant in the Americas at that time, and both sudden victims of a mass extermination 11,500 to 12,000 years ago.

Can we continue to dismiss these people as "gifted savages?" Can we continue to ignore their myths of destruction which spoke of conflagrations and deluges, or their foundation myths, which spoke, invariably, of arrivals by sea? What portent do cyclical periods of destruction and rebirth hold for us, now that we know we may also be approaching the end of a cycle—one that is at the same instance religious, astronomical (scientific), and astrological (mythic)?

The purpose and fate of ancient mankind has remained elusive to modern scientific inquiry. Were we ever once a civilization in harmony with the cosmos? Consider this—the human brain tripled in size from that of early *Homo erectus* to its current capacity with the emergence of *Homo sapiens* over 250,000 years ago, possibly long before. What were our ancestors doing during this long span of time? Can we really believe that human beings with brains of capacity similar to our own wandered the Earth for a minimum of 243,000 years in pursuit of migrating game until suddenly, in an evolutionary instant, they founded great cities at Sumer just 7,000 years ago?

How are we to regard the still-existent Maya, a people who have resisted five hundred years of colonization, and who have persistently challenged our basic materialistic world-view? The Maya continue to live and speak as their ancestors did thousands of years in the past. They continue to view this world as a magical aspect of creation and to understand its beings as recipients of fabulous knowledge. Are we fabulous and magical? If we are not now "fabulous," but seeming victims of continuous warfare, suffering, and continual retribution of past transgressions, as events in the Middle East suggest—has our existence always been thus? We have become a people who expect and anticipate the worst in human interaction. Where did we go wrong? Were we once something different, something more noble, something more intelligent?

Important recent discoveries have given us new perspectives, even as to the kinds of questions we're able to now ask. Can we imagine the sense of accomplishment in the building of observatories and star temples that accurately measured the movements of the sun and the planets 12,000 years ago in the Americas, or in the Earthly recreation of the celestial heavens evidenced in the construction of the pyramids of Egypt and in the great spheres of Costa Rica? Can we appreciate the serenity of purpose in the creation of cave paintings at Chauvet and Lascaux in France, paintings over 32,000 years old that still exhibit a sense of perceptive and dimension that any contemporary artist would envy?[1] Can we wonder at the significance of spit-painting in New Mexico 40,000 years ago, and to rock paintings in Australia that are even older? Can we now feel man's sense of excitement as, 60,000 to 80,000 years ago, he successfully navigated the Indonesian archipelago, exploring, then populating one island only to discover that another lay more distant?[2] Can we now sense the feeling of adventure these early navigators shared as they sailed over open seas, in boats beating against the wind, to islands sometimes a hundred kilometers distant until, in repeated journeys, he had reached Australia and the Pacific beyond? We can envision all of this only if we can recreate and understand our mythical and magical past.

Another significant question needs to be asked—if we have taken some small steps in recovering our forgotten history, why do school books in 1998, from sixth-grade readers to university textbooks still speak of Columbus as the first navigator to reach the "New World"? Why do these texts inform us that the Americas were first populated by primitive hunting bands who wandered across the dry Bering Sea; and why do they continue to tell us that civilized man is the recent recipient of gradual evolutionary progress? These falsehoods will be repeated well into the twenty-first century unless we awaken from our slumber and rediscover the forgotten past.

Historians and archaeologists have steadfastly sought to establish a pattern of land migration for early man. Being academics, and landlubbers, they have viewed the oceans as barriers to contact between civilizations. By contrast, Thor Heyerdahl's basic assumptions sprung from his knowledge that the seas were, and are, virtual conveyor belts that have always *connected* the diverse peoples of the world, not separated them (fig. I5). Though Heyerdahl was wrong in his assumption that man's migration was first from the Mediterranean regions to the Americas, and then from the Americas to the Pacific, his considerable courage and great intuition proved these one-way sea migrations simple to navigate, providing us with a *world-view* long closed. In fact, these migrations were not "one way" but occurred in many directions over great periods of time.

Science and academic authority have replaced myth with a linear and progressive view of history. History has respected Plato and Homer as messengers but has doubted their message. However, the myths they refer to, and their records, preserved in stone, will tell us who we have been and who we might

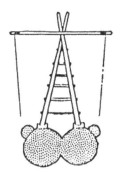

I.5. REED RAFTS. Science and history have taught us that, for ancient man, contact across the seas would have been impossible. But we now know that the Atlantic, with its steady winds and unfailing currents, is far easier to cross than the Mediterranean. We also know that the reed rafts used by Egyptian and Sumerians in the fourth millennium BC would have been more fit to sail across any open sea than the awkward "tall ships" used by Columbus and his contemporaries. Balsa rafts and long dugout canoes that rode close to the waves were used throughout the Pacific in recent centuries and for millennia before. Was there a meeting place between the Mediterranean and Oriental peoples? The thin strip of land that connects the two halves of the American continent contains ancient stelae carved with a variety of faces, from Chinese to Phoenician, in a place that united the great ocean currents. It would have been the logical place to unite diverse cultures, and astronomical knowledge. If ancient man was a navigator he would have repeatedly encountered Central America—the prevailing currents would have left him no choice in this matter.

still become. If there is a perceived implausibility in myth's astonishing tales of impossible events there are also great strengths in myth. Because it is an oral tradition it has been virtually indestructible. There are people alive today, among the Maya, in India, and in Africa who are inheritors of oral traditions, and who retain the ability to memorize thousands of lines of mythic song and poetry. The books of Homer were sung before they were written down. Because myth permits man's involvement in an interplay with the heavens it has torched the imagination of countless generations of listeners.

It is now time to question authority. Must we not now stand in wonder of the story told by myth? Throughout the world myth has been expressed in astronomy, math, and art. And where the essential message of myth has been recorded from diverse cultures, from around the world, it is found to have contained the same message—depicting an essential involvement of lowly man with the greater cosmos. When we view the great megaliths and observatories constructed in the deep past we know, intuitively, that they have a story to tell us, one we must attend to, or forever live in ignorance.

The search for Atlantis is the search for our common spiritual history. And in our beleaguered age we are very much in need of a spiritual connection to the greater universe, a vital connection that man once held freely, without fear or doubt. It was not in religious dogma, nor in ignorant pursuit of game, nor in simple farming, and it was not in recent times that intelligent man was born. If we have arrived at a limited understanding of ourselves, it is because we have unwittingly accepted impositions by a medieval State and Church that have sought to limit, control, and dictate—and thereby humble—our realization of who we are, and where we've come from. Hopefully, this will soon become a vestige of a misguided philosophy and a forgotten world view. But to understand who we are we must also see who we once were.

It was in an ancient exploration of the sea and stars that man transformed himself from a simple competitor among many predators, to a geometer of the world. In his Golden Age, man had become an intelligence in harmony with the cosmos. The key questions remain—when and where did this Golden Age exist, and can mankind hope to regain its vital essence?

Evidence of Plato's Atlantis abounds throughout Mesoamerica and Central America, at the heart of a vast continent, on a thin strip of land that creatively connected the great ocean currents. This center also connected the star-gazers and temple builders, and, at ancient navigational universities it connected the ancient navigators of the world. It's story, yet to be fully retrieved, is evidence of man's purpose, his past, and of his destiny.

1 Ivar Zapp and the Diquis Delta

I N 1940 the United Fruit Company was clearing the Diquis Delta region of southwest Costa Rica of its jungle covering to establish a banana plantation when workers happened upon what would later prove to be vast astronomical gardens. They first found the upper parts of huge stone balls, but when the curious workers dug the surrounding soil out, at some considerable expense of energy, they discovered they had uncovered great spheres, some measuring over nine feet in diameter, and later found to weigh as much as twenty tons. These great balls had once been held aloft by a series of supporting mounds, and had been surrounded by stone statues and stelae. Over time most of the colossal spheres sunk into the ground, some as much as two meters below the surface. The spheres caught the interest of Doris Stone, an archaeologist and the wife of the General Manager of the United Fruit Company in Costa Rica. Stone, in 1949, brought the spheres to the attention of Harvard archaeologist Samuel K. Lothrop while he was in Costa Rica examining other sites.

Intrigued by Stone's reports Lothrop traveled to the Diquis Delta, where he was amazed not only by the size of the granite spheres, but even more impressed by the *precision* with which massive granite blocks had been carved into perfect spheres—having the same diameter and circumference when measured from any point on the sphere. Even the largest were found to be spherical to within a few hundredths of an inch. Lothrop, an established authority on Peruvian and Central American Archaeology, had come to Costa Rica to study the ceramics of the Choretega Indians. But there was nothing that Lothrop had encountered in his investigations of the Choretega, then thought to be the earliest known organized culture in what is now Costa Rica, that suggested the abilities to construct so large and so precise a megalith. And there were hundreds of these mysterious spheres in the Diquis region, and hundreds more, if not thousands, in the surrounding mountains (fig. 1A).

Since the Choretega lacked the technology to build them and since there was no known presence in Mesoamerica of an earlier and more sophisticated culture, the spheres became an enigma. Lothrop declared that the site and the spheres were "out of context." They simply did not fit within any Meso-american context known to Americanist archaeologists. And since the established theories that dated pre-Columbian Costa Rican culture could not be questioned, the spheres themselves had to be dismissed.

Lothrop made no attempt to date the spheres although he expressed the opinion that they were much older than surrounding sites. He took accurate measurements of the spheres and mapped their layouts and their arrangements in groups. Upon inquiry, he managed to correlate the spheres to local folklore and myth that the spheres were related to "the phenomena that takes place in the sky." A few Indians told him that the spheres had something to do with the cyclical movement of "the sun, Moon, and the stars."

1.A. A SPHERE that has been removed from its original site and sits on a lawn in Palmar Sur, Costa Rica.

After Lothrop's brief study of the spheres, presented in *Archeological Remains of the Diquis Delta of Costa Rica,* few archaeologists outside Costa Rica showed any interest in these great spheres. When their evidence was first presented an issue of *Natural History Magazine* (1955) declared that, "It is thought that the civilization that manufactured these spheres must have been highly advanced."[1] But because they did not fit into their preconceived context and pretext archaeologists in general avoided dealing with these megaliths. A few academics and researchers declared that the spheres were the work of the native Boruca Indians—another culture that never showed any ability to construct such megaliths—and casually gave them a probable date of from the ninth to the twelfth century A.D. Over the years the spheres, hidden in the midst of a large banana plantation in a remote and steamy jungle, lay forgotten by all but the occasional looters who found a way to truck them to the gardens and lawns of wealthy Costa Ricans living in the central highlands. Through uncertainty and neglect an important archaeological discovery was categorized as an enduring enigma and abandoned to the banana fields.

When Ivar Zapp entered the picture the spheres had become an all-but-forgotten local riddle. Fascinated by the spheres, Ivar, while teaching in the school of Architecture at the University of Costa Rica in 1981, took his students on a field trip to the steamy Diquis Delta. After an examination of those spheres still *in situ,* he proposed a series of interesting questions to his students: Who built them? How were they built? How were they transported to a place so far from any rock quarries? How were the other spheres, found high in the coastal mountains of Costa Rica, possibly moved there? Then Ivar asked his students to ignore these questions and instead concentrate on another. Since so much thought and effort had gone into the construction, polishing, and geometric perfection of the spheres, what could have been the function of these megaliths? His students, though fascinated by the objects, enigmas in the jungle mist, had no ready answer. But then neither did Ivar. His field trip was meant to be an exercise in awareness of architectural function. But the questions Ivar raised to his students came to dominate his own thoughts. *What could the function of the spheres have been?*

Ivar had long been interested in the work of John Michell, whose orientation of the ley lines of Stonehenge and other sites in Britain pointed to ancient knowledge of the Earth's integral position under the heavenly bodies. Michell's investigation established the relationship of the Celts, through their architectural constructions, not only to solar and astral entities, but also to other ancient structures in Giza in Egypt, to the Etruscans, and to the builders of Baalbek in Phoenicia. Could something similar have occurred in the far distant past in Costa Rica?

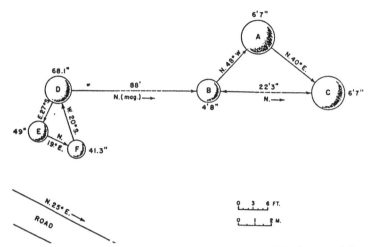

1B. Configurations of the Spheres of Costa Rica. The layout of the spheres as found and diagrammed by S.K. Lothrop. Spheres E and F are now in the Museo Nacional in San José, Costa Rica.

Professor Zapp and his students first studied the layout of the spheres that remained *in situ,* then they consulted the layouts made forty-two years earlier by Lothrop (fig. 1B). They found that, in most cases, the stones were arranged in groups of threes forming a triangular configuration. Ivar noticed that an axis line formed between two major groups of the spheres was oriented to the magnetic north pole, indicating that the builders had a knowledge of the magnetic compass.

Ivar, on intuition, then took a Mercator Atlas and projected the directional lines implied by the layout of the spheres. The implied lines of the spheres missed contact with other significant sites by as much as four hundred miles. But the Mercator Atlas, long used by European navigators, is flat, and the Earth is a sphere. Using a globe, and consulting maps that reflect that dimension, Ivar found that the 19 degree southwest inclination of the line that intersected spheres E and F (Fig. 1C.) projected from the Palmar Sur site in the Diquis Delta leads to Cocos Island, to the Galapagos Islands, and then to Easter Island. In fact, smaller but similarly perfect spheres have been found on Easter Island, but these spheres have been moved, so if they once pointed back to the Americas this access to knowledge is now lost. The directional line implied by spheres D and F project a line that, followed to the northeast, leads to the Straits of Gibraltar, and if projected southwest, leads to the Marquesas. In another group the axis leads to the Great Pyramid at Giza. In another, it leads to Stonehenge. In every case the megaliths of Costa Rica pointed to great megaliths of distant lands and islands(fig. 1D).

1.C. (RIGHT) THE LINES OF SPHERES **E** AND **F** projected from the Palmar Sur site in the Diquis Delta lead directly to Cocos Island, the Galapagos Islands, and then to Easter Island.

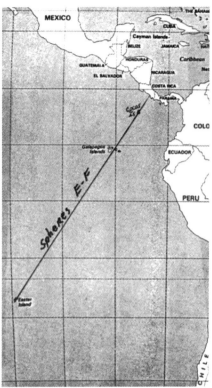

1.D. (BELOW) NAVIGATIONAL DIRECTIONAL LINES OF THE SPHERES OF COSTA RICA (adjusted to fit a flat map). In the Pacific, land comprises less than one-tenth of one percent of the total area. The probability that each implied line would strike an important island group by chance was incredibly remote. That the implied lines would also point directly toward known megalithic sites such as Easter Island, Stonehenge, Malta, and the Great Pyramid in Egypt were beyond any chance probability. Ivar then knew he had made the first step toward an important discovery.

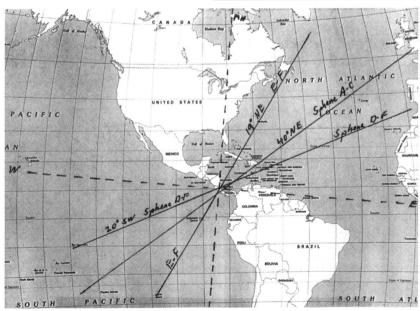

Sight-lines on a flat map, or even a small globe, are one thing; sight-lines on an actual sphere—our Earth—are another. The E-F projection line of the spheres of the Diquis Delta was tested by a pilot-friend of Ivar's using the arc geometry of an on-board computer on a Boeing 727. The result of this test showed that the 19 degree directional line extended over the 7,000 plus kilometers from Costa Rica resulted in a projected flight that missed Easter island by 70 kilometers (42 miles). At first this result bothered Ivar. But a seventy kilometer miss in long range ocean voyaging has been demonstrated by the Polynesians to be a virtual hit. Experienced and able navigators need not make a precise strike on an island destination. By reading swell patterns in waves and cloud formations—both disturbed by the presence of islands—and by observing the presence of land-based birds, such as terns or noddies, navigators can detect the position of an island a hundred kilometers before sighting it.

Were the ley lines of Celtic megaliths and the sight-lines of the spheres of Costa Rica coincidences? If so, why did one implied sight-line, formed by three great spheres point directly to Stonehenge? Ivar was certain that such implied directional paths could not be merely coincidental. He believed that he had discovered something very similar to the "ley lines" by which the Druids of Britain connected Stonehenge and Glastonbury with ancient Greek, Etruscan and Egyptian sites (fig. 1E). He then realized that he had possibly led his university students out of their classrooms in San Jose and onto the grounds of a far more ancient "university."

But the question of function and purpose haunted Ivar. If the spheres rep-

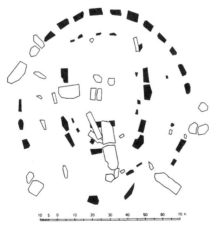

1.E. STONEHENGE, ENGLAND. In *Secrets of the Stones* John Michell was able to determine that not only did the sightlines of the great temples of England and Egypt correspond to particular stars and particular events, such as the summer solstice, they also linked distant temples on Earth.

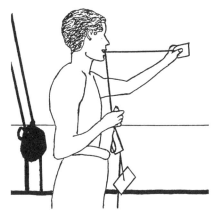

1.F. KNOTTED CORDS. Tim Severin demonstrates the use of the kamal and knotted cord in a *National Geographic Magazine* article in July, 1982. Thirteen years later in an article on Maya murals at Bonampak (*NGM* Feb. '95) knotted cords extending from the mouth—believed by the present authors to be a vestige of degenerated naval traditions—are described as examples of barbaric torture and ritual savagery.

resented terrestrial directions rather than, *or in additon to*, star paths, what were the students of this ancient university being taught? Then it came to him—navigation—surely these students of old were being taught how to navigate both the heavens and the seas!

The implications of such a theory went far beyond anything that Ivar had encountered in his studies. Even John Michell had only expressed his ley lines as sight lines. Navigational theory had not entered Michell's theories or proposals.

Thus, Ivar realized that he would need to look beyond the published archeological record for traces of ancient navigators. Launching an investigation that would dominate the next fourteen years of his life, Ivar pursued the question through an examination at actual sites of the known archeological record, reappraised to include the possibility of navigation as the means by which man's ideas migrated from one continent to another.

On assignment, one of Ivar students, Humberto Carro, found evidence of the use of an ancient sextant used by Arab navigators, that was described in detail in the thirteenth-century manuscript that became the basis for the classic, *The Thousand and One Arabian Nights*. Through the character Sinbad the

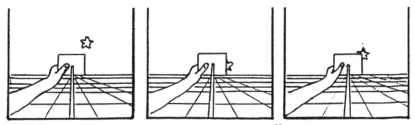

1.G. IF POLARIS APPEARED ABOVE THE HEIGHT OF THE KAMAL THE SAILOR HAD VENTURED NORTH OF HIS DESTINATION. If Polaris appeared below, the sailor was too far south. If the North Star aligned with the rectangle the ship and destined port were on the same latitude and the sailor was on course.[3]

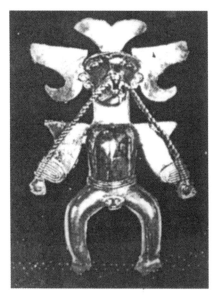

1.H, I. **FIGURES WITH KNOTTED CORDS EXTENDING FROM THEIR MOUTHS**, often tethered to rectangular shapes, have been found throughout the Diquis Delta region of Costa Rica. Surely, these were navigational instruments, not torture devices. R.A.Jairazbhoy (*Ancient Egyptians And Chinese In America*) notes that in both ancient America and Egypt gods are depicted with the odd characteristic of a double twisted rope issuing from their mouths. Another similarity is the Egyptian custom of placing small strips of papyrus with the dead and the Mexican custom of placing bunches of paper with dead.2 Obviously both people had a belief in the power of the written word to transcend Earthly life. But it could not transcend nor long survive the burnings and desecration of less enlightened cultures that followed.

Sailor the tales contained in this classic probably depicted adventures of many "Sinbads" stretching back through hundreds of sailings over thousands of years. It was the use on these voyages of a rectangular sextant (figs. 1F, 1G), called a kamal by the Arabs, that caught Carro's attention. The kamal was made of two wooden rectangles united by a long knotted cord. Each knot on the cord represented the latitude of a known port. Northern ports were represented by knots closest to the rectangle. Ports closer to the equator were represented by knots that permitted a fuller extension of the arm, effectively lowering the "sighting latitude" of the kamal. By holding the knot representing a port in his teeth and extending the kamal with its edge on the horizon and pointing it at Polaris the accomplished navigator could determine his position relative to the latitude of his destination.

What struck Ivar and his student Humberto was that the knotted rope extending from the mouth was very similar to a repeated motif on pottery and gold pendants that Lothrop had found in association with the spheres of the Diquis Delta.[4] Lothrop characterized these numerous items as representing "snakes coming out of the mouth a deity." But Ivar had believed them to be simply units of measure (figs. 1H, 1I). Again, Ivar had questioned their function. Now he felt he had an answer. If his hypothesis was correct it was a geographically large answer. This same symbolism, the knotted cords coming out of the mouth, has also been depicted in pre-Inca burial sites in Peru, and on stelae in the archeological sites of Copan in Honduras, and Bonampak and Yaxchilan in the Yucatán. In India similar depictions have been found in pre-Aryan sites in the Indus valley and among the followers of Shiva, the Hindu god of destruction.[5]

This discovery only made Ivar more determined to find other instruments that could serve a common function among diverse ancient naval cultures. Again, Humberto Carro came up with the key evidence. He found an article (among the reports to the twenty-third Congress of Americanists held in Costa Rica in 1952) by Thor Heyerdahl which explained the technique of sailing balsa rafts against the currents and against the wind. In the article Heyerdahl shows how the ancient Peruvians were able to achieve this counter current navigation by use of removable centerboards called "guara." Functioning like keels, but in use in the Americas for thousands of years before the keel was invented, seven to twelve-foot-long guaras were inserted between balsa logs and lifted or lowered to achieve the desired tacking effect (fig. 1J).

Centerboard navigation in great rafts that carried from fifty to seventy-five men and twenty to forty tons of cargo was in wide use at the time the first Spanish came to Peru. When Francisco Pizarro's fleet reached the northern coasts of the Inca empire they encountered a whole flotilla of balsa rafts car-

1.J. The Incas used guaras, or centerboards, which they thrust down between the logs, and working with sails, could more effectively tack into the wind than any European ships. Since the guaras function in the currents as sails do in the wind they are essentially "sea current sails." By the guara technique a skilled crew could sail a balsa raft in any wind or current to any part of the Pacific.[6] The importance of centerboard sailing was unknown to European boat builders until the late nineteenth century and not understood by scholars until Thor Heyerdahl's 1952 presentation of "Guara Sailing Techniques Indigenous to South America." Even then few scholars trusted Heyerdahl's work.

rying Inca soldiers. The Spanish were surprised by the number of rafts, and by their great size . . . almost equal to their own caravels. But, to the Spaniards, the most amazing thing was that the rafts were moving swiftly toward them, against the current and against the wind. Curious, Pizarro managed to draw alongside several of the rafts. The Incas were as curious about the Spanish and allowed them to board. The Spaniards, initially pretending to be friendly, boarded the vessel, threw eleven of the crew overboard, left four to the raft, and took two men and three women prisoner to be trained as interpreters.[6]

Pizarro's contemporaries recorded the secret of balsa raft navigation, although they didn't fully understand it at the time.Pizarro and his men were told of balsa journeys along the entire coasts of South America. They were also given directions on how to sail to Easter Island, and on to Polynesia. But Pizarro had little interest in sailing techniques or directions to Polynesia, or any obscure or fancied and distant islands. Through his captive interpreters he learned that the reason for the great number of balsa rafts full of soldiers he had encountered was that the Incas were involved in a bloody civil war. Pizarro's quest was for El Dorado, the legendary City of Gold. The civil war gave him the opportunity to use the Inca people against one another. Utilizing the high esteem conferred on him, that of the returning god Viracocha, Pizarro organized an army of Peruvians deeply angry at the Inca regime. His expedition, fortified by thousands of Indians, pushed inland high into the Andes to capture Cuzco, the Incan capital—a city covered with gold.

Within two years the Incan empire fell to the Spanish. Centerboard sailing on balsa rafts survived for a few generations, then was all but forgotten. But historic accounts, most written by chroniclers accompanying Pizarro and other Spanish conquistadors, remain. And wooden guaras, some carbon 14 dated to thousands of years before Pizarro's conquest of Peru, are still being found in the deserts of Peru.

A serious obstacle to rediscovering Costa Rica's past navigational culture is in its climate and soil. Peru's extremely dry climate and sandy soil permitted preservation. Wooden guara boards are not the only objects to survive millennia of neglect. Mummies, three thousand years older than the oldest mummies found in Egypt, have recently been uncovered in the high deserts of southern Peru and northern Chile. By contrast, in Costa Rica's tropical wet climate and highly acidic soil, wood, flesh and bones disintegrate quickly. No record of rafts, ships, or wooden guara boards or the people who used them could survive in such a climate.

In fact, no wooden guaras have been found in Costa Rica. Yet Ivar immediately recognized that a curious event occurred on the "first" encounter of Europeans with native Costa Ricans. Christopher Columbus was long considered to be the first "historical" navigator to reach the Americas from the "Old World." (Lief Eriksson and the Viking discovery of America 500 years earlier was, until 100 years ago, generally considered a myth.) On his first three voyages Columbus encountered only islands, which he believed to be the East Indies, but on his fourth voyage, determined to find the Asian continent, he found instead another continent making landfall near present day Limón, Costa Rica.

Columbus has become a boring topic of discussion. But a his encounter in Costa Rica has particular significance. Because of the size of their ships, Columbus and his party were accepted as great navigators by the native Costa Ricans. Columbus' son, Diego, reported how their party was taken, almost immediately upon arrival, on a two hour walk, to the burial of an important person. Diego describes the lapida that the dead man was laid out on, and describes a prow of a ship underneath him. From this account and other evidence it has generally been accepted that these lapidas were both the bearers and the grave covers of priests and kings. On examining the lapidas what Ivar realized was that the guaras (centerboards) of Peru and the lapidas of Costa Rica were virtually identical in size, shape and ornamentation. No one had noted their similarities before. But no one had been looking for naval implications to Costa Rican sites.

If the stone funeral slabs of Costa Rica were identical to the functional wooden guaras of Peru why have stone slabs at all? They would be too heavy for practical utilization. The use of lapidas as free standing stone slabs on mounds and as part of the statuary of "ceremonial centers" at Guayabo had long puzzled archaeologists. What the archaeologists had interpreted as "ceremonial centers" Ivar saw as astronomical gardens. The stone slabs were found only in sacred astronomical-navigational grounds. Ivar deduced the answer. When he saw the drawings and description of the Peruvian guaras he knew what the function of the lapidas had been—for guaras and lapidas had functioned as the same thing—navigational centerboards! What Columbus and his son didn't realize was that the burial the Costa Rican Indians wanted him to witness was not of a king, but that of another great sailor—an important pre-Columbian navigator whose grave had been covered by a stone lapida. It makes sense that the navigators would be buried under the replica of an instrument that made their long and difficult voyages possible, both as an honor and as a way to steer them in the journeys of the after-life.

Columbus showed little appreciation for symbols of navigation and put no particular emphasis on the encounter. Disregarding the stone lapidas, Columbus's first inquiries of the people he encountered were of the gold pendants, disks, and other adornments they wore. The "Indians" told him that they had obtained their gold from a fabulous people who lived on the far coast of their land. These people were called the Ciguarenses, a sea-going people, and that they brought vast riches in cargoes filled with gold, silver, and precious stones from distant lands.

The following is Columbus's own account, according to Felipe Valentini's work, *The Fourth Voyage of Christopher Columbus*: "In all the places where I had gone, I found it to be true what I had heard; this certified this is true about the province of Ciguare, which according to them, is described as nine days by foot towards west, there they say is infinite gold and they wear corals on their heads, and rings of coral on their feet and arms, and very thick rings, also stools, chests, tables are covered with coral. They also said that the women wore necklaces that went from the head to the shoulders. In what I say all the people from these places coincide and they say so much that I would be glad to have ten percent. They also use black pepper. In Cigueres their custom is to exchange merchandise in the markets; these people tell us this, and they showed me the way they traded cheaply. Others tell us that ships bring canons, arrows, swords, armor plate; the people go about fully dressed; on land there are horses and they make war, they wear rich garments and they

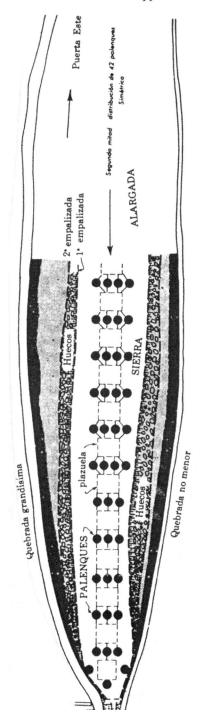

1.K. COCTU, a city built in the configuration of a ship.

have good things. It is also said that the sea forms an arch around Ciguare, and from there ten days walk is the river Ganges. It looks like these lands are as far from Veragua as Tortosa is from Fuentearrabia or Pisa from Venecia."[7]

The local people were apparently indicating two things to Columbus: First, a people different in customs to their own existed on the Pacific coast in southern Costa Rica who called themselves the Ciguare. Second, that the Ciguare possessed naval equipment, gold objects, and a naval culture similar to that which Columbus seemed to represent.

These people, the "Ciguarenese," were never found, although recent finds of gold pendants associated with navigational tools in the Diquis Delta near present day Golfito—about a ten day walk from Limon, and about which the sea forms an arch—indicate that such a naval culture did exist. The great spheres of the Diquis Delta had apparently been long buried, but it is obvious that even as late as the time of Columbus that region was held in high esteem as the center of a naval culture. It has recently been determined by the authors that the site described in the Diquis Delta was no ordinary naval culture but a highly advanced ancient astral-navigation university.

Sixty years after Columbus, Vasques de Coronado, endeavoring to conquer this geographical area, hired several large Indian "piraguas," and their crews. These long canoes had been sailing north from Panama along the Pacific coast. The size of the vessels, with eighteen rowers on each side, and the distances the large boats covered, indicated that sophisticated naval orientations and techniques were present along the Pacific coasts of present day Panama and Costa Rica.

Motivated typically by the quest for gold, Coronado was also seeking a naval passage between the Atlantic and Pacific oceans. Under his command the piraguas began exploring the major rivers of the area looking for a passage to the Caribbean. Between the mouths of the Diquis and Sierpe Rivers, Coronado encountered the fortified city of Coctu, which lay in the Diquis Delta.

Coctu (fig. 1K) could have best been described as a city-state, laid out in the form of a ship. Coronado's description of Coctu, relating an ordered construction and "gardens of great beauty," may well have been a description of the home of the Ciguares. His admiration for the city, which he described as beyond comparison to anything ever seen by the Spaniards, was all the more exceptional since he had lost several men in his efforts to subdue Coctu. With the aid of the Panamanian Indians, Coronado and his Conquistadors eventually gained the surrender of this city of 33,600 people. Although its probable location is known, no trace of it remains today.

After the surrender of Coctu, Coronado and his men encountered a great flooding of the Sierpe and Diquis Rivers. They took refuge with some friendly Indians who lived in houses built on thick stilts several meters above the plain. Coronado did not know it, but the refuge he and his men had taken was only a few miles from giant spheres that would one day help solve a central mystery of the peoples of the Americas.

Based on similarities in jade carvings, pottery, and ornaments, Ivar Zapp felt certain that the peoples who lived in the region of the stone spheres of Costa Rica and the guara navigators of Peru had shared a common navigational culture (fig. IL). The seafaring "Ci-guares" described to Columbus and the "guara" navigators of Peru might have been the same people. The fact that it was in Costa Rica, not in Peru, that the guaras were immortalized in stone pointed to Costa Rica as the likely center for the navigator-priests. Ivar faced two major obstacles in proving his case. The first obstacle was that the indigenous population of Costa Rica virtually disappeared within a few generations of the arrival of the Spanish. Much of the disappearance was attributed to influenza and small pox, and much of it was due to the cruelty of the con-

1.L. STONE LAPIDAS FOUND ONLY IN COSTA RICA CORRESPOND TO WOODEN GUARAS FOUND IN PERU. Comparing lapidas and guaras Ivar found that they are uniform in width, length, and thickness . . . the lapidas are unusually thin for stone carvings, generally less than two inches in thickness. The most striking similarities are in the ornate carvings that form the top borders and handles of both lapidas and guaras. An often repeated motif is that of five to eight carved men standing side by side holding hands. Another repeated motif in Costa Rica depicts twins, sometimes twin birds, sometimes twin beasts, sometimes twin man-beasts . . . and the concept of twins hearkens back to Plato's description of Atlantis, a great empire divided among five sets of twins. The stone arrangements of the twins also often imply navigational directions.

1.M. IVAR ZAPP INSPECTING A SPHERE. After years of study of the mysterious spheres Ivar Zapp noticed the similarity in the lay-out of the spheres to ley-lines found in the British Isles and to sighting-stones found in the Pacific. Suddenly, the thought occurred to Ivar that these were navigational tools. Through an examination of the probable functions of the spheres, Ivar Zapp came to understand that they not only represented celestial bodies but that they also indicated ley-lines that connected the sites of ancient cultures and the routes of ancient navigators.

quering Spanish. No written record of the native people's existence survived the conquest.

However, Ivar has found possible evidence that the more sophisticated navigational peoples of Costa Rica, on hearing of the terrible conquistadors, had simply sailed away, into the Pacific, taking what written records they might have had with them. But they could not take the stone spheres (fig. 1M).

What Columbus and Coronado failed to recognize was, in fact, the last vestige of the great navigational culture of the Americas, one that drew on its memories and lessons back to the Golden Age of navigation, and to traces of man's greatest age on Earth.

What the American navigational cultures had retained knowledge of, and what Columbus almost "rediscovered" was the remnants of the civilization that had given birth to the Sumerian, Egyptian, Basque and Celtic cultures.

While these other cultures had all but forgotten the continent across the sea, only the Phoenicians of Carthage visited there regularly. Whether knowledge of the Americas was a Phoenician rediscovery or simply a continuation of use of trade routes long known to ancient sea peoples is unknown. But there is strong evidence that the latter is closer to the truth.

Ivar realized that if his hypothesis that the spheres were *teaching instruments* of a naval culture was to be tested, he would have to study a known naval culture, one where ancient traditions and techniques were still in use. Ivar sought the advice of archaeologists at the University of Costa Rica. They agreed that his theory was both startling and promising, but none seemed to know of a culture where ancient navigational techniques were still practiced. Then a friend gave Ivar a book that would profoundly influence and confirm his perspective on ancient man.

The book was *We, The Navigators,* by David Lewis. In this book Lewis presents a wealth of information on a Pacific-wide system of navigational learning . . . much of it still alive in the late 1960s when Lewis undertook to recreate the routes of ancient voyagers. Lewis voyaged over 13,000 nautical miles sailing under the guidance of native islanders, on native craft, using native star paths taught to his guides by their fathers and their "father's fathers." Without benefit of any modern navigational equipment or techniques, Lewis and his island mentors never once failed to reach their often distant intended landfall.[8]

Lewis's exploits, primarily accomplished on outrigger canoes, are riveting,

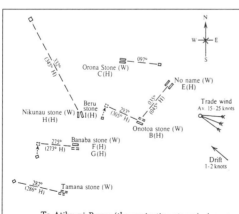

Te Atibu ni Borau *(the navigation stones), Arorae Island. (After V. Ward, pers. comm., 1969). Names of stones from Ward = W, letter of identification from Hilder = H. Bearings as given by Ward, Hilder's bearings in parentheses. All bearings true. Distances: Tamana, 50 miles; Banaba, 448 miles; Nikunau, 75 miles; Beru, 87 miles; Onotoa, 85 miles.*

1.N. "The Stones for Voyaging," Arorae, Gilbert Islands. The directional stones above were found on Arorae, the southernmost of the Gilbert Islands. Similar stones have also been found on Butaritari, the northernmost of the Gilberts. Sighting stones were used to align canoes on taking departure for distant islands. The Gilbertese have a separate word for voyaging canoes, *baurua*, which distinguishes these larger canoes from the ones used in their local group of islands. Like the great spheres of Costa Rica and Easter Island the configuration of these stones were probably used for teaching star and navigational courses.

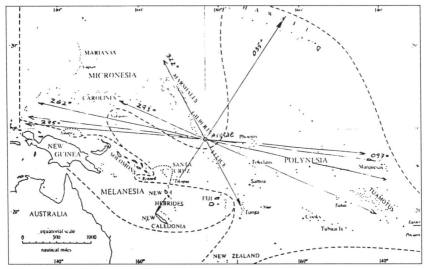

1.0. By extending the expressed lines of the sighting-stones of Arorae the seafarer is led to distant islands and archipelagoes.

yet on reading Lewis's record what first caught Ivar's eye was the description of "sighting stones." Although Lewis's sources spoke of many stone astronomical gardens throughout the Pacific, Lewis was only able to report personally on stones on Niauafo'ou in Tonga and on Butaritari and Arorae, respectively the northernmost and southernmost of the Gilbert islands.

The Gilbertese call the unusual configuration of stones that stand near the northwestern point of Arorae, "Te Atibu ni Borau," ("The Stones for Voyaging"). First mapped by Captain E.V. Ward in 1946 when there were thirteen stones (there are now eight), they were described as "flat slabs of coral about five feet by four feet and about six inches thick . . . set on edge and secured by paving." Lewis describes the voyaging stones of Arorae as ". . . mostly grouped in threes in the manner shown (fig. 1N) to indicate the bearings of islands in the Southern Gilberts and Banaba." Lewis adds, "Sighting stones seem to have been used to align canoes on taking departure in the same manner as natural landmarks, and probably also for recording and teaching star courses."[9]

The sighting stones that Lewis described in the Gilbert Islands of Polynesia were similarly constructed and were laid out in configurations very like those of the spheres of Costa Rica! Zapp examined Lewis's maps and found again that, by extending their expressed lines and angles, they led to the initiation of sea routes that extended to the major archipelagoes of the Pacific Ocean (fig. 1-O). Because 99 percent of the Pacific is open water, could the chance that "sighting stones" led directly to landfall be by chance?

Further research into the oral tradition of the islanders revealed that the stone arrangements of Arorae were used by the navigator caste of the Polynesians to teach star patterns to their sons or daughters. The eldest off-spring were students virtually all their lives learning the names of stars that aligned themselves with the stones on given dates during the year. The stones had been placed in such a manner that these "horizon stars" would align with the stones at the best time of year to initiate a certain sailing course.

In addition to "horizon stars" (fig. 1P) the students were taught sailing by reference to "zenith stars," "star paths" and "star columns," all requiring an exact knowledge of hundreds of stars and star constellations. A navigational "university" was at work in Arorae and had been at work for thousands of years. Most Europeans who encountered the Polynesians regarded their methods and their boats with scorn. But the methods, at least, were far superior to anything the Europeans had devised.

Through David Lewis's research Ivar learned that the people of Polynesia were in possession of highly sophisticated and evolved "know how" about

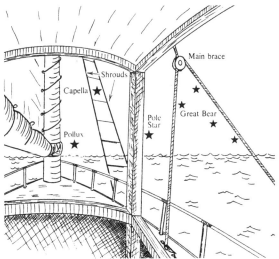

1.P. HORIZON STARS. By steering toward horizon stars at the proper hour, Polynesians always knew the course to follow. After the English, Dutch, and German authorities had banned inter-island navigation, this often meant a departure after midnight. But this was no problem for a Polynesian seeking cigarettes or whiskey—they knew the rising and setting of all the major constellations and knew they could follow the heavenly trek of the stars to their destination. Early Hindu and Egyptian observations and hieroglyphs were also related to horizon stars. The Egyptian hieroglyph for "horizon" is the Sun rising between two mountains. Phoenician sighting instruments for navigation were similarly expressed. Early Hindu and Egyptian observations and hieroglyphs were also related to horizon stars. The Egyptian hieroglyph for "horizon" is the Sun rising between two mountains. Phoenician sighting instruments for navigation were similarly expressed.

navigation. Ivar wondered, could it be that the people of South, Central, and North America also had such knowledge? The spheres of Costa Rica were similar to but far older and far more sophisticated than the sighting stones of the Gilbert Islands. The possible function of the mysterious monolithic stone spheres indicated that, unsuspected by land-based archaeologists, a great naval culture may have existed in Central America. In Ivar's view the directional information contained in the layout of stone spheres demanded a reevaluation of the current perspectives and archeological models applied to the civilizations found in America.

The sighting stones of Arorae and their use as teaching instruments confirmed Ivar's hypothesis. But no reputable archaeologist had ever even hinted that the Pre-Columbian peoples of America practiced the long-range oceanic navigation implied by the stone spheres of the Diquis Delta.

Explorer-theorist Thor Heyerdahl, famed for his voyages on the *Kon-Tiki*, from Peru to New Zealand, and the *Ra* Expeditions in which he voyaged from Egypt to the Antilles, stood alone in realizing the navigational capabilities of early Americans. But Heyerdahl was dismissed as a "lucky adventurer" by the archeological establishment. Heyerdahl's theory of ancient navigation by papyrus boats and balsa rafts, despite his achievements, was not provable as actual historic record. Due to the extremely soft nature of the materials used in their construction no ancient ships were likely to be found. In truth, archaeologists have not, until only very recently, looked for navigational instruments at archeological sites.

For Ivar, by contrast, the discovery of the function of one navigational object led to the search for another. Seeking traces of navigational function in gold pendants, jade knives, huge ceramic pots of the type necessary for storage of water on long distance voyages, stone water mirrors, and other objects, he was rarely disappointed. Among the items that stood out prominently above the others were repeated and dominant themes of the four-sided (sometimes eight-sided) Atlantean Cross and the shallow concave bowls held by four Atlanteans (fig. 1Q). Ivar's investigation of the archeological record showed that Pre-Columbian Costa Rica shared cultural patterns whose origins could be found everywhere throughout the Americas, from the shared Atlantes motif of the Toltecs, to the navigational instruments of the early Peruvians. As such, ancient Costa Rica must have constituted a "melting pot" of navigational cultures, just as cultural port cites today, such as New York and Hong Kong represent a diversity of cultural traits. Ivar was certain that the evidence put Costa Rica squarely in the middle of an ancient navigational culture, one that not only existed contemporaneously with the formative Maya, the Olmecs, and the pre-Incas, but very possibly predated them.

1.Q. Atlantean figures hold up the heavens . . . a repeated theme throughout Mesoamerica. Homer placed the columns on which Atlas supported the heavens far out in the Atlantic. Plato said that Atlas was a son of Poseidon, whose domain was across the "what could truly be called ocean." Later, Classical Greeks, for no apparent reason, placed Atlantis in North Africa, and 19th century theorists placed it in the nearby North Atlantic. The earlier version is confirmed by the predominance of Atlantean figures in the Americas.

Hadn't others made the connection? Ivar studied all the recent publications of Americanists, consulted and interviewed the available archaeologists in Costa Rica. It seemed they had not. Pursuing what we could characterize as a "terrestrial imperative" archaeologists had collectively disdained any navigational abilities of native Americans. With the exception of Thor Heyerdahl, who academic authorities scoffed at as a "lucky amateur," and the distinguished Near East scholar, Cyrus Gordon, author of *Before Columbus*, no voice spoke up for the Americas as a navigational culture. In fact, Central America was considered to be a "backwater" of academic studies that had concentrated their investigations on the great ruins in the Yucatán and Guatemala to the north, and to Peru, in the south.

Ivar found that no archaeologists had investigated the naval techniques by which Pre-Columbian trade was sustained, even though there was ample evidence of movements of goods between all the regions of America, from the south to the north, and vice-versa. No archaeologist had even suggested that the fabulous calendars and observatories of the Mayans, Toltecs, and pre-Incans could have been of more functional use to navigators than to farmers. Nor did any archaeologist seem to question just what the ceremonies might have been that were supposedly conducted at the "ceremonial centers," except to echo the Catholic Church in insisting that pagan rites of sacrifice were somehow responsible for their precise construction.

Ivar realized that "religious ceremonies" attributed by archaeologists to priests and their "ceremonial centers" could actually have been functional "universities," teaching astronomy, celestial navigation, architecture, and other sciences. It had been done elsewhere in the ancient world. For example, in 700 B.C. the Greek astronomer Aratos was building spheres of stone and wood ten feet in diameter to determine "arc-geometrical" values without the benefit of arc- trigonometry. From his work involving experimentation with spheres and their later use as teaching models Aratos established the groundwork that would permit Eratosthenes to later reach an almost perfect description of the Earth's diameter. This knowledge and corresponding knowledge about the sun, moon, and star paths was immortalized in the image of Atlas holding the globe of the celestial vault on his back.

Correspondingly it is known that the Costa Rican water mirror, the device through which astronomers and their students sighted zenith stars and star pillars or columns, was symbolically held aloft by four Atlanteans (Atlanteans is the plural or adjectival form of Atlas), representing the four cardinal directions. David Lewis has shown that Polynesians had studied the stars, their "pillars" or "columns," and their paths in an identical manner.

Had correspondence been established between Greek astronomers and MesoAmerican astronomers? Between MesoAmericans and Polynesians? If navigational and astronomical knowledge, and their symbolic representations, existed in all three cultures, did it not confirm, or at least strongly suggest, navigational contact between these peoples (figs. 1R, 1S)? Why did these

1.R. THE CROSS AS A NAVIGATIONAL SYMBOL. The Maltese Cross, a symbol of navigation carried on the sails of the Santa Maria, supposedly brought the first knowledge of the cross to the "New World" on Columbus's maiden voyage.

1.S. THE MALTESE CROSS had been described in the *Chilam Balam*, depicted as describing the cardinal directions in the Mayan codice of Madrid (below), and inscribed in stone in the Americas for at least sixteen centuries before Columbus. (See also fig. 7R).

three cultures all contain myths of a Golden Age that perished in a great flood? The Greeks gave the name Atlantic to the ocean outside the pillars of Hercules, called Atlantis the great empire of the Golden Age, and stressed the importance of Atlas as both the first king of Atlantis, and the upholder of the heavens and of heavenly knowledge. Yet "atl" is not even a syllable native to the Greek language. It is a key syllable in the Nahuatl and Mayan languages of the Americas. In fact, "atl" in Nahuatl means water as well as the ninth of the twenty day names in the Nahuatl calendar; "Atlahua" was the name given to the patron of fishing among the Mexica who established their capital on Lake Texcoco (now Mexico City); "Atlahuac" was the patron of that city-state's canals and gardens; and "Atlantean" was the name given to the giant figures regarded as the founders of Tula.

Ivar recalled a phrase Cyrus Gordon once used to describe the probable importance of ancient Central America: "The Mediterranean is a sea that connected lands creatively; Middle America is a land that connected oceans creatively."[10] Inspired by Gordon's words, and recognizing the strategic position of Central America in what he had begun to perceive as a vast and ancient navigational region, Ivar now asked how far back in time these correspondences might have existed. The concept of Atlas supporting the Earth, Poseidon's trident, celebration of twins, circular cities, and myths of destruction by inundation all went back to Plato's Atlantis.

Remembering Plato's obsession with circles and his description of Atlantis's capital city, Poseidon, as circular and ringed with canals, Ivar studied the cities and constructions of ancient Mesoamerica. Almost without exception they were circular, and ringed with canals. Encountering again Plato's description of the origins of the Atlantean people and their descent from five pairs of male twins, Ivar looked again at the use of twin motifs in the archeological record of the Americas. It was there in profusion. Everywhere

Ivar looked, from the Atlas figures holding up shallow water mirrors, to the depiction of tridents (Poseidon's symbol), to the circular canal systems that ringed Cuzco and other great American cities the evidence of Atlantis as represented in the Americas is abundant. Was Atlantis what we now call the Americas? Plato in the *Timeaus* had described Atlantis as being *larger* than Asia (the Greek definition basically included little more than what we now call Asia Minor) and Libya (all of Africa except Egypt) combined.[11]

Interpretations of the location of Atlantis have put it in various places—in the North sea, near the Canary Islands, in the Mediterranean, or as Antarctica. On size alone, among known bodies of land, it could not have been any of the first three possibilities, it could only have been the latter, Antarctica. But in Plato's description of a tropical paradise "favored by the sun," Antarctica must be eliminated. So must any concept of a sunken region of the Atlantic. Plate tectonics simply do not show any gap in the coastlines of the Americas in opposition to Europe and Africa; except for a relatively small gap in the Caribbean region, nothing of the size of legendary Atlantis. And this gap can easily be explained by the shallow shoal waters of much of the Caribbean and of the coasts off Florida and Central America, that once must have been part of the Atlantean continent. Before the floods and inundation that accompanied the end of the last Ice Ages, these lands were above ground and provide the fit to the tectonic puzzle.

Eleven thousand five hundred years ago, most the Great Bahaman Bank was exposed land, the Puerto Rican plateau including the Virgin Islands was a single land mass, Cuba and Florida were joined, as were Jamaica and Nicaragua, and the shallow shoal waters of what are now the Windward Islands, very possibly Plato's "bare bones" on a sunken continent, were part of an arching land mass with a few gorges connecting the Caribbean to the Atlantic. The Caribbean, greatly reduced in size from current dimensions, was almost a totally enclosed sea.[12] Ivar's conclusion was that there could not have been a "lost" continent in the Atlantic Ocean, not of the size and scope Plato described. In fact, there didn't need to be a missing piece—America described Atlantis fully.

The importance of Atlantis, of course, goes far beyond geographical or archaeological inquiry. It's importance goes to the heart of man's conscious purpose in the universe, and to the essence of our relationship with the force that created the universe, and made man the observer and measure thereof. If Atlantis was in the Americas, some vestige of cosmic awareness that constituted the heart of the last Golden Age should still be detectable. And it is: The evidence is that, despite a physical destruction of the center of Atlantis and the world-wide destructive activities of mankind, the principles on which

Atlantis was founded have endured. After an age, thousands of years in duration, in which enlightened man was reduced to a simple farmer, the germs of truth, cohesion with the galactic whole reasserted its purpose again in Mesoamerica, probably 5,000 to 8,000 years ago, with the concepts of the Golden Age intact. Flourishing again for millennia it mysteriously self-destructed just several centuries before Columbus. It's record, however, was largely still intact when Columbus arrived in the "New World." Traces of a great navigational culture greeted Columbus at every turn. How could he have missed their implications? How could subsequent science and Archaeology still dismiss the spheres as an "out of context" enigma?

The evidence is far from complete. In looking back into the past we can be sure that for every navigational find we have made, thousands remain undiscovered. Most will never be found, for decay and transformation are part of the immutable laws of nature. Pyramids endure, reed boats and cloth sails perish. Yet evidence of ancient seafarers has been found, and this evidence has been systematically ignored.

Ivar confronted established science with his new perspective on the spheres in Costa Rica. They again responded that the spheres had been constructed by Choretegas, the earliest known people of Costa Rica. Ivar objected that the spheres had been found, even by traditional archaeologists, to be too sophisticated to have been built by any known cultures of the region. Ivar insisted that they must relate to the oldest known culture of Meso-America, the Olmecs, and that they must date back to an age when megalithic structures were being built throughout the world. The establishment answer was simply put, "Do not bother established theory with 'out of context' information." Instead, Ivar enlisted the aid of writer George Erikson. Together, they began a determined search for mounting evidence that would upset accepted science and establish a new paradigm—one that would include the enigmas of the Americas.

2 The Pagan Paradigm: *A Conspiracy of Ignorance?*

A DISASTER *is about to occur . . . It has been a clear and quiet day, almost motionless under a white hot sun that pierces the skin and stifles the air. It is a blue sky, cool in its appearance, yet defying reality. But it has promise. It has been the first clear day since the close passing of a comet, months before brought, at first, relief and exhilaration to the citizens of Poseidon. They had survived that near collision but were not prepared for the aftermath. What followed was a period of great stress for the Atlantean people and their planet. The comet's near miss disturbed the atmosphere, bringing fire storms of dust and debris that stunted the growth of all plant life and destroyed the crops. Thick clouds formed that cooled the Earth unnaturally and obscured the sun for months. The clouds were followed by heavy rains that flooded the land. Giant waves breached the outer walls and subsequent tides have not receded, but have claimed more of the land, so that the capital itself is threatened. The proud Atlantean fleet, badly battered, half destroyed, has put out to sea. Volcanoes and Earthquakes rumble through the countryside daily, instilling constant fear in the people. It is the year 13,133 of the Atlanteans but one day it will be reckoned as 10,513 B.C. The omens—frantic activity of birds, sudden disappearance of insects, the display of bad temper of all mammals, domestic and wild—have confirmed the myth that violent upheaval follows the appearance of a comet.*

In the remains of this first clear day, a loud, nervous crowd has assembled in the center of the "red city," Poseidon. Its citizens have gathered below the ancient observatory desperately awaiting some word of hope from their leaders. The entire population alternately looks to the sky and back at the astronomer-priests who are peering down at the sighting device on an elaborate telescope. The sky quickly darkens and a systematic search by the grim faced astronomers begins. Shouts from the crowd quickly distract them. The crowd grows more frantic, though oddly quieter. As the moon moves across the sky a bright detail distinguishes itself. The chief astronomer realizes that a telescopic scan of the heavens will not be necessary. Focusing on the brilliant object he confirms what has been apparent to the crowd's naked eye—there is a bright object in the sky growing steadily larger and brighter. Near it, slightly fainter, the astronomer sees another object and past it, barely smaller, a third. The astronomer realizes that what the crowd perceives as one bright object in the sky is in reality at least three large asteroids, all loosed from their orbit by the comet, all on a collision course with Earth. The high astronomer-priest turns to his long-faced colleagues. "God is coming," he says softly. "He's coming with a vengeance!"

Below, the crowd has grown silent in confirmation of the words of the priest. Then shrieks are heard as a meteor shower lights the night sky. A great wind appears and whirlwinds and cyclones spiral through the square picking up sand, stones, and rocks, hurling them at the dispersing crowd. In the observatory above them the head priest speaks, "We've got to get to the pyramid, it's our only hope!" Another priest answers, "But it's never been completed. You know it was abandoned centuries ago. The prophesies seemed so remote—until now."

Suddenly a meteor shower reaches the Earth. Thousands of meteors strike the atmosphere at once, dazzling, then blinding the populace. An unnatural heat and great rushes of wind follow. Men, women, and children are lifted into the air and thrown against the stone and marble buildings. Those that can, or care to, see the priests fleeing the observatory, running toward the low mountains that surround the city. The great lantern in the sky grows larger, minute by minute, and small fiery meteorites, rain on the Earth. For several hours the people of Atlantis scramble desperately as a deafening subterranean sound rumbles under their feet. Acts of heroism and cowardice abound—none make the slightest difference. Shortly before midnight an asteroid, over five miles wide, enters the Earth's outer atmosphere. A fraction of a second later it plunges into the Caribbean Sea and strikes its bed, exploding with the force of a million atomic bombs. Temperatures three times the surface of the Sun are created. Distant volcanoes erupt, Earthquakes rock the land, chasms swallow whole buildings, the forests are set ablaze, one ridge, instantaneously, after another. Plants wither and then burst into flames. Skin and hair are singed but cannot be smelled. The shrieks of parrots and pygmy elephants, so beloved by the Atlanteans, can no longer be heard. The remaining population is turned to ash.

The angle of intersection of the asteroid with the Earth begins at a little over 30 degrees, but the Earth's gravitational pull accentuates the descent to an angle of 45 degrees, and greatly accelerates its speed. Striking the Earth in opposition to its east-to-west rotation, the force of the blow slows, and seems to stop the rotation for several minutes. The rotation was slowed, not completely stopped, but the peoples of Asia, on the opposite side of the world, will long remember the event as the day the sun stood still.

The stress on the Earth's crust is immense. Under pressure from the shaking Earth, the great Sphinx of Atlantis cracks then splits in two. The unfinished pyramid crumbles and topples into a newly formed chasm. Poseidon itself crumbles into an empty sea bed, evaporated and blown outward for hundreds of miles around. The sea surrounding Atlantis is virtually dissolved. It will return, soon enough, but not before the rest of the globe feels the effects of the collision. Africa and Europe, shaken by world-wide Earthquakes, will be the first to experience inundation. For, as the Earth slows its rotation the oceans continue to move on. A giant wave, a green mound of water 2,000 feet high, crashes over Europe and Africa. At the same instant a wave 600 feet high strikes the eastern shores of the Mediterranean, flooding the entire coast from Asia Minor to the mouths of the Nile. As the first wave strikes the Pillars of Hercules it is squeezed into a violent chute of water that rises 8,000 feet above the sea floor. When it strikes the Atlantean colony of Malta it is 4,000 feet high as it lifts the great megaliths and throws them eastward. A second, mightier wave strikes the Middle East with a wall of water 2,000 feet high.

At Poseidon the wall of water that rushes in to fill the evaporated sea is 3,000 feet high. Its force, moving 800 miles per hour, carries it thundering through the low hills and valleys. It completely inundates all but the highest peaks of the land, stripping it of life in its path. In only minutes it crosses the narrow center of the continent, the heart of Atlantis, sweeping across from sea to sea.

A few, herders in the mountains and astronomers in the half completed pyramid, temporarily survive, until a gaseous cloud, 2000 degrees centigrade, singes and burns whatever life is left on the surface to a dry and powdery crisp. Even a thousand miles from the impact the oceans are evaporated to a depth of 50 feet and only the smart sea creatures, sensing the coming cataclysm and diving deep, persevere.

The atmosphere above Poseidon is sucked up and away from the Earth by the tremendous heat. Thousands of miles away from the blast at the glaciated northern extremes of Atlantis, and across the barren land bridge in Siberia, the cold land is further refrigerated as the atmosphere is suddenly drawn toward the evacuated atmosphere of Atlantis's heart. Dire wolves, mastodons, and saber-toothed tigers, long adapted to the cold, thin air of the glacial north expire en masse as the temperature suddenly drops 120 degrees Fahrenheit. Ice crystals instantly form in their lungs. Breathing stops. Mammoths freeze while standing upright with undigested grasses in their mouths. The blast is most devastating on the thin strip of the continent facing directly into the blast, that which lies near the equator. In a single day and night, Poseidon, the heart of Atlantis, is destroyed.

Miraculously, even at the isthmus, a few gold miners survive. As the Earth itself shuddered they had huddled deep in protective pockets of the mines. Somehow, days later, a few find their way out. When the ground is cool enough they move down out of the mountain caves, incredulous, delirious, but seeking some evidence of the world they knew, a world that no longer exists. Underneath the thick clouds that have formed from the Earth's evaporated seas there is still enough light . . . red and eerie light from fires and exploding volcanoes . . . that the few survivors can see the ruins of their city-state. There are no remains of terrestrial creatures, none of their fellow men, none of their beasts, none of their pets. Where men had lived, in harmony and honest trade and skills, there are only the remains of creatures from the sea, washed up from the great tidal wave, and the crazed ones cry out that God has turned his people into fish. Others, more forlorn, simply remain quiet. There is nothing to say.

Three Rabbit is among the survivors. In the dim eerie glow he wonders if he is dreaming. But he wonders more about his wife and his young twin sons. Then he stumbles upon the broken balsa logs from a ship that has been thrown up into the mountains, even though he is standing, a mile above and thirty miles from the sea. Three Rabbit then knows that this is a dream that will not pass away. Paradise is lost.

•

A myth? No, this rendering is not one myth. It is a synthesis of many myths from the primitive and archaic peoples of the Americas . . . a continent once called Atlantis. But "primitive" and "archaic" are recent terms used to describe peoples who were once neither, and a myth, accurately transmitted through the ages, is not a simple challenge to history as we understand it, it is often history's true vessel—an oral transmission that endures, despite conquests, tortures, book-burnings, and meticulous revisions by Church and State. Myth finds a way to survive. The Atlantis myth even survived the comments of Plato's student, Aristotle, who scoffed at its account in Plato's *Critias,* declaring, "He who created Atlantis also destroyed it."

Aristotle's seemingly offhand comment was, in fact a repudiation of Plato's Ideas, the circular nature of time, and of myth itself as the repository of truth. Aristotle's condemnation of the Atlantis myth not only demonstrated the significance of the rift that developed between these two philosophers, it also helped mark a turning point in how man regarded himself and his place in the cosmos. Plato and his notion of a magical and intelligent universe hearkened back to an earlier age. Aristotle's world view looked forward to a scientific age. And time has demonstrated that mankind—his philosophy, his politics, and his concept of history—was to take Aristotle's side of the argument. Myth, as the portrayer of finite man's interaction with immeasurable cosmic truths, was replaced by the concepts of categories, and measurable reality, and later, with the distinct aid of Sir Isaac Newton, by empirical science. These measurers of the new sciences of man created in their wake a mechanical and dead universe, more resembling a clock than a living organism.

Of course, the mythic vision of our past never had been solely Plato's to create, nor was it Aristotle's to destroy. In vast reaches of the world, untouched by the Eurocentric world view, among primitive peoples, and among sometimes sophisticated navigators and astronomers, the myth of Atlantis endured. The Atlantis myth was and is a universal Myth of the destruction, by conflagration and deluge, of a people who had grown too proud, and who had lost harmony with the gods of the heavens. This same myth has been repeated a hundred times over in cultures from around the world, under different names, set in different locations, and ascribed to seemingly different times. But Plato, aided by the knowledge of ancient Egyptians, had given it a particular name, a particular location, and a particular time.

That place was the Americas, the time was about 11,500 years ago, and the inhabitants of this advanced culture were navigators, architects, and astronomers—both in Plato's rendering and by the evidence of later cultures

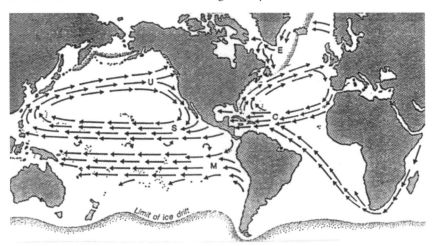

2A. THE PREVAILING WINDS AND CURRENTS OF THE WORLD'S OCEANS AND THE SEA ROUTES NAVIGATORS WOULD HAVE USED. The Atlantic Ocean could not have been home to Atlantis 11,500 years ago, but it could have been a sea-way, a virtual conveyor belt to the "lost continent." It is far easier to sail across the Atlantic from Iberia to the Americas under steady winds and a favoring current than it is to sail even half that distance in the Mediterranean where currents are tricky and winds can blow hard from any direction and then dissipate into a sailors' nightmare—a complete calm.

rebuilt from myth (fig. 2A). But before presenting new evidence that the heart and center of Atlantis and of the Americas were once the same, we must undertake a re-creation of the past. We must reexamine those factors—the mis-interpretation of evidence and mis-application of theories—that have led conventional authorities to presume that advanced civilization in the Americas is a recent and isolated event. It is time to question authority. Only then can the repudiation of the antiquity of America's ancient civilizations be put in perspective. Believers of the concept of a living universe have been judged ignorant, their beliefs and constructions called "pagan." Was it conspiracy, ignorance, or a "conspiracy of ignorance" that led the Catholic Church, European historians, and Americanist archaeologists all to confer the "Pagan Paradigm" on native Americans?

On suddenly and unexpectedly encountering a continent with great cities, circular canals and monuments obviously geared to observance of the heavens, one might think that its discoverers would exult in finding "so glorious a new world," and that some would even infer that the source of the legend of Atlantis was at hand. A few of those that followed the discoverers actually did just that, reporting that they had found the true identity of Atlantis. Columbus himself boasted of finding the original Garden of Eden. These reports were largely ignored. Most of the followers of the discoverers and Conquistadors were too busy conquering, plundering, and subjugating the peoples of the Americas to entertain the question of just who and what they were plundering. Reports of gold and of the possible location of El Dorado were really all that interested the Spanish crown and most of its subjects. The Roman Catholic Church had other interests (fig. 2B).

The reports by Cortez's chroniclers of a great city at the inland Aztec capital of Tenochtitlán, in particular, caught the attention of both Church and State. The Church of Spain quickly sent emissaries to the New World. One scholar-priest, Don Carlos de Siguenza, befriended the descendants of the Mexican kings, learned the Nahuatl language, and studied the manuscripts and codices of the Toltecs—the people who had preceded the Aztecs in Mexico. Siguenza, a Jesuit priest, was as well a poet, a mathematician and an astronomer. As such he was able to gain the confidence of Aztec priests who had hid sacred texts from the invading Spanish. They shared their remarkable manuscripts and drawings with the learned friar, including calculations based on eclipses of the sun and the moon and paintings depicting the passing of comets. From the evidence, Siguenza concluded that the Toltecs and their predecessors, the Olmecs were an ancient race, descended from a continent or group islands that must have been Plato's legendary Atlantis.[1]

The Americas, as an expression of Plato's "ideal state," reflecting his canons

2B. A "WATER MIRROR" FROM COSTA RICA. The "pagan paradigm", first expressed by the Catholic Church, viewed Mesoamerican culture as primitive and barbaric. As a justification of the conquest and decimation of the native Americans they called their star temples "ceremonial centers" in which evil ceremonies were performed. Indented slabs of stone like the one shown above were dubbed "sacri-  ficial altars," on which beating hearts were pulled from living victims. Americanist archaeologists have repeated the Church's version. We believe, however, these figures were shallow water mirrors used to teach astronomy and navigation.

of proportion and divine harmony in both their architecture and in their social organization, may have been lost on soldiers and seekers of El Dorado. It was not lost on the authorities of the Church. Siguenza was expelled from the Jesuit order. Although he retained many friendships in the order and was allowed to keep his books and manuscripts, publication of his work was denied. On his death most of his treasures were seized and burned by representatives of the Catholic Church in Spain. But some of his manuscripts were preserved by the Jesuits in Mexico. Unfortunately, the Jesuits were commanded to quit Mexico in 1767, many to face trail and execution in Spain for being too sympathetic to pagan cultures. Siguenza's treasures were also confiscated and either destroyed or transported back to Europe and possibly buried in some archives, (some say in the great hidden library maintained by the Vatican.)

If Friar Siguenza's voice was stilled, others were not. Another perplexing problem for the Church was presented by Friar Diego de Landa's report from the Yucatán peninsula that the Maya had a sophisticated science of astronomy that had recorded celestial events from the distant past. De Landa also reported that they had an equally sophisticated numbering system that traced their present age to 3113 B.C. by European reckoning, and that the Maya traced a preceding age back to 8238 B.C. This date was well before the date the Church had given as the origin of the world—5,500 years B.C. The Church was disturbed that the Maya had an obviously earlier date for creation. The discovery that the Maya had a calendar of eighteen months consisting of twenty days with an added five day "unlucky" period at the end of the year further alarmed church scholars. The Maya calendar was identical to the 360-day calendar of the oldest known Egyptians. Worse yet, some church scholars were aware that the Egyptians believed the god Thoth had brought the calendar and knowledge of mathematics, astronomy, and language to the Egyptian people from somewhere far across the sea.[2]

Other reports were equally disturbing to Church officials. The great pyramid at Cholula (fig. 2C), reminiscent in its stepped structure to the Ziggurats of Babylon, was believed by Toltec legend to have been built at the command of one the seven giants that survived the universal deluge. The purpose of the pyramid, built on the largest known base of any structure in the world, was to enable its builders to reach heaven. According to legend the Gods destroyed the pyramid with fire and confounded the language of the builders—so that they could no longer understand each other. Thus in one pre-conquest myth the Toltecs revealed a story very similar to biblical accounts of Noah and of the Tower of Babel.

Even more difficult to accept were the reported teachings of the "God-who-walked-as-a-man," Quetzalcoatl. His principle lessons of love and charity bore a striking similarity to the teachings of Christ and Buddha. If the existence of heretical thought and the worship of idols were perceived as a threat by the Church, how then was the information that in this distant land there may have been vestiges of a distinct civilization that was far older and, possibly, far more "enlightened" than any found in the Bible? Could the Holy Fathers accept the brilliance of a civilization that pre-dated their authority?

The Church recognized the importance and the potential threat of the astronomical sites and of their possible antiquity, and immediately sought to destroy and discredit them. They represented a challenge to the absolute authority of the Church, which, of course, could not be tolerated. However, when the chroniclers also reported that the natives indulged in pagan rituals, and provided detailed descriptions of human sacrifices, the Church and State breathed a sigh of relief. These reports were all the justification they needed

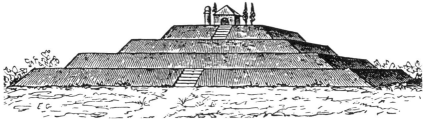

2C. The Great Pyramid at Cholula. Circular layouts of many ancient Central and South American cities reflect and echo the circular layout Plato gave for Poseidon, the capital of Atlantis. This structure has the largest base of any known pyramid in the world. It is believed to have once been crowned by a jade image of Quetzalcoatl but it was looted and destroyed by the Spanish. Its stones were used in building many of the churches that dominate present-day Cholula.[3]

2D. THE DESTRUCTION OF CHOLULA. Among the worst of the infamous acts of the Spanish was the massacre at Cholula. By one account, when he passed through the gates of Cholula, "Cortes was greeted by girls singing, dancing, and playing on instruments, while others brought bread and fowl. Nobles chieftains, and common folk, unarmed, with eager and happy faces, crowded in the great courtyard of the Temple of Quetzalcoatl to hear what the white men would say." Cortez and his men sealed the gates, raised their weapons and fell upon the Cholulans without warning, commencing to hammer, hatchet, and spear their guests until all had been slaughtered. "Those of Cholula were caught unaware. With neither arrows nor shields did they meet the Spaniards. Just so they were slain without warning. They were killed by pure treachery." Europe had come to the Americas. The accomplishment of the Greeks in creating a modern world can be attributed to the philosophy of Aristotle, just as its expansion can be attributed to his warring student, Alexander the Great. Meeting success, the state, no longer a concept, consolidated its base of power and presumed to banish the gods. To accomplish this they had to discredit myth, the container of man's relationship with his gods. And they did. But not without a struggle. The power of the newfound state, having forfeited its divine power, rested solely on military dominance. As the dominant power of the Greek military deteriorated, it was replaced by an authority that no longer rested on man's relationship with the gods, (Romans were permitted access to their borrowed Greek gods only as long as it didn't interfere with the business of the government of Rome), but on man's relationship with a law-giving and authoritarian state.

As the power of Rome itself deteriorated, the Church of Rome seized upon its organizational powers. Originally conceived as a Christian vessel the Church soon became a state unto itself replacing the content of its message with the authority of its message until its message was simply authority. Where man had once stood naked and responsible before his gods, he now stood, cloaked in dependency to an artificial creation without hope of enlightenment except through prescribed obedience to an omnipotent church-state. The Church, fearing disorder, embraced an immovable Earth, an unshakable Church, and obedient subjects. The decree was expressed thusly by Pope Pius IX, "The rights of the individual are great indeed, but the rights of the Church are Greater." Which effectively meant the rights of the individual were no more. For the individual, when one dared surface, the threat of loss of life, or loss of loved ones, surpassed any thought of disobedience. So it was with the Romans, so it was with the Roman Catholic Church. The Dark Ages were hard upon the people of Europe. The ideas embraced by the Dark Ages would soon devastate Mesoamerica.

for the complete domination and destruction of the natives peoples of the Americas.[4]

Under the direction of friars and bishops, the Church undertook the virtual obliteration of all vestiges of ancient civilization (fig. 2D). While soldiers plundered precious gold objects containing sacred hieroglyphs and astronomical observations and melted them down into gold bars to be shipped to Spain, men of the cloth, notably Bishops de Landa and de Zumarraga, aided by enslaved natives, smashed thousands of stone "idols," and razed temples to the ground. The stones of the destroyed temples would later be used to build Catholic Churches on top of the ancient sites, a practice that had been common throughout "pagan" Europe as well. The paintings and writings of the ancient Americans were gathered and publicly burned. Those who opposed the will of the Church were labeled "idol worshippers" and were ceremoniously burned at the stake.[5] Even the Americans who greeted the Spanish as liberators from Aztec rule met a cruel fate.

Exuberance over the discovery of a new and ancient world excited the peoples of Europe. Yet, all travel to Mexico was forbidden by the Spanish Crown. Writings sympathetic to Native Americans were suppressed, burned, or buried in archives.[6] Scholars in the 19th century, controlled by the Church, pronounced that the astronomical gardens of Mesoamerica had no such purpose but were merely devices to remind the people when to plant crops! (Does any farmer need an elaborate astronomical garden to tell him when spring has arrived?) When Mexican scholar Leon y Gama marveled at the intricacies of the Aztec stone disc, declaring it to be a sophisticated calendar, the Church quickly suppressed his writings, arguing that the "calendar stone" was a sacrificial altar whose intricate markings were merely ornamental, the work of "irrational and simple-minded beings."[7] The mission to dominate, destroy and discredit, was not a mere zealous mistake on the part of the Catholic Church and was certainly not done out of blind ignorance. It was a coldly calculated and brutal erasure of traces of civilizations that predated, not only Christ, but sites "sacred" to the Old Testament as well. Their utter success in obliterating the native American cultures laid the basis for a profound ignorance that would endure for centuries.

While the Catholic Inquisition took harsh exception to any scholarship that praised the achievements of Native Americans, subsequent Protestant depiction was often worse. Unable to distinguish between a culture that in its decline practiced human sacrifice, but in its millennias of glory, hearkened back to Golden Age of human existence, European historians—their own history the product of generations of brutal warfare, their cities ringed with intricate defenses—accepted and embraced the stories brought back by messengers of the Church that told of hideous child sacrifice and ritual brutality (fig. 2E).

There is a great deal more evidence that for hundreds and thousands of years the builders of star temples lived peacefully in city-states, inter-connected by great limestone roads, called *sacbeob*, as well by an intricate system of canals that ran between the city-states, and connected them all to the sea. In Mesoamerica all these city-states stood open to each other, built without walls, without protective barriers, so that any man or band of men could enter another city without having to overcome, moats, bastions, catapults, or burning oil.

Walled cities and warfare as a means and end of life had ruled Europe and

2E. AZTEC STONE CALENDAR. The Aztec Stone disc was not a "sacrificial altar." It was an intricate calendar that measured the movements of the gods—the stars and the planets. In myth as in classical legends man's fate lay both in his own hands and in the hands of the gods who, invariably represented movements by the heavenly bodies, which (who) could behave in a benevolent and orderly fashion, or could behave in disorderly manner, whimsically, and unleash great violence. In Mesoamerica the nature of all things was determined by flowing interaction between the individual (the microcosm), and the heavenly gods (the macrocosm). Nations really had no significant role in this interplay. The greatness of nations sprang almost solely from the greatness of their leaders and their leaders relationship to the gods. However, in Greece, primarily in the city-state of Athens, a new concept of nation arose. A body politic emerged that eventually banished the whimsical powers of the individual and of his gods. Political stability, a state undreamed of in prior Greek myth or Homeric legend was achieved. But a price was paid. First the individual mind and then the minds of the gods themselves became subordinate to the glorified state.

the Near East since the terrible coming of the age of iron, around 1,000 B.C. For century after century, cities and states were burned and looted, women raped and murdered, men and children impaled on stakes or nailed to crosses. Their slow tortuous deaths were put on public display as a cruel lesson to the vanquished few still alive. By contrast, for 2,000 years the builders of cities without walls in the Americas lived in a very different world from that of the Europeans, and their huge rampaging armies. These same builders of sophisticated, organized cities, were branded "savages" by the conquering Europeans, an epithet still in wide use to this day. Yet instead of wholesale slaughter, disputes between states were settled among warriors in organized games played out on ball courts. In the aftermath a few brave men were ritually sacrificed. It was only much later, perhaps in the eighth century A.D., that more war-like tribes of Toltecs and Aztecs descended on Mesoamerica and carried out large scale massacres that resembled what had long been going on across the Atlantic. Even then Aztec cruelty may have come to resemble the ways of the "Old World," but it never saw its equal until the Conquistadors of Europe arrived on that fateful day that Cortez landed in Mexico.

Despite some wonderful scholarship, mostly by priests of the Catholic Church, the true nature of the peoples of the Americas was neither understood nor fully recorded. The portrayal of the Americans by European historians was one of arrogant denigration. Although few ventured to visit the actual ruins of palaces and temples described by the conquistadors' chroniclers, historians were quick to proclaim these constructions as primitive and degenerate. William Robertson, the 18th century's leading authority on the Americas, portrayed MesoAmerican architecture "as more fit to be the habitations of men just emerging from barbarity than to the residence of a polished people. . . . These structures convey no high idea of progress in art and ingenuity. . . . If buildings corresponding to such descriptions ever existed in the Mexican cities, it is probable that some remains of them would still be visible . . . the Spanish accounts appear highly embellished." Robertson concluded that both the people of America and their constructions were not "entitled to rank with those nations which merit the name civilized." Robertson's' word on the matter was not only accepted by academia, *it went unquestioned for a hundred years.*[8]

In this manner, the truth of who the peoples of the Americas had been was itself sacrificed to the mandates of a narrow Eurocentric point of view. Was it pure ignorance of what truly still existed in the Americas, or can we lay the blame on the Church's quick decimation of temples and records, that so highly regarded a historian could have been so wrong? In the end it doesn't really matter. European historians fed on each others accounts, increasingly belittling the architectural record of the Americas, so that by the end of the eighteenth century Cornelius de Pauw, a leading historian, would write, "the so-called palace occupied by the Mexican kings was a hut."[9]

The list of misconceptions that the Eurocentric mind fostered in its on-going appraisal of the Americas is endless. From the time that Church and State, separately and in concert, began to issue decrees and judgments on the Americas, an apparent conspiracy of ignorance has grown wider and wider. Historians and archaeologists have, perhaps unwittingly, done much to confirm each others' misperceptions. Since the time of Columbus's "rediscovery of America" to the later decades of the twentieth century, educators have been wrong on almost every count in their assessment of the antiquity and significance of civilization in the Americas. Those of us who attended grade school, high school and college in the middle decades of this century were subjected to an accumulation of misinformation concerning the history of the peoples of this "island-continent"—an aggregate "knowledge" without even a resemblance to the truth.

Item: When it was determined in the aftermath of Columbus's voyages that the "Indians" he had encountered were not Asian, but native to a New World, two questions arose: Who were these people, and how did they get there? The first question was itself two-fold and was answered by the Church. Were these natives truly human beings, and, if so, were there two separate creations? It took the puzzled Church until 1537 to answer the question with a decree that, yes, they were human beings and, yes, that there had been a single creation. The Indians had migrated to the American continent and were likely to have come from the Ten Lost Tribes of Israel.

The second question was answered by science—or so it seemed—and it apparently contradicted the Church's earlier pronouncement on American origins. Schoolbooks to this date still tell the story of migrations of primitive hunters from Asia. These hunters crossed the floor of the Bering Sea, laid bare by Ice-Age depletion of the seas, most likely between the years 11,000 B.C. and 9,000 B.C. when a six-hundred-mile-wide land link between Asia and America (Beringia) had been exposed by the heaping of ice on the continents, causing a lowering of the oceans by several hundred feet.

In fact, the idea of Beringia migration was first broached in 1590, not by a scientist, but by a padre of the Roman Catholic Church. Fray José de Acosta, in an apparent attempt to explain man's presence in the New World without giving too much credit to the Lost Tribes of Israel, or to Israel's possible connection and claim to the Americas—positions the Church had first broached and then later became uncomfortable with—proposed an extraordinary account of ancient events. Under apologist Acosta's theory the Americas were settled by primitive hunters who had originated in the most remote and primitive part of Asia—Siberia.[10] Thus, although human, the early Americans were judged descendants of among the most backward and isolated races of humanity, and were thought to have barely improved on their dreary origins.

The Church had long employed the most gifted theorists, and handsomely endowed them. Frey Acosta apparently had come up with a theory that pleased them greatly! Later, science seized on the idea, and, as it often has, followed the Church's lead, incorporating religious dogma into scientific dogma. A rather flimsy theory, based on no actual research, received universal acceptance from the scientific community and found its way into our body of scientific knowledge. It has remained there long enough that it is now considered conventional wisdom.

It made little difference that Acosta neither visited Beringia nor any part of America in support of his theory, and, subsequently, it has made no difference that the theory itself makes little sense. *It has been accepted. You can read about it in any textbook.* But these questions remain: Would Siberian hunters really follow migrating caribou farther and farther into the cold and dreary north during an Ice Age, with no knowledge of what lay ahead, until they'd reached warmer climates on another continent several thousand miles away? Could they have? The Arctic area at the end of the last Ice Age was very dry, and as a result, it was free of glaciers (as today Greenland is glaciated at its southern tip but bare in the north for lack of moisture). But the cold at that time was intense, probably more severe than that found today on the Antarctic continent where even today no Eskimo could long survive.

Beringia (fig. 2F) was portrayed by migration theorists as lushly vegetated, a natural lure for migrating caribou and their pursuers. But recent analysis of the ground that borders the present Bering Sea have revealed little or no pollen at the layers that existed during the last Ice Age. Apparently the land was ice-free but it was also plant free. It was so cold nothing could grow. Beringia was a dry and dusty plain barren of any vegetation. Could such a place have attracted the caribou and mammoths that supposedly, in turn, attracted the hunters?[11] It now appears unlikely that there was any game to follow. Even if these primitive hunters could have survived this bitter cold, and lack of food, and been foolish enough to want to follow some misbegotten, lost, and starving caribou, or even if they had some purpose in their trek that we do not understand, they would have been eventually thwarted in their effort—when coming down the North American continent, they soon would have run into an impenetrable ice sheet two miles thick and covering thousands of miles.

A melting period began about 14,000 years ago and continued for 2,000

Land ■ Glaciers ☐ Ocean

2.F. BERINGIA, THE REPORTED SITE OF PRIMITIVE MAN'S MIGRATION FROM SIBERIA TO THE AMERICAS. We must question Beringia theory. Hunters were unlikely to have survived a very cold crossing of the dry and barren Beringia plain. Caribou were also unlikely to have survived. They would have had no vegetation to eat, and the cold temperatures would have frozen their lungs, as well as the lungs of any human pursuers. Even if they could have crossed Beringia they would have still have had to cross over a two-mile-thick ice sheet for two thousand miles before they found anything to eat.

years, but rather than open a narrow corridor down the west coast of Canada that could have enabled land migration, the melting undoubtedly created wide and swiftly running rivers of icy water. Crossing these rivers would have required boats or canoes, vessels the American school of anthropology has insisted they could not have had. Even then the journey would have been extremely hazardous.

A better argument than that of a two-thousand mile ice-trek would be that man migrated along the same route but in canoes closely following the coast. Dana and Ginger Lamb proved that such a trip was feasible (at least in much warmer waters) in their journey in a dugout canoe from San Diego to Panama in the 1930s as recorded in their book, *Enchanted Vagabonds*.[12] But close-to-shore navigation is fraught with perils; unpredictable tides and currents, disturbed winds, rocks, shallows, and reefs. The experienced sailor is *always* more comfortable with the usually constant conditions of the open sea.

How did we get stuck with Beringia theory? In the early part of the twentieth century other proposals for migration were made, notably navigation. Proposals were made that man took an easier route to America, following and flowing on steady ocean currents that crossed the open seas. But Franz Boas, who from his post at Columbia University dominated the American Museum of Natural History and all American Indian Anthropology in the first half of this century, stated in 1925 that "the broad expanse of water made immigration impossible."[13] Thereafter it was uniformly agreed, among scholars, that primitive peoples throughout the world lacked the vessels and navigating skills, and more importantly, the will, to cross the oceans. Closed book. Boas has spoken.

Based on the Boas pronouncement S.K. Lothrop, the investigator who stated that the spheres were "out of context," was able to declare Peruvian balsa rafts unfit for oceanic navigation (fig. 2G), commenting that they "could not travel as far as to the Polynesian islands, not even to the Galapagos group, a few hundred miles offshore." In 1932 he published "*Aboriginal Navigation of the West Coast of South America*" asserting that the balsa raft ". . . absorbs water rapidly and loses its buoyancy completely after a few weeks. Owing to this characteristic it was necessary to take the Jangada (balsa raft) apart at intervals, haul the logs ashore, and there allow them to dry out completely." It did not matter that Lothrop was personally unacquainted with balsa rafts or with sailing in general. Academia took his word on this matter, just as it would later accept his assessment of the spheres as "out of context."

In *Early Man And The Ocean*, Thor Heyerdahl points out that Lothrop had based his opinion on the writings of G. Byam, a nineteenth-century British traveler who had only once spotted a balsa raft in the distance. Byam's opinion of the raft's capability was based on theories propounded by the captain of his ship, who also apparently had no first hand knowledge of balsa rafts, but did have a contempt for them. Nevertheless Lothrop's conclusion, based on Byam's account of an unnamed captain's opinion, was taken as doctrine. Based on Lothrop's assessment, Inca authority P.A. Means wrote of the balsa that "it was obviously a type of boat that would awake nothing but scorn in the breast of shipbuilders of almost any other maritime people in the world."[14] (This is but a further example of how research on the Americas has "progressed.")

Heyerdahl also pointed out that the negativity toward Peruvian balsa rafts was based not only on prejudice but on a key misapprehension: Old dry balsa logs (the kind described by Lothrop) did get waterlogged when exposed to sea water; freshly cut green balsa logs that the Incas (and pre-Incas) actually used retained their own sap, and *never* became waterlogged. Further, Heyerdahl theorized that the "wash through" construction of the rafts "allowed all entering water to disappear as through a sieve." Waves that would have swamped or severely tossed a hulled boat simply passed through the wave-hugging balsas. Heyerdahl not only pronounced the balsas more fit, *he proved it*. In 1947 he

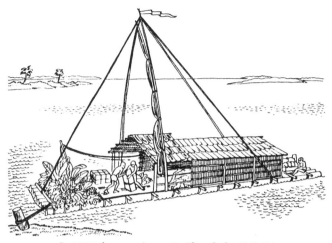

2.G. BALSA RAFTS. In 1932 the prominent Pacific scholar R.B. Dixon presented evidence that the sweet potato had been carried by man from Peru to Polynesia in Pre-Columbian times and suggested that balsa navigators had carried the plant across the ocean. The leading scholar on Polynesia, Sir Peter Buck responded in *An Introduction To Polynesian Anthropology,* "Since the South American Indians had neither the vessels nor the navigating ability to cross the ocean space between their shores and the nearest Polynesian islands, they may be disregarded as the agents of supply."[15] Dixon, on learning of Lothrop and Buck's assessment of the balsa raft, quickly backed down. There was no question of the sweet potato's genetic origins in South America. And it is still called by its Quechua name, *kumara,* in both Peru and Polynesia. But Dixon knuckled under to the weight of superior academic authority and recanted of the notion of navigational contact. How then did the sweet potato get from Peru to Polynesia at dates of 12 to 15,000 years ago? Did some bird carry its large tubers across the ocean? Did those tubers arrive with an attached name tag, or had it been carried by another, genetically American life-form, the parrot, with the parrot squawking its name throughout its journey?

sailed the balsa raft *Kon-Tiki* from Peru to the Tuamotu Islands, a voyage of over 4,300 miles, in 101 days.

Reaction to Heyerdahl's achievement in academia was mixed at best. Just because Heyerdahl proved the Incas and their predecessors could have sailed across the Pacific doesn't mean they actually did it. And why, after all, would they attempt so dangerous an undertaking? They could have better asked why man would wander thousands of miles over huge glaciers to migrate via the Bering Straits. But they didn't. Reasons for voyaging over the open sea are manifold: trade, adventure, new fishing grounds, prestige—provided you return with the right goods or interesting tales—and even the exiling of undesirables. And all of this could be accomplished in a year or two, not over several generations of wandering through icy fields. The sea was warm, the ships were seaworthy, the sailors competent, the wind and currents favorable. But the established authorities considered primitive man and his craft incapable of such voyages. Heyerdahl's theories and actual accomplishments could not change the accepted paradigm.

Later Heyerdahl reopened the book by demonstrating in the *Ra* Expeditions just how easy it was to sail across the Atlantic on re-creations of reed rafts in use 6,000 years ago on Lake Chad in Africa and on Lake Titicaca in Bolivia. From examinations of skeletal remains we now know that navigators from south east Asia settled in Australia 80,000 years ago, crossing a broad expanse of open sea in their voyages. And we know that subsequent Melanesian and Polynesian voyages peopled most of the now-inhabited islands of the Pacific in antiquity. In fact, the Polynesians were not limited to the Pacific. Mitachondrial DNA evidence shows that the inhabitants of Madagascar 3,000 years ago were Polynesians, a people who lived an ocean-and-a-half away. But, in academia, the terrestrial paradigm for migration had been established, the navigational paradigm dismissed, and the establishment has forced the terrestrial view upon us ever since. In fact, Dr. Glyn Daniel, former general editor of the Thames & Hudson archeological books, called Heyerdahl's achievements "academic rubbish."[16]

Item: In 1975 more than twenty large stones, hand-shaped in the form of cylinders and doughnuts, were found in 30 feet of water off the coast of southern California. The stones were evidently anchors, evidenced by groves and drilled holes to which heavy ropes could be secured. Since identical stones have been found in China for thousands of years and have not been in use there for more than 500 years a few anthropologists have been bold enough to speculate that the stones proved pre-Columbian contact between China and America. Noted historian Frank J. Frost scoffed at the idea, contending that nineteenth century Chinese immigrants lost the anchors while fishing at sea. Yet photos and records of nineteenth century Chinese craft show that they used iron anchors, made in America![17]

Item: Sylvanus Morley, the Carnegie Institute investigator whose work in Guatemala in the 1930's made him the leading authority on MesoAmerican Archaeology, wrote, "The ancient Maya emerged from barbarism probably during the first or second century of the Christian era." Morley based his opinion on dates he gleaned from stelae at Tikal and Uaxactun; it was an opinion that required acceptance of several assumptions. It assumed that Tikal and Uaxactun, both located in the Peten region of Guatemala, were the oldest Maya sites (fig. 2H).

Morley also assumed that the calendrical system and the systems of writing and numerals, including the concept of zero, that were incorporated on these stelae, had emerged as suddenly as the stelae themselves without the thousands of years of development such sophisticated systems would normal-

2H. TIKAL, GUATEMALA. Hooded, steep pyramids at Tikal suggest a culture that could rival, in scariness and intimidation, the Pittsburgh Steelers, or Hollywood's Darth Vader and Star Wars, whichever you fancy. The indication that such structures were built more for show than with any evil intent, is clearly shown by the fact that, despite the ability to create great stone structures, walls were almost never built around the city-states of Mesoamerica.

Sylvanus Morley had overseen the excavation of Tikal. When the work was done Morley declared that it was the most ancient and powerful site in Mesoamerica. In fact, after Morley's death, great Maya sites such as El Mirador, which contained pyramids larger than those at Tikal, were found to be several hundred years older. And the Mayan site of Cuello in the jungles of nearby Belize has been found to be at least 2,000 years older than Morley's date for Tikal.

---

ly take, and without the thousands of years of observation their astronomical records would require. He shrugged off the question of development with the observation that the Maya were simply "the most brilliant *aboriginal* people."[18] Apparently, among "brilliant" aborigines, no development of astronomical centers, no formative stages, and no trial and error were necessary.

Morley helped establish the academic paradigm—the Mayans were the most ancient indigenous Americans, and not much had been happening with them, except primitive agriculture, until the first century A.D.. He also established that Tikal, the excavation under his direction, was the oldest Mayan site in Mesoamerica. At that time there were only a few dozen known sites. Now that there are more than ten thousand, most unexcavated, we must question whether the one Morley presided over was, in fact, the oldest.

The Church had had no way of dating MesoAmerican civilization. They simply decreed that it was more recent than Jesus Christ, systematically destroyed all records to the contrary, and then sat back hoping they wouldn't be proven wrong. Centuries later, the Church's favor to science was repaid. Morley, Americanist Archaeology, and science confirmed the Church's decree.

The mandate of American Archaeology has been that the first major sites discovered by preeminent archaeologists had to be the grandest and the oldest. Morley's excavation of Tikal had to be the excavation of the font of Maya culture. At that time, of course, the Americanists thought that they would never encounter another site to match Tikal's grandeur, or that the significance Morley attached to this one site could never be challenged. Then Caracol, in the Mayan mountains of Belize, a country long considered a "backwater" of the Maya, was discovered. Caracol matched Tikal in power, boasting in its stelae of military victories over Tikal, and dwarfed it in size. El Mirador, on the Guatemalan border with Mexico, had larger pyramids and was hundreds of years older. Cuello, in Belize was at least two thousand years older. Nearby Cerros, mostly hidden under waters that rose at the end of the Pleistocene, could be *very* much older, and when finally excavated, very much grander. And all these sites exhibited mathematical and astronomical knowledge that Morley had not found at Tikal. Yet cautious investigators have been very slow to understand or to relate understanding of these more recently discovered sites.

Yet Morley's arbitrary (and self-enhancing) dates became so entrenched in the minds of archaeologists that when, in the 1950s, radiocarbon dating gave Teotihuacan (site of the Pyramids of the Sun and the Moon) a probable date of 900 B.C., the report was greeted with ridicule. Later tests have yielded dates in excess of 1400 B.C.[19]

Item: When archaeologist Matthew Stirling discovered a colossal Negroid head at the Olmec site of Tres Zapotes, and later found others at La Venta (south of present day Veracruz, Mexico), he proposed a date of 600 B.C., for Olmec culture (fig. 2I). Academic laughter at such an early date ensued. Curiously, Michael Coe, Yale Professor of Archaeology, and a leading MesoAmerican historian, did not dispute the dates (they were later confirmed by a National Geographic-Smithsonian-University of California expedition as 814 B.C., and are now conservatively dated as 1200-900 B.C.). But Coe emphatically denied that the stone faces were Negroid. He contended that the reason the stones had African features was that the primitive tools used to cut them were too blunt to make sharper noses or thinner lips! But how would he explain the intricately carved braids or short kinky-haired beards on the stones? How did he explain smaller carvings displaying Phoenician-like images of sharp noses and thin lips found in immediate proximity to the stones and dated to the same period? How did he explain the small terra cotta (clay) figures found lying about the great stone heads, all of them depicting figures with thick lips, broad noses, kinky hair, and goatee beards? Coe responded to this last question in a *Science Digest* interview in 1981 by saying he was "unaware" of the clay figurines, even though they have been well documented and are on display in the Museum of Anthropology in Mexico City. Very recently historians have had to concede that, since blacks from the Sudan dominated Egypt during the period from 1200 B.C. to 900 B.C., the Negroes portrayed at La Venta were likely not only to have traveled *with* Egyptians of the classic period, they very likely *were* the Egyptians of that era.

It is a habit of the "establishment" to ignore or to dismiss that which doesn't fit into their theoretical paradigm. Thus the colossal heads at La Venta weren't Negroid because there could have been no African contact with America in 800 B.C. Academia could not admit the possibility of contact because, to do so, they would have had to revise theory they held sacred—the neo-darwinian hypothesis of a separate evolution, with various civilizations appearing similar due to man's inevitable response to similar problems.

Other anthropologists, called mavericks by some, admit a Negroid influence, theorizing that Phoenician sailors brought Negro slaves with them when they colonized America. But one must wonder how likely it is that such

2.I. OLMEC HEAD AT LA VENTA, MEXICO. The Olmec culture predated the Mayan "Classical Period" by over two thousand years, according to traditional dating. Actually, they were contemporaries. The Aztecs, who came much later, and who were curiously eager to please the conquering Spanish, told them that the Toltec god, Quetzalcoatl, (the Mayan god Kukulcan), was a tall, bearded white man. But they were saying this to bearded white men whom they feared. The truth is that Quetzalcoatl, the kind god who denounced any form of human sacrifice, was more often depicted as a black man, but most often depicted as a red man.

colonists, if they were Phoenician, would have left behind small plaques of their own likenesses, while erecting huge monuments to their slaves—some eight feet tall, eighteen feet in circumference, and weighing over twenty-four tons! Since the stones from which the heads are carved had to be transported from many miles away through thick jungle, this would have been quite a testimony to the Phoenicians' love for their slaves. Could it be that the archaeologists have got it all wrong, that the Africans were the masters, the Phoenicians their vassals, employed because of their seafaring skills? Even that suggestion would overturn concepts of dominance between the races that Eurocentric minds hold dear (though few admit it). This notion of Western white dominance is simply a modern imposition on a world that had no idea of our prejudices, no anticipation of our limited thought. Call it ethnocentrism, call it prejudice, call it the preeminence of the "Western" world, something the dominant mindset inherited from the Greeks . . . it isn't valid.

In our dynamic world, current values simply can't be applied to past civilizations. The ancient world was as different from our own as the future world will be; not accessible by our standards, and not susceptible to our re-creations, no matter how well or despicably motivated.

There have been a few cracks inflicted upon the ivory tower of academic isolationism. Alexander von Wuthenau's *Unexpected Faces In Ancient America* details a multitude of African, Mongoloid, and Semitic portraits in the art of ancient America which he attributes, in part, to voyages of Nubian Kushites who gained great power in Egypt from 1200 to 800 B.C.—although evidence suggests that the Negroid heads at La Venta and Tres Zapotes are much older than these dates. Ivan Van Sertima found Egyptian presence in the Americas a thousand years before Christ (figs. 2J, K, L, M). Professor Barry Fell found ample evidence of Phoenician writing throughout the Americas. And, with meticulous scholarship, Professor Cyrus Gordon confirmed the Paraiba Stone, found in Brazil in 1872, to be an authentic Phoenician inscription of the sixth century B.C.[20] (Later we will present evidence of navigational encounters between the lands of the Mediterranean and America, and between Asia and America, that span millennia before these dates).

But the cracks are being quickly plastered over. As evidence that the Morley-Coe paradigm still holds conventional sway, Charles Pellegrino in *Unearthing Atlantis,* a well received book published in 1991, boldly describes the year 1478 AD as "a world full of disparate civilizations that had yet to find one another."[21] And Irene Nicholson in *Mexican And Central American Mythology* flatly states of the gigantic head at La Venta, "This example has Negroid features, though there were no Negroes in America at such an early time."[22] How did she know that? Is it any wonder philosopher Immanuel

2.J. WARRIOR WITH MUSTACHE (PHOENICIAN?) AT EL CEIBAL
2.K. RULER WITH CHINESE FACE AT COPAN
2.L. OLMEC (NEGROID)
2.M. SEMITIC FIGURE FROM EL SALVADOR

All of the above have been dated to from 1,400 to 4,000 years BP. We must ask, "Are these the faces of Ancient Americans?" Contrary to what we would expect, the further we go back in time the more diversity we encounter. If America had been isolated, then populated by Mongoloid nomads crossing the Bering Strait, and then isolated for millennia more, wouldn't early Americans have a more homogenous look? Wouldn't their DNA have been less diverse? Instead Americans, at the time of Columbus, had the most diverse DNA of any people in the world.

Velikovsky called college teachers "purveyors of fossilized notions offered as ultimate truths?"[23]

Item: At Chichen Itza, the famed Maya center in the Yucatán, temples adjacent to the main ball court are decorated with mythological warriors and battle scenes. Depictions of gods include a deity who is both winged and bearded. Distinct from the gods, but carved on walls and columns throughout Chichen Itza are depictions of triumphant warriors who have distinctly Eastern Mediterranean features and full beards.[24] Since the Maya had no facial hair it is obvious that some other people, possibly Phoenicians, had once lived there and exerted a considerable influence on the decorators of the monuments. Yet Americanist scholars have long denied the existence of "foreign peoples" in ancient America. They claim that the depicted figures did not have true beards but wore "false beards" akin to the depicted nobility of Pharaonic Egypt. But this argument begs the question, if the Maya were imitating a bearded race with false beards just who was it they were imitating (fig. 2N)? If there was no contact where did the notion of beards and of ceremonial false beards come from?

Item: In *Voyagers To The New World*, Nigel Davies correctly points out a flaw in Thor Heyerdahl's theory. Heyerdahl questioned how it would be possible for New World cultures to have arisen so rapidly unless they were imported from another continent. Davies points out that for a time it was thought the vast Chavin site in the Andes, whose cut stones are almost identical to

2.N. "Uncle Sam" at Chichen Itza. At the North Temple (also called "The Temple of the Bearded Man") a bearded figure supports the heavens.

those of the great Egyptian pyramids, had appeared suddenly. But later information has proved that Chavin culture developed over many millennia, not by a sudden introduction. Michael Moseley has shown that "the growth of Chavin was a long-drawn-out process." Dates of elaborate construction in the ceremonial areas in Peru now predate accepted dates for Egyptian constructions. Mummies, similar to those found in Egypt dating to 5,000 years ago, are now being dated as at least 8,000 years old in Peru. In fact, it is in Egypt, Mesopotamia and China that great civilizations seemed to spring suddenly into view. But citing anthropologists who point to an abundance of similarities, including female deities, between Chavin and the mid-Chou (tenth to eighth centuries B.C..) period in China, Davies concludes, "nevertheless the latest dating shows that Chavin beginnings long predate the mid-Chou period, so that the likelihood of the Peruvian feline deity being an imported product is correspondingly diminished."[25]

Why would these feline figures, described by Gordon Willey as displaying "disturbing similarities," both as to content and style, have to have been imported to ancient Peru? Heyerdahl has already shown that ancient balsa rafts could easily sail with the dominant currents and trade winds across the Pacific. Why couldn't contact between ancient Peru and China have come from the "New World"? We now know that both Davies and Heyerdahl were mistaken—each solved half the puzzle. Davies recognized at least some antiquity and some development in the Americas but failed to grasp that early man could travel on the seas. Heyerdahl recognized and championed man's diffusion through the sea but somehow failed to grasp man's antiquity in the Americas.

Nigel Davies later accuses Arthur Posnansky, the leading expert on Andean Archaeology, of indulging "in flights of fancy" when he dated the older Tiahuanacu site in Bolivia as 12,500 years old (fig. 2O). Davies concludes that "if the site was really ten thousand years old . . . then all the radiocarbon figures for Peruvian cultures become sheer nonsense, together with most of the writings of Peruvian scholars."[26]

Maybe most of the writings of twentieth century Peruvian scholars *are* sheer nonsense. A distinguished team from the German Astronomical Commission measured the obliquity of the Kalasasaya astronomical observatory at Tiahuanacu and concluded that it was built to measure equinoxes and solstice extremities in years from 10,000 B.C. to 9,300 B.C.[27] Similar equinox and obliquity measurements have been found recently by archeoastronomers reexaming the Sphinx in Egypt as well as sightlines to the Orion constellation as it appeared 12,500 years ago.(See Chapter 10). Even Davies, a defender of isolationists, admits that "the problem of American links with the eastern Mediterranean is complicated by the fact that leading theories were formulated before the true antiquity of Olmec and Chavin was known to science."[28] Nonetheless, the leading theories have not changed.

Item: In *Mankind In Amnesia* Immanuel Velikovsky demonstrates that man is not only capable of forgetting what has been known to past generations, but is also capable of forgetting, for the sake of convenience, what he, in his own era, has learned. When the naturalist Charles Darwin circumnavigated the Americas in his ship the H.M.S. *Beagle* he was continually amazed at the evidence of sudden annihilation of mammoths, mastodons, giant sloths, the American horse, as well as smaller birds, mice, and so many other animals,

2.O. SUN DOOR AT TIAHUANACU, BOLIVIA. Cut out of a single block of stone weighing over 100 tons the archeaoastronomical sightlines of the megalith have been dated by Posnansky to around 9,500 BC, concurrent with Atlantis.

all at the same time—in a geologic instant that we now call the end-Pleisto-cene extinction.

Darwin recognized that the scenes of destruction of so many species were beyond the ability of a few bands of hunter-migrators. But he could find no other explanation. He wrote in his *Journal* in 1834, "It is impossible to reflect on the changed state of the American continent without the deepest astonish-ment. Formerly, it must have swarmed with great monsters: now we find mere pigmies. . . . The greatest number, if not all, of the extinct quadrupeds lived at a late period . . . what then, has exterminated so many species and whole genera? The mind at first is irresistibly hurried into the belief of some great catastro-phe; but thus to destroy animals, both large and small, in Southern Patagonia, in Brazil, on the Cordillera of Peru, in North America up to the Behring's Straits, we must shake the entire framework of the globe. It could hardly have been a change of temperature which at the same time destroyed the inhabi-tants of tropical, temperate, and Arctic latitudes on both sides of the globe."

Darwin concluded, "Certainly, no fact in the long history of the world is so startling as the wide and repeated exterminations of its inhabitants."

Twenty-five years later Darwin published his *Origin Of Species By Natural Selection.* In it he proposed a very slow evolutionary process of all life with elimination of the least fit within any one species, and a gradual extinction of entirely "unfit" species over thousands and hundreds of thousands of years.

Darwin rejected the idea that species could become extinct as a result of cataclysms. Having done no new field work since his voyage on the Beagle, where he witnessed and marveled at the sudden extinction of so many life forms, Darwin still wrote, in the concluding pages of the *Origins Of Species,* "As all the living forms of life are the lineal descendants of those which lived long before the Cambrian epoch we may feel certain that the ordinary succes-sion by generation has never once been broken, and that no cataclysm has desolated the whole world."[29] Darwin's conclusion, which contradicted his own field work, was almost universally accepted and applauded. Myths of cat-aclysms were out; materialism and exploitation of the less fit, nature's way, was now justified. Colonial Empires and industrialists loved and embraced it. Darwin's theory of evolution became the law of reason.

Item: In 1943 naturalist Loren Eiseley became aware of great carnage in Alaska associated with the end of the Pleistocene period, 12,500 years ago. Heaps of bones of every type of now extinct North American animal, mixed with splintered trees, covered tens of miles in every direction (fig. 2P.). The scene was very like that of the Siberian forest after a close encounter with an asteroid in 1908. Shortly after the time of Eiseley's observation he wrote, "We are not dealing with a single, isolated relic species but with a considerable variety of Pleistocene forms, all of which must be accorded, in the light of cultural evidence, an approximately similar time of extinction. . . . In certain regions of Alaska the bones of these extinct animals lie so thickly scattered that there can be no question of human handiwork involved. Though man was on the scene of the final perishing, his was not, then, the appetite nor the capacity for such giant slaughter."

Of this same wholesale extermination of fauna, Velikovsky wrote, "Fit and unfit, but mostly fit, old and young, with sharp teeth, with strong muscles, with fleet legs, with plenty of food around, all perished." Eiseley stated, "It seems odd that a fauna which had survived the great ice movement should die at its close. But die it did."[31]

What could have happened 11,500 years ago to account for a disaster of the dimensions noted by the young Darwin and the young Eiseley? Peter Tompkins in *Mysteries of the Mexican Pyramids* cites the work of Professor Cesare Emilini, head of the department of Geology at the University of Miami. Emilini suggests that melting icecaps alone may have caused worldwide cataclysms. Working with graphs of deep-sea core samplings taken in the Gulf of Mexico, Emilini found evidence indicating glaciation and deglaciation occurring in cycles of about every 20,000 years over the last 700,000 years. He also discovered that the last major deglaciation occurred in 11,600 B.C. when something caused the waters of the Caribbean to rise 130 feet in a very short period of time, perhaps only a few weeks or months.

Geologists almost universally agree that deglaciation permanently raised the level of the oceans world wide by over 425 feet. But most have thought that the process was gradual. And while others admitted that sea levels actually changed little over long periods at the end of the Pleistocene, they have remained skeptical of large and sudden changes in the sea level. However the evidence of eroded seashells that formed distinct beach-heads recently found in the Mediterranean now suggests that sea levels have risen in a series of sudden events, with intervening periods of up to two hundred years in which sea levels hardly changed at all.

What could be the mechanism for the sudden and undoubtedly catastrophic rises that would have moved some coastlines back by tens of miles? Emilini speculates that the 130 foot rise of 11,600 years ago occurred when ice water from the melting Wisconsin icecap suddenly broke through the confines of Lake Nippissing and poured down the Mississippi Valley. A similar rise today would leave New York and the entire eastern seaboard under water! The Florida peninsula and the central valley of California as well as much of Europe would meet a similar fate.

A significant question remains—what caused the sudden destruction of

2.P. HEAPS OF BONES, IVORY, AND WOOD AT CRIPPLE CREEK, ALASKA, DATING FROM THE END OF THE PLEISTOCENE. This photograph is similar to the world depicted by naturalist Loren Eiseley on his visit to Alaska in 1943. At that time Eiseley wrote that this evidence of mass extinction "drives the biologist to despair as he surveys the extinction of so many species and genera." Later, Eiseley, in deference to Neo-Darwinian gradualist theory, denied that catastrophic events ever occurred.[30]

the moraine banks that held Lake Nippissing? Many scenarios could be posited in which a collision, or near-collision by a comet or asteroid are not needed. But without a singular event of such magnitude how can one explain the sudden extinction of the great mammals of North America?

Since they occur in the same time frame could the mass extinctions have been related to the end of the Golden Age and to the destruction of Atlantis? Myths of destruction by flood can be found not only in the religious and historical records of Hebrews, Sumerians, Egyptians, and Greeks, but can also be found in preliterate traditions (myths) of almost every primitive people known. How could beliefs and myths so widely held have no basis in fact?

A scientific mechanism for cataclysmic destruction was unknown in Darwin's or in Eiseley's time. But these naturalists had been personal witnesses to the effects of a great cataclysm. Would Eiseley, the naturalist, oppose Darwin, the theorist? The answer came quickly. Seventeen years after his personal encounters with the effects of cataclysm, Eiseley published *The Firmament Of Time*. In this work he firmly closed the door on cataclysms by stating, "After the passage of two centuries of scientific endeavor, man in the mass (is) still enormously susceptible to the appeal of cataclysmic events, however badly sustained from the scientific point of view. . . . Catastrophes, in essence, may be said to have died of common sense."

Darwin and Eiseley dismissed it all, apparently because their early observations were in conflict with theories they later developed. How shall we weigh the testimony of two authorities who seemingly "forgot," or later repudiated their own field work; or even the efforts of "two centuries of scientific endeavor" against the combined myths, the sacred beliefs of over one hundred cultures throughout the world?

These are just a few examples of apparent academic myopia and misguided views that, stated from a position of authority, have become entrenched in our body of knowledge. They have been become dogma, questionable theories long accepted without questioning. Thus, the obvious question arises: How can so many people (experts) be so obviously wrong about so many things? Is it finally time to question authority?

Anthropology attributes the origin of our present civilization to those civilizations that existed on the shores of the Mediterranean Sea, namely, in an order reaching back into greater antiquity—the Romans, the Hebrews, the Greeks, the Minoans, the Babylonians, the Egyptians, and the Sumerians. Yet that progression takes us back only, at most, into the last 7,000 years of the four million that man has been on Earth. (This date significantly coincides with the date the Roman Catholic Church has given for man's existence on Earth.) In a universe over 15 billion years old the presumption that civilization is so recent staggers the inquiring mind. Did the world grovel, unintelligently, all that time, only very recently realizing it's potential through a linear progress of technology in these last few centuries? The question seems absurd, yet that is what we're taught in our school textbooks and even in our higher institutions.

Was the Catholic Church mistaken in declaring the universe to be 6,002 years old, or the world flat, or all divine authority theirs? Were they just as wrong in giving us Beringia theory as science, or in calling Meso-Americans recent, though gifted, aborigines? Science has rejected their year of 4,004 B.C. as the year of creation for the universe, and no one believes in a flat Earth, or even the Earth as the center of the universe. Yet men of science have continued to pursue Beringia theory!

The destructive role played by the Catholic Church cannot be overemphasized. They even kept score of their deeds by establishing, in Spain, the Commission for the Destruction and Expiation of Idolatry. A 1621 report by Father Joseph de Arriaga listed over 5,000 "objects of idolatry" that were obliterated by breaking, melting, or burning.[32]

In arrogance and ignorance, self-righteousness and greed, conquistadors and emissaries of the Church alike, destroyed, pillaged, murdered, and mortally infected the descendants of a civilization that, if not technologically superior, was at least its equal—a civilization that in its understanding of man's place in the world far surpassed those who destroyed and desecrated it. Europeans carried with them diseases that had not existed when the Golden Age of Navigation met its decline around 1000 B.C. Diseases sprung from animals that had been subsequently domesticated and confined to pens where foods could mix with defecation—notably pox from cowpox, and influenza from swine flu. These new diseases, unknown in the Americas, and therefore without resistance, decimated whole populations.

All of this destruction of American aboriginals was justified on the grounds that the Spanish were dealing with pagans and idol worshippers who performed the most savage human sacrifices. Cortez's chronicler, Diaz, accused the Aztec priests of performing 50,000 human sacrifices a year, of constant drunkenness, and of performing sodomy and cannibalism on their victims. But Cortez himself wrote that he actually never witnessed a single human sacrifice except those of captured soldiers during battle. That the Aztecs practiced ritual human sacrifice in an attempt to please angry gods and prevent a cataclysm cannot be questioned. But it is also evident that the Spaniards grossly exaggerated the nature and number of the sacrifices in order to justify their own brutality.[33]

Voltaire's observation that "Antiquity is full of the praises of another Antiquity still more remote," reflects the belief of the intelligent mind in the integrity of ancient myth. It also described the "situation" in the Americas that the Church had come to face. It was the fear of the discovery of this "other antiquity," one that could question their creation theory, that drove the Catholic Church and the Spanish crown to minimize the achievements and the antiquity of ancient American cultures.

They reacted to the challenge with swift and certain cruelty in the Americas but with rational justification in Europe. They sought to show the intelligentsia of their era that their actions were just and reasonable. They created, historically, a "*New* America"—primitive, pagan, and hopelessly evil. The views they instilled in Eurocentric academics is in the end no more justified than rewriting of history of, say, the Aryan takeover of Dravidian India, the Germanic takeover of Gaelic Britain, the Tudor revision of English history, or the Roman vanquish of the artistic Etruscans. But revisionist history was predictable during the many centuries that academics were controlled by the absolute authority of Church and State.

Once twentieth-century history and science emerged in their own right, no longer to be held accountable by Church and State, what, we must wonder, provoked them to pursue the Church's pet theory of Beringia migration, and to continue to ridicule myth and the notion that man in ages past faced great cataclysms?

Is history truly a conspiracy of ignorance? Is there some collective guilt in the Eurocentric mind over its decimation of the Native Amerinds that has led them to accept the Church's edict that the destroyed culture was pagan and primitive? Or has mistaken and misguided theory fatally blurred the investigation into our collective past? Or, sadly, has simple greed compelled the Europeans to embrace the "Pagan Paradigm?" We will discuss the complicated answers to these questions in the next chapter, focusing the pillar of the "pagan paradigm"—Clovis man.

3 From Clovis to Chaos

THREE RABBIT had once been a warrior. He had sailed with an expeditionary fleet to put down an uprising in Kumar, a colony that lay at the far end of the great enclosed sea east of the Pillars of Hercules. The revolt had been easily subdued. Three Rabbit himself had seen no action. But during night watches on the long journey he had been befriended by one of the navigators and had learned about the stars and the star paths . . . secret knowledge known only to navigators and to the astronomer-priests. Three Rabbit learned the holy names of the constellations and of their migrations across the sky. He learned how to sight the horizon stars, how to trace their arc across the sky, and how the appearance at midnight of zenith stars, or the magnetized needle floating on a piece of cork in Chac-Mool's bowl, would mark the course to follow. But when he'd returned to Poseidon after a year at sea he'd discovered that his wife had given birth to twin boys and he had vowed never to go to sea again. He became a gold miner and his knowledge of the stars went unused . . . the priests would never have admitted him to their inner circle . . . he hadn't asked.

After the cataclysm Three Rabbit could only weep and mourn for his lost family, and his lost city, now mostly submerged under the ever rising tides. He could no longer bear to look at it. He returned to the hills. Then a miracle happened. Three Rabbit saw a man come crouching out of a cave carrying a dead child. Then behind them he saw two tiny figures, standing erect. Under the fiery red glow of the sky the roof of the cave cast a dark shadow over the pair but Three Rabbit recognized them at once—his twin boys had survived!

Life was hard for Three Rabbit and his twin boys. Before the cataclysm food had always been plentiful in Atlantis. Hunters and herdsmen had brought game from the hills, farmers had brought fruits and grains from the fields, and the sea had provided a rich variety of food. All that had changed in a single day and night! And the process of destruction did not end when that night was over.

75

When the asteroid came to Earth it evaporated the top layer of the sea into a dense cloud of moisture that rose and grew to encircle the Earth. The sun grew dimmer and all the surviving people of the Earth lived in twilight. Rains fell, storms raged, the seas were constantly agitated and murky. Without the warmth of the sun the Earth cooled quickly and the rain throughout the world turned to snow. Only at the equatorial zone did the falling snow melt, and even there it grew terribly cold. As an Ice Age was ending it appeared another had begun.

All of this had been foretold. Three Rabbit had learned from the navigator priests that the appearance of a comet, although beautiful to watch in the night sky, could presage disaster. And it had come. What had not been foretold was how difficult life would be for the few who survived the disaster (fig. 3A).

Three Rabbit was amazed that of all the survivors he encountered, none of them had anything more than the simplest notion of star paths, few had any concept of agriculture, less knew anything about architecture or plumbing; and while many claimed to know the sea and how to harvest it, they all lamented that this new sea seemed lifeless, and unmanageable in the poor boats they could fashion.

The game had disappeared; there were no mammoths, no camels, deer were rarely seen, and there were no horses. Only carcasses and drying bones remained, spread over the surface of the land. There were vermin in the ruins of the city, in fact there were droves of rats. Some of the survivors who lived by picking through

3.A. An Olmec emerges from a cave carrying a dead child. The common Olmec image of a man emerging from a cave, carrying live or dead infants, has often been characterized as the power of the elite to pass between the spirit and real worlds. Certainly most Olmecs never lived in caves. However, the presence of dead infants in the arms of the saddened Olmec parents may reflect a long memory of an emergence from a time of devastation, just as the myths of Atlantis told of a few survivors emerging from caves high in the mountains.

the remains of fallen temples and houses actually learned to hunt them and eat them. But Three Rabbit was saddened by what he saw of the ruins of Poseidon, not because men had become hunters of rats, he understood that, but because what had once been so beautiful and ordered was now so disfigured and chaotic. Contact with the heavenly gods could no longer take place.

On his one visit to the sunken city Three Rabbit took an atlatl, a boomerang, and the broken remains of a calendar and made his way to the high plains above Atlantis. There he made a wonderful discovery: He found the great spheres of the astronomical university. It was as magical and as timeless as the clear nights on the ocean when the navigator-priest had turned mentor-friend to Three Rabbit and had described these very fields to him. The sphere that represented the sun, 13 feet high, and 13 feet across in every direction, was undisturbed by the upheavals. The spheres that represented the planets, though their onyx shells were cracked, still lay, for the most part, close to their original positions. But the smaller spheres that represented the stars and their astrological configurations had been scattered haphazardly by the Earthquakes and giant waves. Three Rabbit realized that the knowledge gained through millennia was now lost.

Three Rabbit noted that the fields that surrounded these spheres were plentiful with the animal from which he took his proud name, rabbits. There were no longer any dire wolves to hunt them. Three Rabbit built a hut of thatched palms on these grounds, cared for his children, and taught them the use of the atlatl and the boomerang, skills in which they quickly exceeded him. They lived off the rabbits and from the fruits and berries of the standing trees. Then Three Rabbit reconstructed the broken celestial calendar, and from that he began to reconstruct the celestial configurations. The work was slow, nights were invariably rainy and breaks in the clouds occurred only after months of waiting, revealing stars for only fleeting moments. It was fifty years before normal skies reappeared. During most of that time Three Rabbit had only the calendar and his memory to work from.

Passing hunters and foragers at first thought Three Rabbit was a little crazy. But when they realized he was recreating the heavens, recalling the stars they remembered but could no longer see, they gladly went to his aid in moving and repositioning the spheres.

When his work was done Three Rabbit waited. He had been to the colonies and he felt sure that Atlanteans from the colonies would return to rebuild Atlantis. There was little to do but wait.

The Search for Clovis Man

As the authority of the Church waned and the State's power to suppress history occupied itself with current affairs in Europe, the "anti-antiquity" or "Pagan Paradigm" found a much needed third ally . . . twentieth-century science. The possibility of an Atlantean presence in America, along with America's great antiquity had been obvious to the Europeans who arrived after Columbus's voyage initiated the "Age of Discovery." But their intuitions were quashed by the Church.

Four centuries later the antiquity of American cultures should have been equally obvious to the fledgling Americanist school of anthropology. At least the *possibility* of antiquity should have been considered and pursued through open-minded excavations of the great sites in Mesoamerica. But armed with only the scantiest historical data, and having excavated (mainly by looting) only a few sites in Mesoamerica, early twentieth-century American archaeologists announced boldly to the world that "our knowledge of the past is limited only by our theoretical and methodological shortcomings."[1] Excavations might reveal some interesting (and valuable) artifacts, but the sites themselves would reveal little about the history of the people. Their true history would be determined elsewhere—presumably in the meeting rooms of great universities and museums.

However, despite their boasts, American Archaeology in the early years of this century really had no viable theory to explain man's presence in America. Stone Age discoveries were being made, and they were found at stratigraphic layers that indicated dates thousands of years before accepted theories. But just as quickly as their discovers would claim great antiquity for their finds, Ales Hrdlicka, the Czechoslovakian born head of physical anthropology at the United States National Museum, would quickly ridicule these claims. Hrdlicka set an absolute limit for man's presence in the Americas of 3,000 B.C. From his eminent post Hrdlicka quashed all claims of man's antiquity before that date. Resistance to his authority among students led to academic failure. Hrdlicka's views were relentlessly enforced. Resistance by academics lead to many destroyed careers.[2]

Hrdlicka and his anti-diffusionist contemporaries weren't merely cranky old men. Their stance had another, "more philosophical," motivation. Their task was to show that the principles of Darwin's Theory of Evolution and Natural Selection could and would operate independently in the Americas. Their absolute view has been phrased thusly: "If it can be shown that civilizations arose in the Americas in complete isolation from similar complex societies of the Old World, a strong case can be made for the argument that there is an inherent tendency for simple human societies to become progressively more complex under certain conditions, and that this process of cultural evolution is amenable to scientific generalization and even prediction. In other words, if complete isolation is assumed, the American continent can be seen as a sort of giant island laboratory, onto which a few humans have been cast

3.B. CHARLES DARWIN, 1868. Darwin's famous statement ("False facts are highly injurious to the progress of science, for they often endure long; but false views, if supported by some evidence, do little harm, for every one takes a salutary pleasure in proving their falseness") reflects Darwin's innate sense of fairness. His inheritors, the Neo-Darwinians who seized on his theory, lacked this sense of fair play when, led by Ales Hrdlicka, they relentlessly destroyed the careers of anyone who disagreed with them.

ashore, allowing scientists to observe what kinds of societies and behavior patterns they generate, starting from scratch and receiving no external clues."[3]

The question of dating was critical to this dogged resolve to "prove" Darwin's theories of evolution (fig. 3B). MesoAmerican and Peruvian cultures were viewed as the only possibilities of civilizations arising from contact with other civilizations. The Americanists wanted to prove that "no contact" was possible between the "New World" and the ancient peoples of Asia, Egypt and Sumer. Otherwise their model of independent evolutionary development could be questioned. If the development of American civilization, particularly pyramid building, could be demonstrated to be much later than both the rise and the decline of pyramid building in Egypt and Mesopotamia, then their evolutionary "laboratory" would remain in intact. The Americas would then have been isolated by both an ocean of water and vast sea of time. The Americanists accomplished their goal, much as the Church had done before them, by "authoritarian" declaration. Apparent facts to the contrary would simply not be admitted. All such evidential facts *had* to be declared "out of context" and of no consequence.

Darwin could not explain an event we *know* happened—the cataclysmic destruction of megafauna of North America. However his followers were successful, to the academic mind, in explaining a circumstance that *never* occurred—isolation of all the accomplishments of the vast American continent from the mainstream of civilization.

Under the Neo-Darwinian model, mirroring the needs of Inquisition theory, it was important to find that the initial peopling of the Americas should have occurred in an isolated and primitive setting. The Beringia explanation was appealing to Americanist archaeologists for the same reason it was appealing to the Catholic Church—it linked only primitive and isolated cultures. But Beringia Theory lacked anything that resembled conclusive proof.[4]

Then in 1927, in a gully near Folsom, New Mexico, J. D. Figgins excavated a spear point lodged between the ribs of a long-horned bison that had become extinct at the end of the Pleistocene, over 10,000 years ago.[5] Archaeologists flocked to the area. More Folsom spear points were found, and a few years later traces of an earlier Paleo-Indian culture were discovered: At Clovis, New Mexico, bi-facially flaked spear points (fig. 3C) were found

3.C. CLOVIS POINTS.

lodged within the rib bones of Ice Age mammoths.[6] Although radiocarbon dating of the Clovis site would not be available until 1949, the presence of man in direct association with a mammal that became extinct at the end of the last Ice Age literally blew the lid off Hrdlicka's imposed dates. However, because these were obviously *primitive* hunters, the theory of isolated civilizations remained intact. In fact, it was reinforced. The Neo-Darwinians were certain they were on the right trail. As more sites of Paleoindians armed with Clovis-type points were discovered throughout North America—some as far away as Nova Scotia—the isolationists were convinced that they would find the land link between Asian and American man. Clovis man would prove Beringia theory. In doing so it would put to rest any wild theory of navigational contacts between ancient civilizations. Clovis man might have even provided a side benefit for the evolutionists—an explanation for the mass extinction of thirty-two species of mammals at the end of the last Ice Age.

Extinction is not a recent phenomenon. It has been with our ecosystem for hundreds of millions of years. Yet often when one species disappears, a better adapted species has been seen to "fill in" the niche left by the extinct variety. At least that is the theory of Darwinian evolutionists. According to this theory, the explanation for the disappearance of the large American mammals at the end of the last Ice Age had to center on replacement theory. Clovis-pointed humans were the only culprit available. Accordingly, evolutionists have pointed to man's arrival in the Americas to explain the demise of all large American mammals.

Paul Martin's explanation (fig. 3D) places the blame on a hundred or so hunters, and their offspring. But the truth is that the cause of such extinctions were beyond Clovis man's ability. Mammoths, dire wolves, short-faced bears, and saber-toothed tigers would have been the most difficult (and fruitless) to eliminate. Bison, elk, and caribou made the easiest targets. Yet records of the hunting activities of nineteenth-century American Indians, riding horses and armed with bow and arrows, and later with rifles, show that they killed only

3.D. MAMMOTHS. THIS COMPLETE CALF WAS FOUND IN SIBERIA IN 1977. Paleontologist Paul S. Martin proposes that the first humans to traverse the ice-free Beringia passage arrived in Alaska 12,000 years ago, already armed with the Clovis point. A mere band of one hundred people, he reasons, survived the ice-free corridor and happened on to large herds of mammoth, bison, caribou, horses, saber-toothed tigers, and all the other large American mammals. Because the large mammals had no prior knowledge of man's ruthlessness they were easy kills for the Clovis pointed hunters. With food so plentiful the hunting bands doubled in population every twenty years, so that in 500 to 1000 years they became a group of bands that had grown to number 600,000 people, all hunters, all successful in their hunts. Despite their success they pressed on, ever southward so that by the end of their first thousand years on the new continent they had reached Tierra del Fuego at the tip of South America, and had established settlements throughout the Americas. However, along the way, the great mammals disappeared under their onslaught. The Clovis hunters, armed with their superior point, had been so successful they had driven the mastodon, mammoth, camel, American horse, saber-toothed tiger, dire wolf, etc., to extinction. It is an absurd theory. Yet because it so neatly fits the "survival of the fittest" model, Martin's theory is still entertained by Neo-Darwinians more interested in advancing their precepts than in discovering what really happened. If a band of 100 "Clovis" hunters could have somehow survived a crossing of Beringia and a three thousand mile walk over ice sheets or along the cold marshes cut by raging river of cold melt waters from those ice sheets, they hardly could have increased their numbers during such a demanding migration.

slightly more than 400,000 bison each year. Since at the time of European contact there were more than 40 million bison, the number killed was less than the annual increase in herds. Four million American Indians, armed to the teeth, did not reduce the numbers of bison, they simply took the overflow away for their own needs. Could a few hundred starving "Clovis" men, hunting on foot with spears, have decimated to extinction so many species of great beasts in a few centuries?

The notion is not only preposterous on its own merits, it runs counter to every understanding we have of "primitive" hunters—they had reverence for their game, they celebrated their kills with reference to their ancestors whose spirits were thought to have found rebirth in the bestial world. It is not likely that any primitive hunter, even given the means they surely lacked, would have slaughtered entire populations of the beasts they hunted.

Bison were later exterminated to the point of extinction by European hunters who killed in vast numbers, apparently solely for the value of the bison tongues and pelts—a dark episode in our history that has been wonderfully and terribly recreated in the movie, *Dances With Wolves*. In fact, tongues and pelts were only additional bounty to the real reason for the destruction of the bison. Actual U.S. Army policy statements have been found that document another motive—a calculated military campaign to destroy native Indian society by eliminating their most sacred and valuable resource. But in the time of the Clovis hunters there was no international market for buffalo pelts, no nefarious military, no means, and no reason for such a vast overkill (fig. 3E).

Neo-Darwinians have promoted and trumpeted the extinction of animals by man to counter any possibility that cataclysms could have occurred. But extinction itself was really only a side issue to their general theory. What Neo-Darwinians needed was the discovery of actual sites that would prove to be progressively older as the investigation moved northwest toward Siberia. They would also need to demonstrate some link between PaleoIndians and PaleoSiberians. But, although Clovis sites were easily and often found in Colorado, Oklahoma and even in Massachusetts, none were found in Alaska nor in northwest Canada that even remotely matched the older dates for Clovis man in the southwest. Yet the Clovis-Beringia paradigm has persisted, and has been incorporated into the textbooks of both universities and high-schools throughout the United States. Beringia migration from Asia, with Clovis spear-pointed hunters leading the way south was accepted, without any proof, as fact.

It was only after sixty years of intensive search that the first find of Clovis man was made at the Mesa site in Alaska in 1992. Here, Clovis presence has

3.E. SABER-TOOTHED TIGERS (*SMILODON*). The game Clovis man is credited with decimating would not have been such easy prey as Martin envisions. Wild horses, we know, are
skittish, and they are fast. Mammoths and mastodons, if they in any way resemble bull elephants, would have been a very formidable opponent for a small stone age band armed
only with the Clovis point. Saber-toothed tigers would have been an even more difficult
opponent. The idea that they too would have become extinct by reason of deprivation of
their game, is contradicted by the very premise on which Martin's theory rests, that the
Clovis hunters had become so efficient at killing, and so enamored with the sport, that they
killed vast numbers of game in every region they went to, decimating the population. If so,
they must have left most of their kills uneaten. Saber-toothed tigers and dire wolfs could
only have flourished in such a scenario. All carnivores depend on their speed and strength
in bringing down a kill, but they live, in the most part, on easy game—kills brought down
by something else in which they can share. Clovis hunters would have left a bounty for the
tigers and dire wolves, fearless animals that would have followed man's trek and his abundant kills from Alaska to Tierra del Fuego. Their numbers should have expanded, particularly in the southern regions. Instead they disappeared.

---

been determined to be have occurred around 9,300 B.C. But in proving
Beringia Theory or in confirming Clovis man as the instrument of man's peopling of the Americas from Asia, this is a case of too little, too late.

Neither this lone site nor sixty years of Clovis and Beringia theory can stand
up to new evidence of man's earlier presence in the Americas, at sites that had
nothing to do with Beringia migration, including Meadowcroft near Pittsburgh,
Pennsylvania 14,500 years ago, Monte Verde in southern Chile in stratigraphical-
ly aligned sites that range from a now undisputed 12,500 years ago to possible
occupation 33,000 years ago. Nor can Beringia/Clovis theory account for man's
artistic presence in Brazil at Pedra Furada 32,000 years ago. This northeastern
Brazilian site contains paintings in unfaded natural colors that have had prelimi-
nary radiocarbon datings of 25,000 and 32,000 years before present. These dates
not only precede Clovis and Bering Sea migration by a minimum of 13,000
years, they predate the famous Lascaux, France cave paintings of Cro-Magnon

man.[7] Although a contemporary date of 32,140 B.P. has recently been established for Cro-Magnon paintings at Chauvet, France (fig. 3F).[8]

And if Clovis man was the initial migrator from Asia 11,500 years before the present how are we explain handprints in the nearby Peddejo Cave in New Mexico, discovered by the distinguished archaeologist Richard S. MacNeish, that have been carbon 14 dated to 40,000 years ago?

Excavations in the Valsequillo region of central Mexico, near present day Puebla, have revealed late Pleistocene human artifacts that include knives, scrapers, and unifacially worked spear points. These cultural remains, found in association with mammoth kills, have been radiocarbon dated at just less than 24,000 years before present. Dating based on local geological strata has arrived at even earlier dates for the Valsequillo material. At Tlapacoya, southeast of

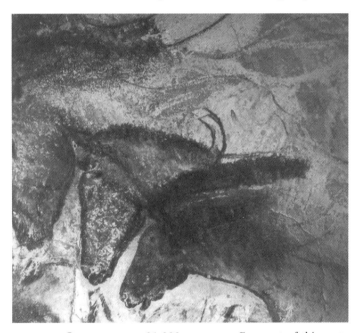

3.F. PAINTINGS AT CHAUVET CAVE, 31,000 YEARS B.P. For most of this century it has been assumed that the more primitive paintings at Chauvet and other sites in France— stick figures and paintings that lacked artistic perspective and dimension—must have been the oldest, and that Cro-Magnon man's artistic ability must have evolved over the 31,000 to 11,500 year B.P. period in which the paintings were accomplished. It has recently been determined that the most magnificent depictions of horses and lions, occurred, at least, 30,000 years B.P. In *Chauvet Cave: The Discovery of the World's Oldest Paintings,* Jean Clottes writes: "We now know that sophisticated techniques for wall art were invented . . . at an early date. The rendering of perspective through various methods, the generalized use of shading, the outlining of animals, the reproduction of movement and reliefs, all date back more than 30,000 years."[11]

3.G. BERINGIA. The photo above is of a current Asian desert. But studies of late Pleistocene Beringia have revealed no vegetation, high winds, extreme cold, and barren dunes of a lifeless sand. What were the winds like in Beringia with no trees, no moss to ease their buffeting, no vegetation to stabilize the ground and prevent it from blowing away? What would it have been like if a Pleistocene hunter had crossed these life-less dunes and climbed an ice sheet of over two miles in height? With no food to support game, what would he have hunted? Why would he have climbed such an ice sheet? A recent movie suggests it could have been done in a "Quest dream." But how many quest dreams, each successful, would it take to move a founding population through three thousand miles of ice sheets?

Mexico City, a very finely made blade of obsidian, uncovered in 1967, has been carbon dated as 23,000 years old. Both sites revealed human cultural remains more sophisticated, and 10,000 years older than the finds at Clovis, upon which archaeologists have based their Asia to Patagonia migration theory.[9]

Nor can Clovis theorists account for *the total lack* of any Clovis points in Siberia. More surprising, and finally disheartening to Beringia theorists, are the results of recent excavations of the famous Choukoutien site in northeastern Asia. There isolationists expected to find a primitive and uniform predecessor of Clovis, hopefully in the 10,000 to 20,000 B.C. framework. Instead the Upper Cave at Choukoutien was found to contain several skeletons from 20,000 B.C. that display few modern mongoloid features.[10] The renowned anatomist, Franz Weidenreich, saw one female's skull as similar to a Melanesian's, another as resembling an Eskimo's, while a rugged male's skull was comparable to a modern European. One conclusion is inescapable—divergent human types were interacting in Siberia twenty thousand years ago!

Clovis theory ultimately disproved what it had sought to confirm—Beringia migration from Siberia to the Americas (fig. 3G). Except for the lone Mesa site in Alaska, the sites for Clovis became increasingly more recent as the observer moved from the southwest to the far northwest, suggesting that the main body of Clovis migration (and possibly Beringia migration—if it *ever* existed), occurred in a reverse direction than that posited by Clovis theorists—until it hit a wall of older and more diversified cultures in Siberia. Given this, let's repeat the question—can we be sure, given the extreme difficulty, that Beringia migration occurred at all? And if so, was this a sparse and probably inconsequential migration, likely by canoe, northward, along the Pacific coast, after the Earth warmed, and actually across Bering Sea from America to Asia?

That is the view taken by E. James Dixon, former Professor of Archaeology at the University of Alaska, and current curator of the Denver Museum of Natural History. Dixon himself had long advocated Beringia and Clovis man theory, and had long led archeological searches for proof of these theories. But the proofs he found invariably negated the theory he had been defending. His recent book, *Quest For The Origins Of The First Americans*, presents compelling evidence that Paleoindians had migrated from the high plains of the American continent *northward* to the Arctic regions some ten to twelve thousand years ago, after most of the melting had occurred. Dixon's theory has been confirmed by Gerald Shields, professor of biology at the University of Alaska. Using DNA as an evolutionary "blueprint" Shield's Institute of Arctic Biology has been able to determine that Paleoindians from the states of Oregon and Washington and province of British Columbia are at least "twice as old" as peoples from the far northern groups—the Eskimo-Aleut, Athabascan, and Haida.

The discovery of Clovis culture effectively opened one door to real history in pushing back the dates for early man in America beyond Hrdlicka's arbitrary dates. However, the prolonged search for Clovis man also meant that while the body of archeological research focused on primitive sites to the north, the great sites of civilization in Mesoamerica, many far older, and far more sophisticated, were virtually ignored—except by looters, museum collectors and a few adventurers.

Clovis man, dated to around 9500 to 9,200 B.C., was a decidedly primitive hunter. Anna Roosevelt, an archaeologist from the Field Museum and the University of Illinois, Chicago, led a team of archaeologists who discovered that the Monte Alegre site, situated on the Amazon River, provided a home to peoples with a very distinct tool kit from Clovis man, and that they developed clusters of vegetation, enjoying in their diet, cashews, Brazil nuts, fruits of various palms, a variety of seafood, as well as the meats of animals hunted in the forest. They also created sophisticated cave paintings (see fig. 3H).[12] Their world, carbon 14 dated to a minimum of 11,200 B.C., was more diverse, and less desperate than Clovis man's, supporting a new "Pre-Clovis" hypothesis.

3H. A ROCK PAINTING AT MONTE ALEGRE, BRAZIL, reveals hand prints, concentric circles, and an inverted figure. An April, 1996 article in *Science* reports, "Several subtropical Brazilian rock art sites and open sites with flaked stones, rock painting spalls, and possible hearths have numerous, *consistent* pre-Clovis radiocarbon dates going back to 50,000 years BP, but human presence that early has been questioned."[12] Mitochrondrial DNA evidence has also suggests the earlier dates for man's presence in California going back at least 50,000 years, long before a land-based migration through Beringia was possible. And if linguistic diversity is used as an indicator of man's presence in the Americas it must be noted that the greater diversity in the languages of native speakers is found far south of glaciated regions, indicating that man's presence there was far

earlier. Studies of mitochrondrial DNA—genetic material inherited at a relatively constant rate, but only maternally—by Alva Hicks, have in fact indicated much earlier dates, suggesting the emergence of modern man in the Americas and not in Africa. This complicated argument is still in its infancy but has been attracting a growing number of supporters.

But was this outpost on the Amazon the most sophisticated of that time? Probably not. It was likely a fringe culture that, predating Clovis man, coexisted with even more diverse and sophisticated cultures.

That Clovis man was a hunter-gatherer is indisputable. What is disputable is the inference that there was a uniformity to the cultures and technologies of ancient man, and that Clovis man, in his activities and knowledge, represented the evolutionary forefront of man's activity in the Americas. Could a sophisticated man, skilled in mathematics and architecture have co-existed with more primitive men? The answer is obvious. Even as we approach the twenty-first century, with massive jet travel and world-wide communications networks there are peoples in Africa, South America and Arctic who live a similar hunter-gathering existence. The history of civilization has always been, at any one time, uneven. And it has not always been a uniform advance from the more primitive to the more civilized. Indians of North America erected great mounds and pyramids at Memphis a thousand years before the most recent wave of European contact. Yet in the eighteenth century the only Indians the "White Man" encountered were nomadic hunters. Are we missing something?

Archaeologists, finding the remains of Clovis man in New Mexico, decided that they had found not only the earliest inhabitants of the Americas, but the most advanced. Why? What could have led them to so arbitrary a conclusion?

As noted, recent evidence at Pedra Furada, Monte Verde, and in Costa

Rica and Nicaragua, indicate that the "Clovis Man" found in New Mexico and Colorado lived at the northernmost fringes of a vast American civilization.

His presence at the northern extremes of what was a very cold continent twelve thousand years ago was probably by his *own choice*. In response to a warming of the environment and to the expansion of a civilization he did not understand Clovis man moved north toward Canada and later to Alaska, once again seeking the wet and cold hunting grounds that the pursuit of game, and his way of life, demanded.

Was Clovis man an Asian migrator to the "New World?" Recently one of the most complete and oldest human skeleton ever found the Pacific Northwest was discovered. The bones of this early American, discovered by James Chatters, have been carbon 14 dated to 9,300 BP by scientists at the University of California, Riverside. But he was not a Siberian entry into the "New World." Because of his "long narrow skull, and prominent nose," among other characteristics, he has been judged to be a *Caucasian!*13 What was this Caucasian doing here at this time (fig. 3I)?

At the same time that primitive Clovis hunters were making spear points in anticipation of hunting megafauna, probably following herds of caribou moving north on a warming American continent, an earlier and more civilized society flourished to the south, probably outside of their realm of knowledge, or of concern or caring. South of these migrating hunters, ancient MesoAmerican cultures were constructing spheres to teach star paths at celes-

3.I. AN "ARYAN" FACE IN MESOAMERICA. But was he a white supremacist, or was he merely a navigator?[17] Some anthropologists and current inhabitants of the lands of ancient cultures are reluctant to believe that their adopted predecessors were not the builders of their adopted monuments. They protest, often angrily, that proof of an outside influence dilutes the integrity of the indigenous people, treating them as primitive recipients of some other cultures know-how. Often, as in the Americas, this argument is voiced by descendants of the very people who destroyed, infected, slaughtered, and overran the people whose integrity they now pretend to defend. Can the Spanish descendants of the Conquistadors really lay claim to the integrity of the Mayans, the Aztecs, and the Incas? Can Americanist anthropologists from the United States and Europe pretend to fashion a defense of native peoples that disregards and suppresses evidence of earlier, perhaps more highly developed peoples? If so, by what right?

tial universities and ancient Peruvian cultures were erecting great megaliths as star temples. The art of navigation, the only possible explanation for early man in the Americas, was being taught.

At one time you could justify the apparent ignorance of the American and Eurocentric archaeologists by noting that they simply must have known nothing about sailing and could not appreciate its possibilities. But archaeologists could only ignore the feats of Thor Heyerdahl and his successors for so long. Hundreds of amateur sailors have demonstrated that any seventeen-year old or any seventy-year old with a modicum of navigational ability can cross the Atlantic. And they can do it in almost any kind of ship, boat, or raft. But still the archaeologists stubbornly refuse to consider diffusion of cultures through navigation. Why?

The Neo-Darwinians were not the only force in American Archaeology in the twentieth century. Franz Boas, America's most prominent anthropologist, commanded attention. To his credit Boas, denounced the preoccupation with Beringia migrations and with Neo-Darwinian evolutionary theory as unproductive speculation. He urged his students to concentrate on individual sites themselves and to disregard their regional implications.[14] Out of his work, and the work of his followers, the actual sites of early man in the Americas were meticulously recorded. From the functional evidence Boas fashioned a counter proposal. His "Eskimo wedge" theory simply plotted and traced the actual dates for man's habitation of sites and found they described a northwestern migration, *after* the end of the Ice Age, as lands were freed of ice, and *from* the Americas to Siberia. This migration occurred *after* Beringia was again a shallow sea. (*See sidebar, page 84*)

The often brilliant, and inspired work of Franz Boas seemingly anticipates the discovery that the central regions of the Americas were a home to advanced civilizations, with only rogue explorations at their northern perimeter. However, Boas soon came to be identified with a marked intolerance for early dates for MesoAmerican civilization and with any suggestion of Pre-Columbian cultural contacts between the Mediterranean and American peoples. The Boas bias against navigation (it was "impossible"), unchallenged in academia, demonstrated that he himself was theoretically driven against the possibility of a great prehistoric American civilization. How had Boas, an anti-theorist, who emphasized the collecting of hard data from specific sites, become the champion of an intolerant theory—one that dismissed the navigational possibilities of early man?

The answer relates, oddly, to race. Unlike most of his contemporaries Boas was a humanist and felt highly uncomfortable with suggestions that American "aborigines" could not have built a sophisticated culture on their

A Significant Change of Mind

A S CURATOR AND PROFESSOR of Archaeology at the University of Alaska Fairbanks E. James Dixon had long led teams of researchers looking for proof of Beringia migration through Alaska. He eventually came to realize that land migration theory had it all wrong. He expected that his published reports of migration by sea would find some acceptance. In 1987, while Monte Verde (Chile) excavator Tom Dillehay met with Dixon and a small group from a variety of sciences, to discuss the antiquity of sea contact, Brian Fagan, author of *The Great Journey,* played to large audiences gathered at the Alaska Anthropological Association meetings. Fagan's conservative view, that there is no credible evidence for man in the Americas prior to around 12,000 B.P., was cheered by large audiences of archaeologists. Dillehay and his finds were all but ignored. Dixon was advised by an associate that his hints that humans may have colonized the America via the Pacific should be dropped, or he would face losing credibility within the profession. Dixon lost his job.[18]

However, the times may be "a changin'." Brian Fagan recently reviewed Tom Dillehay's work *Monte Verde: A Late Pleistocene Settlement in Chile* (Smithsonian Institution Press, 1997) in the March/April issue of *Archaeology.* In his review Fagan, to his great credit, described Dillehay's research as "exhaustive, exemplary, and extraordinary", admitting that Dillehay's dating of 12,800 (prior to any known or even theorized Beringia dates) was unassailable. Fagan conceded, "Monte Verde was so unexpected that some archaeologists, this reviewer among them, wondered if the site really was an undisturbed cultural layer. We were wrong. Dillehay . . . has shown that we must think of the initial settlement of the New World not as a set of simple migrations, but as a process of complex and diverse adaptations to a myriad of unfamiliar environments."[19] Actually, Monte Verde is only one of a vast number of sites that contradict the establishment view of ancient history in the Americas. And although it predates any culture the establishment has been willing to accept, it was probably a fringe element of a greater culture.

own. His objection was not really on scientific grounds but rather a seeming "gut reaction" to contemporaries of his age who claimed that "white" intervention and influence could be the only explanation for advanced cultures in the Americas. In 1940, in response to Nazi racial classifications that used skull types to determine who should be sent to the gas chambers, Boas successfully demonstrated that head and body forms varied more greatly within populations than between population groups.[15]

Boas was particularly appalled by an inner circle of Nazis who called themselves the *Thule Gesellschaft*, taking their name from a legendary North Sea island thought to have been a refuge for survivors of Atlantis. Hitler himself apparently believed that Aryans had originated in Atlantis and had used Thule as a springboard to reintroduce a race of purity and greatness to Europe. As we shall see later, Aryans had little to do with the diverse peoples who inhabited Atlantis, and Hitler's concept of government was antithetical to the concepts of harmony of the Golden Age. Yet Hitler, arousing justifiably negative reaction to his perverse ideals, managed to discredit the legend of Atlantis and of myth itself.[16]

Thus by rejecting the "myth" of White Supremacy and intent on proving the uniqueness of the Mayan, Toltec and Aztec cultures, Boas effectively discouraged any dating of American sites that would permit cultural diffusion from or to other "Aryans," notably the Sumerians, Egyptians and Phoenicians. In doing so, out of noble intentions, Franz Boas obscured a true view into our collective multi-racial, multi-cultural and interconnected past. And he set the table for the arguments of Neo-Darwinian isolationists.

In *Prehistory Of The Americas* Stuart J. Fiedel clearly sets forth the isolationist point of view: "Diffusionist theories have often rested, explicitly or implicitly, on the racist assumption that Native Americans were backward savages, incapable of devising sophisticated cultures without the benevolent assistance of more advanced white-skinned tutors . . . American archaeologists have felt compelled to counter such denigration of Native Americans' abilities by demonstrating that complex societies developed independently in the New World."

But didn't this outlook, supporting the concept of isolation from a humanistic point of view, reinforce Neo-Darwinian evolutionary theory, supporting isolation as a springboard for independent evolution, and bring us right back to the past views of Church and State? It did. But few seemed to notice.

We have seen that bad concepts in science (Beringia theory) lead to bad concepts of history, and that bad motives of Church and State have lead to suppression and utter destruction of man and myth. But in the case of Franz

Boas it was a matter of good motives leading us away from the observable truth.

The students and followers of Boas dominated the chairs of the anthropology departments of American universities until well into the 1970s. It was not until his philosophical heirs began to vacate their chairs, from attrition, that the American archaeologists began to admit that the archeological record was less than complete, to say the least. By that time hundreds of new sites in Mesoamerica were being excavated and thousands more were being pinpointed by satellite photography. Even then America's antiquity in the archeological record could not be fully admitted; to do so would jeopardize the reputations and the life-long work of our universities' leading physical anthropologists. The reputation of the students of these leaders was similarly at risk. And they have succeeded to the positions of their mentors. Admission in errors in dating has progressed slowly. Admission of a fundamental error in not altering theory, as new discoveries have come to light, has not yet arrived.

Under the established academic paradigm a young Norman Hammond in 1975 excavated the site of Lubaantun in the Maya Mountains of southern Belize. Nicknamed "The place of the fallen stones" because of its jumbled rows of stones (figs. 3K, 3L), Hammond determined that Lubaantun was a late-classic Maya "ceremonial center" probably built after 650 A.D. and that it was destroyed by a large Earthquake in about 890 A.D. It has long been a habit

3.K. PHOTO OF AUTHOR ERIKSON AT LUBAANTUN, BELIZE. We can compare Lubaantun and other sites where stones are precisely fitted without the use of mortar to "Three Windows" at Machu Picchu, dated by archaeoastronomy to 2,300 B.C. Called a "ceremonial center" by traditional archaeologists, there is strong evidence Lubaantun was a navigational center built long before the rise of classic Maya cultures.

3.L. JUMBLED ROWS OF STONES AT LUBAANTUN. Although archaeologists claim it was destroyed by an earthquake local Maya tell of its destruction by looters who dynamited this site in the early part of this century.

of traditional archaeologists to call sites "ceremonial centers" when they didn't understand the site's purpose.

Lubaantun is considered a "Maya ceremonial site" despite evidence that it wasn't a Mayan center of any description. It lacks stelae, hieroglyphs, or other evidence that would indicate it shared a common culture with other Mayan sites in Belize, the Peten, and the Yucatán. Its precision-cut stones, fitted without mortar, resemble much more ancient sites such as Tiahuanacu in South America and Cheops in Egypt. Santiago Coc, a Mayan archaeologist who worked with Hammond in excavating Lubaantun in the 1970s and has been the resident guardian ever since, does not agree with Hammond's dating of the site. Coc laughs softly at the notion Lubaantun is late Maya. Although Coc himself is a Maya, he believes that Lubaantun was built by peoples who pre-dated the Maya civilization in Mesoamerica. Santiago Coc is more than a traditional archaeologist, and unlike Norman Hammond, he is beholden to no academic theory, paradigm, or university. He knows that the Americanist theory that Lubaantun was crumpled by an Earthquake is wrong because his own grandfather had witnessed the destruction of the site by archeological looters who blew it up with dynamite. He knows that Lubaantun is much older than nearby Mayan sites, such as Nim Li Punit, because the oral tradition of the Maya had always acknowledged a more ancient civilization that built great cities out of perfectly fitted stones that required no mortar, just as Lubaantun had been built. He knows, because he has listened to the myths and oral traditions of the Maya, that they were not the first people but that they had inherited and attempted to rebuild the structures of the people of the Golden Age. Lubaantun, to the Maya, belonged to a long ago age. If Coc is right, could Lubaantun be a rare MesoAmerican site that was not later built over, as typically happens, but like the Sphinx, Stonehenge, and Sacsahuaman has survived in its original form?[20]

The fanatic search for Clovis man has led archaeologists to ignore significant finds or to place them in contexts where they do not fit. It has obscured real history. Clovis theory cannot account for the diversity and brilliance of cultures that peopled the central areas of the Americas. But something significant did occur about the time that Clovis man inhabited sites in New Mexico—a time when the great mega fauna of the American continent suddenly disappeared. An event occurred that spelled the end for the American horse, camel, mastodon, mammoth, dire wolf, and for the advanced cultures that existed at the heart of the continent—Atlantis. And that event cannot be explained by the "Inquisition theory" of primitive man's migration across Beringia. It can, however, be explained by a new computer-enhanced field—chaos science.

4 Cataclysms, Myth, and Chaos Science

Turning and turning in the widening gyre
The falcon cannot hear the falconer;
Things fall apart; the centre cannot hold;
Mere anarchy is loosed upon the world,
The blood-dimmed tide is loosed, And everywhere
The ceremony of innocence is drowned;
. . . what rough beast, its hour come round at last,
Slouches towards Bethlehem to be born?
                              —*The Second Coming*, W. B. Yeats

ON THE ONE HAND we have had myth—not any one culture's myth—but repeated myths from every ancient culture, that have told us that catastrophes shaped and reshaped the world. Myths of destructions by floods and conflagrations were almost invariably related as the consequence of celestial upheavals, with man seen as an active force, most often as the worker of some misdeed that agitated the celestial storm.

On the other hand we have had the traditional sciences.

Geologists have described great changes that have occurred on Earth, emphasizing, however, that these changes have taken place very gradually over immense periods of time. Evidence of planetary collisions have long been apparent in the tens of thousands of pock marks visible on the Moon and Mars, and recently detected on Venus. And, although it has been accepted, through simple mathematical probability, that the Earth also received tens of thousands of these "hits" it has also been assumed that most, if not all, occurred before the formation of our present continents and that they are remnants of collisions from the deep past. Probably because it has been very uncomfortable to think otherwise, scientists assumed that all planet building

ceased many hundreds of millions of years ago. Cataclysms capable of suddenly changing the course of life on Earth during man's recent tenure were
considered "impossible" and "too fantastic to be true."

Yet some great force has plunged us willy-nilly into a series of Ice Ages that
began as early as a million years ago and that have dominated our planet for
the last 130,000 years. Despite science's designation of our present period as
the Holocene, or post-Ice Age, this dominance of fluctuation has not yet sub-
sided. We are living in an era of celestial disturbance. If traditional science has
been right, myth wildly wrong, and planet building has ceased to be the cause,
then what is the mechanism of this disorder? In our textbooks astronomers
have assured us that deviations of the Earth's orbit has been to blame. A
slightly greater distance from the sun has caused a slightly cooler Earth. Over
many years, according to this accepted theory, the cooler Earth retains more
snow and ice, reflects more of the sun's rays back into space, and eventually
results in an Ice Age. If this conventional theory of Ice Age formation is to
hold sway it must be demonstrated that the small deviation in the Earth's
orbit could cause significant cooling and that the Earth cooled gradually. But
the evidence contradicts this "scientific" notion. In recent years the theory of
slight orbital disparity has been questioned. Present day Earth is actually farther from the sun during the North American summer than it is during the
winter. Yet in the northern hemisphere we have continued to have hot sum-
mers and cold winters. More significantly, geologic evidence has recently been
found that before each of the Ice Ages the Earth went through a considerable,
sudden, and very short-lived, *warming period.*

John Hamaker, an amateur scientist who has been dismissed as a "loony"
by conventional scientists, was the first to propose a pre-Ice-Age warming.
But recently, prominent Ice-Age geologists, including Anne de Vernal of the
University of Quebec, and Gifford Miller of the University of Colorado, have
found that the Ice Ages were preceded by a short period of warming.[1] What
caused these warming periods is unclear. But it definitely could not have been
caused by a gradual distancing of the Earth's orbit from the sun's glow.
Something else triggered the Ice Ages. Miller states, "People are taught in high
school that when the world gets cold, an Ice Age begins . . . the geologic record
is showing us that this is not so."

Models for such a "warm/cold" scenario have been established in recent
years. These include the "nuclear winter" that would result from a world-wide
detonation of nuclear armaments. But cataclysms need not be man-made.
Any great cataclysm that inflicts a great and sudden heating of the Earth will
result in a "nuclear winter." All it really takes is for something to cause a great
evaporation of the world's water, resulting in a world-wide cloud formation

that blocks the sun's warming rays, reduces the world's temperature, and permits the moisture, trapped in these clouds to fall to Earth as snow. An encounter, a terrible encounter, with either a comet or a large asteroid would fit this bill precisely.

Thirty years ago world-wide cataclysms were considered too incredible to be true. Before 1978 hardly anyone accepted Velikovsky's description of *Worlds in Collision* as a modern scientific concept. Then a group of scientists from the Lawrence Berkeley Foundation and University of California discovered a thin layer of iridium in a 65 million-year-old layer of rock. Iridium is very heavy, and is assumed to exist in some density near the core of the Earth but is barely traceable near the surface. Yet it does exist in very traceable amounts in a dark clay stratum that surrounds the Earth corresponding to a date of 65 million years ago. The presence of iridium, common in meteorites, occurs at what has come to be called the K-T boundary (the end of the Cretaceous period, the beginning of the Tertiary). The record of the catastrophe that ended the life of the dinosaurs is written in this world-wide ring of iridium!

This iridium "layer" has led scientists to propose that an asteroid six to ten miles wide collided with the Earth at a speed fifty times the speed of sound. The site of the collision is now generally accepted to be at sea, off the northern end of the Yucatán peninsula. It's effects were devastating. Its impact created temperatures three times the surface of the sun. A firestorm was created that devastated the flora and fauna of Mesoamerica. Vast amounts of earth and sea, in the form of steam, were thrown into the outer atmosphere. All phytoplankton in the Gulf of Mexico and the Caribbean Sea were exterminated. For a large portion of the world it was an end to photosynthesis on both land and sea. In short order the food chain was destroyed. But the immediate effects of the stress on the Earth's surface were earthquakes and volcanic eruptions of immense proportions. A tidal wave, perhaps several miles high at its inception, circled the globe. Floods and violent winds reached far into the interior of the continents. A fireball was created in the space that surrounds the Earth. A cloud cover resulted, dense enough to create a nuclear winter that lasted up to fifty years.

How does this event, at the K-T boundary, relate to our current views of our own past? Only in the sure truth that history can and does repeat itself. Only in the recognition that celestial forces will most certainly recur, to profoundly effect human destiny. We are certain that this scenario describes how the age of dinosaurs ended. But is this also how the Ice Ages began—not with cold but with incredible heat and fire that created dense clouds, similar to those that encircle Venus, but without that planet's internal heat?

All comets do not contain iridium. Few asteroids do. We have definite evidence of one collision. But what about other possible collisions in our past? The temporary heat of such an event would have evaporated the top twenty feet of the oceans, a cloud cover would have obscured the sun, and eventually the moisture would have returned to Earth, at first as rain, but, as the planet slowly cooled, for lack of direct sunlight, as snow. An Ice Age would have been born by a mechanism that has nothing to do with the Earth's slightly elliptical pattern, but that has everything to do with a celestial collision.

It can no longer be doubted that a cataclysm of immense proportions occurred at the K-T boundary. Seventy-five percent of all animal species suddenly became extinct, most plankton died out, and the greatest outpouring of lava the world has known occurred at this time. On one side of the K-T boundary dinosaurs dominated the Earth, and had for 140 million years. On the other side, during the Tertiary, dinosaurs were a thing of the past (fig. 4A). There was no gradual decline in dinosaur numbers or diversity prior to the "event." Both continued to flourish right up to that K-T boundary line. In fact, diversity had been increasing in Asia.[2]

The basic tenet of the Darwinian theory of evolution, that more fit species will gradually supplant the less fit, did not work as the "engine of evolution" for 220 million years of Earth's history. That is, it didn't work to the benefit of

4.A. THE SUDDEN EXTINCTION OF THE GREATLY ENDOWED T. REX CHALLENGES THE DARWINIAN THEORY OF EVOLUTION. All true theories are subject to independent confirmation. "Survival of the fittest" cannot be challenged or confirmed because it is not a scientific theory at all. The idea that random mutations will be rewarded by survival of the most fit is a circular argument that defines who and what is most fit by observing who and what survives. "Natural selection" requires that the survivor must be better adapted to his local environment. Thus suddenly, by that measure, after 150 million of dominance, dinosaurs with their extinction, are judged "unfit," because they could not survive a major blow to the Earth by a comet or large asteroid. Could man withstand such an impact? It is

doubtful. But insects, frogs, and burrowing creatures could. An even more critical challenge to Darwinian "theory" lies in its inability to explain the development of complex organs, such as the complex eye. No single mutation can be seen to increase vision in the eye's development, yet a series of many thousands were required to create the organ that we enjoy today. How were any of these series of mutations locally rewarded? The eye surely evolved, but it did not encounter preferential selection on its journey. Natural selection cannot anticipate the future of any particular change that is not immediately, and locally rewarded. Yet the complex eye evolved. The mechanism for evolution has yet to be described by our current sciences. Mathematical mammals, who we now assume are the highest form in creation. Mammals relentlessly dug themselves into dirt, or scurried away from dinosaurs for millions of years. Neither did it work to the benefit of dinosaurs, who ruled the world during those same 220 million years. Throughout the Jurassic and Cretaceous Ages, from 220 million years ago until 65 million years ago, dinosaurs and mammals coexisted. Dinosaurs flourished, evolving into a wild variety of species. Mammals stayed much the same, small squirrel like creatures hiding in the brush and burrowing into the ground.

At the K-T boundary the dominant dinosaurs, the "fittest" for over a 150 million years, Tyrannosaurus Rex and Cyclopteas among them, met their end. It secms, in fact, that in times of cataclysms the rule of "survival of the fittest" is reversed. The fittest, those who openly rule the world, are the most vulnerable, while the least fit, those who must hide in caves and at the fringes of life, are in the best position to survive.

David Jablonski of the University of Chicago, a leading extinction theorist, provides one possible answer. "Mass extinctions change the rules of evolution. When one strikes, it's not necessarily the most fit that survive; often it's the most fortunate.

"When their environment is disrupted, groups that had been healthy can suddenly find themselves at a disadvantage. Other species that had been barely hanging on, squeak through and inherit the Earth.

"The best example is mammals. Dinosaurs and mammals originated within ten million years of each other about 220 million years ago. But for 140 million years dinosaurs ruled, while mammals stayed small and scrambled around hiding out in the underbrush. Mammals all basically looked alike—squirrelly or shrewish and no bigger than a badger—until the dinosaurs disappeared. Then they took off. Within ten million years there were mammals of all shapes and life-styles: whales and bats, carnivores and grazers. Mammals just couldn't do anything interesting until the dinosaurs were out of the way."[3] Mammals then had their chance. The Neo-Darwinian model of evolution when applied to separate but equal developement of cultures, down to the manufacture of similar tools, temples and ways of constructing star temples,

confirmation of theories is not new. But with computers you no longer have to be an Einstein to participate. The Wistar Institute measured Darwin's theories according to mathematical probabilities, and has found that there has not been enough time in the universe, let alone in the development of mankind, for selection of random mutations to have resulted in higher forms of life. In fact, on a time chart, the greatest developments have occurred in the least space of time, contrary to the gradualist theory of the Neo-Darwinians.

does not work. But the evolutionary principle of succession does. When a niche is created, some animal quickly moves to fill it.

However, niche replacement does not confirm the Darwinian principle of "survival of the fittest." It simply cannot explain why the niches have been created in the first place. In *The Origin of Species* Darwin admitted, "No one can have marveled more than I have done at the extinction of species. When I found in La Plata (Argentina) the tooth of a horse embedded with the remains of Mastodon, Megatherium, Toxodon, and other extinct monsters. . . . I was filled with astonishment; for seeing that the (present) horse, since its introduction by the Spaniards into South America, has run wild over the whole country and has increased in numbers at an unparalleled rate, I asked myself what could so recently have exterminated the former (American) horse under conditions of life so favourable."[4]

Darwin's wonder is more than understandable. Since the European introduction of the horse less than five hundred years ago that animal has thrived in the Americas.

Indeed the modern horse arose in the Americas and later migrated to other continents. Today, despite the urbanization of an entire continent, it survives in wild bands in Argentina, as well as in Wyoming, Montana and Canada. The idea that a few greedy bands of Beringia hunters wiped out the American horse—which was little different from (and ancestor to) the Asian, Arab, or European horse, together with the dire wolf, saber-toothed tiger, mammoth, etc.—from the face of the Earth 12,000 years ago is unlikely. Some force other than Darwin's "survival of the fittest" was at work.

Yet, discounting cataclysmic theory and myth, Darwin insisted that "rarity precedes extinction" and that the decline of a species must always be gradual. Although Darwin saw the emergence of dominant species as an extremely slow process he declared the "the utter extinction of a group is generally . . . a slower process than its production."[5]

It now appears that each of the great geological periods were attended, at their end, by a cataclysm. A great extermination marked the end of the Devonian period 365 million years ago. A sudden disappearance of ninety percent of the Earth's species accompanied the end of the Permian age 225 million years ago (fig. 4B). The Triassic ended in upheaval 210 million years ago. The Jurassic and Cretaceous ended 65 million years ago with the extinction of the dinosaurs, who had dominated this planet for 140 million years. And the Pleistocene ended 12,000 years ago accompanied by the extinction of 32 large species of large mammals (megafauna) including the mammoth, mastodon, saber-toothed tiger, American horse, and dire wolf.

Total decimation of the majority of living species, with a slant toward

4.B. A VOLCANO DOMINATES TINY OMETEPE ISLAND, LAKE NICARAGUA, NICARAGUA.
A few geologists think that the action of spewing volcanoes alone may have accounted for
the "Great Dying" that marked the end of the Permian period 225 million years ago. That
mass extinction, perhaps the greatest on Earth, witnessed the demise of 70 percent of all
land-dwelling species and 95 percent of all ocean-dwelling species. But to look to volcanoes as the sole cause of a great extinction would be reckless. Something caused sufficient
stress on the Earth to cause volcanoes to go berserk. The acid rain that accompanied the
end of the Permian suggests changes in atmospheric chemistry as the result of the impact
of a comet or large asteroid. (Plato's account of the destruction of Atlantis includes the
description of volcanic eruptions. To find Atlantis we must first look to those areas of the
world that have volcanic activity and there are few areas where there are more active volcanoes than Central America).

eradication of the most successful species within each period, can't be coincidence. Nor can the fact that each mass extinction was attended by wild swings
in global sea levels. The Neo-Darwinian attitude that "We don't need a cataclysm to account for the demise of species, it could happen without a catastrophe" begs the point. You could construct a model without them, just as
you could construct a model of the Americas as a totally isolated continent. It
didn't happen that way. The catastrophes were there. They happened. Its
record is written in iridium. Too fantastic to be true? No, in this case we have
the smoking gun, the iridium, and we have the victims, the dinosaurs. And
while evidence of the collision at the K-T boundary is *believed* to exist in a
giant crater on a scarred sea floor off the Yucatán, hidden by sediments, the
Manicouagan crater in Quebec, half the size of Connecticut, is *known* to have
been formed 210 million years ago, corresponding to the end of Triassic.[6]

The question persists, have cataclysms happened within the collective
memory of man? Has their record lingered in myth? Could the Pleistocene,
and a civilization defined by Atlantis, also have ended in a similar fiery cataclysm a "mere" 12,000 years ago? Science's answer has been an emphatic no!
But that "no" has found itself on very shaky ground in recent years. For most

101

of this century geologists have been quick to assure us that the age of celestial collision was part of our very distant past. They calculated that it would be another 26 million years until the next sizable asteroid or comet struck the Earth, if ever. Not to worry, scientists have tried vainly to reassure us.

But recent evidence has been to the contrary. Collisions within our solar system have always been underestimated. Archaeologists have long been cognizant of large craters created in much more recent times. The Barringer Crater in Arizona, over three-quarters of a mile wide and 640 feet deep, has been dated to the collision of a meteorite a mere 100 feet wide 25,000 years ago. But even a relatively small asteroid chunk of this size could have greatly affected climates and species (fig. 4C). What about larger asteroids? In February of 1986 the asteroid Adonis, five miles wide, passed within 186,000 miles of the Earth. If it had struck the Earth it would have effectively ended our age. We've recently learned Adonis is one of over three dozen large asteroids in the Apollo group that have orbits that regularly cross the Earth's orbit.

On March 23, 1989, an asteroid more than a half mile wide missed the Earth by just 700,000 miles. It came undetected and if it had arrived on the

4.C. EFFECTS OF AN IMPACT. IN 1908 A HUGE EXPLOSION, BELIEVED TO BE AN ASTEROID SKIPPING ACROSS THE ATMOSPHERE, DEVASTATED OVER THREE THOUSAND SQUARE MILES OF FOREST IN SIBERIA. A firestorm sweeps across the face of the Earth. Dust blankets the world, the sun isn't seen for several months and when it reappears it has become a faint red ball. (According to Wendy Wolbach of the University of Chicago, the amount of soot generated by the K-T impact shows that "as much as 90 percent of the world's forests must have burned.")7 Huge tsunamis encircle the globe. The Earth, deprived of sunlight, cools. Global cloud reflects heat of the sun. The atmosphere, thick with evaporated moisture, begins to rain (an acid rain) and then to snow. An Ice Age is born, draining the shallow seas, pushing coastlines tens to hundreds of miles out into what had been the continental shelves.

same path just six hours later it might have wiped out 90 percent of the world's population. A NASA panel estimated in 1992 that there are up to 4,000 asteroids that cross Earth's orbit and are bigger than a half mile across, a size that could send civilization back to the Stone Age.[8]

The idea that significant collisions could occur only every 26 million years was replaced in the 1980s by the notion that they could occur every 300,000 years. By the end of 1997 that figure was revised to account for cyclical periods in which collisions were deemed possible to every 26,000 years by some and to every 12,000 years by others! Astrophysicist Jack Hills of the Los Alamos National Laboratory calculates that an asteroid only 600 feet in diameter could have struck the Atlantic ocean and created a massive tidal wave 600 feet high . . . large enough to destroy coastal cultures such as the fabled Atlantis. What happened to account for so significant a change in our scientific thinking? Simple observation of the Earth and cyclical patterns of destruction of vegetation and animal life, and more sophisticated observation of the skies.

With the Hubble telescope in orbit and more careful tracking of celestial

4.D. UNCHARTED ASTEROIDS. On June 3, 1996 *Time Magazine ("A Shot Across the Earth's Bow")* reported that only a week before a previously uncharted asteroid, about a third of a mile in diameter, had passed the Earth at a distance of 280,000 astronomical miles, establishing a new "known" record for a near miss by an object of that size. The asteroid had been first spotted by Timothy Spahr at the University of Arizona's Steward Observatory only four days earlier when two telescopic images shot a half-hour apparently revealed a bright dot with a small tail. Two days later a second set of photos, and confirmation by Carl Hergenrother who picked up the asteroid on the 90-inch telescope on Arizona's Kitt Peak, revealed that the asteroid had doubled in size and speed. The observers then realized that they might be witnessing the potential destruction of a sizable portion of the planet with too little time for anyone to do anything about it. Traveling at 58,000 miles per hour the asteroid's near miss was the equivalent of its showing up less than six hours too early for a potential collision with Earth. That collision would have generated more destructive energy than all of the nuclear weapons of the USA and the former Soviet Union combined, and would have sent the Earth into an extended "nuclear winter."

bodies by land-based telescopes around the world, we now know that collisions aren't as remote as we once suspected. Is it only by chance that now that we are able to detect such objects that we are detecting them in abundance? Have we been blithely "secure" for centuries while asteroids and comets have been whizzing by dangerously close and undetected (fig. 4D)? The answer lies in a synthesis of Chaos Science with the myths of ancient MesoAmericans. But since the computer-based Chaos Science is so new, and myth has so long been dismissed as "unbelievable," we may be left with little time to find out.

We also know something else. Something that is common sense to all but the most narrow-minded theorists: *Events have happened that have nothing to do with Darwin's evolutionary theory.* Within the past twenty years, with information available through super-computers, and space launches, scientists

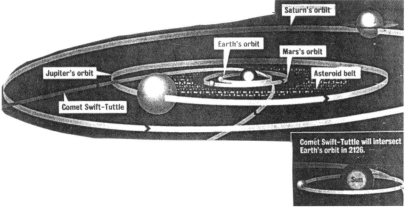

4.E. ASTEROID BELT. Once thought to be contained within the asteroid belt between Mars and Jupiter it is now known that thousands of "rogue" asteroids roam freely throughout the solar system. In early 1996 the United States government initiated a serious effort in searching the skies for asteroids and comets that could cause planetary disasters. Air Force military telescopes, previously used to track spy satellites and NASA electronic cameras were used, for the first time, in a combined effort to discover potentially deadly objects in the heavens. Eleanor Helin of NASA's Jet Propulsion Laboratory in Pasadena heads the new team called the Near-Earth Asteroid Tracking Project. They had fully expected to find some potentially dangerous asteroids but to their amazement they had, as of July 1997, found over 5,000 potential Earth crossing asteroids. Some are too small to pose a world-wide threat and some were previously known. However, ninety-nine are over one kilometer in diameter. Striking the Earth at incredible speeds any of these ninety-nine would likely destroy more than ninety percent of life on Earth and turn life for the surviving ten percent into a nightmare. None of the "new Earth-crossers" are likely to hit Earth within the foreseeable future but the surprising number of them signal the likelihood that thousands of Earth crossing objects of considerable size have yet to be detected. NEATP had by July of 1997 only mapped 10 percent of the sky. Helin stated in April of 1996 that with the new system in place, "Within two month's, I've discovered as many asteroids as I'd found in my whole career."9

have realized a different perspective. A new, formidable, and enlightened branch of natural science has emerged within the space of a few decades, one that has come to dwarf the search for Clovis man. At first glance it seemed to have nothing to do with Archaeology, but in its implications it has everything to do with man's history of Earth. What was once denounced by Darwin and his considerable following as "catastrophism" and called "cataclysm theory," and dismissed as oddball speculation by enlightened twentieth century scientists, is now "Chaos Science," endorsed by many fields of science that understand the workings of the super-computer. This new science has come to challenge classical physics as well as Neo-Darwinian evolutionists and their "gradualist beliefs." The Church waged a costly battle against those who questioned the concept of the universe and stars as fixed and the immovable Earth as the center of the Universe. Science took the same position with those who questioned Sir Isaac Newton's laws. But with the arrival of Chaos Science there can remain few thinkers who will defend Newton's concept of a fixed and immutable pattern to the motion of the Earth and the solar system or to Lamarcks' determinism (fig. 4E). The message contained in the imagery of myth, that of cataclysmic events that visit the Earth with regularity, a concept that had been dismissed by scientists as "impossible" has suddenly found support from within the scientific community. Chaos Science reaffirmed the possibility of myth. To rephrase W. H. Auden, "a crack in the teacup *has* opened a lane to the land of the dead."

What is Chaos Science? Chaos Science is most easily explained in situations where it is least commonly apt to occur . . . in our stable solar system, for example. With the aid of sophisticated computers, science has discovered that Newton's laws of gravitational attraction in determining an order to the universe really only work to create a fixed and stable state when there are two bodies involved (Earth and Sun, Earth and Moon, etc.) Add a third body to the equation and you have lost predictability. Add several planets, their moons, 4,000 known asteroids, and the activities of comets lurking in the Oort cloud and you have the potential for chaos. This is not a chaos you can see on a day to day basis, as you can in weather systems. Chaos in our immediate section of the heavens will not reveal itself every year or even every century, for our solar system is one the most ordered observable entities we've measured. But like a pendulum swinging in an only slightly uncontrolled arc it will lead us to short periods of inevitable disorder, and possibly, cosmic disaster. Little of this was understood before the birth of Chaos Science, and to many minds, it seems, little will ever be understood. (See Sidebar, following page).

Some of us, notably the young and the inveterate risk takers, may cheer this

The Butterfly Effect

CHAOS, the irregular side to nature, was first observed in the workings of our atmosphere, in which, unlike our solar system, chaos is at work every day. In fact it was through attempts to predict the weather through ever more complex mathematical and computer models that Edward Lorenz discovered that where the components of a system are unstable and nonlinear, order and prediction are impossible.[10] The implications of this discovery can best be illustrated by what has come to be known as "The Butterfly Effect" in which, as preposterous as it may seem, the beatings of wing of butterflies in China actually can effect the weather in Europe two months later.

revolutionary theory on philosophical grounds, for there is clearly a beauty in the infinite patterns of chaos and there is a greater order contained within.

We've long known weather is unstable (fig. 4G). But chaotic patterns, despite Newton, despite Aristotle, may also occasionally hold the upper hand with what were thought to be fixed bodies of the universe. Although the main variable, friction, rarely comes into play in space, galaxies do collide. Black holes swallow other stars. And even our solar system has free bodies, asteroids and comets running loose in irregular patterns.

If chaos exists in the movement of bodies in our solar system it must be a very confined chaos. Otherwise the environment of the Earth could not have enjoyed the millions of years of apparent stability that has existed here and that has permitted life as we know it. In fact, in a seemingly ordered system only one factor need be chaotic to make the whole system potentially, and periodically, chaotic. The orbit of the first eight planets around the sun are stable and predictable. All are only slightly elliptical, confirming Newton's theory of attracting bodies, and none are likely to veer off and collide with each other.

The exception is the orbit of the ninth planet, Pluto. While predictable, Pluto has an orbit that is definitely elliptical beyond explanation by Newton's gravitational theory (Newton, in fact, was not aware of Pluto's existence). While Pluto's orbit is normally outside the orbit of Neptune it is currently closer to the sun than Neptune and will remain that way for the remainder of this century. The point is that there are occasions when the orbits of Pluto and

Neptune will intersect. The likelihood of collision is minuscule, given the varying lengths of the orbital paths and vastness of space, but it does exist.

Pluto's orbit confirms the existence of a chaotic state—within a much greater ordered state—of the solar system. For if any planet's orbit is chaotic, then the entire system, technically, is potentially chaotic.However, Pluto is an unlikely candidate for the role of initiator of periodic cataclysms. Pluto, one-fifth of the Earth in circumference and one-five hundredth of its weight in mass, is probably not even a planet. It could be a trapped comet, or, smaller

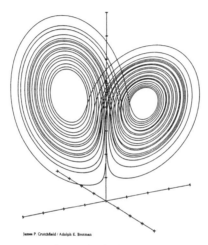

James P. Crutchfield / Adolph E. Brotman

4.G. THE LORENZ ATTRACTOR. The work of Edward Lorenz marked the breakthrough for the new science. Hoping to discover that super computers, if fed with enough information, could greatly assist in determining weather prediction world wide, Lorenz one day typed in a sequence of numbers that differed from the computer sequence by one- one thousandth part. The unexpected result of this slight change in input (Lorenz had rounded off the number. 506127 to.506) was that within two months the entire weather pattern world wide was chaotic. Lorenz had expected to find that if you began exactly the same circumstances (which is not really possible) you would get exactly repeating results. And if you began with similar circumstances (nine hundred and ninety-nine of a thousand would be very similar) you could at least expect somewhat similar results. He discovered the opposite. Given even the slightest change in initial conditions no two weather patterns will ever arrive at the same results. Change any one of a thousand variables even slightly and the resulting patterns will change exponentially. General patterns emerge.[16] Thus you can anticipate spring storms in the southern and midwestern regions of the U.S. But you cannot predict whether these storms will ravage Texas, flood Iowa, and bypass Oklahoma, causing drought. Some, all, or none of the above could happen in any one year, or could reoccur for several years in a particular area, such as the drought that created the "dust bowl" of the 1930s or the repeated floodings of the Missouri and Mississippi river valleys in the 1990s. Our computer models offer millions of possible scenarios for weather patterns to duplicate each other, but none do. Out of the discovery that long range weather prediction was impossible Chaos Science was born.

than our own moon, Pluto could itself have once been a moon, a satellite of another planet that somehow was dislodged. If so, the force that dislodged it must have been considerable. (Pluto has its own moon, Charon, which may be another dislodged piece of a celestial collision that has not resolved itself to the larger chunk, or may have been a foreign body subsequently captured. Pluto remains little understood).

If the chaos contained in our solar system were confined to Pluto's wanderings we could all feel pretty secure. It is not. The phenomenon of resonance is a much more likely candidate for creating chaotic conditions that could effect Earth. Resonance is best demonstrated when a planet and orbiting moon are both at furthermost point from the sun (aphelion) and in conjunction exert great tidal stress upon each other. In the lunar systems of Saturn and Jupiter, where several moons are involved, the resonance can produce great Earthquakes and very uneven orbits. It is Jupiter's resonance with the more than 4,000 charted asteroids (and many more yet uncharted), that occupy the wide area of space that separates Jupiter from Mars that provide the greatest potential for chaos. Logically there should be a planet between Jupiter and Mars. It could be that the asteroids represent a planet that never formed, due to Jupiter's massive gravitational effect, or one that formed and was smashed to smithereens by some outside force. In any event, there is no planet, only a seeming random collection of odd-shaped asteroids.

In 1867 the American astronomer Daniel Kirkwood noticed that the asteroids did not, in fact, randomly occupy their vast territory. Using resonance models constructed for the relationship of Jupiter to it moons (fig. 4H), he

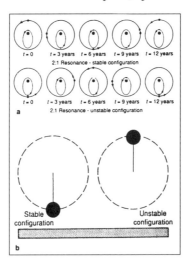

4.H. Resonance and its effect on Asteroids in the Kirkwood Gap.

found there were no asteroids at the 3:1 resonance configuration. Since distribution of asteroids should have been random and thus fairly even, where had the asteroids missing from the 3:1 belt (now known as the Kirkwood gap) gone? In 1981, more than a century later, Jack Wisdom of the California Institute of Technology found an answer. Wisdom demonstrated that any object at the 3:1 Jovian resonance would undergo substantial and unpredictable changes in orbit. The asteroids, during certain conjunctions involving the Sun, Jupiter, and Jupiter's moons, and other disturbances, have been cast or drawn out of the containment of the asteroid belt, many in eventual potential collision courses with Mars and the Earth.

Is the Kirkwood gap now empty? If so, has all danger finally passed? Unfortunately, the danger may be increasing. Very few Kirkwood gap asteroids are likely to have been cast out of the solar system entirely. Some may have collided with Jupiter but the vast majority are traveling in chaotic and unpredictable orbits that may eventually intersect with our own. Moreover, Kirkwood only knew of about 100 asteroids in the 3:1 gap, less than five percent of the number known today. There remain not only many more potentially Earth-bound asteroids in the 3:1 gap, but there are as yet unleashed asteroids in several other gaps that have been subsequently discovered.

A collision with an asteroid six miles wide ended the era of the dinosaurs. We now know of over 200 asteroids that are in excess of sixty miles in width and probably many thousands of a size that could end, or significantly alter, man's reign on Earth. We are certain of their sizes because occasionally one will "occult," that is, pass between us and the sun. Because of their relatively small size, when this event happens the sun's rays will pass in an almost parallel line around and past them. Thus their shadow will equal their diameter. The passing of 2 Pallas revealed its diameter to be 558 kilometers (about 375 miles) in width![11] The periodicity and the exact dates of their potential unleashing has not been determined by Chaos Science. But we know that movement of larger asteroids out of the Kirkwood gap is irregular and sporadic. Thousands of years have passed with only smaller chondrites, meteorites with only a few million years of exposure to cosmic rays, reaching the Earth's surface (fig. 4I).

Recently we have witnessed a renewed activity out of this chaotic zone. In 1989 an asteroid approximately one mile in diameter passed within 500,000 miles of the Earth. Change its course by only four hours and you will have a collision with the Earth. The Swift-Tuttle asteroid passed within 110 million miles of the Earth on November 7, 1992 and is due to return, perhaps on a collision course, in August of 2126. An asteroid named "1989 A.C." will pass close to the Earth in 2004. Two other large asteroids, Alinda, and Quetzalcoatl, are in resonance with Jupiter and may soon be unleashed in our general direc-

4.I. CELESTIAL ROCKS AND "DIRTY SNOWBALLS." Meteors, mainly the debris from asteroids and comets, strike the Earth with great frequency, particularly during the Perseid showers that come every August to the northern hemisphere. These meteors are all very small and most burn up in our atmosphere. Only a few strike the Earth as meteorites. It has recently been speculated that as many as 30 ice chunks of over 30 feet in diameter, debris from comets, strike our planet every month. Yet there is no particular reason why only small objects would come to be on a collision course with the Earth. The asteroid Ceres is 1,000 kilometers wide and is subject to the same forces that sent the celestial body that struck the Earth and resulted in the formation of the moon. That body must have rivaled Ceres's size (it is likely that the moon itself is mainly expelled Earth matter while the object that created it is now part of the Earth, probably lying under the Pacific). Are the possibilities of such collisions now extinct? They could easily be viewed that way, just as Mount St. Helens, prior to its devastating eruption, was considered "probably extinct."

tion. Are we entering a period of renewed exposure to planetary disaster? As the Age of Pisces draws to a close and the year 2013, the date that marks the close of the current Maya age, approaches, can we expect more activity from the unstable reaches of the asteroid belt?

Scientists now calculate that, based on the activity of asteroids and comets of which they are aware, the chances of any single individual on Earth today dying as a direct result of a collision of one these objects with the Earth is roughly three times as great as the chances of an individual suffering a fatality from an airline crash.

Evidence of direct strikes are not needed to explain great exterminations. A "near miss" can be quite catastrophic. How close would a "near miss" need to be to devastate life on Earth? Particularly if it came at an inopportune time, such as the close of an Ice Age? An asteroid or comet would need not be on an exact collision course to wreck great havoc. Our planet's gravity could pull a near miss into an intersecting trajectory. At the same time it would greatly accelerate the speed of the asteroid, just as our astronauts face magnified speed as they return to Earth. Since an asteroid would be approaching from behind us and at an oblique angle to the Earth (asteroids orbit the Sun in the same direction as the Earth), the increased speed may have caused some asteroids not on a true collision course to "bounce off" our atmosphere much as smaller meteorites do with regularity. And what a "bounce" it would be. A near-near miss of a large asteroid with the Earth (if you could describe a violent brushing with our atmosphere a "miss") could very well account for the sudden fate of tens of thousands of mammoths and other large mammals in Siberia and Alaska 11,500 to 12,000 years ago—without any trace residue of iridium. Have asteroids entered our atmosphere recently? In this century there have been two such occurrences in Siberia, in 1908 and again in 1947. There were conflagrations in the atmosphere caused, probably, not by the impact of asteroids, but by a small asteroid or chunk glancing off the atmosphere, much like a stone will skip off the surface of water. Both times wide ranges of the Siberian forest were devastated and most animal life was completely wiped out.

Mastodons and Mammoths were able to move north through cold river valleys and icy streams at the close of the last ice. It seemed there was no climatic extremity that they could not endure. Yet at an instant in geologic time they disappeared.[12]

It was within that time frame that Plato said Atlantis was destroyed, being hit first by a conflagration and then by a deluge. A "near miss" by a comet or asteroid of great proportions would first set the sky on fire and then unleash a terrible tidal force upon the seas. Coastal civilizations worldwide would have been affected, but those closest to the passing body would be inundated. In the case of large mammals, many met their end in valleys near the northern seas. But even a great distance from the seas would not have protected them. For if the heat of such a conflagration in the sky above them had not killed them, the sudden loss of oxygen would have meant instant extinction in a suddenly breathless world. Only the smaller burrowing mammals, reptiles and insects, with their own private cells of oxygen could have survived. This

4.J. A DEFORMED FROG LACKING ONE OF ITS BACK LEGS. Frogs have the ability to live in suspended animation in hard baked clay for up to fifty years. Long assumed to be the most delicate of animals, they proved long ago to actually be among the most sturdy. Unfortunately, while the frog has proved durable in the face of celestial cataclysms it now appears helpless against the onslaught of man-induced pollution. Frogs around the world are disappearing because they are born deformed and incapable of reproduction.

would explain why frogs (fig. 4J) and toads didn't disappear with the dinosaur or with the mammoth.

Changes in the Earth's elliptical orbit have been cited as the cause of the Ice Ages, but, discounting collisions and near misses of asteroids and comets as "unbelievable," science has been unable to describe just why the Earth's rotation around the Sun, stable for tens of millions of years, would have become deviant. The answer is now becoming clearer, one closely associated with myth—irregular movements in the heavens and increased comet activity.

The myths of early man universally regard the appearance of comets as the harbinger of disaster. Since comets, by our standards, appear so infrequently, and usually pass millions of miles from us, we must wonder why they were so fearful. A viable explanation is that one individual comet passing through the asteroid belt could dislodge the paths of ten of hundreds of asteroids from the asteroid belt that lays between Mars and Jupiter. Thus a comet would not have to pass close to the Earth at all to bring at least the threat of devastating subsequences. If you question how primitive men could have linked the two events, since asteroids destabilized by the passing of a comet probably would not immediately threaten the Earth, remember that in terms of the heavens primitive man was anything but primitive . . . he was a master of the skies.

On the other hand not all "primitive" societies had developed sophisticated astronomy and yet comets are feared in pre-scientific cultures throughout the world. Why? A strong case can be made that their fear was based on the occurrence of at least a close and catastrophic miss by a comet, and perhaps even an actual collision by a comet fragment or small asteroid sometime within the collective memory of man—a memory that would have been an undeniable part of man's oral tradition.

As if to remind us of what has been our past fate, and what most likely will be our destiny, we witnessed, in the summer of 1994, the spectacular collision of a series of comet chunks, pieces from the disintegrating comet Shoemaker-Levy, [9] with the surface of the planet Jupiter. Many of the explosions that resulted were larger in diameter than the Earth itself, and they produced a fireball fifty times brighter than Jupiter. Shoemaker-Levy had first made a close pass with Jupiter that tore the comet apart into thousands of fragments and dozens of large chunks. Then, with its orbit bent by Jupiter's huge gravitational field, Shoemaker-Levy returned to collide with the planet with the force of millions of atomic explosions. Could life on Earth survive such a fireball, equal to millions of hydrogen bombs, with temperatures at the impact point many times that of the surface of the sun?

Clearly the collision of a comet with the Earth would be every bit as devastating as that of a large asteroid. But even at the beginning of this decade the

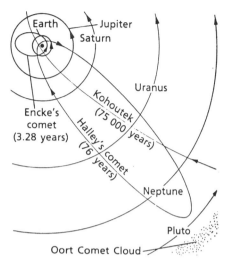

4.K. THE KOHOUTEK AND HALLEY'S COMET. Asteroids aren't the only potential problem. Comets, thick chunks of frozen gas and assorted matter sometimes described as "dirty snowballs" lie waiting in the Oort Cloud just beyond the apogee of Pluto's orbit and in the Kuiper Belt which may stretch half-way to the closest stars. For reasons unknown one of these "snowballs" is occasionally stirred into action and lunges into the heart of our solar system. One comet, the Swift-Tuttle, passed 110 million miles from the Earth on November 7, 1992, and in August of 2126 will pass much closer. Some scientists give it a 1-in-10,000 chance of hitting Earth on that date but others feel that the odds are more perilous. What is certain, however, is that such collisions have not been uncommon in our past, nor are they likely to be uncommon in our future. Once considered a rare, or unlikely event, Hal Levison of the Southwest Research Institute in Boulder, now estimates that "there are something like 10 million comets that cross the paths of planets in the solar system."[13]

chances were regarded as less likely for three reasons: there appeared to be fewer comets (at least there were fewer that entered the planetary scope of the solar system), their orbits normally covered a much wider range than those of the asteroids, and, coming out of the egg-shaped Oort Cloud their orbits followed a different plane—comets would only rarely and briefly cross the Earth's orbit (fig. 4K).

Data gleaned from the Hubble space telescope has changed much of that thinking. The Hubble team of astronomers that surveys our solar system has recently reported that comets that visit our inner solar system come, predominately, not from the Oort Cloud, but from the Kuiper belt. Much of the Kuiper belt lies closer to the planetary solar system, encompassing the planet Pluto. The Hubble team, led by Alan Stern, now estimates that the Kuiper belt contains over 200 million comets including many over 125 miles wide. Moreover, the belt lies on the planetary elliptic, answering the question of why the solar system appeared to have a sharp edge ending at Neptune (Pluto's small mass could not help define a symmetry to planet configuration), rather than a classic bell-shaped distribution of matter. The bell shape, squashed by tidal forces to a very low trajectory, exists, but the outer matter is dispersed into hundreds of millions of planetoids, or comets that reach, perhaps, half-way to the nearest star.[14]

The important point for us on Earth is that comets exist, and interact on our planetary plane, rarely deviating from our angle of orbit by more than eleven degrees. Thus the potential for interaction, to use a mild term, is increased greatly beyond past expectations. Whose past expectations? Myth emphasized these portents of doom.

Could what we now call "Early Man" have been so sophisticated in his astronomical observations that he made the connection between the appearance of a comet and the resulting reign of disaster on Earth? But why should we call ancestors from twelve thousand years ago "Early Man"? From what we now know of the world, man of that time was very intelligent, and very much in tune with the celestial world that surrounded him.

Human memory, preseved through myth, is long enough to understand why comets, despite their beauty in the night sky and the excitement they engender, are universally feared. Only 12,000 years, a few seconds of geologic time, have lapsed between what was likely a comet's or asteroid's collision, or a very close (and destructive) encounter with the Earth, and the July 1994 collision of fragments of the Shoemaker-Levy 9 comet with Jupiter. With Halley's comet regularly menacing Earth for the past several centuries, science may have to conclude that we are currently smack in the midst of an age of comets, very possibly similar to the one that caused the extinction of the dinosaurs 65 million years ago, and of the mammoths and American horse 12,500 years ago, the event that most concerns us here.

We know that something significant happened around 12,500 years ago. We know that the event marked the demise of vast numbers of megafauna, just as the K-T event doomed the dinosaurs. We know that myth relates this time as the end of man's first try at survival, and we know that enough humans survived that test that man, was given a second chance. But for this date we lack the positive proof of an iridium trail. Could it be that an asteroid or comet passed or that one only a half-mile in circumference impacted, or that a larger one "bounced" off our planet? The evidence may still be outstanding. Yet the effects are known.

Asteroids and comets have usually been considered separately. Yet it stands to reason that the same force that disturbs the Oort Cloud, and the Kuiper Belt—whether it is a closely passing star, an undetected and eccentrically orbiting tenth planet, or dark matter of the Milky Way galaxy—would also affect Jupiter and tend to stir up the millions of chunks of matter in the Asteroid Belt. Comets themselves passing through the asteroid belt may be responsible for sending large meteorites Earthbound.

Chaos Science has enabled us to reappraise not only our traditional "predictive" sciences, it has enabled us to reassess the information contained in the myths of ancient peoples (fig. 4L). Does Chaos Science ultimately disprove

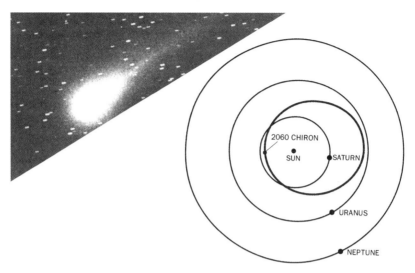

4.L. PHOTO OF 2060 CHIRON, A COMET THAT HAS LEFT THE KUIPER BELT AND NOW HAS AN EARTH-CROSSING ORBIT. The Maya and pre-Maya, in millennia of charting the heavens, knew of many more returning comets than our recent return to astral science has been able to observe. The Maya system of reckoning time described distinct ages marked by conflagrations that ended one age and began another. The current age, by their calendar, is due to end on December 23, in the year 2,012. Will this date be marked by the arrival of a great comet civilization has forgotten?

Einstein's famous objection to the "uncertainty principle," when he stated that "God does not play dice with the universe?" It has clearly dealt a "death blow" to the doctrine of scientific determinism—that the universe and everything in it is completely predictable. Yet, it may be there by a design of which we are unaware.

We cannot rely on the words of scientists who viewed the cosmos from a purely mechanical point of view. As Stephen Hawking has pointed out, without expansion and resulting chaos, Newton's static universe would long ago have started to contract under the influence of its own gravity, and would now be in full collapse.[15] Chaos exists—and interaction, free will, and the Platonic concept of flow thus reenters any equation of knowledge. Indian mystics well understood this concept when they described the universe as "a cosmic dance."

5 Bones of Contention: *Is Archaeology Science?*

T HE FIRST ATLANTEANS *to return to their homeland came from the colonies on the west coast of Africa. It took them fifty-two years. Although at the moment of the cataclysmic event the great wave had initially moved away from the west coast of Africa, leaving the ships in the ports lurching in thick mud, the sea returned and destroyed most of the Atlantean colony's fleet. The effect of the reversal disturbed the Atlantic so greatly that all except the Atlanteans had come to think of it as a sea of mud. Nine thousand years later a Greek philosopher named Plato still described the mud shallows of the Atlantic as unnavigable.*

Meanwhile, Atlantis was rebuilt—at least an attempt was made to its rebuilding. Three Rabbit's twin sons, Red Bird and Seven Stars were among the builders. This time the great pyramid was an obsession, believed to be the only defense against another visit from messengers of the Sun God. The new Atlantis could not be built on the ruins of the old, as was the custom, because the great stone boulders used in its older construction were submerged. Still, the Atlanteans naturally wanted to live close to the life-giving sea. The new Poseidon, capital off Atlantis, was built two hundred feet higher, at the edge of new coastline, from smaller rocks, not perfectly fitted, but held together by mortar. But there were other problems. Building skills were lost. No one could remember how the metal orichalc, a brass rich in zinc, was made. And because the proposed structure was so massive, the Atlanteans brought foreign peoples from distant colonies to help in its construction. At first it was required that all spoke the Atlantean tongue, the universal language, but the workers resisted and the idea was dropped. Crews on the pyramid worked in several different languages. Rivalries grew, and fights broke out. The omens were dire—the sea was visibly rising, and the days were getting hotter. One season no longer followed the other. In what once had been the moderate capital of Atlantis, it was sweltering summer year round.

To the north and to the south the great ice caps were retreating. The melting Wisconsin glacier filled huge Lake Nippissing until it began to overflow into the Mississippi valley. Antarctic ice sheets broke off icebergs the size of cities. One day with a roar and unimaginable rumble an ice sheet a thousand miles wide broke off from Antarctica and plunged into the sea. The Earth's crust, already imbalanced, was suddenly thrown into turmoil. Great earthquakes rippled the Earth's surface. A great rift opened and the waters of the great Lake Nippissing poured down the Mississippi valley. Within a day the gigantic flow raised the level of the Mexican Gulf and the Caribbean Sea by 200 feet. It was equaled by the wall of water coming up from the Antarctic. The two waves met at the New Poseidon, on the thin strip of land at the center of the great Atlantean continent, at the crest of the long delayed, not quite completed, pyramid. Thus, within a generation, Atlantis was destroyed twice, the first time by fire, the second by flood.

The deluge was universal. All the great cities had been built on the sea coasts. All were destroyed. Those that survived the deluge finally learned a valuable lesson . . . to move inland from the coasts and find higher ground. Remnants of a culture oriented to the sea sought and found a new home along large river valleys. In a warming world climate they moved away the seacoasts and from Atlantis's heart. Some even crossed the Atlantic and settled in what would later become Sumer and Egypt, where the people became dispersed and agricultural, forgetting the practice of their naval heritage. They remembered that greater time only through myth.

Four thousand years later a lone expedition crossed the Atlantic to what would later be called the Windward Islands. Before the destruction of Atlantis this area had been above the waters and formed an outer rim that all but enclosed the Atlantean sea. Now it was mostly submerged with only the mountain tops still visible above the risen sea, as a reminder of what had once been. There was no way to regain the knowledge that had been lost. Myth alone survived. Narratives of the Golden Age, when Atlanteans roamed the seas and built great cities, have been kept throughout millennia, accompanied, in a few places, by the hope it could be revived.

•

Is traditional Americanist archaeology a science or is it an attempt to fit new information into old paradigms? The question of man's past has too long been left exclusively in the hands of archaeologists and historians. Most historians can only report on what is there in the written record, without a thought to considering the living record contained in the oral tradition and culture of peoples who still maintain the "old ways." Most archaeologists are basically diggers, working under Victorian and Darwinian ideas of man's relevance in the world. They are careful diggers, to be sure. However, Americanist archaeologists have long been working under an outdated terrestrial model of primitive land migration that they have shown little will to question, even when confronted with significant information that challenges their model. In fact, academic acceptance has continually rooted out any dissidents to the Neo-Darwinian model. They have been able to report on the obvious food gathering and tool and weaponry making techniques of the ancient remains they have encountered, but they have been unable to tell us what a man of two thousand years ago, or of twenty thousand years ago, thought, or how he acted, or why he built what he built.

Encountering pyramids that in their construction recorded precise movements of the planets and star constellations, encountering wide roads that interconnected the great cities of Mesoamerica, built without defensive walls, and encountering megaliths that describe distinct sight-lines marking pathways through the seas to distant civilizations, the academics have been unable to grasp the greater implications of their finds. They have told us that these were "ceremonial centers." But they have been unable to tell us what ceremonies were conducted at these "ceremonial centers." Encountering great astronomical observatories and entire city-states laid out in harmony with celestial bodies, the academics have again missed the point and declared that they were built as a farming aid—a means to tell the farmer when to plant his crops. Further, Americanist anthropology has viewed the construction of the great Mayan sites in Mesoamerica as a linear undertaking. Under this model when one city-state fell, it was replaced by another in prominence. Thus Tikal in Guatemala replaced Uaxactún; Caracol, in Belize, replaced Tikal; Chichen Itza, in the Yucatán, replaced Tula, in the Valley of Mexico, etc. However, it is

5A. Sacbeob interconnect the great city-states of Mesoamerica.

now becoming clear that many major sites not only coexisted without the defensive walls that marked "Old World" civilizations, they were interconnected by wide limestone roads, called sacbeob, intricate canals, and a wide range of traded goods (fig. 5A).

A new breed of scientists—biochemists, and astronomers among them—equally interested in our past, have encroached on the private realm of established archaeologists. They have concluded that there was a different purpose to precise knowledge of the heavens. It wasn't farming—farmers have always known when to plant and when to reap. Purpose and intent must have been built into the precise construction of star temples and that purpose had to be in an exact definition of astronomy—a measuring of the stars. Similarly, the exact layout of the spheres of Costa Rica was based on another science—navigation. In fact naval astronomy may have come thousands of years before the cataclysm that gave astronomy a second function—that of careful watching for signs of another cataclysm. But archaeologists could not see the navigational functions inherent in star temples. Nor could they see the function in the great calendrical and numerical systems of the ancients. American physical anthropology has languished under obvious misconceptions unable to break free from the theories that embraced MesoAmerican cultures as an isolated and recent event.

The view from inside a narrow frame of reference and theory is often self-righteous, and blindly "self-fulfilling." Thus American Archaeology became convinced of its own authority as the dispenser of knowledge and, absorbed in its own conceit, issued declarations beyond the questioning or measurements of outsiders. In summary, their story is that the universe has been here for 12 to 15 billion years, life on this planet for 600,000 years, man for 4 to 5

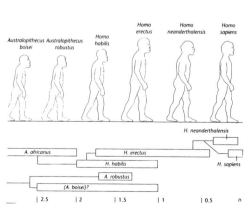

5.B. Homo habilis. Among L.S.B. Leakey's discoveries in East Africa was that of a hominid who knew how to make tools and to organize his life. When Leakey came to understand the characteristics of this hominid he gave him the name Homo habilis, "handy man". Whether we evolved from this little fellow or from some cousin of his is still unclear, but what has been very clear is that the main body of archaeology has noted little change in the habits of mankind from his time, 1.8 million years ago, until 7,000 years ago.

119

million years, Homo sapiens for 200,000 to 270,000 years, but civilized thinking man has been around for a scant 6,000 to 7,000 years . . . before that everything was pretty much a dumb groping for survival (fig. 5B).

Mankind has, collectively, always wanted to believe that we appear as we are—and were meant to be as we are—in Stephen Jay Gould's words, by "a natural result of inevitable improvement constructed by a process (natural selection) that continually makes successful creatures better and better."[1]

Those are Stephen Jay Gould's words, but Gould, now considered the world's leading theorist on large-scale patterns of evolution, rejects this arrogance. He has demonstrated that natural selection has never worked to any advantage in the context of a great period of time, nor in a great diversity of environments, but only in local environments where greater specialization, and an associated lack of flexibility, has insured survivability. Humans, in their short existence on Earth, have defied the process, first by generalizing their responses to local environments, and secondly by delaying their sexual maturity until well into their second decade of existence. In other matters, including cannibalism and an extreme passion for revenge against others of their own kind, Homo sapiens has positioned itself as a temporary and, per-

5.C/D. WHEELED TOYS. We can compare similarly depicted wheeled toy animals in Sumer (left, center) with wheeled toy dogs found at Popocatepetl and Veracruz in Mexico (5.D right). If the people who eventually built the great civilizations in Mesoamerica had migrated across Beringia as hunting bands they would have undoubtedly taken their dogs, the Siberian spitz and husky, with them. But there are no traces of the Husky or Spitz or any thing like them in ancient Mexico and Central America. However, short-haired dogs like those found in ancient Egypt and Sumer (Mesopotamia)have been found depicted in wheeled toys from Mexico to Panama. Does this point to Sumerian settlement of the Americas? Possibly. But the presence of mummified "Sumerian" type dogs in Peru dated to 8000 B.C., two thousand years before the traditional dating of the rise of Sumerian civilization, would seem to indicate that dog migration, at least, was from the Americas to the Mediterranean.3 The very question of the domestication of dogs from wolves may prove to be as complicated, and as little understood, as the rise of diverse peoples. Working from the earliest known fossilized bones, archaeologists have long argued that the domesticated dog is, at most, 14,000 years old. Yet working through mitochrondrial DNA evidence Robert K. Wayne, a UCLA evolutionary biologist, contradicts archeological evidence with DNA proof that dogs have been domesticated for at least 100,000 years.4

haps, absurd, ruler of the Earth. In any event, despite his temporary rule, mankind has much to prove. Although some last much longer the average species survives for about four million years. Our species, Homo sapiens is about 250,000 years old. Man has many uncharted millennia to endure to prove that he is worthy to rank significant mention, let alone dominance, among the creations of this world.

Americanists have viewed natural selection as an imperative that has inevitably worked towards man's emergence and dominance. Simply put, God favors humans. At least, that is the argument of both the Creationists and the Neo-Darwinists. If so, why did God wait so long to introduce humans into the picture? And did they arrive by necessity? If this is the argument, that man is a necessary product of either divine design or evolutionary process, only the Creationist argument can hold any merit. Darwin's gradualist theory of evolution cannot account for man's dominance or even for his presence. Gould, referring to his wonderful book, states "Wonderful Life asserts the unpredictability and contingency of any particular event in evolution—and emphasizes that the origin of Homo sapiens must be viewed as such an unrepeatable particular, not an expected consequence."[2]

When faced with the likelihood that mankind spread over the Earth much as crabgrass spreads through a yard, interconnectedly, academic anthropology has countered that the Earth and its oceans were too vast, and its peoples too isolated, for any significant contact to have occurred. How could they have known that the oceans were not navigable 12,000 years ago? They could have known it only if they had misinterpreted data and then written this very wrong data into their textbooks, as indisputable fact. When outsiders, like Thor Heyerdahl, have proven their theories wrong, they have discarded the contradictory evidence and called the outside investigators "amateurs." Archaeologists do not like outside interference with their pet theories—like most academic specialists they are very "territorial."

Archaeologists and historians have been misled by the concept of the history of humanity as a series of events tied together as a linear imperative instead of attempting an understanding of the complexity of man's endeavors (figs. 5C, 5D). In their view, if they found man making Clovis points anywhere on the North American continent it meant that the most advanced men anywhere in the Americas were making Clovis points, hunting mastodon, and building charcoal fires. In truth the history of man on this planet is more convoluted than strictly linear. Even today, we repeat, primitive man coexists with more technologically advanced man.

In the 1940s some American anthropologists, notably the followers of Franz Boas (see earlier mention), became aware that British Functionalists, particularly Radcliffe-Brown and Malinowski, stressed the value of viewing sites and their evidence on their on merit, eschewing attempts to make sites, or artifacts from those sites, fit theory.[6] For a brief period, the emphasis on spear points and pottery, was replaced, by a few, with an appreciation of structures.[7] But that is not how most Americanists have viewed the evidence. In Mesoamerica scientists in the fields of paleontology, morphology, and geology have insisted on integrating a Darwinian gradualist mechanism into their interpretation of ancient sites. When dates of the sites have conflicted with Neo-Darwinian ideals—ideals intent on describing the Americas in both an independent and more recent cultural context—older dates have invariably been the ones questioned and disbelieved. Thus the spheres of Costa Rica have been declared "out of context." "Out of context" designation, a simple throwing away of evidence that does not fit established theory, has provided a needed reinforcement for the Americanists. In the Diquis Delta the spheres were viewed as too old and too sophisticated to have been constructed by documented cultures, such as the Choretega. As indicators of civilization the builders of the spheres were viewed as too advanced to fit within the academic paradigm of the Americas as a recent citadel of civilization. So they have been designated an enigma, and then ignored. The pursuit of fitting American sites into a Darwinian model has been devastating to independent thought and to independent sites.

By the early 1950s the Americanist reliance on fitting sites to preconceived theories was reinforced by the use of carbon 14 dating. Carbon 14 dating gave the archaeologist an absolute date making cultural context and patterns of behavior within an integrated whole unnecessary. However, carbon 14 dates themselves are inaccurate (see facing page), and the method by which they have been used has taxed credibility.

Rocks and megaliths, like the spheres of Costa Rica, have in themselves no value that can be dated by the C-14 method. They are simply too old. What C-14 dating can do is approximate associative material, like charcoal or fired pottery shards, with the sites. Thus if we find an ancient site where truly primitive hunters were fashioning spear points and find fires that we can date to 12,000 B.P. (before present) and find corroborative evidence of extinct mammals from an associative date we can pronounce, fearlessly, that these hunters lived at a particular date.

The problem occurs when we find evidence of charcoal fires associated with sophisticated structures. For example, Napoleon ordered the surrounding sand cleared from the Egyptian Sphinx down to its base. A few of his soldiers may have built fires at that level. After the French withdrawal some Egyptians could have fired pottery at the same level. Or they might fire pot-

Carbon 14 Dating

CARBON 14 is a radioactive isotope that is regularly absorbed from the air by green plants. When animals eat the green plants they also ingest the carbon 14 and it becomes part of their tissue. When other animals eat this tissue they also ingest the carbon 14. And so on. When a plant or animal dies it can take on no more carbon 14. At that point radioactive decay begins. According to Willard F. Libby, who first effectively dated samples in 1949, the dead organism will lose half its radioactivity in 5,568 years. Half of the half that remains will dissipate in another 5,568 years. "Half-lives" can be measured effectively for up to 50,000 years by measuring the remaining C-14 in any uncontaminated material that has ever been alive. But Libby's figure proved to be wrong when dates of 2,600 B.C. were obtained for objects of the first Dynasty of Egypt—in this case calendrical dates showed that the objects and cultures involved were five or six hundred years older. Libby believed that the amount of C-14 in the atmosphere was a constant but actually it was much more prevalent in earlier times. Thus any creature that lived in a time when C-14 was richer will appear much younger than it really was. Studies that include known measurement of C-14 in the atmosphere have proved that an organism with a date of 3500 B.C. actually dates from 4375 B.C. in real years. A C-14 dating of 11,200 B.P. is really 13,200 B.P. and by 20,000 B.P. there is a discrepancy of 3,500 years. Despite this unchallenged re-calibration of the dates of organic matter Eurocentric archaeologists and our major texts have held on to the un-calibrated dates.[5] Calibrated dates for sites often put them before those that fit into the established paradigm. The earlier dates, even when archaeologists admit they must be correct, often prove to be embarrassing. So they are ignored.

tery during the next decade or century. If a sandstorm in the next century were to have buried and preserved these activities, and a subsequent cataclysm struck, say in the year 2,013, what would the record be a thousand or ten thousand years from now? By associative carbon 14 dating you could safely assume, by this method, that the Sphinx dated to 1800 to 2,000 A.D., contemporary with the American experiment with democracy. Preposterous? No, that is simply the way Archaeology works.

We must remember that if one piece of charcoal or pottery is dated as 5,000 years old that does not mean that other objects found in association with it could not be centuries or millennia older. Often, the very people responsible for assigning dates to sites forget that simple fact. Yet, when artifacts such as pottery shards or fire pits can be dated by carbon 14 techniques—the holy grail of archaeologists—these dates are given as an absolute dating of the site involved.

Historians and archaeologists at first declared any proposed find that predated Christ "absurd" or "out of context." But they have had to grudgingly push back the dates for their interpretation of early American man's evolution as a civilized being—at first by hundreds, and recently by thousands of years. Thus, for example, Teotihuacan is believed to have arisen not in 100 A.D., as long reported, but in 900 to 1,400 B.C. Despite these revisions, archaeologists have continued to insist on their gradualist paradigm. What they persistently misread and ignore is that an intelligent, civilized, human presence had been in existence for thousands of years, perhaps tens of thousands of years, before the dates for their selected site of civilization's emergence in the Americas.

We must reemphasize that the neo-Darwinian model has been mistaken in two very significant ways: in its decree that evolution is gradual and inevitably favors the fittest, and in its rejection of catastrophes, relegated to the fancy of "myth," as an important operative in the function of evolution. Darwin based his model of evolution on the work of botanists and zoologists of the nineteenth century. They were certain that they represented the forefront of scientific endeavor in artificially combining optimal breeds to create healthier stock. Darwin believed that this "artificial" process of selection was not limited to new science but mimicked a process that had been naturally and gradually occurring throughout the entirety of life on this planet. In his view, natural selection, a very gradual rewarding of the fittest, and a gradual eliminating of the less fit had been an ongoing process from the beginning of time. Of course, this was a notion, not quite a theory, and it was not scientific fact. And, as indicated earlier, it contradicted significant observations Darwin, himself, had made.

Darwin often doubted his own theory. It required a belief in history as a

continual step-ladder with one species supplanting another, becoming dominant by being better able to adapt to changing circumstances. But the industrial society of the nineteenth century loved this theory. While contradictions
in Church theory (Do unto others . . .) sometimes impeded their world-view,
Darwin confirmed the place of both the Church and the industrialists as
inheritors of the world. They had survived, they were rich, therefore the world
had arrived at its highest point, and was in perfect order.

This "step-ladder" approach to evolution was not significantly challenged
until 1989 when Stephen Jay Gould published *Wonderful Life*, based on the
long-ignored discovery by Charles Doolittle Walcott of a myriad of fossils at the
Burgess Shale in southern British Columbia. Gould called Walcott's 1909 discovery "the Holy Grail of paleontology." And Gould's revelations of the mechanism of evolution have turned gradualist Neo-Darwinian concepts upside-
down. The idea that new species evolved through great struggles over immense
periods of time was contradicted by real evidence that almost all phyla, families,
and the basic masterplan of species of life were generated in an "evolutionary
moment." This evolutionary flash occurred in a long ago period called the
Cambrian, and the flash itself is now known as the Cambrian explosion.

In that period all of the phyla of life that now exist, and many others now
extinct, were born within a span of a few million years, from 530 to 525 million years ago. A minimum of 10,000 new species were born, and phyla arose
that did not endure, including five-eyed creatures, jelly-fish with shrimp-like
tails, and elongated beings that confuse the investigator as to what end was up
and which end marked the beginning. But more importantly Arachnids (spiders, crabs), Insecta, Chordates (those with spines—ancestors of fish, mice,
and men), and all the other animal phyla—the complex body forms that continue to dominate our planet today—suddenly appeared in the Cambrian.
Nothing like these creatures existed before this explosion of life forms, and
nothing new has been created since.

It appears that the significant events in the evolutionary history of our
planet have occurred through a mechanism and process that has had nothing
to do with Darwinian theory. *Evolution is an indisputable fact.* But Darwin's
theory of gradual replacement of inferior species by newer, more adaptive,
and more fit species—"survival of the fittest"—does not appear to have been
the valid mechanism for the origin of species. Some other mechanism surely
prevailed and accounted for the wonderful diversity of life Gould describes,
but it was not the one described by Darwin, nor by any of his followers.

The question of Darwinism versus Creationists essentially represents the
head and tails of the same question, with differing and very wrong answers.
Although both have been used as rationales for exploitation of the planet's

resources, neither provides true scientific discovery nor do they provide definitive answers. Neither view contains an actual basis in how man or his predecessors has behaved nor, despite their pretensions, is either view enlightened in its concept of how man should behave. If we have attained evolution's highest order, the lesson of history appears to be that not only does God favor humans but that God favors humans who destroy other humans, their past, and their resistance to existing powers. Is this an absurd notion? Have we not lived through an absurd century?

Gould's view is that because of "the unpredictability and contingency of any particular event" biological evolution culminating in mankind is a chance event. This refutes the traditional Americanist and Darwinian view that man is the necessary product of a gradual process of "survival of the fittest." The idea that we are the inevitable result of evolution must be reexamined. Darwin and Neo-Darwinian dogma have not been reinforced by science but has, in fact, been disproved by the observations of biological science and the mathematics of probability.[8]

If Darwinism cannot explain biological evolution, can neo-Darwinism explain parallel and inevitable duplication of step-pyramids, and exact replication of cultures without contact? The Roman Church maintains that man was created in God's image. Ancient beliefs, expressed in myth and animal totems, have maintained that all of life was created in God's image.

Darwin was not only mistaken in his view of how species were gradually created, he was doubly wrong in his theory of a gradual mechanism for the extinction of the less fit. Followers of Darwin have trumpeted their belief that he had successfully refuted pagan beliefs in catastrophism. Yet five great periods of extinction have marked the demise of creatures that, until their extinction, ruled without significant contest to their rule . . . species that within the context of their environment could not be questioned in their fitness to dominate. These five extinctions have been recently recognized and documented by Richard Leakey, David Jablonski, Stephen Jay Gould, among others, and have been recorded as end-Ordovician (440 million years ago), late-Devonian (365 million years ago), the end-Permian (225 million years ago), the end-Triassic (210 million years ago), and the end-Cretaceous (65 million years ago). None of these great extinctions, which cumulatively extirpated two-thirds of the species that have ever arisen on Earth, was either gradual nor resulted in the elimination of the "least fit." The greatest extinction, the end-Permian, un-selectively wiped out 95 percent of the species that then existed. Seemingly it was those species that dominated for hundreds of millions of years that were eliminated. Gould writes, "There is no separate problem of the extinction of the dinosaurs . . . The history of life has been punctuated by brief episodes of mass extinction."[9]

We repeat, we have yet to account for the most recent extinction, when the mastodon, mammoth, saber-toothed tiger, dire wolf, American horse and camel, and thirty other species of mega-fauna became extinct at the end of the last Ice Age, around 11,500 years ago. Why did these large animals that appeared to dominate the Americas, suddenly disappear, all at the same time? The only explanation that makes sense is that of a celestial collision of a comet or asteroid with the Earth, the catastrophe graphically told in myth, the results of which were once witnessed and described by Darwin, only later to be denied.

As Boas suggested, we must return to the sites themselves, but looking beyond confirmation of misguided theory, including racial and cultural prejudices, and instead to an examination of *function*. The great constructions of Mesoamerica were not ceremonial sites, they were sites of learning, of "science."

While we must rely on archaeologists for at least the initial investigation and excavation of digging sites, to rely on archaeologists to translate their findings into the definitive record of man's history on Earth is folly.

Sadly, archaeologists have repeatedly disdained and dismissed the measurements other sciences—in fact they have been trained to do so. As a result they operate within a narrow perspective, effectively an insulated paradigm of ignorance. Even today, there are few archaeologists who understand or even admit archeoastronomy or Chaos Science as an operative in world history. Probability science is simply ignored. Myth has been ridiculed.

Isolationists have been unable to admit that genetic evidence would, within their own century, firmly link Asian sailors who reached the shores of Australia over 80,000 years ago to modern Africans and Europeans (fig. 5F). Nor have they understood the implications of "multi-regional development," that the contact between humans in all parts of the world has been intermittent and two-way for at least 270,000 years. But on the basis of the evidence available to them they could have at least admitted the possibility.

Was it conspiracy or simple arrogance? Perhaps their ignorance, considering how young their profession was, and how much there was yet to learn, is excusable. But their attitude—that they could make pronouncements based on scanty and misconceived evidence, as well as on matters of which they knew nothing—is astonishing. Knowing as little as they knew, it is the arrogant disregard of the scope of their pronouncements—indicating that they were the font of all knowledge and were beyond questioning—that is what is so appalling. Their theories have significantly hindered revelations of the truth—about particular sites, their true dates, and the intelligence and spiritual cultures of "early man."

5.F. ART IN AUSTRALIA. Circular depressions carved in the face of a 13-foot-tall sandstone monolith. They have been dated to a minimum of 60,000 years B.P. In 1992 Richard Fullagar, an archaeologist at the Australian Museum in Sydney discovered a series of thousands of inch-long depressions in a sandstone monolith at Jinmium in northwest Australia. The indentations formed arcs and parallel lines that stretched for hundreds of yards suggesting shapes and information not yet understood. What is understood is that they were not arbitrary but deliberate, and that they were forged by a human presence that also left tools below sediment layers that have been dated to more than 116,000 years ago. There was no land bridge from Asia to Australia at such ancient dates, or at any time since. There were only hundreds of miles of open sea between Asia and Australia. Toolmakers must have also been navigators of seas for well over 60,000 years ago but their activities probably reach another 60,000 years into our past.[10]

We argue that Archaeology, if it is to be considered a science at all, must not only be open to questioning of its own established rules and theories, but must also be measurable by other sciences. We are beginning to learn from Chaos Science that any nonlinear entity is "sensitive dependent on initial conditions."[11] The number of variables in the formation of any culture and of its artistic and architectural expression are manifold, complex, and nonlinear. A few changes in initial conditions—even a small battle won or lost—could change the nature of that culture. Has the history of mankind been, in essence, unalterable? If so how could the isolated event of Montezuma's error in mistaking Cortez for Quetzalcoatl have spelled doom for an entire civilization? Or in our century could the makeup of the world have been different if Nazi Germany had won World War II? Or were both these outcomes somehow predetermined?

A preposterous conclusion? No, not under the imperatives of Neo-Darwinism. It is our position that no science can flourish independently of other sciences. Science and knowledge are always measurable by other sciences and other knowledge. Chaos Science, genetics, mathematical probability, language studies, multi-regional development, astronomy, logic, physics, navigational science, archeo-astronomy, functional architecture, and a reassessment of myth itself as a vessel of history all present an alternative view to the theories taught in our schools. We must attempt to measure conventional archeological wisdom by these other sciences and by other knowledge and see which view makes the most *sense.* The world is, after all, both intelligent and unpredictable, as well as both discernible and magical, and all of its possibilities can happen at the same time.

It wasn't until the late 1970s that some of our leading archaeologists would come to reluctantly admit that the preoccupation with Clovis man was possibly pointing in the wrong direction, and that the dates assigned for Uxmal, Chichen Itza, and Tikal were not only wrong, but that these cherished sites may have been only relatively recent manifestations of a far older culture. Of course, changes in our textbooks come very slowly. Discoverers are loathe to give up claims that their finds are the oldest and, hence, the measure of all to come. And museums want to continue to brag that the artifacts they've purchased and the excavations they've funded are *the finds*, incontestable testimony to their powers of discovery and accumulation. Yet many archaeologists now openly admit that the arbitrary dating of Paleo-Indian presence in America as to no more than 12,000 years ago and advanced civilization in Mesoamerica as no more than 2,000 years ago bear little resemblance to man's actual antiquity in what we now call the Americas.

How incomplete was the record? Until twenty-five years ago years ago only well-excavated sites such as Chichen Itza in the Yucatán and Tikal in Guatemala were considered to be important. Tikal was thought to be unchallenged in its domination of the Mayan lowlands whereas Belize was not even considered as an area for study. Now Caracol, in Belize, is known to have been a major site with a possible population of two million occupants. Recently deciphered glyphs at Caracol boast of military victories over Tikal. And at Caracol a central royal burial tomb was found in 1992. (Isolationists have long claimed that Mayan pyramids differed from Egyptian pyramids because they had no burial tombs). Discovery after discovery have followed, and Belize, which today has a population of less than two hundred thousand, is now thought to contain as many as a thousand major Mayan sites and to have supported a Pre-Columbian population of over four million people. Another ten thousand sites, some major, are acknowledged to exist in that small country. How was this been overlooked for so long?

Commenting on the plethora of new evidence of early civilization in the Americas, Norman Hammond, professor of Archaeology, Anthropology and Classics at Rutgers University, and director of the university's archeological research program, recently wrote: "A decade ago it was thought that classic Maya civilization sprang into being quite suddenly during the third century A.D. The preceding period, called Pre-classic or Formative, was believed to have been an age of humble village farming societies. Since 1975 many discoveries and reassessments of known evidence have radically changed the accepted picture of Pre classic culture. It has been found that intensive agriculture above the slash-and-burn level was developed far earlier than had been thought (fig. 5G). Huge buildings that have been dated to Pre-classic times imply substantial social and economic organization. Recent excavations show that standardized tools were made in large-scale workshops and traded over great distances. It even seems that some elements of the classic intellectual culture were widespread in Formative times. . . . It now seems likely that the forbears of the Maya and their descendants inhabited their territory continuously from around the end of the last Ice Age, (over) 10,000 years ago."[12]

Yes, this is the same Norman Hammond who, as a young man, investigated Lubaantun and pronounced it a recent Maya site, even though Mayans themselves have called it pre-Maya. But the now-seasoned Hammond is pushing back the dates of civilization in Mesoamerica by thousands and tens of thousands of years. In the last twenty years Belize has been transformed, in the eyes of American Archaeology, from a country with a few minor Mayan sites, mostly from the late Classic period (600–900 A.D.) to an area with potentially tens of thousands of Mayan sites, many of major dimensions, that stretch back to the formative Maya period (Cuello is dated by Hammond at 2500 B.C.), and to thousands of years earlier.

Why has so little of the real history of Mesoamerica been discovered? At the same time that young archaeologists were investigating the significant sites, their academic superiors were controlling the education and publishing systems, writing, editing, advising, and reviewing the books and articles on early man. As overseers of the work, research, degrees, and the professions of

5.G. CUELLO, BELIZE. For a century-and-a-half archaeologists have combed Mesoamerica looking for Mayan centers. Most of the searches have concentrated Mexico's Yucatán Peninsula and Guatemala. When a few Mayan sites were discovered in the tiny country of Belize they were quickly dismissed as "satellites" of the main Maya culture. Within the last twenty years excavation at Cuello has determined that it dates back to at least 2,500 B.C., two thousand years older than the Yucatán's more famous Chichen Itza.

young scholars, significant finds that linked ancient navigators from cultures around the world were being made. These were conveniently ignored, swept under the collective rug, and termed "out of context." The result? No one really was looking *(see below)*.

In dramatically pushing back the dates of civilized man's presence in Belize,

---

Scholarship . . .

THE PROBLEM with nineteenth and twentieth century scholarship has not been that students have not sufficiently loved the truth, it has been that they have respected those peoples in positions of authority more. Scholarship has demanded that the work of students seeking higher degrees must not express ideas radically different from the published theories of those dispensing the degrees. Degrees are and have been issued on the basis of conformity and affirmation of taught principles. And since having a degree is useless without a job, it has been equally important for the young scholar to submit research that does not contradict those who control the jobs. To rise from a lower position to a more loftier one the academic must publish work that conforms to the theories and opinions of department heads. At a certain point the academic has so much invested in conformity to existing principles that to repudiate them would be to repudiate his own life work and that of his teachers and peers. Thus the "half-baked", though scholastically venerated, ideas of one generation of scholars becomes doctrine for the next generation of scholars . . . and so on. This system of confirmation of dogma has been called the "power principle," but really it is the "knuckle under the authority principle." It is a useful and expedient approach for acquisition of positions and eventually power within institutions but useless for apprehension of knowledge. Yet our "halls of knowledge", our universities, the museums they control, and academic authority itself, have all long suffered under this system.

Hammond is still only addressing the *land-based aspects* of the Mayans and preMayans. Isolationists have continued to question why, if they ever existed, has so little evidence been found of ancient navigators? There are several answers. The first is that advanced navigational cultures flourished before the deluge in seaports that are now buried hundreds of feet under the sea where little excavation has ever been done. The second answer is that boats and navigational instruments have been made from perishable goods. A third, and most important, answer is that there is evidence and quite a bit of it, but that no one operating within the traditional paradigm has been looking for it. Under a terrestrial academic paradigm that amounts to little more than self-perpetuating dogma the evidence that has been found has been ignored or dismissed.

The Platonic (idealist) view of history, in which each event can be under-

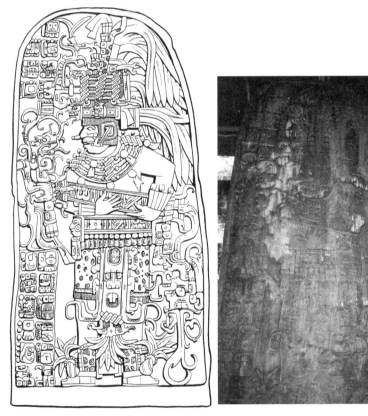

5.I. EL CIEBAL, EL PETEN, GUATEMALA. Comparing the authors' photo to an artist's portrayal of stela 10 at El Ceibal we can appreciate one of the dangers of excavation—despite a canopy the stela has weathered badly. Soon the thick mustache that indicates the figure as a probable Phoenician will likely be indistinct.

stood only if the whole process is understood, has been misplaced, forgotten through twenty-three centuries of stony sleep. The cultures of Central America have been viewed through a terrestrial and linear paradigm. The entire field of Archaeology awaits a new paradigm that recognizes the Platonic flow to all things universal. The staid and static Aristotelian and Newtonian models must be reexamined and abandoned before the diggers can begin to understand just what it is they are digging up, and what has already been dug up (fig. 5I).

We simply cannot emphasize strongly enough: A reassessment of the archeological record of the Americas is required. The evidence of the last few decades firmly shows that advanced navigational cultures have long flourished, and that these cultures have been promulgated by red men, black men, yellow men, and even white men. The evidence also clearly shows that no culture advanced in mathematic principles, astronomy and architecture has ever arisen in isolation. Contact and exchange of information have been crucial to the development of advanced cultures.

The Aztecs that the Conquistadors conquered and subjugated had themselves overran an earlier people, the Toltecs. The Aztecs, only partially understanding their cultural booty, took the Toltec cities, their temples, and even their gods as their own. From the cities they earned riches, from the temples they learned little, from the gods they learned much, but they feared the knowledge of these ancients, and despite the Toltec admonition against human sacrifice, they sacrificed their young, and the young of conquered tribes, in appalling numbers.

Apologists for the Church and the Conquest of America, historians, and sensationalists have spent a lot ink on the savage conduct of the Aztecs, focusing on their behavior as "typical" of American savages. The overwhelming evidence is that long before the Aztecs ever gained power in Mesoamerica, and long before the Toltecs, very different peoples prospered there. Teotihuacans, Mayans, proto-Mayans, and Olmecs and other diverse peoples shared the Americas. Africans, Orientals, Caucasians and Semites left their traces at the navigational center of the world, that thin stretch of land at the heart of the American continent that creatively connected the great Pacific and Atlantic oceans. These traces, now slowly being uncovered, include some of the most startling monuments in the world (fig. 5J).

Legend and myth tell us that there was once a race of peoples who ruled this land and that through arrogance and natural disasters they were destroyed. A change in the heavens and a resulting cataclysm was the instrument of that destruction. Through the use of super computers and Chaos Science the mechanism for these fabled cataclysms has been found. Could

5.J. COPAN, HONDURAS. At Copan author Erikson points at a figure described on the stela as the Mayan ruler Eighteen Rabbit, although his features are distinctly Chinese and the stela is flanked by depictions of elephants. Throughout Central America the record is the same . . . at each significant site there is a record in stone of a diversity of peoples from distant shores that predated Columbus, some by a few hundred, some by a few thousand, some by several thousands of years.

ancient man have been aware of Chaos Science? He was, but he had no need for sophisticated computers. He had first hand experience: He had his own "computers" of the sky built into his every day existence.

Ancient myths, when studied with an open mind, can lead to solid discoveries. For instance, less than a hundred years ago scholars were certain that Homer's *Iliad* and the fabled Troy were myth. Amateur archaeologist Heinrich Schlieman's attempts to find the historic ruins of Troy in Asia Minor were greeted with derision. When Schlieman found the ruins, right where Homer said they would be, he proved that Troy and the Trojan wars were both a Greek myth and a historic fact. In fact, if we keep an open mind, there is no reason to believe that one excludes the other (fig. 5K).

Myth, the interaction of finite man with immeasurable cosmic truths, ultimately answers the question of why ancient man was so obsessed with the heavens. Myths predate megaliths and all the great stone structures and complexes associated with ancient man. Many of these great structures are astronomical sighting devices which trace the movements of the sun, planets, comets, and stars. The emphasis of these observatories, from ancient Peru to present day Mexico City, and from Stonehenge in England to Cheops in

5.K. TROY. An interesting note on Troy is that in his enthusiasm Schlieman and his followers uncovered eight layers to Troy, one built on top of another. Homer's Troy was at level II. But the Troy of level VII, predating the Troy of Helen and Paris by 2,000 years was by far the most sophisticated level, both architecturally and artistically, revealing wide trade contacts.[13] This mirrors findings in Mesoamerica, where deeper and older levels now being uncovered reveal higher levels of sophistication at more ancient dates.

Egypt, was in tracing the limits of celestial movements, principally by defining equinoxes, and solstices, but also by other methods not fully understood today. The precise layout and wonderful construction of these temples required an incredible array of knowledge spanning the fields of architecture, astronomy, calendar-making, and navigation. The accuracy and intricacies of these structures imply purpose and function. Long before many of these structures were built, knowledge of these sciences were carried forward by a people who remembered that purpose and function. The apparent reason for this precise science was to detect deviations and to predict the deluges and conflagrations both remembered and foretold by myth.

Functional inquiry finds the traditionalists to be sometimes slightly wrong, and sometimes very wrong in their dating of sites in the Americas. But it is not in finding the true age of sites mistakenly dated that is most important—it is the agelessness of the ideas and purpose these monuments of intelligence represent that is most important. Sophisticated astronomy and worldwide navigation go back thousands of years in the Americas, to a time before the most current reconstructions at Coba and Tikal, and to a time when the heart and center of the Americas was a land, known to its first European chronicler, Plato, as Atlantis.

Plato described Atlantis as an island continent with a sophisticated naval culture at its center. A look at the globe shows that only one continent could have had a sea faring culture at its center. Plato's tale about an advanced civilization across the great sea that was suddenly and forever destroyed was off target only in one detail, albeit a major one - "forever" was too long a time. The civilization was destroyed, the capital and all the great coastal cities did sink, but the continent, after great flooding, and great destruction remained. That continent is what we now call the Americas. But then it was Atlantis, home to a seafaring people who had almost slipped from memory. Plato did not merely preserve their name. He put them in their rightful context . . . at the heart of the Golden Age of Myth.

Experts have long been telling us that the Golden Age of Atlantis never existed, that deluges and worldwide floods never happened, that the sun has never varied from its present path and glow, and that complicated architectural structures such as pyramids and astronomical observatories, common to civilizations oceans apart, are merely coincidences, or exist in answer to an "evolutionary imperative." These experts have also told us that myths are "old fables," stories by primitive man about a primitive world that he hardly understood. It is the "experts" who have not understood (fig. 5L).

If we of the twentieth century have been living in a conspiracy of ignorance, we are not alone. The process has been going on for two and a half millennia.

5.L. ATLANTEANS, TULA, VALLEY OF MEXICO. The Greeks were always in awe of Atlas, the man-god who held the sky above them. His domain, as a son of the sea-god Poseidon, was far away. Homer placed the mountains that he dwelt in, far out in the Atlantic. Today we can see fifteen-foot-tall sky-bearing Atlanteans in the artifacts of Mesoamerica.

In Plato's *Timeaus* the Egyptian priests warned Solon: *"You Greeks are all children . . . you have no belief rooted in old tradition and no knowledge hoary with age. And the reason is this. There have been and will be many different calamities to destroy mankind, the greatest of them by fire and water, lesser ones by countless other means. . . . you remember only one deluge, though there have been many, and you do not know that the finest and best race of men that ever existed lived in your country; you and your fellow citizens are descended from the few survivors that remained, but you know nothing about it because so many succeeding generations left no record in writing."*

Yes, myths are older than megaliths, they are also the *reason* for their construction. There is no way to date a myth. But we can now date some of the deluges and conflagrations that gave rise to myth. We can now begin to appreciate ancient knowledge that found its expression in the myths of the world, and we can begin to understand its precise and immense demonstration in ancient architecture. And if we can prove Darwin and his denial of catastrophism wrong, we can begin to understand the great events that predated our sorry (or wonderful) existence.

In the next chapter we will finally take a longer look at our earliest written source for the myth of Atlantis, Plato, and address his telling of it in terms of what we know about geography, oceanography, and early map-making.

6 Plato's Atlantis: *From Myth to Reality*

WHERE WAS the Atlantis of myth? If you are presently upright in any part of the Americas you are standing on it. Plato tells us in the Timaeus and again in the unfinished Critias that Atlantis was a real, not imaginary, island-continent, and that it was located beyond the Pillars of Hercules (Straits of Gibraltar) in, or across, the Atlantic Ocean.

In or across? It is an important distinction. Most scholarly translations, from that of Sir Francis Bacon, a proponent of Atlantis in America in the early 1600s, to Sir Desmond Lee, the Cambridge mentor whose work on Plato led to his being knighted in 1961, place Atlantis "opposite the strait," or as "the opposite continent."[1] But Ignatius Donnelly's translation of Plato, in his heralded and popular nineteenth-century work, *Atlantis: The Antediluvian World*, translated "opposite continent" as an "island in front of the straits," a phrase that has led to much misunderstanding. For brevity and clarity we will present the following excerpt from Desmond Lee's translation of the *Timaeus*. But because Donnelly's work has most often been relied on as the source book of Atlantis's location we will also represent that translation where it conflicts with Desmond Lee's interpretation.

The legend of Atlantis concerned a people who dominated the world in the "Golden Age" when man fearlessly navigated the great oceans and lived in harmony with the gods. In the *Timeaus* and again in the unfinished *Critias* Plato told the tale of Atlantis, a tale Critias learned from his grandfather, who had learned it from Solon, a prominent Greek statesman and historian who had visited Egypt in 590 B.C. Solon in turn learned the tale from priests, who held access to secret libraries and who told Solon about earlier times and events known to them. They told him of many different calamities that had destroyed mankind and they told him of Deucalion and Pyrrha, descendants of the first man, and how they had survived the first flood. Solon was anxious to hear details of this great era and of any heroic doings by his remote ancestors. The priests obliged him with a story of a war fought by the ancient Athenians against the great power from across the Atlantic.

From the *Timaeus*:

"There is in Egypt," said Critias, "at the head of the delta, where the Nile divides, a district called the Saitic. The chief city of the district, from which King Amasis came, is called Sais. The chief goddess of the inhabitants is called in Egyptian Neith, in Greek (according to them) Athena; and they are very friendly to the Athenians and claim some relationship to them. Solon came there on his travels and was highly honoured by them, and in the course of making inquiries from those priests who were most knowledgeable on the subject found that both he and all his countrymen were almost entirely ignorant about antiquity. And wishing to lead them on to talk about early times, he embarked on an account of the earliest events known here, telling them about Phoroneus, said to be the first man, and Niobe, and how Deucalion and Pyrrha survived the flood and who were their descendants, and trying by reckoning up the generations to calculate how long ago the events in question had taken place. And a very old priest said to him, "Oh Solon, Solon, you Greeks are all children, and there's no such thing as an old Greek."

"What do you mean by that?" inquired Solon.

"You are all young in mind," came the reply: "You have no belief rooted in old tradition and no knowledge hoary with age. And the reason is this. There have been and will be many different calamities to destroy mankind, the greatest of them by fire and water, lesser ones by countless other means. Your own story of how Phaethon, child of the sun, harnessed his father"s course and so burnt up things on the Earth and was himself destroyed by a thunderbolt, is a mythical version of the truth that there is at long intervals a variation in the course of the heavenly bodies and a consequent widespread destruction by fire of things on the Earth. On such occasions those who live in the mountains or in high and dry places suffer more than those living by rivers or by the sea; as for us, the Nile, our own regular saviour, is freed to preserve us in this emergency. When on the other hand the gods purge the Earth with a deluge, the herdsmen and shepherds in the mountains escape, but those living in the cities in your part of the world are swept into the sea by the rivers; here water never falls on the land from above wither then or at any other time, but rises up naturally from below. This is the reason why our traditions here are the oldest preserved; though it is true that in all places where excessive cold or heat does not prevent it human beings are always to be found in larger or smaller numbers. But in our temples we have preserved from earliest times a written record of any great or splendid achievement or notable event which has come to our ears whether it occurred in your part of the world or here or anywhere else; whereas with you and others, writing and the other necessities of civilization have only just been developed when the periodic scourge of the deluge descends, and spares none but the unlettered and uncultured, so that you have to begin again like children, in complete ignorance of what happened . . . in early times. So these genealogies of your own people which you were just recounting are little more than children"s stories. *You remember only one deluge, though there have been many, and you do not know that the finest and best race of men that ever existed lived in your country; you and your fellow citizens are descended from the few survivors that remained, but you know nothing about it because so many succeeding generations left no record in writing.* For before the greatest of all destructions by water, Solon, the city that is now Athens was preeminent in war and conspicuously the best governed in every way, its achievements and constitution being the finest of any in the world of which we have heard tell."

Solon was astonished at what he heard and eagerly begged the priests to describe to him in detail the doings of these citizens of the past. "I will gladly do so, Solon," replied the priest, "both for your sake and your city's, cut chiefly in gratitude to the Goddess to whom it has fallen to bring up and educate both your country and ours—yours first, when she took over your seed from Earth and Hephaestus, ours a thousand years later. The age of our institutions is given in our sacred records as eight thousand, and the citizens whose laws and whose finest achievement I will now briefly describe to you therefore lived nine thousand years ago; we will go through their history in detail later on at leisure, when we can consult the records. Consider their laws compared with ours; for you will find today among us many parallels to your institutions in those days. First, our priestly class is kept distinct from the others, as is our artisan class; next, each class of craftsman—shepherds, hunters, farmers—performs its function in isolation from others. And of course you will have noticed that our soldier class is kept separate from all others, being forbidden by the law to undertake any duties other than military: moreover their armament consists of shield and spear, which we were the first people in Asia to adopt, under the instruction of the Goddess, as you were in your part of the world. And again you see what great attention our law devotes from the beginning to learning, deriving from the divine principles of cosmology everything needed for human life down to divination and medicine for our health, and acquiring all other related branches of knowledge. The Goddess founded this whole order and system when she framed your society. She chose the place in which you were born with an eye to its temperate climate, which would produce men of high intelligence; for being herself a lover of war and wisdom she picked a place for her first foundation that would produce men most like herself in character. So you lived there under laws I have described, and even better ones, and excelled all men in every kind of accomplishment, as one would expect of children and offspring of the gods."

"Among all the wonderful achievements recorded here of your city, one great act of courage is outstanding. *Our records tell how your city checked a great power which arrogantly advanced from its base in the Atlantic ocean to attack the cities of Europe and Asia. For in those days the Atlantic was navigable. There was an island opposite the straight which you call (so you say) the Pillars of Hercules, an island larger than Libya and Asia combined; from it travelers could in those days reach the other islands, and from them the whole opposite continent which surrounds what can truly be called the ocean. For the sea within the strait we were talking about is like a lake with a narrow entrance; the outer ocean is the real ocean and the land which entirely surrounds it is properly termed continent.* On this island of Atlantis had arisen a powerful and remarkable dynasty of kings, who ruled the whole island, and many other islands as well and parts of the continent; in addition it controlled, within the strait, Libya up to the borders of Egypt and Europe as far as Tyrrhenia. This dynasty, gathering its whole power together, attempted to enslave, at a single stroke, your country and ours and all the territory within the straight. It was then, Solon, that the power and courage and strength of your city became clear for al men to see. Her bravery and military skill were outstanding; she led an alliance of the Greeks, and then when they deserted her and she was forced to fight alone, after running into the direst peril, she overcame the invaders and celebrated a victory; she rescued those not yet enslaved from the slavery threatening them, and she generously freed all others living within the Pillars of Hercules. At a later time there were Earthquakes and floods of extraordinary violence, and in a single dreadful day and night all your fighting men were swallowed up by the sea and vanished; this is why the sea in that area is to this day impassable to navigation, which is hindered by mud just below the surface, the remains of the sunken island."[2]

Donnelly's translation differed slightly from the italicized section above. We will cite a part of it:

"*These histories tell of a mighty power which was aggressing wantonly against the whole of Europe and Asia, and to which your city put an end. This power came forth out of the Atlantic Ocean, for in those days the Atlantic was navigable; and there was an island situated in front of the straits which you call the Columns of Heracles (Hercules): the island was larger than Libya and Asia put together, and was the way to other islands, and from the islands you might pass through to the whole of the opposite continent which surrounded the true ocean; for this sea which is within the Straits of Heracles is only a harbor, having a narrow entrance, but that other is the real sea, and the surrounding land may be most truly called a continent.*"

There have been many translations of the *Timaeus*. But notice this sequence which invariably shows up. There is a *named sea,* the Atlantic, well known to the Greeks, and the source of the power that threatens the Greeks. There is a *second named sea,* the Mediterranean, "*the sea which is within the Straits of Heracles (Hercules)*" and it is described as "*only a harbor, having a narrow entrance.*" And there is an *unnamed sea,* "*That other, is the real sea (ocean), and the surrounding land may be most truly called a continent.*"[3]

If the Mediterranean is only a harbor, and the Atlantic was the way to an island larger than Asia Minor and Libya combined, and a bridge to other islands, what sea could truly be called ocean, and what land could "*most truly be called continent*"? Our answer is that the named sea is the Atlantic, the bridge or "way to other islands" is Mesoamerica, the other "true ocean" is the Pacific, and the true continent, seemingly not an island, is Asia. (Actually the continent is Eurasia though it may not have been understood then that Europe and Asia were, in fact, one continent, and, by the Greek definition, an island itself, being completely surrounded by sea!) It seems, even then, the vastness of Asia prevented it from being called "island" although it truly is. But it did not prevent the ancients form recognizing the Americas as an island. We must remember that the Greeks had no limitation of size in their definition of island. An island was simply a body of land completely surrounded by water, as the Americas most certainly are. More importantly we must also realize that, although the northern and southern extremities of the Americas were known to some ancient navigators, the perception of the many more who visited Poseidon and the ports at its heart, in what we now call Central America, were encountering a continent that, at places, divided great oceans by only a dozen miles. Is it any wonder that navigators, able to transverse a land by only a few days portage would call that land "island?"

Plato called Atlantis an island-continent, and later reemphasized that it "may truly be called 'island,'" meaning that unlike Europe, Asia, and Africa, there is no land connection to another continent. Plato, writing in 347 B.C., clearly put Atlantis at the far side of the ocean. That Plato meant some small island in the Mediterranean, like Minoan Thera (figs. 6A, 6B), is preposterous. Atlantis is described as being larger than Libya (then defined as all Africa west of Egypt), and Asia (a term by which the Greeks meant Asia Minor and lands west of the Indus) combined. Thera, destroyed by an immense volcanic eruption in around 1500 B.C., did posses many of the materially advanced characteristics attributed to Atlantis—hot and cold plumbing, multi-storied buildings with terraced gardens, and an active seaport among them. But on geographical grounds alone, Thera, (now the small island of Santorini) could

6A. Minoan civilization in the Mediterranean has been associated with artistic bulls; sophisticated plumbing systems; elegant frescoes depicting great sailing fleets, seemingly vessels of trade, not war; an appreciation of leisure and of woman's equal role in society; and great palaces at Crete, 2,100 B.C., and (depicted above) in Mycenaean Greece 1,600 B.C. That these small islands could have recreated aspects of Atlantis is probable. That they could have been that great island-continent is absurd.

6.B. Evidence of an earlier civilization has also been uncovered at Crete. The ceramic disc pictured below is made of a clay not found in the eastern Mediterranean and displays hieroglyphs not yet deciphered.

hardly qualify. Yet, that tiny island, only a few hundred miles off the coast of Greece, and well known to Greeks and Egyptians of the sixth and fourth century B.C. has recently been posited as Atlantis. Similarly, small island groups from the Canaries off Africa to the islands off Scotland have been proposed as the true Atlantis. But there is no geological evidence that any of these islands were part of a continent-sized land any time within the last 100 million years. In fact the evidence, plate tectonic theory and sonar observations of the ocean floor included, is all to the contrary.

How have so many people been mislead to believe Atlantis was *in* the Atlantic, and not *across* from it? Donnelly's translation that placed Atlantis "in front of" the straits must have misled many. The use of the term "island" must have thrown many others off, although Atlantis is referred to as a continent as well as an island. But island or continent, an Atlantis larger than Libya and Asia combined simply could not have fit within the Atlantic. Libya was considerably smaller than what we now know Africa to be, but so was Asia, as the extent of present Siberia was not known, and the Americas and Antarctica were missing. Thus Libya comprised about 20 percent of the Earth's surface. Plato's statement that Atlantis was "larger" than Libya and Asia combined cannot be interpreted as "smaller," nor can "opposite continent" in reference to the Atlantic be interpreted as within the Atlantic (or within the Mediterranean). Even by the limited parameters of Greek geography, Atlantis had to lie across the Atlantic. It could only have been the Americas (fig. 6C).

Because Plato most often dwelt on "the appearance" of events in the mundane world, as in opposition to the "ideal," which, to him, represented a higher truth, his insistence on the fact of the existence of Atlantis and of its location is doubly curious. It was unlike Plato to insist on geographical facts. For that reason alone we should pay particular heed to his words, which he never used mischievously or lightly. Atlantis's size is clearly stated. Libya (all of

144

Africa except Egypt) and Asia Minor combined comprise just under 13 million square miles, the Americas (North and South) cover 16 million square miles. No other island-continent can fulfill Plato's description since the other island-continents, Antarctica with 5.5 million square miles and Australia with less than 3 million square miles are simply too small.

The common misperception has been that Plato was not giving Atlantis a specific location in the *Critias*, that he was only generalizing the physical description of Atlantis. Writing in Athens in the early fourth century B.C. it has been thought that his understanding of geography, like all Greeks, was limited and that he could not have known of the Pacific, or islands in the Pacific as a bridge to the true continent. But Plato simply wasn't like all Greeks. He had studied with Pythagoras, whose teachers, like Pythagoras, had studied with the Egyptians; even if Plato did not understand geography his Pythagorean teachers and his Egyptian teachers did. Indeed Plato demonstrated that he understood the scale of worldwide geography by identifying the Mediterranean as a "harbor."

Denial of Plato's possible knowledge, learned through the school of Pythagoras and Egyptian records, of a true notion of geography of the Earth has resulted in a recurrent misreading of his actual words. Nor can there be much credence to the repeated argument that Egyptian priests in the beginning of the sixth century B.C. could not know of the Atlantic Ocean, let alone lands beyond. We know that the Egyptians for hundreds of years before this time had regularly employed the Phoenicians as merchant marines and they may have learned much from these "sea-peoples." But any Phoenician knowl-

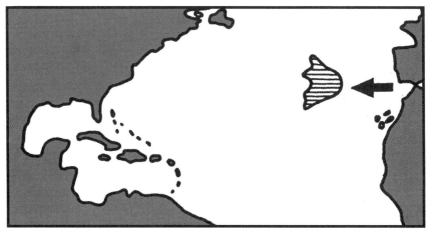

6C. Plato said Atlantis was larger than Libya and Asia combined. Yet popular misconceptions often depict Atlantis as a "continent" the size of the Iberian peninsula.

edge gleaned was much more recent than that already contained in the ancient archives of the Egyptians. In fact the priests seemed almost to be giving Solon, perplexed because the events they described did not fit within the Greek reckoning of time, both a geography lesson and a history lesson when they told him,

"You Greeks are all children . . . you have no belief rooted in old tradition and no knowledge hoary with age. And the reason is this. There have been and will be many different calamities to destroy mankind, the greatest of them by fire and water, lesser ones by countless other means."

Could ancients have actually known the true geography of the Earth? The Piri Reis map (fig. 6D), presented by Charles Hapgood in his *Maps of The Ancient Sea Kings* gives us information on the maps of a Turkish admiral, rediscovered in Istanbul in 1929. These maps, painted on the parchment of the Admiral Piri Reis in 1513 correctly identify the longitudinal relationship between Africa and South America, describe South America's coastline in detail, and describe, almost without a flaw, the coastline of Antarctica when it was free of ice. The Piri Reis map was reportedly drawn after information presented in maps of classical antiquity, and its description of South America mirrored that of Ptolemy's Map of the World from the second century A.D. The map itself contains notations (in Arabic) that it was based on Arab maps of the fourth century A.D. and that these maps were based on maps drawn by navigators in the days of "Alexander, Lord of the Two Horns," known to us as Alexander the Great.

Based on knowledge of what has been lost of classical Greek writers, including Aristotle's literary works (all lost), Plato's scientific and technical works (all lost), the works of the Greek tragedians, Aeschylus, Euripides, Sophocles (all lost), much of what we know to have once been written, by surviving references, has been irretrievably lost. It has been estimated that ninety percent of the world's knowledge has been lost to pillaging and burning by conquering armies and conquering theologies. That strikes us as a highly conservative figure. What we have lost that we have no reference to must be far greater. Most of this must be scientific in nature. And if the conquest of Mexico is any example, it is in the nature of conquering theologies to destroy all written records, to dismantle temples, but yet to fail to eradicate the continued existence of myth and belief, heroes and villains, and gods and devils. The latter persist no matter what is done to the people; old gods and demons are simply renamed in the new religious and political order. Meanwhile the science and technology of the past has been erased.[4]

Arabs considered any science not contained in the Koran to be blasphemy, and its destruction an imperative. Medieval Christians considered any science

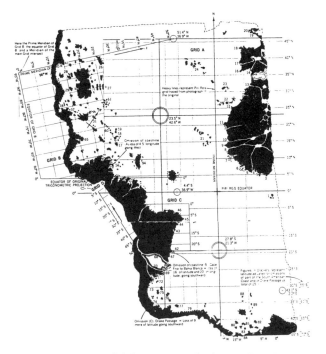

6.D. THE PIRI REIS MAP. How did the ancient sailor know where he was going? He had to have past experience, training with someone with past experience, or a good map. Chances are he had all three. Such maps were the ancient equivalent of our treasure maps because they pointed to true treasures, where to mine tin, where to trade for incense and myrrh, sugar and coffee. The Piri Reis map is possibly the only extant map of the ancient mariners that survives to this day. The Chinese reportedly had similar maps.

not in their doctrines to be works of the devil. Chinese emperors, including the builder of the Great Wall destroyed all past knowledge because it posed a threat to their stature and power as an imposition of god's will on Earth. Has it not always been so?

But if the maps, mathematics and technology of invaded and defeated civilizations has been systematically destroyed a large question remains. Are there any exceptions? Where did the information contained in the Piri Reis map come from? It's exact use of longitude challenges the European belief that the ability to determine longitude was discovered in the eighteenth century. Its precise description of the coastline of South America and Africa and proportional distances between the two continents was confirmed in the nineteenth century. The map is known to have been in continuous circulation since 1520 and is reported to have been seized by the Turks from a navigator who sailed with Columbus, yet its description of the coastline of Antarctica was long held in disbelief—Antarctica was only discovered by the modern world in 1820![5] And it was only in the International Geophysical Year (1957) that Antarctica was sounded through the Ice Sheet and effectively charted. Yet those recent charts, now confirmed through satellite measurements, confirm the Piri Reis map as precise in its definition of Antarctica's outline. The map's authenticity can no longer be disputed, nor can it's antiquity. It could only have been charted from space or by navigators who encountered Antarctica when it was *completely free of ice*, approximately six to seven thousand years ago.[6]

Spaceship theories aside—they may have been there at that time, but would they have shared information with a terrestrial map-maker?—the Piri Reis map clearly demonstrates ancient knowledge that has been presumed lost or forgotten. The map itself in the copy discovered in 1520 is obviously just a fragment of a far larger map.[7] Did the original maps, drawn over five millennia before Piri Reis, include similar detail in their descriptions of the Pacific? We may never know because the usual processes of forgetfulness, namely destruction, burning, torture, and genocide and natural cataclysms have seemingly erased the records of early navigators. But if ancient navigators could have charted Antarctica, a continent encircled by the most violent seas in the world, in such detail, they could have gone anywhere.

Confirmation of ancient navigational abilities does not of itself confirm the existence of Atlantis in the Americas. It cannot prove the relevance of the Antilles, which now so resemble Plato's description of the "bare bones" of the lost continent nor can it prove that the heart of Atlantis, its capital of Poseidon, must lay in a location with easy access to the major trade routes of both the Atlantic and the Pacific. But ancient knowledge of seamanship, only reconfirmed within the last half century, strongly suggests a middle American base. And we must realize that we may not have lost as much as we have thought. We have simply misinterpreted what we have already found. As one historian puts it: "It may be . . . that the science we see at the dawn of recorded history was not science at its dawn, but represents the remnants of the science of some great and as yet untraced civilization."[8]

In the *Critias*, describing the natural properties of the continent of Atlantis Plato states, *"Poseidon's share was the island of Atlantis . . . at the center of the island, near the sea, was a plain, said to be the most beautiful and fertile of all plains."* This *"center of the island"* has also been translated by Sir Desmond Lee as "midway along its greatest length." We challenge you to find a continent, other than America, with the possibility of a capital at the center of the continent and also near the sea. In Eurasia that capital would be a little east of the Ural Mountains, in Africa it would be in Zaire, in Australia somewhere in the outback. Only on the American continent (remember, North and South

America do not constitute separate continents even if they have different names) does the shape of the land taper down so that at its center, approximately Costa Rica, it is both the heart of the continent and on the navigable sea. In fact, the center and heart of the Americas (Atlantis) is situated on two great oceans, the Atlantic and the Pacific.

To those who protest that Atlantis of myth was "swallowed up by the sea and vanished" we can only answer that they are quite right. The *heart* of the civilization of Atlantis was destroyed by the sea, just as almost every antediluvian civilization, built by the sea, was similarly destroyed during the great deluge. What has somehow eluded most investigators is the statement that "the island of Atlantis was *similarly* swallowed up by the sea and vanished." We have emphasized the word "similarly" because the context is *"At a later time there were Earthquakes and floods of extraordinary violence, and in a single dreadful day and night all your fighting men were swallowed up by the Earth, and the island of Atlantis was similarly swallowed up by the sea and vanished."* In other words the great catastrophe that befell Atlantis was similar and concurrent with the disaster that befell Athens, and the entire antediluvian world. Yet there remains to this day an Athens, and even if it is not the same Athens (and we believe it is not), the loss of the Athens that existed in the legend put forth in the *Critias*, and that is now probably buried in the Aegean Sea, did not result in the permanent vanishing of the European continent. Similarly we believe that Poseidon, the capital of Atlantis, was destroyed by a deluge and that the city itself, the heart of Atlantis was destroyed and is now somewhere submerged, along with most of the great Atlantean cities. A civilization was destroyed but the continent of Atlantis, after some considerable upheaval, survived. You most probably, we reassert, even be standing on it.

One could wonder about some matters on which Plato was misled. After all he did speak of the Atlantic as "hindered by mud just below the surface." This is undoubtedly a reference to the Sargasso Sea and in this instance reflects Plato's reliance on the diminished and limited naval technology of his time and of his country. The Sargasso Sea, an area of the Atlantic as large as the Caribbean, that lays midway between the Straits of Gibraltar and the center of the Americas (Atlantis), is confounded by brown sea kelp that rises to the surface of the sea. The Greeks, in limited encounters with this vast sea, chose to sail north of the steady trade winds. They must have sailed at the worst time of the year, late summer, and had been frightened by tropical storms. Their route, through the Sargasso Sea, hindered by kelp at the surface and by moderated or stilled winds, had determined their judgment—the Atlantic was unnavigable. The Phoenicians knew better, as evidenced by their appearance at La Venta, in Mexico, 1600 years before Plato wrote the *Timaeus* and *Critias,* but the Phoenicians had reasons to encourage wild rumors among the less seaworthy nations (fig. 6E).

Was there an Atlantis? Skeptics claim that because only Plato wrote about this mythical land, that he was creating a fable, a teaching model for his students. Plato could have been telling a story, a cautionary tale, as some suggest, for the purpose of awakening indolent and slothful minds. That, after all, was

6.E. PHOENICIAN VESSEL. Strabo's *Narrative* describes a Phoenician ship trading with the Cassiterides ("The Tin Islands"). The Captain of the ship became aware that a Roman ship was following him, intent upon discovering the Phoenician's source of tin. So the Phoenician lured the Roman ship into shoal waters, and both vessels were wrecked. The Phoenician Captain survived and on his return he received from the State the value of his cargo. He had served his people well, keeping their secret from the Romans.[10] Fooling the Greeks, Romans and Egyptians had to be a source of constant joy to the Phoenicians. It also preserved their status and way of life. Because after the Hittites destroyed their base in Asia Minor the Phoenicians depended on their supremacy of the sea for their status, livelihood, and very existence.

The "Cassiterides" have been associated with the British Isles because that is where the ancients discovered mined deposits of tin, the scarce metal necessary to the production of bronze. But tin deposits in the British isles were well known and were quickly exhausted. The Phoenicians were reported to have knowledge of a secret and massive source of this much-sought-after treasure, although they often referred to their source as the "tin mountains" rather than the "tin islands". Since we now know that the Phoenicians traveled regularly to the Americas for thousands of years before Strabo's narrative, and that they had detailed maps of the coast of South America, we can probably surmise that Phoenician tin came from the region of Lake Titicaca, high in the Andes mountains in present day Bolivia, which is still one of the world's primary sources of tin.[11]

his technique in his university, fashioned after his teacher, Socrates, and it was the purpose of his dialogues. But Plato made it clear, always, when his tales were pointed, and when they referred to actual events. Of Atlantis, he repeatedly told us that it was "a fact and not a fiction." Plato stressed that there were written records, first in libraries of the Egyptian priests, then in translation from Egyptian to Greek, and later in a manuscript compiled by Solon, of which Critias' grandfather (also named Critias) had passed the original copy on to his grandson.

Charles Pellegrino in *Unearthing Atlantis* complains that, "More than two thousand years later, all we have is Plato's word that Solon's manuscript ever existed."[12] In fact we have much more than Plato's word. The character that Plato tells Atlantis's story through, Critias, was a famous philosopher and statesman. It is a matter of historical record that Solon, himself an important statesman as well a respected historian, made the journey Plato describes to Egypt, where he visited the priestly colleges of Sais and Heliopolis in 571 B.C. Solon's own account of his visit with the Egyptians and of their tale of Atlantis survived him by several hundred years. The Roman historian, Plutarch, confirmed its existence. But sadly it is now lost.[13]

The Greek historian Crantor visited Sais some 300 years after Solon and was taken by Egyptian scholars to the temple of Neith. There, according to the Roman philosopher, Proclus, he was shown a column whose hieroglyphics retold the history of Atlantis. The priests confirmed to Crantor that the story told by the hieroglyphics was fully in accord with Plato's' tale, with which they were familiar. The priests then translated the hieroglyphics on the column and presented Crantor with a written copy. This column, well-known to Greek and Roman historians, has never been found by twentieth century Egyptologists, and the written copies of both the original hieroglyphics and their Greek translation are believed to have been destroyed in the burnings of the library at Alexandria.

Cyrus Gordon in *Before Columbus* cites the writings of Greek authors who wrote of Phoenician knowledge of the new world. Theopompus, a fourth century B.C. historian, wrote in the *Meropis* of an enormous "continent, outside the Old World, inhabited by exotic people living according to the strangest life-styles." Theopompus described this continent as a "land with cities where gold and silver are so common they have less value than iron." The Greek collection *Concerning Marvelous Things Heard*, attributed to Aristotle's school describes a great "island" with navigable rivers discovered by the Carthaginians (from the Phoenician colony of Carthage founded on the northern shores of Africa in the ninth century B.C.).

Diodorus Siculus, a Greek author who lived in a Phoenician city on Sicily in first century B.C. told of a "vast island" in the ocean that lay many days to the west of Africa. He described this land as "mountainous but favored also with beautiful plains," describes navigable rivers and states that the people on the "island" possessed advanced agriculture and architecture, and irrigated gardens and groves. Diodorus wrote that the remote distance of the land caused it to remain undiscovered until the Phoenicians chanced upon it.[14] Had the Carthaginians discovered a new world, or a much older one?

References to Atlantis from all these sources, some of which pre-dated Plato, clearly show that he was not alone in his belief of Atlantis's existence. But even without testimony from others, we should give more than a little credence to Plato's word. It may even outlive Pelligrini's.

We know politicians, generals and historians lie. But there are voices of truth that have come down to us through the ages. Socrates (through Plato), Buddha, Jesus, come to mind. Like the others, Plato's word has stood the test of time. If he said Atlantis existed we can be sure he must have believed that it did. Indeed the myth of Atlantis is one of those rare instances of a belief that is both universal and timeless.

And perhaps more important than any one individual writing of Atlantis is the fact that whole cultures have made knowledge of this island-continent, and its fate, part of their lore.

The Berbers of North Africa have the legend of Attala, a land across the sea, that was once rich in gold, silver, and tin, but that was submerged by the sea. The Basque peoples of northern Spain and southern France believe that they are descendants of the ancient Atlanteans whom they refer to as the Atlaintika. Ancient Celtic legends have a different name, Avalon, for the continent reclaimed by the sea god. But they put their mythical homeland in a nearby geographical location, in the North Sea—a location in which it is impossible to confirm Plato's description of tropical fruits. Arabian legends refer to the land of Ad, located across the western ocean, and reputed to be the cradle of civilization. In the Puranas and Mahabharata, the ancient writings of India refer to a continent called Atyantika, positioned in the ocean half a world away from the Indian sub-continent and the scene of a catastrophic destruction.[15]

When was Atlantis destroyed? In the *Critias* Plato gives us many more particulars of the nature of Atlantis, reminding us first—as the Egyptian priests told Solon—that "in all nine thousand years have elapsed since the declaration of war between those who lived outside and all those who lived inside the Pillars of Hercules."[16] Since Solon's visit to Egypt occurred in 571 B.C., Poseidon was destroyed, just as ancient Athens was destroyed, about 11,570 years ago, or 9,570 B.C. (fig. 6F).

6F. CALENDAR OF DENDERAH WITH HOUSES OF ZODIAC PORTRAYING LEO AT THE VERNAL EQUINOX. Because of prescession of the equinoxes this calendar refers to a date of between 10,950 and 8800 B.C.,[19] and corresponds to the period in which the Sphinx was eroded by water, the pyramids of Giza were built in perfect alignment with the constellation, Orion, and the mastodons and American horse and camel disappeared. It also corresponds to the date Atlantis was submerged.

Why should we give any credibility to this date? To many it seems incredibly ancient. But Mayan, Egyptian and Hindu calendars go back much further. There are some significant coincidences with the date Plato gave for the physical destruction of Atlantis. Arthur Posnansky, who spent a lifetime studying the massive astrological and megalithic centers of Bolivia, gives 9,550 B.C. as the approximate date construction stopped on the Sun Temple at Tiahuanacu.[17] Zoroastrian chronology give us the year 9660 B.C. as the date "when time began."[18] Flavio Barbiero posits 10,000 to 12,000 years ago as the date when either a comet or asteroid struck the Earth causing great upheavals including the melting of icecaps in Europe and the melting of the Wisconsin ice cap in North America.

Plato's date for the destruction of Atlantis roughly corresponds to the end of the last Ice Age. If these events are associated they may share a single cause. We have been taught that the melting of the great ice sheets happened gradually, over a long period of time. But evidence now exists that some of the melting and some of the worldwide 400 foot rise in the level of the sea may have happened very suddenly. If so a large portion of what is now shallow water in the Caribbean and the Gulf of Mexico, and a sizable portion of Central American and Mexico's Yucatán Peninsula would one day have been above water and could have been the site of Atlantis's major seaports, including it's capital city of Poseidon, and a few days later been under water. It would have remained there in Plato's day and it would still be there today.

In fact there is much evidence of a high civilization now buried under the sea. It is now known that a great cedar forest once grew on the Greater Bermuda seamount, now under water, and that remains of that forest have been radio-carbon dated to around 11,000 years ago.[20] (Later we will present evidence that the rise in sea level was catastrophic and that there are significant ruins in the seas off Mesoamerica.)

Plato gives us a great deal of information on the physical characteristics of Atlantis. In the *Critias* he again tells us that Atlantis was "larger than Libya and Asia put together," and that it was an island—i.e. completely surrounded by water.[21] However, Plato goes much further with the description in the *Critius*, telling us that the god Poseidon by Cleito, the daughter of "one of the original Earth-born inhabitants, begot five pairs of twins, brought them up, and divided Atlantis into ten parts, each to be governed by one of the ten twins. The elder of the eldest pair of twins was given the central province, Atlantis, which was equipped with 'godlike lavishness,' and was made King over the other nine provinces as well."[22]

Plato gives us the names of the other nine twins and tells us that they were "made governors, each of a populous and large territory," and that "they and their descendants for many generations governed their own territories and many other islands in the ocean and . . . also controlled the populations this side of the straits as far as Egypt and Tyrrhenia." It is apparent that the "island" of Atlantis is in fact a great empire and many of us have searched Plato's words for indications of the nature and characteristics of all ten provinces. But after reconfirming the notion of empire by describing the combined wealth and power of the ten governors as "greater than that possessed by any previous dynasty of kings or likely to be accumulated by any later," Plato makes little mention of the other provinces and islands of the greater Atlantis. Instead he concentrates his tale on the central "island," a province also called Atlantis, and on its capital, Poseidon (figs. 6G, 6H).

It seems that most investigators in trying to determine the size of Atlantis took only the one-tenth part, what Plato describes as the central island and its characteristics. Having mistaking Atlantis's size they also mistook its location.

The *Critias* also provides us with great detail of the flora and fauna of Atlantis—although it is obvious that in his descriptions of a lushly vegetated land Plato is addressing only the central province of Atlantis, a one-tenth part of the continent. Descriptions of the other nine provinces are missing from the incomplete *Critias*. But given Atlantis's great size and Plato's placement of the time of its downfall in the late stages of the last Ice Age most of greater Atlantis's climate must have been fairly severe.

Addressing the heart of the central province Plato speaks of "a plentiful supply of timber for structural purposes, and every kind of animal domesticated and wild, among them numerous elephants . . . and plenty of grazing for this largest and most voracious of beasts, as well as for all creatures whose habitat is marsh, swamp and river, mountain or plain. Besides all this, the Earth bore freely all the aromatic substances it bears today, roots, herbs, bushes and gums exuded by flowers or fruit." Plato goes on to describe known cultivated crops, grains, and fruits of every kind saying "all these were produced by that sacred island (fig. 6I), then still beneath the sun, in wonderful quality and profusion."

Plato also states that the grove of Poseidon "was full of trees of marvelous beauty and height," and that all of the abundance of Atlantis was "sheltered from the north winds." From the characteristics described in the *Critius*—a tropical climate with lush vegetation and two crops a year—it is curious that

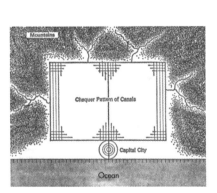
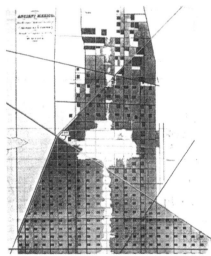

6.G/H. PLATO'S ATLANTIS.[23] Compare the checkered canals in the depiction of Poseidon (the capital city of Atlantis) in Desmond Lee's translation of the *Critius* (left) with a map of Tenochtitlán Montezuma sent to the King of Spain (right) This map shows how the city was divided into squares with floating chinampa gardens linked by canals and pathways.[24] Does this make Tenochtitlán Atlantis? No. But the method of canal building around city-states in Mexico, Guatemala and Belize suggest a knowledge of ancient methods that are similar to Plato's account of Atlantis.

6.I. "BUCKMINSTERFULLERENES." Carbon arranged in a perfect geometric solid as an icosahedron, constructed of 60 carbon atoms. Do they allow the Earth to both transmit and receive information?

Plato called Atlantis "a sacred island." He also described the Earth as a living and magical entity, a crystal that receives information from the greater cosmos through a system of spherical ley lines that are connected at sixty points, forming a dodecahedron of twelve pentagonal slabs. Plato said that the energy of "the Earth, viewed from above, resembles a ball sewn from twelve pieces of skin." This "soccer ball-shaped" analogy with inter-connecting ley lines of power has long been considered the most absurd of Plato's theories, leading to a great deal of mirth in the established scientific.[25]

They may be laughing less heartily now that Richard E. Smalley, Robert F. Curl, and Sir Harold Kroto have been awarded the 1996 Nobel Prize in chemistry for their discovery of the existence "Buckminsterfullerenes", a previously unknown form of carbon, that is made up of 60 carbon atoms, arranged in the form of a sphere—like a soccer ball or geodesic dome. This hollow cage of 12 hexagons and 20 pentagons of carbon exhibits the strength of a diamond and the elasticity of rubber. The Nobel winners have pronounced this form of carbon, the element on which all life is based, ubiquitous, existing everywhere simultaneously in the universe, although this has yet to be proved.[26] Russian scientists have found evidence of faint magnetic lines which appear to run around the Earth in ley lines that define a dodecahedron superimposed on an icosahedron, essentially itself a "fullerene". These finds confirm Plato's assertion that the Earth itself acts energetically by pulsating between the icosahedron and the dodecahedron. This pulsating energy is characteristic of the crystal, but it is a very weak force in crystals of the size that we have known. However, evidence that the Earth's core, a body the size of the moon, is a *single* spinning crystal, has also been posited during the past year. Was there truly a harmonic principle known to ancient man, and somehow harnessed to assist him, but lost to science for millennia?

---

so many investigators have put Atlantis in the North Atlantic Ocean. Atlantis flourished and was destroyed at the end of the last Ice Age, around 9550 B.C. At that time great ice sheets, though in retreat, still extended deeply into the American continent (on provinces of Atlantis not described in the *Critius*) and into the Eurasian continent. The ocean that lay between them, at northern latitudes, had to be very cold as well.

In placing Atlantis in the middle of North Atlantic it must have been assumed that such an island would have been bathed by the warm waters of the Gulf Stream. But ocean currents may have been very different during this period. There is no evidence that the gulf stream even existed at that time. Geologists studying past distributions of two species of *Foraminifera,* a small sea animal that produces a leftward coiling shell spiral in warm waters, and both a leftward and rightward spiraling shell in cold waters, have concluded that warm Gulf Stream waters could not have reached Europe before 8000 B.C., almost two thousand years after the demise of Atlantis.

If the gulf stream existed at the time of Atlantis, and followed its present course, it must have been much colder than it now is and could not in the North Atlantic have nourished the abundant tropical and sub-tropical fruits and vegetation Plato describes. In fact, all of what we now call the American continent north and west of the Yucatán peninsula would have been much too cold. From fossil records we know that the northern extremes of the Caribbean, 22 degrees above the equator, were too cold for the formation of corals twelve thousand years ago. The idea that an island situated from 32 to 45 degrees north of the equator could have been Atlantis is simply not supported by what science now knows about the Earth's climate at the end of the last Ice Age.

However, one area of the Americas could easily have fit Plato's description of a land "sheltered from the north wind." Even today, from the Yucatán to San José, Costa Rica, locals complain about the "northerlies" or "New York winds" that bring sudden cooling in December and January. At the end of the Ice Age these dips in the jet stream had to have been much more severe. But

6.J. Robert Stacy-Judd's "The Destruction of Atlantis."[27]

the Diquis Delta, in the southwest corner of Costa Rica, where the great spheres have been found, is protected from north winds by the mountains of central Costa Rica.

If the importance of Atlantis to Plato was in its value first as a cautionary tale, and not in its physical location, why do we attach so much importance to its geographical location? We might as well search for Phaeton's chariot, beams from Noah's Ark, or the physical site of Homer's Troy, to name a few "impossibilities." But Schliemann found Troy, the landing place of the Ark is now generally considered to be Mount Ararat, and Phaeton's "chariot" that in myth burned the face of the Earth may not be impossible to find . . . if you look for the right asteroid.

Because interpretations of the myth of Atlantis have, for the past several hundred years, placed its physical location in the middle of the Atlantic Ocean, and because geologists have found no traces of a sunken island-continent there, both the scientific interpretation and the popular conception of the term "myth" have suffered. It has become increasingly important to find the true physical location of Atlantis both as historical fact and as a confirmation of myth. When we compare Plato's description of Atlantis in the *Timaeus* and the *Critias*, and then compare those descriptions against what we can now measure by our sciences it becomes apparent that Atlantis could have had no other location except in the heart of the great island-continent we now call the Americas (fig. 6J).

7 Myth & Magic: *Messages from the Deep Past*

Eight Rabbit giggled. He knew he would when the priest mentioned the turtle, the turtle that carried the world on its back. He had been determined not to giggle. But when the time came he giggled anyway. Then all his young friends laughed with him, nervously. Now they all had to contend with the stern look on the priest's face. The priest then brought up the topic of the Jaguar, and how it would quickly devour the unbelieving. Eight Rabbit stopped giggling. He truly feared the Jaguar, and he knew that without the help of the priest's guidance he would not know how to deal with this creature.

Man is indispensable for the completion of creation; he himself is the second creator of the world, who alone has given to the world its objective existence.

—C. G. JUNG[1]

IF ATLANTIS was real why do we call it a myth? The problem with myth, both ancient and recent, lies in our present understanding of the word. Seen from our current mechanistic perspective there is a fatal weakness in myth as a container of history. Myth describes a world unfamiliar to us, where man communicates openly, often defiantly with gods, and challenges them on Earth and in the heavens. In myth not only could men act as gods, gods acted as men, with appetites for food, sex, and revenge. Because the cosmos of myth was described as alive with jaguars, scorpions, and winged serpents our modern view, driven by quantitative technology, has assumed that myth does not describe actual events. Myth has come to be associated with "mistaken primitive concepts" at best, or as "a belief which modern science will easily disprove." The problem, to state it simply, is that, to our current way of thinking, myth is not believable.

Science has replaced myth with a linear and progressive view of history. But if myth cannot be believed by the truly empirical investigator, then, neither can history. History, by design of reason, is rendered believable. But history, by the design of conquering armies and dominating theologies that have obliterated past knowledge, lacks continuity. Moreover, history, written from a presumed neutral position, has never been neutral. History has always been partial to ruling ideologies. As they say, history is written by conquerors. Myth has also been exceedingly partial, but it has also retained a relevancy to the past.

If there is a weakness, from the rationalist perspective, there also is a strength in myth. Because it is primarily an oral tradition it has been resistant to the destructive habits of invading armies. And because it admits man's involvement in the heavens it has torched the imagination of countless generations of listeners (7A, B, C, D). Throughout the world, myth has been expressed in astronomy, math, and art. Where the essential message of myth has been recorded from diverse cultures found around the world, and found to be essentially the same story, must we not stand in wonder at the tale told by myth?

Archaeologists have long maintained that it was only around 7000 B.C., with the gradual warming associated with the decline of the last Ice Age, that man began, in a limited number of river valleys—notably along the Nile, Indus, and Tigris-Euphrates rivers—to establish stable agricultural cultures. Early herdsmen and farmers began stock breeding, grain cultivation, and irrigation, and resulting food surpluses permitted the first true division of labor. This stability led to a diversity of architectural, political and artistic expression which provided, in turn, the cornerstones of civilization—writing, the wheel, codes of law, and trade.

7.A-D. A supernatural animal (left) participates in an important ritual in the Mayan underworld; the plumed serpent, the creator; the jaguar, the destroyer; and Anubis, a god associated with the cult of the dead in ancient Egypt.

7.E. MYTHS OF EXPLORATION BY SEA. Huwanwa, a fire-breathing giant, killed in Sumerian myth by the adventurer-king, Gilgamesh. The myth of Gilgamesh, King of the Sumerian city of Uruk, around 2600 B.C., depicts the fabulous sea journeys of a man in search of a rare fruit plant, but also in search of his own immortality. To find either, Gilgamesh had to cross the "Sea of Death." The adventures of Gilgamesh, recounted in Sumerian myth and recorded in stone, were very similar to those of Odysseus, of whom we have a written record. Their adventures were incredible, and the events that they experienced were, to our minds, beyond what any one man could have experienced and endured. Yet the great myths of ancient Sumer, Egypt, and Greece always refer to experiences at sea, on great voyages of discovery. Can the myths refer to the experiences of many sea-farers, neatly wrapped up in the tales of a few heroes?

These academic archaeologists have based their theories on discoveries of simple agricultural villages that existed, by current dating, from a few hundred to seven thousand years in our past. Each time the discovery of a wholly different culture has been made, the discoverers have interpreted the "new" find to be not only the most advanced, but also the oldest example of the new culture. Thus, although far less than ten percent of all the known archeological sites in Iraq have been excavated, a smaller percentage in Mesoamerica, and almost none at all in the shallow ocean waters of the world, archaeology and history are certain that they have arrived at the universal implications of their meager finds. In doing so they have had to ignore and dismiss the universal memory of mankind, myth (fig. 7E).

Man has been a toolmaker for over 700,000 years. Probably he has used language for as long. Homo sapiens has not demonstrated any evolutionary changes in the past 100,000 years—although an evolutionary digressive Neanderthal sub-species flourished from 270,000 to 30,000 years ago—Homo sapiens is both older and newer. Yet twentieth century paleontologists have accepted the conceit, promulgated by the Catholic church, that civilized man can be no more than seven to nine thousand years old.

Even within the framework of Mediterranean cultures the timetable of traditional archaeology makes little sense.

How do they explain the artistic expression found at the Lascaux Cave in southwest France, dated to 22,000 B.C., where the elegance and strength of the paintings led the Abbe Henri Breuil to note that the expressions found in the art was "suggestive in their own way of the early Renaissance."[4] Pablo Picasso, after examining the Lascaux artwork and comparing it to advances in twentieth century modern art exclaimed, "We have invented nothing!"

The argument has been put forth that, since most of the paintings depicted animals, this was a case of primitive hunters idling away their torchlit night hours depicting the migratory game they intended to hunt in the morning. But the cave contains over 600 paintings, 1,500 engravings, and a vast number of geometric figures (fig. 7F). Complex mixtures of dyes and minerals, sturdy scaffolding, and long hours had to have been committed to even one small portion of this great undertaking. A sophisticated and extensive source of lighting would have been required—simple torches would have left a carbon residue, and none has been found. These intricate and highly stylistic paintings exhibited a sophisticated sense of perspective in even the earliest paintings—an expression of perspective that was not found again, in Europe, until

7.F. CRO-MAGNON CAVE PAINT-ING OF A NOW EXTINCT ELK WHOSE ANTLERS SPANNED THIR-TEEN FEET. The Irish Elk flourished in Europe for thousands of years but met extinction at the same time the great fauna of the Americas met their doom, about 12,000 years ago.[3]

7.G. VENUS OF BRASSEMPOUY. Carved ivory bust of a Gravettian woman's head at Landes, France, circa 20,000 B.C. How do twentieth century paleontologists explain the sophistication of the above figure or the carved ivory bust of what has been called an Ice Age "hunter" found in a field near Dolni Vestonice, Czechoslovakia and dated as about 26,000 years old?[9] They make no attempt to. Nor do they explain baked clay figurines dated to 25,000 years ago at a nearby site. There is no explanation of 15,000 years old ivory figurines found in Siberia, nor of the exquisite ivory head known as the Venus of Brassempouy (France) that has been dated as 22,000 years old, nor the carved body of a man excavated in a 32,000-year-old level in a cave at Hohlenstein, West Germany?[10] Nor do they explain the head of an Ibex, an intricately carved engraving on a bone staff, dated, very conservatively, at 15,000 B.C., and found in association with Magdalenian cultures at Basses-Pyrenees, France. The stylistic unity of the sculptures and of the paintings, not only at Lascaux and Chauvet, but throughout the region, suggests that a class or school of artists were responsible.

---

the fifteenth and sixteenth centuries A.D. The paintings date from 10,000 to 22,000 years ago with some displaying sophisticated perspective and some displaying stick figures. If a linear Neo-Darwinian model had been at work at Lascaux these paintings should exhibit a gradual evolution of art. Yet it has been well established that the paintings created over 22,000 years ago exhibited the *most* sophisticated styles, while the most recent paintings were primarily stick figures. Moreover, their creators did not live primitively in the caves but used the caves only as a gallery for their works. The evidence is that these paintings simply had to be the work of sedentary artists who were part of a culture that had long before become freed from the demands of nomadic hunting and gathering.

Lascaux is not an isolated example. Magdalenian (Cro-Magnon) art can be found in nearly 200 painted and engraved caves extending over hundreds of square miles in southern France. At many of these sites, some over 75 kilometers from the Mediterranean and 150 kilometers from the Atlantic, finely carved bones used for harpoons, and spearpoints, as well as a variety of seashells, have been found. Could these artists have fished as a daily activity while painting took up their night time hours? Hardly. Only a sophisticated and complex culture could have supplied seafood, minerals and dyes from over great distances, and provided the time needed for the creation of these paintings. The stylistic unity of the paintings, not only at Lascaux, but in artistic expression throughout the region (fig. 7G), suggests that a class or school of artists were responsible.[5] In Stephen Jay Gould's words, "We are . . . surprised, even stunned, to discover that something so old could be so sophisticated."[6]

We now have evidence of man in America at sites dating back to at least 33,000 years before present. Conservative archaeologists, when they have admitted these dates, have told us that these were all "primitive" men. At Monte Verde, in Chile, early excavations by Tom Dillehay first found man's presence dated to 12,800 B.P. This culture was diverse, "exploiting a wide range of environments including forest, estuaries and seacoasts, all identified from plant remains . . . studies of different houses revealed variations in the use of local and nonlocal materials."[7] The diverse food resources alone prove Monte Verde to be more sophisticated than primitive bands of Clovis hunters in North America, but the fact that it was at least 1,000 years prior enables Monte Verde to debunk Beringia theory by itself. Moreover, at deeper levels Dillehay and his team have recently uncovered a culture that flourished 33,000 years ago. At these lower stratigraphic levels investigators have discovered an agricultural basis to the culture that included a variety of tubers including the potato.[8]

Similarities in rock art at Pedra Furada, in Brazil, and at the widely separated site of Monte Verde, in Chile, confirmed contact across a vast continent. An artistic, agricultural, and culturally diversified civilization existed, actually flourished, in the Americas over twenty thousand years before the more primitive Clovis man supposedly migrated across Beringia.

7.H. A CAVE PAINTING OF GIRAFFES. From the Erongo Mountains in Namibia, Africa. Cave paintings in southwest Africa have been dated at some sites to 26,000 B.P., 10,000 B.P., 3,500 B.P. and 500 years B.P. They mark a continuity of a sophisticated expression of culture that span many millennia. Sadly, the art of painting has disappeared among the San peoples (formerly called Hottentot) within the past few hundred years—years marked by acrimonial contact with modern Europeans. Yet the myths and lore of the San still describe an original creation of a people who were too stupid to survive, and who were destroyed by a conflagration. And they describe a second attempt at the creation of man, that resulted in the San people of today.[17] Is it a coincidence that their myths reflect those of the Maya, or that their paintings share the style of 20,000-year-old paintings in France, some 5,000 miles distant?

7.I. TRANSFORMATION. A man ritually transforms himself into an Armadillo so that he can dance at the place Hunahpu descended into the underworld.[11]

Expressions of art and ceremonial burials, from Brazil to the Czech Republic, among Cro-Magnon, Neanderthal, ancient Africans (fig. 7H), and people yet to have found a designation, speak of the presence of myth and civilization in fruitful coexistence for tens of thousands of years before the "birth of civilization." Since it is clear that advanced civilizations with intricate divisions of labor, existed long before, and, in their range of achievements, far beyond the scope of incipient agricultural cultures in Mesopotamia, what happened to their historic record? Traditional Archaeology, advised and guided by the theory of gradual and slow evolution and progress, simply has no answer. *Myth does.*

Taken figuratively, allegorically, or as the portrayal of actual events in story form, myth has related to our intuitive senses in ways that scientific measurement and historic renderings have not. Often myth has told its story while addressing the difficult questions of existence—death, transformation, formlessness, and creativity—without losing track of actual and significant events. Myth has had a way of preserving its tales in their original form. In myth there are recurrent ages, cycles of enlightenment and darkness, war and peace. Apprehended by a different mindset than our own, myth has survived through a series of transcendental images, often allegorical, often animist (fig. 7I).

Encountering tales of a man lassoing the sun, or turning himself into a coyote, or an owl, or a jaguar, the empirical scientist has thrown his hands up

7.J. AINU OF JAPAN. Transformation, the key tenet of myth, is expressed by the ceremonial burial of the dead, and the worship of ancestors. To our current knowledge both were first practiced by Neanderthals in Europe. However, the Ainu, who preceded the Mongoloids in Japan, have the curious idea that to some of the departed, *this* world is more attractive than the hereafter. Thus ancestors occasionally return, disguised as animals—seals, bears, deer, and other honored guests. But in their animist disguise they are trapped, without hope of becoming human again, and without passage to reenter the next world. Hunters provide the answer to their dilemma by slaying them, and providing a final passage to the next world.

and dismissed all myth as fable. In doing so he has missed the point. Myth, told among peoples who lived in close harmony with the Earth and the sky, had to be expressed in vivid images that reflected man's magical association with the Earth, its animals and with the movement, at times erratic, of the heavens. If it had been told in the dry, factual manner that historians of the past several centuries have employed, it would have been discarded and forgotten. The recognition of human mortality has inspired the need, now considered among many of us as impossible, to transcend death. For mythic man transcendence was obvious. It only needed a description. The purpose of myth is to describe the transformation of the individual into a different, often lesser and sometimes greater realm of being. Thus the transformation was at times described as a rebirth as owls, at other times as beasts, and sometimes as stars. Lacking the poignancy of immediate human involvement these records would have been committed to a written form and no longer conveyed orally. Probably man's history has been told both ways, concurrently, for tens of thousands of years, but for a variety of reasons, including systematic destruction of the written records of defeated cultures, only myth has survived.

Science, sadly, insists that the universe is so big, and individual man is so small, that no connection between man and the cosmos is possible. The essence of myth is that size has nothing to do with it. Intuitive knowledge of nature combined with precise measurement of the movements of celestial bodies is the unifying force between man and creation, not the quantitative dimensions of the observer and the observed. In myth, man, as the geometer of the universe, becomes the vibrant point of existential knowledge (fig. 7J).

Our modern view has separated myth from science and history, seeing them as contradictory forces. Myth disagrees. In years carefully recorded by the ancient Egyptians and Sumerians, and in numbers devised by the ancient Maya, early man has told us a far different story. "Primitive man" in search of myth has been supported by his sciences, notably his mathematics and his astronomy. In fact the mathematics by which we can now independently confirm astronomical observations and quantum mechanics, were developed and understood by a "primitive" people, the Maya, to a degree unmatched in the world until late in this century. The ancient view incorporated myth and science as well as myth and history as part of a balanced and holistic view of the world. Myth, by recent believers, has been called "history in disguise." It is sometimes a considerable disguise. But the true test of myth, as a container of fact and history, is not whether man's participation in the events it describes is verifiable, but whether myth describes verifiable events.

In myth all of the founding gods of the great civilizations were navigators— Thoth in Egypt, Quetzalcoatl and Kukulcán in Mesoamerica, Sume in Brazil, Oannes in Sumer, Viracocha in Peru. Myths of arrival by sea are universal, yet there have been no myths of migration across land bridges. Even in North America there are no myths of "great journeys" across the Bering Sea and over glacial terrain. Foundation myths have invariably told of arrivals by sea.

In the thirteenth century B.C., a Babylonian priest named Berossus wrote in Greek an account of his native Mesopotamian culture entitled *Babylonica*.

7.K. BAS-RELIEF OF OANNES AT NINEVEH. Symbols of foundation invariably describe arrival by sea, from the symbol of the fish in Sumerian myth to its adopted use as a foundation symbol for the early Christian church. The symbol of the fish also represented the Great Lord Vishnu in Hinduism and Set, the founding god of the Egyptians (Set is also represented as a boat). Poseidon, the sea god of the Greeks and the founder of Plato's Atlantis, is always depicted with a trident. To some the trident is only a spear for catching fish, but others interpret its parallel lines as representing the equator and the lines of the tropics of Cancer and Capricorn. Others have interpreted it as representing knowledge of longitude. The cross may also be regarded as a symbol of sea peoples since its representation in the skies, the Southern Cross, occurs in the southern hemisphere, a realm only accessible, in ancient times, to seafarers. Displaying the cross may have been a proud symbol indicating that its bearers knew of the southern seas.

In it he ascribes all the arts and sciences to a primal being, half-man half-fish, named Oannes, who came out of the sea, and "taught man everything there is to know," including "the use of letters, sciences and arts of all kinds, and rules for the founding of cities, and the construction of temples."[12] According to the Babylonian myth Oannes (fig. 7K.) was one of seven founders to arrive from across the sea, adding "Since then nothing excellent has been learned though much has been forgotten."[13] Significantly Oannes is described as father of metallurgy. Since no metals of any significance have ever existed in Mesopotamia, Oannes had to come from across the sea. If he was a bringer of bronze, as he was described, he likely brought copper ore from Isle Royal in Lake Superior, and tin from Lake Titicaca in Bolivia.

A Nahuatl myth (central valley of Mexico) describes an arrival by sea that is preserved in the Codex Boturini with a series of paintings depicting sea boats and a God whose symbol was an *ilbal*, which has variously been interpreted as a book (a place to see) or as a "seeing instrument attached to an elliptical rod." His arrival, according to the long count, was in 15,600 B.C., and it founded an age that did not end until the deluge almost 5,000 years later.[14] Mexican foundation myths of the ancient Toltecs were still known to the Aztecs when the Spanish chronicler Friar Sahagun recorded their myth of "Panotlan" as the landing site. Panotlan means "place of arrival by sea."

In Egypt the concept of arrival by sea is accompanied by the myth of departure by sea, to the underworld. The departure is described as a journey to the west, to the land of origins.

The Minoans, who before recent excavations at Thera, were considered a "mythical" people, had myths handed down from a far earlier past. Their just kings were honored during their lives but honored even more in death. For in the afterlife they became the Gods that sat in judgment of the dead. Minos became such a judge, as did his brother, Rhadamanthus. Together they ruled the afterlife from a land across the great ocean. It was the land from which they had come and it was the land, if they lived just lives, to which they would return. In Strabo's words, "They were assured an eternity of bliss, *far to the west* in the splendid Isles of the Blessed . . . soft winds wafted to them the treble songs of birds. Fresh fruits grew just overhead for their delight. There friends and lovers were eternally young, eternally reunited, eternally at peace. On all sides stretched the silver summer sea that languidly lapped the shores of their Atlantis."[15]

The *Popol Vuh* (fig. 7L), or "Council Book" of the Quiche Maya of the highlands of Guatemala describes the four known ages of man as four attempts to get it right. In the third try the gods attempt to make man out of wood. The Popol Vuh describes it thus:

"This was the peopling of the face of the Earth: They came into being, they multiplied, they had daughters, they had sons, these manikins, wood-carvings. But there was nothing in their hearts and nothing in their minds, nor memory of their mason and builder. They just went and walked wherever they wanted. Now they did not remember the Heart of Sky . . . And so they accomplished nothing before the Maker, Modeler who gave them birth, gave them heart. They became the first of numerous people here on the Earth. Again there comes a humiliation, destruction, and demolition. The manikins, woodcarvings were killed when the Heart of Sky devised a flood for them. A great flood was made . . . they were not competent, nor did they speak before the builder and sculptor who made them and brought them forth, and so they were killed, done in by a flood.

"This was when there was just a trace of early dawn on the face of the Earth, there was no sun. But there was one who magnified himself; Seven Macaw was his name . . . He was like a person of genius in his being . . . (He said) 'I am great. My place is now higher than that of the human design. I am their sun and I am their light, and I am also their months.' . . . And so Seven Macaw puffs himself up as the days and the months, though the light of the

7.L. DESTRUCTION MYTHS OF THE MAYA. The only books to survive destruction by the Catholic Church, the *Popol Vuh* of the Quiche Maya, and the *Chilam Balam* of the Yucatán Maya, describe the destruction of a civilization similar to Atlantis. However, three codices of Mayan hiero-glyphs, smuggled out of Mexico, eventually showed up in Europe. Glyphs from the so-called Dresden Codex describe the deluge pictorially. Torrents of water pour from a serpent in the sky. Under the signs of Venus, Jupiter, Mercury and Mars two additional vast streams pour down from the heavens. The Moon goddess, symbol of death, pours more water from an inverted vase, while an evil god drives two arrows of destruction down upon the Earth. The meaning can only be that all the forces of nature rained on the Earth. Myth and art are one. Myth and history are one. But can myth and scientific verification be one?

sun and moon has not yet clarified. He only wished for surpassing greatness. This was when the flood was worked upon the manikins, woodcarvings."[16]

How does this story of the proud and defiant Seven Macaw and the flood visited upon his people differ from Plato's story of the proud Atlanteans advancing on Greece or with biblical stories of pride and downfall by the forces of heaven, or with any similar story retold through hundreds of cultures through countless years? Compare it to the Greek myth of Deucalion and Pyrrha descending from Mount Parnassus after the deluge, the only humans left in a dead world.[18] In the Hindu version the people lose their faith, the Lord Krishna departs, the Age of Kali descends, and the ocean rises to destroy the unbelievers, and the people are sustained only by the belief that Kalki will bring a new age. It is the same story, universally told.

Genesis 11 refers to an age of international builders. After the flood (narrated in Genesis 7-8) talented men, sharing a common language ("one set of words" —Genesis 1.1) set out to build the Tower of Babel.[19]

We can compare this biblical account to the myth told of the founding of Cholula (south of Mexico City near Puebla) "At the time of the cataclysm, the country . . . was inhabited by giants. Some of these perished utterly; others were changed into fishes; while seven brothers of them found safety by closing themselves into certain caves in a mountain called Tlaloc. When the waters were assuaged, one of the giants, Zelhua, surnamed the Architect, went to Cholula and began to build an artificial mountain (a pyramid), as a monument and a memorial of the Tlaloc that had sheltered him and his when the angry waters swept through all the land. The bricks were made in Tlamanalco, at the foot of the Sierra de Cocotl, and passed to Cholula from hand to hand along a file of men—whence these came is not said—stretching between the two places. Then were the jealousy and the anger of the gods aroused, as the huge pyramid rose slowly up, threatening to reach the clouds and great heaven itself; and the gods launched their fire upon the builders and slew many, so that the work was stopped. But the half-finished structure, afterward dedicated by the Cholultecs to Quetzalcoatl, still remains to show how well Xelhua, the giant, deserved his surname of the Architect."[21] The Cholula Pyramid is still the largest known structure, in terms of cubic content, in the world. But, according to myth, it was never completed. The gods destroyed the pyramid and confounded the language of the builders.[22]

Myths of foundation (fig. 7M) are almost invariably intertwined with myths of destruction by cataclysms. The Dresden Codex of the Maya says: "The sky approached the Earth and in one day all perished. Even the mountains disappeared under the water." Another Maya myth speaks of "an inundation, which swept across the world, swallowing all things in its mountainous surges."[23]

7.M. Itzamna arriving from the East as depicted in the codex Troano. Mayan myths say that their ancestors came from the ocean. Like the Nahuatl people to their north they describe more than one foundation. The mythical civilizer Itzamna, carrying the letters of what would become the Mayan language, arrived from the east, to found one age. Itzamna came across a sea with twelve paths through it (in the celestial sea the zodiac has twelve paths). Later, in a different age, another migration came from the west, led by Kukulcan, the Mayan equivalent of Quetzalcoatl. Like the peoples of Mexico who described several incarnations of Quetzalcoatl and like the Hindus who described many appearances of their lord-god Krishna, the Maya myths had Kukulcan arriving several times. One appearance was in the form of Tonaca, a migrating seafarer. In Peru the Quechua say Tonapa, a seafaring incarnation of Viracocha, left into the Pacific to found civilizations in Oceana.[20]

In Peru the Incas describe two separate creations by Viracocha, the first having angered the god, so that he brought about their destruction by a great deluge. The "children of the sun . . . had a full account of the deluge. No living thing survived except a man and a woman." then the creator fashioned out of clay one person for each nation; "then he gave life and a soul to each one, men as well as women, and directed them to their designated places on Earth."[24]

The Gila of America's southwest desert have the following myth: "The Eagle came to warn the prophet, and to say that all the valley of the Gila should be laid waste with water: but the prophet gave no heed. Then in the twinkling of an eye, and even as the flapping of the Eagle's wings died away into the night, there came a peal of thunder and an awful crash; and a green mound of water reared itself over the plain . . . When morning broke, there was nothing to be seen alive but one man."[26]

A testimonial to the strength and endurance of myth is that deluge myths are common among people who, in recorded history, have never seen the sea, or great rivers.[27] Of course flash floods are common in the desert. But Doug Vogt has pointed to the fact that many of the legends describe waters as passing over the tops of mountains, and that, even in America's desert southwest (and in Asia's Gobi desert), the flood is described as "a green mound of water passing over the land."[28] Local floods do not pass *over* mountains and they produce *brown* water, not green! Only great floods, cataclysms, can cause the oceans to sweep over mountains and through the interiors of continents.

A myth of the Guaymis Indians of Costa Rica says: "Angered with the world, the mighty Noncomala poured over it a flood of water, killing every man and woman; but the kindly God Nubu had preserved the seed of man, and when the waters had dried up he sowed it on the moist Earth."[29]

In Aztec legends one version is told of a catastrophic flood that covered the whole world, causing the fourth race of men to turn into fishes, except one pair of humans who were warned to embark in a hollow cypress tree. Another version tells of an escape by Giants who survived in caves:

"This first age, or 'sun,' was called the Sun of the Water, and it was ended by a tremendous flood, in which every living thing perished, or was transformed, except, following some accounts, one man and one woman of the giant race. . . . The second Age, called the Sun of the Earth, was closed with Earthquakes, yawning of the Earth, and the overthrow of the highest mountains. Giants, or Quinames, a powerful and haughty race, still appear to be the only inhabitants of the world. The third Age was the Sun of the Air. It was ended by tempests and hurricanes, so destructive that few indeed of the inhabitants of the Earth were left; and those that were saved lost, according to the Tlascaltec account, their reason and speech, becoming monkeys.

The present is the Fourth Age. To it appear to belong the falling of the goddess-born flint from heaven, the birth of the sixteen hundred heroes from that flint, the birth of mankind from the bone brought from Hades, the transformation of Nanahuatzin into the sun, the transformation of Tezcatecatl into the moon, and the death of the sixteen hundred heroes or gods. It is called the Sun of Fire, and is to be ended by a universal conflagration."[30]

The Aztecs were more recent, as a civilization, than the Mayans or the Sumerians. However, their myths were borrowed from the Toltecs and from the pre-Toltecs. The Aztec account is not just the myth of a deluge, with few survivors, but a description of the birth of sacrifice, as well as the story of the unfinished pyramid, "threatening the clouds and the great heaven itself," which is so reminiscent of the biblical and Sumerian tales of the Tower of Babel. Also of importance is the introduction of Xelhua as a great architect.

The destruction myths of the Quiche Maya of Guatemala (contained in the *Popol Vuh*) are virtually identical to the destruction myths of the Maya of the Yucatán, and to the myths of the Aztecs of central Mexico that were inherited from the Toltecs. Moreover they are identical to the Hebrew myths found in the Old Testament and to the myths of Sumer. The *Popol Vuh* also described how the tribes, in a time of unrest, had to leave their land, and that they "crossed the sea, the waters having parted when they passed."[31] We can compare this myth to the tale told in Exodus.

The Toltec version of the Deluge was given by the native Mexican historian, Ixtlilxochitl:

"It is found in the histories of the Toltecs that this age and the *first world,* as they call it, lasted 1,716 years; that men were destroyed by tremendous rains and lightning from the sky, and even all the land, without the exception of anything, and the highest mountains, were covered up and submerged in what was *fifteen cubits* (caxtolmolatli); and here they added other fables of how men came to multiply from the few who escaped from this destruction in a 'toptlilpetlocali;' that this word nearly signifies a closed chest; and how, after men had multiplied, they erected a very high 'zacuali,' which is today a tower of great height, in order to take refuge in it should the second world (age) be destroyed. Presently their languages were confused, and, not being able to understand each other, they went to different parts of the Earth.

"The Toltecs, consisting of seven friends, with their wives, who understood the same language, came to these parts, having first passed great lands and seas, having lived in caves, and having endured great hardships in order to reach this land; . . . they wandered 104 years through different parts of the world before they reached Hue Tlapalan, which was in Ce Tecpatl, 520 years after the Flood."[32] The Toltecs traced their migrations back to a land they knew as "Atlan."

The deluge has been described again by the Ute Indians of the Lake Tahoe area—"The Great Spirit sent an immense wave across the continent from the sea, and this wave engulfed both the oppressors and the oppressed, all but a very small remnant. Then the taskmasters made the remaining people raise up a great pyramid so that they, of the ruling caste, should have a refuge in case of another flood."[33]

Myth, of course, is not found only in the Americas. Virtually all the peoples of the world have had their own stories of their origins and foundations. The stories contained in these myths have differed sharply with the gradualist and land-based theories of traditional Archaeology. The myths almost invariably speak of ages of man, of cataclysms and floods, and of recurring creations and destructions of civilizations. In opposition to the short view of gradualists, that myths of destruction are too fantastic to be true, we must adopt a longer view; some fundamental idea must be behind these stories, some fundamental and universal experience had to have occurred. Myths and legends so widespread must have basis in fact.

In Egypt a 3,000-year-old twelfth-dynasty papyrus tells the story of a survivor of an earlier age and of the deluge. The survivor is said to be from "The

Island of the Serpent." Before he leaves what is described as a vast island, the survivor is told, "After you leave my island you will not find it again as this place will vanish under the sea waves." Describing the catastrophe that followed, the author of the document states: "A star fell from the heavens and the flames consumed everything. All were burned but I alone was saved. However, when I saw the mountain of corpses I almost died of grief."[34]

A Samoan legend states, "In early times there was a flood which destroyed all beings, except one man, Pili, and his wife, who took refuge on a rock, these survivors subsequently becoming the ancestors of mankind."[35] While throughout Polynesia there are two versions of the legend of Tawhaki, one stating that Tawhaki "caused a deluge by stamping on the floor of heaven, which cracked so that the water flowed through and covered the Earth." The other says that, "Tawhaki wishing to be avenged for the attempt to kill him, called upon the gods to send a deluge to overwhelm the world after he and his friends had taken refuge on the top of a mountain."[36]

In the Philippines the sages of the Ata tribe tell how a flood visited the Earth and covered it with water, and all the people were drowned, except two men and a woman who were rescued by an eagle.[37]

In China the legend of Yahou describes a time when "an immense wave that reached the sky fell down upon the land. The water was well high in the mountains, and the foothills could not be seen at all."[38]

India's Satapatha-Brahmana tells of the adventures of young Manu who one day goes to water to wash. A small fish jumps into his hands and speaks to Manu asking for protection, that he may avoid being eaten by larger fish and grow large himself. Manu agrees to the request, puts the fish first in a jar, then digs him a pit. The fish grows very large under Manu's care and is taken to the ocean. When it is released the fish thanks Manu for caring for him. He then warns Manu, "In such a year the great flood will come. Thou shalt attend to my advice by preparing a ship; and when the flood has risen thou shalt enter into the ship, and I will save thee from it."[39]

In ancient Greece the writings of Hesiod describes how the fourth race of men, produced by Zeus, were like demi-gods. These were destroyed by the ocean. The fifth race of men now lives on Earth. This race Hesiod calls "the race of iron," and describes us thus: "Men never rest from labor and sorrow by day . . . the father will not agree with his children, nor the children with their father . . . nor will brother be dear to brother as aforetime . . . not knowing the fear of the Gods one man will sack another's city, for might shall be their right."[40]

In the *Oera Linda Book,* Norse legends relate a history of the Frisian race, a matriarchal blue-eyed, blond-haired people who averaged over two meters in height and who dwelled in a land called Atland. Atland, which enjoyed a warm and nourishing environment was destroyed by a cataclysmic deluge. Its survivors migrated to the Mediterranean and under the Frisian warrior-princess, Minerva, founded Athens and ancient Greece. The Greeks eventually became weary of their rule and united under Cecrops, the son of a Frisian girl and an Egyptian priest, drove the Frisians out of Athens.[41]

The *Oera Linda* legends present some conflicting scenarios. Atland was reported to have existed off the coast of present day Norway in a time when the North Atlantic was much milder, before the great flood, and a possible tilt in the axis of the Earth effectively sent that region to the northern climes. But references in the *Oera Linda* also describe Atland as being to the southwest, across the vast sea, making an axis tilt unnecessary in describing its lush tropical climate. An interesting aspect is the description of Cecrops as "half man and half serpent" reflecting the serpent as a prime mover in ancient events. The pre-Columbian peoples of Mesoamerica regarded the serpent in exactly this way. The *Chilam Balam*, the native Yucatán chronology of the Mayan people, describes a flooding almost identical to the account in the *Popol Vuh*, but in the *Chilam Balam* the fiery rains and floods were accompanied by a celestial convolution as "the Great Serpent was torn from the sky . . . skin and pieces of its bones fell onto the Earth. . . . Then the waters rose in a terrible flood. And with the Great Serpent the sky fell in and the dry land sank into the sea."[42]

Another poignant aspect is the reference to the Frisian invasion of pre-Ancient Greece—"founding" is a term invariably used by invaders—which was eventually repelled. This myth confirms Plato's description of this series of events put forth in the *Critias*, with the early Greeks warding off the invaders from across the sea.[43]

A myth of the Aravecs of Guyana states that the Great Spirit sent a double calamity to the world: first it was struck by fire and next by a great flood that covered the Earth.[44] Both Canaanite and Mayan hieroglyphs relate that the purpose of sacrifice is to avert deluges and cataclysms.

The Roman poet Ovid wrote of the great Flood: "There was such wickedness once on Earth that Justice fled to the sky, and the king of the gods determined to make an end of the race of men. . . . Jupiter's anger was not confined to his province of the sky. Neptune (Poseidon), his sea brother, sent the waves to help him. Neptune smote the Earth with his trident and the Earth shivered and shook. . . . Soon there was no telling land from sea. Under the water the sea nymphs were staring in amazement at woods, houses and cities. Nearly all men perished by water, and those who escaped the water, having no food, died of hunger."[45]

Josephus Flavius, the Jewish historian of the first century, told us that Nimrod built the Tower of Babel for the purpose of providing shelter in the event of another deluge. As noted, Ixtilxochitl, the Mexican chronicler, gave us a parallel Toltec motive for the construction of the pyramids.[46]

It is interesting that although historians have persisted in referring to Sumer as the "cradle of civilization" the Sumerians themselves, in profuse writings still being interpreted, disagreed. In tablets dated to the fourth millennium B.C. from the Mesopotamian city of Ur the Sumerians claim that long before their time there was a civilization of great cities that fell in disfavor of the supreme god. The god decreed a great flood to wipe out mankind. According to the Sumerian records Enki, the ocean god (equivalent to the Greek god Poseidon), warned King Ziusudra, advising him to build a very large boat, to save himself. Ziusudra built the boat and saved himself and certain livestock from the flood.[47] In this telling the primal flood myth of the Hebrews (Noah and the Ark) is predated by a Sumerian myth of the fourth millennium B.C.

The true history of man on Earth can be found in the stories contained in myth. These tales refer back to a time when men and women lived in relative peace and acceptance of the cosmos in a Golden Age of human achievement and understanding. What we have presented are excerpts, bits and pieces from myths from the Americas and around the globe. But they represent hundreds of other such myths that speak of a world-wide deluge as well as a common knowledge of its cause, proud defiance of the celestial gods, and its source, the gods of heaven reigning down on the disbelievers.

How far back in man's memory does myth go? We think we have invented the telescope, the wheel, agriculture, art, religion, and intelligence itself. The message of myth, tells us otherwise, and more. And when we truly learn to evaluate the sites of ancient man, their physical record will confirm myth as history in disguise.

History has not occurred in a straight or even line of descent. It, like myth, has had retrograde curves, zigzags, and revolving circles. But more significantly there are times when it comes to a dead stop. If we had a cataclysm today—of a scale that destroyed all our cities, and melted all our surface metals—what evidence of our twentieth century existence would remain? The pages of books and wood on land burn, wood under water rots, metals and glass melt. *The only things that would remain are those made of stone, or where man's memory persists among survivors, those ideas that can be expressed in an oral tradition—myth.*

The great Aztec Stone calendar (fig. 2D) found at Tenochtitlán in an excavation beneath Mexico City (as the result of excavation for a subway) describes the four past eras as well as their causes of destruction, namely Water, Wind, Storms and Jaguar. The Aztec description (actually Toltec) is confirmed by Mayan hieroglyphics. According to the Codex Vaticano-Latino the four ages have had varying lengths; the first lasted 4,008 years and ended in a deluge, a cataclysm in which the oceans covered the Earth, sparing only one man and one woman; the second lasted 4,010 and ended in a conflagration of fire; the third lasted 4,081 years and at its end the present age was founded in our year of 3113 B.C. Our current age, by Mayan reckoning, will last 5,125 years and end on Sunday, December 23 of our year 2,012.[48] Counting back from the projected year of 2012 as the year of the destruction of the fourth age to the current date of 1998, the first age, as related by both the Nahuatl and Mayan peoples ended by flood 13,202 years ago, or 11,202 B.C.

Is this a preposterous date? If we think Mayan myth faulty we must remember that the mathematics and astronomy they devised could predict eclipses of the sun hundreds of years in the future to within thirty-three seconds of the actual event, and that their ability to reckon time surpassed any other known method, including our Gregorian calendar, until the invention of the atomic clock. Their abilities, however, were not based on any of our sophisticated sciences but rather appear to be based on simple observation over a very long period of time. But we would do well to try to understand their long-lived observations of the heavens because they appear to have never mistaken a great event in the heavens, and they predict another just sixteen years into our future.

If myth is collective memory of true events, when did this world-wide deluge occur? What could have happened 13,200 years ago to account for such a disaster? As mentioned in chapter 2, Peter Tompkins cites the work of Professor Cesare Emilini, who found evidence indicating glaciation and deglaciation occurring in cycles of about every 20,000 years over the last 700,000 years. The last major deglaciation, Emilini discovered, occurred in 11,600 B.C. when ice water from the melting Wisconsin icecap suddenly broke through the confines of Lake Nippissing (the combined glacial melt waters that now, reduced, have formed the Great Lakes)—and poured down the Mississippi Valley causing the waters of the Caribbean to rise, in a few days, by 130 feet.[49]

Other geologists have speculated that at the end of the last Ice Age a chunk of the Antarctic ice sheet, perhaps as large as Texas and California combined, broke off from the continent and created a wave of water over a thousand feet high, permanently raising the level of the oceans world wide by over 400 feet.

Earlier investigators with no ties to either the Church or conventional history, Alexander von Humbolt, Brasseur de Bourbourg, and Le Plongeon, independently arrived at the same conclusion—that primitive cultures could be seen as the debris of higher civilizations that had been destroyed by great catastrophes. These men had no knowledge of Chaos Science nor of the random plucking of comets from the De Kuyper belt. They simply believed the myths they encountered that were associated with the ruins of ancient civilizations in Mesoamerica. They believed that myth could be history in disguise.[50]

Brasseur de Bourbourg, writing in mid-nineteenth-century, interpreted the Troano and Chimalpopoca codices as a history of an ancient people who had come from a large continent that had spread across the Atlantic. A series of four periods of cataclysms, caused by passing comets and accompanied by temporary shifting of the Earth's axis had resulted in the demise of this civilization. Brasseur placed the date of the final destruction of this continent in the year 9937 B.C. Noting the similarities in astronomy, astrology, physics, and religious practices, as well as records of almost identical myths among Egyptians, Sumerians and Mesoamericans, Brasseur deduced that one had been the founder of the other two. Since Central American civilization was, in his eyes, older, Brasseur believed Egypt and Sumer to be colonies of the survivors of the earlier advanced civilization. He believed the Carians of Central America were that people.[51] Mistakenly, Brasseur envisioned this continent as having stretched from Central America and across the Atlantic as far as the Canary Islands. But whether he thought the codices said this or whether he conjectured that particular geographic confirmation on his own is not known. A glance at the map of Mesoamerica and the basins of the Gulf of Mexico and the Caribbean (figs. 13A, C) clearly shows that the land mass, prior to the deluge that accompanied the end of the last Ice Age, was far more extensive than it is today.

We don't know for certain what caused the sudden and violent end to the last Ice Age but the tales of a passing comet contained in the codices Brasseur found are a very likely cause. Passing close enough a comet could cause deviations in the Earth's rotation, deviations in the axis and great stress on the Earth's plates. Tremendous Earthquakes would ensue and possibly unleash the waters of the Great lake Nippising formed by the melting North American ice mass and could break off a huge chunk of the Antarctic ices sheet. Tremendous flooding would almost immediately follow the great Earthquakes. Destruction by flooding of such a large area of land, with navigational cities located on or near ancient shorelines, could surely be recorded as destruction of a continent. Brasseur just had the continent in the wrong place.

In Hindu mythology the beloved god Krishna, avatar of Vishnu, the preserver, is shot in the heel by the hunter, Jara, who represents the aging of the gods and the arrival of egoistic man. Wounded, Krishna leaves this world, and the Age of Kali begins with a deluge. (Homer's myth—now confirmed history—of Troy and the wound to the heel of Achilles should be kept in mind).

"And on the same day that Krishna departed from the Earth (god of light), the powerful dark-bodied Kali (god of destruction) descended. The ocean rose, and submerged the whole of Dvaraka."[52]

Remember that in 590 B.C., Solon is warned by priests in Egypt, a country where history and great megaliths go back over 2,500 years before that rendering, that the lesson is that the memory of the past has been forgotten, wiped out by deluges and cataclysms, which are periodic and recurring in nature, and of which there are but a few survivors. The cataclysm that befell both ancient Athens and Atlantis is described as "the greatest of all destructions by water."

Plato's telling of the story of Atlantis was in the tradition of myth, in this case a destruction myth. And like all myth it had elements that do not necessarily ring true to the empirical mind (fig. 7N). They call on a higher truth. If the essential truth of the destruction of Atlantis was not actually believed, what would inspire such diverse peoples as the Sumerians, Chinese, Egyptians and ancient Americans to erect precise mathematical monuments to measure the movements of the celestial heavens as a forewarning of a repeat disaster?

7.N. TWIN MOTIFS IN ATLANTIS. To the archaic mind myths were real, living entities, just as the sun and stars above, were living entities. Empirical reality was not ignored, but had a subjective counterpart that complemented the objective world to form a unified whole. Thus natural events, even the cosmological, had human participation. Heroes held up the heavens on their shoulders. In mythology each tale can be interpreted at different levels, the human (or animal), the cosmological (or celestial), or as a  balanced unity of both. Light contrasts with darkness, ignorance with enlightenment, good with bad, and life with death. The ephemeral was balanced by tales of transformation. Balance of the two sides to any matter was essential to a definition of existence. This balance was often described in pairs, essential opposites, in which the distinct figures display conflicting and complementary aspects of the whole. The Yin and Yang of China, the repeated twin motifs of Atlantis repeated throughout Mesoamerica, and the legend of Gilgamesh of Sumeria are but a few examples. (Gilgamesh was a solitary figure, but because of this he was described as a man out of balance, without a counterpart). Today we exist as a society without balance because the known is plentiful but without intrinsic or mythic meaning. The unknown is a vast emptiness of space and time. There is no balance. Yet man has a significant role in the universe. He has simply forgotten his role.

Plato's story of Atlantis in fact contains another myth. In the *Timaeus* Solon is reminded of the Greek story of how Phaeton, child of the sun, harnessed his father's chariot, but was unable to guide it along his father's course and, as a result, burnt up things on the Earth, and was himself destroyed by a thunderbolt. Is the story of Phaeton a mythical version of the truth that there is at long intervals a variation in the course of the heavenly bodies and a consequent widespread destruction by fire of things on the Earth? We know that Plato regarded this destruction as both cyclical and celestial because he describes cataclysmal variations in the sun and heavens elsewhere. In the *Statesman* he writes of a reversal: "I mean the change in the rising and setting of the Sun and other heavenly bodies, how in those times they used to set in the quarter where they now rise, and used to rise where they now set."

Plato was not alone in his belief that something periodically went wrong with the sun. Mayan myths warn that "Under the might of Ah Uuc Kin . . . is the seat of the 12-Ahau katun, Yaxan Chuen, Great-monkey-craftsman (the sun). It is the countenance he will display during his reign in the heavens. That which is in the heavens will come forth on 12-Ahau."[53] This could refer to a devastating comet or even to an asteroid. But the Toltecs are more specific in describing the sun's involvement in a solar catastrophe: "There fell a rain of fire; all which existed burned . . . the sun itself was on fire, and everything, together with the houses, was consumed."[54]

Aztec myths related that the building of the pyramids was undertaken as a defense against the "all-consuming fire from the heavens."[55] Even the Voguls (Russia) had a version of the cataclysm describing the "Earth burning at both ends of the sky," possibly indicating that Asia was on back side of the Earth when a celestial cataclysm occurred.[56]

The following tale of the Fifth Sun has versions in Aztec, Toltec, and Mayan myth. We present the Toltec version:

The Nahuatl myth of the Fifth Sun tells of a time when there had been no sun in existence for many years. So the Aztec Gods assembled in Teotihuacan and gathered around a great bonfire to discuss how they might rekindle the light of the world. The gods decided that one of them must cast himself into the bonfire and that he who did so would have the honor of being transformed into the new sun. A boastful God named Tecciztecatl claimed he would be the one to cast himself into the flames and become the new sun. But the other gods, doubting him, asked for a second volunteer. None came forth until a lowly god called Nanahuatzin, who was afflicted with scabs, came forth and announced he would be the one.

For four days the other gods did penance and built a tower to Nanahuatzín and Tecciztecatl as big as a mountain. Then they all assembled on the tower and offerings were made to the great bonfire beneath them. Tecciztecatl's offering was of fine feathers, nuggets of gold, precious stones, red coral, and the finest copal. But Nanahuatzín instead of feathers offered nine green reeds tied in bunches of threes, instead of gold and red coral he offered hay an maguey thorns anointed in his own blood, and instead of copal he gave the scabs from his sores. The other gods judging Tecciztecatl's offering superior said: "Now Tecciztecatl, jump into the fire!" Four times Tecciztecatl tried but four times he was unable to summon the courage. Nanahuatzin was then summoned and he flung himself into the fire. He crackled and burned in the flames and Tecciztcatl, now ashamed, followed Nanahuatzin into the fire.

Then the gods began to peer through the gloom in all directions for the expected light, and to make bets as to what part of heaven the new sun should first appear in. Some said here and some said there; but when the sun rose they were all proved wrong, for not one of them had fixed upon the east.

This story of a humble, suffering god who sacrifices his life to save the world is just one of many myth motifs that can be found in virtually all prehistoric cultures. Like the deluge and creation myths it can be heard in stories from all times, and wherever human beings have lived and passed the memory of their purpose on to their descendants.

To the sixteenth century European mind, represented by Spanish missionaries, the Myth of the Fifth Sun was repugnant because it paralleled the teachings of the Church, which would admit no parallels, and because it was the apparent origin of the concept of human sacrifice among the Toltecs and Aztecs and their ancestors. To the nineteenth and twentieth century scientific mind it was repugnant because it represented a world view steeped in superstition and magic. Mistaking technological and authoritarian political development as a corollary for animal evolution, science saw mankind as progressing from magic to true religion and on to empirical science. There could be no turning back to a reality based on myth.

The view of the Roman Catholic church is understandable, even if unforgivable. But man's belief in myth and his eternal place in the cosmos has also been impaired by those whose who fail to understand the message in myth . . . and who fail to grasp that myths are not just fantastic stories, but are cautionary tales based on real events. Even scholars who stress the importance of myth in man's understanding of the cosmos can miss the point. In his important examination of myth, *Hamlet's Mill*, Giorgio de Santillana declares that Greece is not submersible, and that "it is evident that events of the Flood in the Era Epic, however vivid their language, apply unmistakably to events in the austral heavens and to nothing else."[59] A large area of the Greek peninsula, above sea level during the last Ice Age was submersible, and is now submerged under hundreds of feet of water. The Athens of Plato's account, coastal at the time of the attack by Atlanteans, had to be many miles from any present coastline, and must now stand under about 400 feet of water. *That Athens was certainly submersible* (fig. 7O).

Until less than a hundred years ago Troy was considered a "myth," Sumer was considered a myth, Jericho was considered a myth, Noah and the tale of

7.O. THE PROBABLE COASTLINES OF GREECE BEFORE THE DELUGE. Greece was a much larger country at the time of the cataclysm that ended Atlantis and when the Mediterranean was much smaller. In fact NASA infrared photography has revealed that the Mediterranean was once three separate bodies of water and the farthest to the east was a fresh water lake fed by a spectacular waterfall that plunged over a thousand feet from the Nile north of present day Alexandria. However the Mediterranean of Plato's Atlantis was a continuous sea, though greatly reduced in size from today's boundaries.

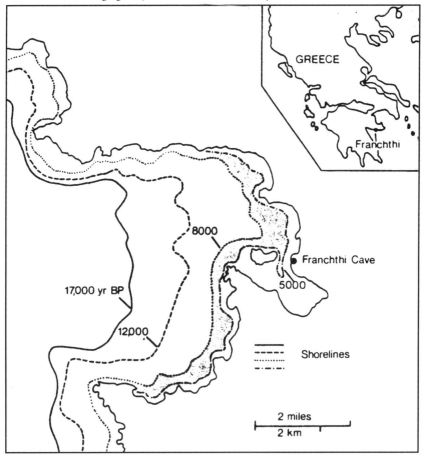

his Ark was considered a myth. Myths of King Minos and an earlier civilization in Crete, more advanced in the sciences than the classic Greeks, were considered preposterous. But all these are now known archeological sites with dates far earlier than what has been taught. The people who pursued lost civilizations on the basis of myth were laughed at, hounded, and publicly scorned by academics. The Sumerian clay tablets listed kings, notably Mes-anni-pad-da, who went back thousands of years before the supposed inception of simple farming in Mesopotamia seven thousand years ago. Scientists scoffed at the existence of this founder-god. But Sir Leonard Woolley found an ancient temple, near Ur, that placed Mes-anni-pad-da as the actual founder of the third dynasty after the flood.[60]

Today, the discoveries of Schliemann, Woolley, and Sir Arthur Evans are regarded as important finds. But unimaginative academic voices now tell us that there is nothing more to be discovered by this unconventional approach. They are wrong (fig. 7P)!

The ancient peoples of Central America have left a legacy of myths that are incomprehensible to the logical mind, and they have also left the records of an exact astronomy and architecture that is marveled at by modern scientific thought. Yet they surely both spring from the same source, from the same minds. Is archaic thought unfathomable, hopelessly contradictory? Or is there something very wrong in the way we perceive it? An investigation into what constitutes "archaic" must be attempted. It is a difficult concept for us to digest but, for the archaic mind, myth and empirical science were not opposed, but worked in harmony. How else can we explain their fascination with precise measurements in astronomy, architecture and mathematics? How could a mind that believed an owl or coyote was a long-lost relative also devise the concept of zero and plot the stars accurately for 26,000 years? Yet the notion that there is a reality that transcends empirical knowledge persists.

The purpose of myth, after all, was to make the world intelligible to man. Myth provided the answer to philosophical questions of origins, purpose, and place. Questions which science and philosophy no longer try to answer. More importantly myth was man's attempt to reconcile the conflicting principles of matter and spirit. Through myth man's spirit participated in the great physical events of creation and destruction. Through myth man played a part in the great celestial events that determined his destiny. Yet myth did not arise so much from need as it did from observation of the skies and of heaven. For it was there, in the visible heavens that man saw the dramatic interplay of flux and constancy.

To archaic man this drama was divine. The players, the sun, moon, and stars were living entities, like himself. They contained spirit, hope and despair, like himself. And like himself, they could be vengeful, cruel, kind, life preserving and life taking. Why did mythical man spend so much time gazing at the stars? Because, unlike us, he didn't see them as cold mechanical objects, so distant as to be irrelevant. He had been schooled under a far different frame of reference. He saw them as gods, angry and just, benevolent and wrathful, inhabiting celestial realms.

Mythical man's interest in the stars verged on the fanatical. Was his eyesight superior to ours? Probably. Did he possess instruments that made knowledge of the heavens a more precise science? Probably. Did he live in an

7.P. URKESH. (Persian Seal). The ancient Hurrian people of what is now Syria had a myth of a boy, Silver, who believed that he had no father. One day, when his mother thought Silver had grown old enough, she told him that his true father was Kumarbi, father of all gods, and that Kumarbi could be found in the sacred city of Urkesh. The myth involved Silver's quest to find his father, and although he never succeeded, his father was reported to be in the mountains to the north, he finds Urkesh and his father's people.

Based on the myth, two Los Angeles based archaeologists, Marilyn Kelly-Buccellati and Giorgio Buccellati, began excavating a site near the present day village of Tell Mozan in 1983. In the summer of 1995 they found cylinder-shaped seals, the size of a small finger, marked by Sumerian words that identified the site as Urkesh. These personal seals identified the king of this radiocarbon dated 4,300-year-old site as Tupkish, its queen, Uqnitum. The seals from this city-state of an estimated 20,000 people are similar to those found at Ur in Sumer (Iraq), and also to the fired clay cylinders still used in South America.[53] Silver's tale, according to the Buccellatis, symbolized the mining of metals in the mountains and their journey to the markets of Urkesh. But myths really were never that mundane. Our interpretation is that Silver represented his people in a quest for their origins. Silver, fatherless, represented the forgotten memories of a race of people.

The Los Angeles Times called the physical discovery of Urkesh, long considered mythical, "somewhat akin to finding the lost world of Atlantis."[58] They are right. But what the Buccellatis found was but one piece of an immense puzzle.

environment without pollutants to diminish the night skies? Definitely. Regarding the celestial bodies in their movements across the heavens ancient man could experience a sense of order and grandeur, predictability and wonder. Imbued with life they represented a stately procession of the spirit that man could experience directly. It is little wonder that man sought to measure their movements, record them, predict them, exult in them, and in rare instances, sacrifice to them. Thus mythical man, in harmony with the cosmos, was able to participate in "ultimate" events. And he was, by the power of myth, more than just a watcher, man was the geometer, the conscious mind through which the movements and activities of the heavens could be understood.

Archaic man was not very different from modern man in one respect. His fondest hope was that everything would run predictably and smoothly. Legends of great events were fine fare for the storytellers, but no one was anxious to witness their recreation. The Golden Age, after all, was a time of perfect equilibrium. Myth ended as the dominant force in life when society became too big, kings refused to die, and societies wanted to reign through eternity. Transformation of the individual was rejected. Kings and leaders wanted their legacy to survive. They sought to overthrow the basic law of nature, individual man's immediate access to the gods, and to make the world fixed and eternal, according to their rules. A new myth was born—The "Myth of Authority" of Church and State. If myth is misconception, then the new "myth" surely has met that criteria.

Under the "myth of authority" the biblical story of Noah and his Ark, while disregarded as literal history, or an exaggeration, has nevertheless provided a focal starting point for a straight and continuous line of human development for mankind under Judaic-Christian authority. In truth a story so widespread must be based on a factual event, probably under-exaggerated because modern man has been unable to grasp the worldwide destruction of the deluge. And because it is so widespread a myth it cannot support any one line of authority. Especially one, that while maintaining temporal and material power, has insisted it has a "divine right" to do so (fig. 7Q).

The voyages of Columbus seemingly created a new "myth": that the Age of Discovery, as we call it, created the *first* links between the Old and the New World and gave birth to worldwide navigation. Out of this mistaken view came world-wide domination, engendered by the tall ships of the English, the Dutch, the Spanish, the Portuguese, and even the Germans: Colonialism, as the vessel of civilized laws and authority. We've called this new authority not only "The Age of Discovery," but the "Age of Reason." Yet it appears that all Eurocentric man was doing was substituting new myths for the old.

7.Q. SEATED FIGURE. Quirigua, Guatemala. As José Arguelles puts it in *The Maya Factor,* "The myth of scientific progress and technological superiority could receive no greater blow than to discover that a more advanced civilization existed prior to the rise of the myth of progress, practiced by a people who, by modern estimation, were still in the Stone Age."[61]

"Substituting" is, of course, not the correct word. Closer to the truth are words such as "genocide" and "forced extinction."

On the American continent a new "myth" within the frameworks of the European "myth," took hold: the myth of American superiority. The great American Myth was engendered by the resourcefulness displayed by the hearty descendants of European immigrants in subduing what they thought was a vast virgin wilderness. Actually that "wilderness" had been civilized, if not "subdued," at least 30,000 years before Columbus, and probably had a population throughout the Americas of over 40 million people when these most recent wave of explorers arrived. It had sustained sophisticated and stable civilizations in the Ohio and Mississippi valleys for thousands of years before the coming of the Europeans (mound builders of the Hopewell and Memphis cultures). And it had been linked to a great navigational center in Mesoamerica.

The "myth" of authority could have no greater champion than that engendered by the voyages of Charles Darwin aboard the "Sea Beagle" and the subsequent publication of Darwin's doctrine of evolution and natural selection—although clearly, this theory has been used in ways Darwin would have considered unimaginable. In fact, Darwin's observation of "survival of the fittest" is now no longer theory. It is a belief of mythical proportions. Every authoritarian ruler, every tyrant, indeed, and every successful business man can justify his or their position, no matter how ignobly achieved, as just as things should be. The "fittest" have survived and inherited the world. Yet the true record of man and the emerging lessons of Chaos Science reveal that the "fittest," in Darwinian terms, are not always the survivors. There is a greater game being played in the cosmos than the theories of Darwin and his followers can imagine.

How do we finally define myth? Myth as a container of truth has an arbiter that no authority can repress—it is the measure of time. The particular "myth" of the triumph American ingenuity against great odds in subduing and conquering North America already is failing that test. The John Wayne movies and Zane Grey novels that depicted handfuls of heroic men overcoming great odds to subdue a barbaric and untamed land are really no longer taken at anything resembling historical reality. The tremendous success of *Dances with Wolves,* which portrays a caring and pastoral Native American tribe being pursued by a relentless and brutish U.S. Army, demonstrates that we in the west might finally be ready to adopt a more enlightened view of our history and our (lack of) purpose. We still hold on to a myth central to Western thinking—that of American superiority, although this "myth," an inherited relic of British colonialism, is sustainable only by the ultimate shield of authoritarianism—a superior war machine.

Myth has moved armies, built civilizations, destroyed others, and has rebuilt civilizations from distant memory (figs. 7R, 7S). Myth has kept a record of man's deeds and his ideas. The stories contained in true myth are often terrible, sometimes cataclysmic. They most often refer to an authority over events which any given state or church, at any given time, cannot control. It is really no wonder that the first item of business of any scientific regime

7.R. THE SWASTIKA. This Indo-Persian cross, depicting a steady wind at the back of the cardinal points was a symbol of "good luck" for navigators. In one of the most sordid chapters in history's most sordid century, Adolph Hitler attempted to create an Aryan "myth" of superiority and destiny. Seizing on ancient symbols, like the swastika, utilizing the music of Wagner and the philosophy of Nietzsche, artists in touch with true myth, Hitler hoped to provide a conduit to a "mythical" past. The Nazi conduit to myth had nothing to do with true myth, man's interaction with the cosmos, but instead foisted a terrible and authoritarian rule on a people who no longer had any belief in myth, but were simply looking for an avenue to power and revenge. We must distinguish between myth that endures and may truly be called Myth and myth that cannot endure, but for a brief time has its own, often ugly, "usefulness."

has been to discard all previous knowledge as myth, just as the first order of business of any religion has been to reject past religions as pagan idol worshippers whose gods should be rejected and destroyed and whose remaining followers should be laughed at, stoned, persecuted, or executed. What any society, itself bereft of a coherent myth, cannot tolerate is knowledge of true myth.

When we refer to the "myth" of unlimited resources waiting to be exploited or to the "myth" of white supremacy we must ask this question—how is the term to be used? If myth was a vessel of truth and intuitive knowledge among the ancients how has it come to be known as a misguided and intrinsically flawed belief? In common use today it is almost invariably the latter, but there is no other adequate term to accurately describe the veracity and integrity it once represented. Substituting legend for myth begs the question. Legend and myth after all have their own meanings, with legend referring to a specific event, a singular act of heroism, while myth refers to an intrinsic belief, a cosmic background, in which a legend can find its particular glory. There is and there has been, both a legend and a myth of Atlantis. Mere legends did not build the ancient world. It was the belief in myth, the forces of chaos, and the divine and uncertain dance in the ordered cosmos, that both predated and necessitated great cultures and their constructions.

7.S. THE MALTESE CROSS. At Palenque, Chiapas, author George Erikson points to the record, written in stone, of a Maltese Cross on a wall which was constructed circa 100 B.C. Earlier dates of this symbol of navigation have been found throughout the Americas (see also figs. 1R, 1S in Chapter 1).

8 The Serpent and the Cross

"Our only measure of truth is . . . our perception of truth. The undeniable tradition of metamorphosis teaches us that things do not remain always the same. They become other things by swift and unanalysable process. It was only when men began to mistrust the myths and tell nasty lies for a moral purpose that these matters became hopelessly confused."

—Ezra Pound

"The best lack all conviction, while the worst are full of passionate intensity."
—The Second Coming, W.B. Yeats

A DISASTER IS OCCURRING. Not in a single day or a single night, but in a wave of ignorance, warfare and retribution reign on the land. The sky is darkened by the terrible acts of men. Should they not know better? The old ways are being forgotten. Bloody sacrifice is everywhere. The people are tired of wars. They are walking away from their cities.

•

The Serpent and the Cross are both symbols of knowledge. The Serpent repeats itself throughout diverse ancient cultures and myth as a symbol of power and knowledge. In Mesoamerica, as in India, it was also the symbol of the benevolent god. The Cross similarly has represented knowledge and power. The Maltese Cross (figs. 1R, 7R) has generally been interpreted as knowledge and power in the four directions; the Christian Cross was meant to carry a message of kindness and forgiveness of sins. But the truth often poses

189

a threat to power. And the Cross under the medieval Church became the antithesis of knowledge and benevolence.

These powerful symbols clashed head-on in the sixteenth century in the Americas. The Cross, carried by the conquistadors and a vast array of following adventurers, prevailed. But the followers of the Cross were not independent rogues. They all had to answer to the Crown and to the Church. The Crown wanted gold. The Church wanted converts, as well as gold. Hernando Cortez provided the needed conquest. His soldiers and their adjuncts admirably satisfied the needs of the Holy Office in Spain. But a few priests, consigned to take the Holy word to the pagans, instead brought the pagan's words back to Spain. (see Chapter 2).

Bernardino de Sahagun had arrived in the Yucatán in 1529. He learned the Nahuatl language and, instead of being shocked by what he learned of these people, he was simply curious. He undertook to record everything he could of them, and he enlisted their friendship and aid in this undertaking.[1] From all of his informants Sahagun and his Indian scribes composed a twelve-volume codex (now called the Florentine Codex) describing every aspect of Aztec life, from descriptions of the foods they ate, to their obsession with astronomy, counting, religion, and how they buried their dead—usually entombed with a piece of jade in their mouths to serve as a heart in their next lives (figs 8A, 8B, 8C).[2]

Sahagun also learned that the Aztecs were relatively recent arrivals, having conquered the far more developed Toltec culture only a few hundred years before. The war-like Aztecs, having migrated from the northwest, had a sense of wonder for the people they had conquered. They had arrived in the central valley of Mexico having little idea of mathematics or architecture, but instead of simply destroying the Toltec culture, they copied it and learned Toltec con-

8A-C. JADE PIECES. Two Olmec jade pieces (a reclining figure [left], *La Venta,* and a jade "dragon spoon" from Costa Rica) and a Shang Chinese K'uei dragon (right). Friar Sahagun probably did not know that the Olmecs also put a rounded jade piece in the mouths of their dead before burial, nor that jade was used to depict dragon gods associated with water, Earth, and royalty. He certainly did not have any inkling that the same jade was highly revered in China where it stood for water, caves and the emperor. Nor could he have likely known that the word jade meant "precious" in both languages. Jade, traditionally highly prized in China, does not naturally appear anywhere in that country. Either the Chinese discovered it elsewhere or someone introduced it to them. The uses and symbolism of jade in Mesoamerica and China, in ancient times, exceeds coincidence.[3]

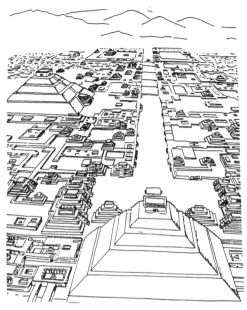

8.D. A RECONSTRUCTION OF THE CENTRAL EXCAVATED CITY-STATE OF TEOTIHUACAN. The Pyramid of the Moon is at the center. The Pyramid of the Sun is to the left. Friar Sahagun describes a Nahuatl legend that the Valley of Mexico was peopled by a people who originated from the south, in a land called Tamoanchan, "where they devised the count of years, the book of dreams." From the teachings of these ancient peoples—whose knowledge included the concept of zero—sprang the civilization of Teotihuacan and its monumental pyramids and observatories dedicated to the sun and the moon.

cepts. Rather than vanquish the peaceful Toltec gods, they incorporated them into their beliefs, and made them equal to their own gods of war.

Sahagun described Teotihuacan, as a city-state built by the Toltecs (though they had only come to conquer it long after its construction by the unknown Teotihuacans), and in a manner that resembled the Greek colony of Alexandria. Teotihuacan, the present site of the ruins of the Pyramid of the Sun and the Pyramid of the Moon, had flourished for thousands of years, and then had been abandoned in the sixth century A.D. Yet the Aztec priests Sahagun encountered had a very clear memory of it, even though the Aztecs had arrived in the central valley of Mexico much later than the Toltecs, probably in the fourteenth-century. Teotihuacan had been a city devoted to learning, to scientists and philosophers, and to the recording of accumulated astronomical and mythological knowledge. It also was known as the burial place of kings, where those who died became gods, ascended into the heavens fig. 8D). Death rites include the use of the sacred mushroom ("the flesh of God"), and water rites that resembled Christian baptism.[4]

Disturbing as this information might have been, the Church faced a potentially more devastating revelation. Similar to the foundation myths, the Aztecs (Nahuatl) also described a far more recent arrival by sea, that of the Toltec god Quetzalcoatl, the law giver. Quetzalcoatl, the Serpent god, forbade the sacrifice of humans and animals and taught a doctrine of brotherly love. His arrival has been variously described as from 2,000 to 1,400 years before present (but some accounts put his arrival at shortly after the deluge). Through Sahagun, the Church learned that the Serpent God of these people was not a monster, as they'd presumed, but a man—a very curious man. Depicted almost universally as tall and bearded and as having come on a ship from across the sea to the east, Quetzalcoatl, The Plumed Serpent, appears to have been half man, half legend. His beard by some is said to have been blond, red by others, and black in other accounts. Those who say he walked the Earth at the time of Christ give him Semitic features and a swarthy complexion. Aryans say he was fair-skinned and blue-eyed. Those who favor his arrival from Ireland say his skin was green. Those who say he came from Atlantis say he was a giant and that his skin was red.

By some accounts he was a king, in others he was the Wind God. But all accounts of Quetzalcoatl agree that he was first and foremost a teacher.

8.E. ATLANTEANS AT TULA. Greek myth describes Atlas as supporting the world. Mayan sites portray Atlanteans supporting the heavens. Could there be a connection? When we look at the great astronomical constructions of Mesoamerica we are looking at a continuation of the belief in myth. The first female child of Atlas, the first king of Atlantis, was named Maya. In the temples of Mesoamerica a constancy with Myth, a belief in the magical, the eternal, and man's connection with one through the other, endures. And it survives even today.

Quetzalcoatl taught his followers math and astronomy and the secrets of temple building. He was a great law-giver and so loved all life that he couldn't bear to hear of harm to any animal. He respected the peoples' belief in sacrifice but he advised them to sacrifice only snails, flowers and butterflies, never other humans. But his main teaching was of compassion and love for humanity. Quetzalcoatl gave the Indians maize and taught them all their crafts. He walked throughout southern Mexico teaching the merits of brotherly love and forgiveness of sins. He related how he had been tempted by demons wanting him to sacrifice a human heart so his people could be spared of a cataclysm. But he had abstained from their deceit and treachery, and it was the demons who were vanquished.

According to legend Quetzalcoatl was also tempted by wine, sex, and the desire for glory in battle. Quetzalcoatl was able to overcome all the temptations. But Tezcatlipoca, Quetzalcoatl's opposite force, poisoned the food of Quetzalcoatl's followers in Tula (fig. 8E), and then disguised himself as an old woman toasting delicious maize. The maize had been drugged by Tezcatlipoca, and the starving Tulalans were soon in a stupor and easily slain.

Aggrieved, Quetzalcoatl realized that deification could come only through suffering. He burned his gold and coral houses and cast his treasures into the water. Deprived of all worldly riches he set out on foot to find Anahuac, the "place at the center, in the midst of the circle" (Anahuac has also been translated as "the land between the waters").[5] In all, it bears a striking resemblance to Plato's description of Poseidon, the capital of Atlantis. Quetzalcoatl, originally the gift giver, had now become the man of suffering. At the onset of his journey he was followed by thousands. But when he entered the mountains only a few hunchbacks and dwarfs remained at his side. He cherished his following but they died of cold following Quetzalcoatl up through the pass between the volcanoes, Popocatepetl, and Iztactepetl.

After he left, Quetzalcoatl's legend grew. Those that believed in his teachings but had not followed him on his journey built temples at Tollan, and in other Toltec cities, in recognition of Quetzalcoatl. The great pyramid at Cholula is said by early European witnesses to have been adorned at its summit by a jade statute of Quetzalcoatl several feet in height.[6]

Recently, at Tula, deciphered codices describe a conflict between the Toltec priests at Tollan. Dissatisfied with a prolonged drought and upset about recent military losses, some of the priesthood called for a return of human sacrifice. But the older priesthood, still loyal to Quetzalcoatl, rejected the idea of human sacrifice. After much turmoil the older priests quit Tollan. They were accompanied by a large following of the common people, unhappy about the conditions the drought had inflicted on their marginal lives, and

8.F. GREAT BALL COURT AT CHICHEN ITZA. Quetzalcoatl spent many years wandering and teaching. He and his followers built ball courts and temples throughout Mesoamerica.[8]

displeased with the authority of the state. Thus a vast migration of the Toltecs, loyal to the humanitarian teachings of Quetzalcoatl, was underway, culminating in their reunification with him in the Yucatán (fig. 8F).[7]

Legend states that one day Quetzalcoatl sailed away to the east on a raft of Serpents. It would appear that the handsome Tezcatlipoca, the Lord of the Material World, and Quetzalcoatl's nemesis, had triumphed over him. But the Nahuatl reading of these events differs. They say it was the Plumed Serpent who finally triumphed because he had learned how to fly, and he had risen above the material possessions of the world.

When Quetzalcoatl left he promised to return from the sea "to judge the living and the dead". He promised that return in the year and on the day of 1 Reed, a date that recurs once every fifty-two years. It was by chance that on this day, in the Christian calendar, April 22, of the year 1519 A.D., that Hernando Cortez's ships arrived in Mexico.[9]

Thus only ten years before Sahagun had arrived to tell their tale to the Church and record their history, the Aztecs had faced their moment of truth—the return of Quetzalcoatl. Though fearful, they thought they were welcoming the gentle Toltec Serpent-God. Instead they were greeting the Cross of the Inquisition. Death and destruction would soon follow.

What could Montezuma have thought on hearing that Quetzalcoatl had returned? Of course it is pure speculation to attribute motives to people long gone, but it is easy to conjecture that his reaction was not one of joy. The Aztecs were not the people who had been taught by Quetzalcoatl, not the ones who had followed him through personal sacrifice, not the ones on whom he'd bestowed undying kindness and love. They were the usurpers, the conquerors of the Toltecs and their gods. They were the borrowers of gods of an earlier, more sophisticated, navigational culture—about which they knew very little.

Yet they believed in Quetzalcoatl, and they sacrificed to him. And that in itself was a serious problem. Quetzalcoatl had taught that sacrifice was wrong.

Some Aztecs believed that their "borrowed" god, Quetzalcoatl, was right about the evils of sacrifice. Yet when turmoil presented itself, when the sun god was out of sorts, they could not refrain from appeasing their own angry gods with the sacrifice of a youth. After all, Quetzalcoatl was only the wind god, an idealist, not the giver and taker of life itself! But he was still a god. He had great powers. And he had reason for great anger.

Hernando Cortez displayed this "god-like" anger when he arrived at Cholula in 1519 on his march from the sea to the fabled Aztec capital of Tenochtitlán (fig.8G). But his anger was not an expression of the god's dismay at human deviance from the rules of heaven. His anger was one of defiance of the gods, and of any order of the heavens. Under a jade image of Quetzalcoatl,

8.G. PALENQUE. THE "Temple of Inscriptions," containing the tomb of Pacal Votan. The Spaniards were correct in their assumption that the pyramids had not been built, original-ly, by the Aztecs. But the Spanish conclusion, that they were built by devils, was absurd. The pyramids were built by a great and ancient people, perhaps a synthesis of many races, at a time when navigators ruled the world.

8.H. QUETZALCOATL. The Mayans had another name for Quetzalcoatl. They called him Kukulcan, which in their language means the Plumed Serpent. He was the same person, the bearded and loving teacher, and the same Wind God. The Incas called him Viracocha, and said he was white, bearded and lived in the great age before the Deluge. Viracocha and his followers built the great megalithic structures at Tiahuanacu and at Sacsayhuaman above Cuzco, and taught their people astronomy and all the arts and sciences. All had promised their return. And for the peoples of the Americas, involved incessantly with calendars both daily and celestial, their return was anticipated with both hope and dread. But it was mapped out daily just as the constant movement of the stars were mapped. In the *Bhagavad Gita* Krishna is described as having appeared to Arjuna as Garuda, the flying Serpent. The Serpent is knowledge. At first it strikes us as something terrible, beyond our control. But to the even and experienced mind we can come to regard it as a friend, a tool, and even as a deliverance.

set in the center of the Cholula pyramid, Cortez and his men slaughtered over 6,000 Cholulans.[10]

After the massacre at Cholula (fig. 2D) became known throughout the Aztec Empire, Cortez and his four hundred men had an easy path to Tenochtitlán and the Aztec emperor, Montezuma. A cowered Montezuma vacillated between his perception of Cortez as the second coming of Quetzalcoatl, and his recognition of Cortez as a brute. Before he could make up his mind, Montezuma, and many of nobles, were slain. Montezuma's faithful guard turned on the Spaniards, killing and wounding many, but somehow the Spanish were able to escape to Teotihuacán, site of the pyramids of the Sun and the Moon. The Spaniards regrouped and, during months of recruiting, enlisted tribes that had suffered under Aztec rule. They returned a year later to destroy Tenochtitlán, leaving a quarter of a million people dead from wounds, starvation or disease. Those Aztecs who survived the Spanish onslaught may have met a worse fate. They were enslaved, branded on their foreheads, and subjected to torture, rape, and every form of abuse the Spaniards could think of.[11]

It is ironic and tragic that the man the Aztecs mistook for Quetzalcoatl, the teacher of brotherly love, the abhorrer of sacrifice or any form of harm to living beings, would turn out to be a slaughterer and torturer of human life (fig. 8H).

Of course, neither Cortez nor the Church had any understanding of the nature of Quetzalcoatl when Cortez pillaged Cholula and Tenochtitlán. Nor did they know of the Mayan Serpent god, Kukulcan, nor did they know the nature of the Inca god Viracocha, whose golden calendar had been melted down by Pizarro's soldiers, and shipped back to Spain. It would take four decades for this information, largely supplied by Friar Sahagun to reach Spain. But when it did it arrived like the first thunderclap of a gathering storm.

Quetzalcoatl's flight from oppression and injustice, recorded in the Codex Anales de Cuauhtilan (preserved by Sahagun), mirrored the story of Moses and his people's flight from Egypt, but with a significant twist—knowledge of a personality that forbade human sacrifice to the gods already existed in Mesoamerica. The people and their leading priests were willing to emigrate from their land in defense of the teachings of Quetzalcoatl, not in anticipation of him. This version of mankind's history put knowledge of the savior (Quetzalcoatl) ahead of knowledge of the deliverer (the unnamed equivalent of Moses).

The similarities between the story of Quetzalcoatl and the Jewish legend of Enoch, son of Cain, could not have been lost on the Church. Just as Quetzalcoatl's followers had frozen on the mountain pass of Popocatepetl, Enoch's followers had perished in snow and hailstones at the spot were Enoch ascended into heaven.[12] Indeed, Tenochtitlán, the Aztec capital and the city founded to honor Quetzalcoatl means "land of Tenoch." Could Tenoch have been an earlier name for Quetzalcoatl? Could the Nauatl language with its penchant for prefixing Ts on important place names have changed Enoch, the city founded by the son of Cain, to Tenoch?[13] In sixteenth century Europe speculation abounded that the Americas were the land in which the banished Cain had eventually settled. If so, Cain would have to have become a seafarer.

The parallels to Sumerian, Persian, and Indic legends are every bit as compelling. In Iran the followers of the epic hero Kai Khusrau, and the five palladins, are left to perish in a snowstorm as Kai Khusrau ascends the Ivory throne to Heaven.[14] In the Hindu epic, the *Mahabbarata*, when Yudhishthira sets out on a pilgrimage in the mountains the citizens of his city follow him for some distance. He sends them back and thereafter is followed only by his wife and his four brothers. They—like the five followers of Enoch, the five followers of Kai Khusrau, and the followers of Quetzalcoatl—perish while Yudhishthira "entered Heaven in his mortal body, not having tasted death."[15]

Could such parallel legends develop among widely geographically divided peoples in antiquity without contact? What the Church faced was a realiza-

8.I. MOHENJO-DARO'S CIRCULAR CITADEL. Indus valley.[16] Until the discovery of Dravidian people of the Indus valley 50 years ago, pre-Aryans were considered primitive. History had taught us that Aryan invasions of India 1750-1400 BC imposed the rule of civilization on a spiritually and materially inferior people. After many years of excavation at Mohenjo Daro, Harrapa, and other Dravidian sites along the Indus valley we now know they have had a far more advanced civilization than their Aryan conquerors.[17]

tion that the contacts, or the common origin, could have occurred long before the date they had given to the creation of the world (fig. 8I).

Sahaguns' intense interest in recording the record of the Aztec people, and their legends of a far earlier people, was more than upsetting to the Church authorities. The Church was not pleased at reading Sahagun's' descriptions, particularly the concepts of trial on Earth followed by the promise of a happy afterlife. Only the Church could promise that. In the eyes of the Inquisition Quetzalcoatl could well have been a Jesus to rival Jesus (see facing page). Jesus of Nazareth, offering direct communion with God to his followers, was himself one Jesus too many for the Inquisition. Thus, when the time came, the Church of Rome, unable to truly follow the teachings of Jesus, did not turn the other cheek when confronted with heretics.

In the Yucatán, the Church had another problem. A Franciscan friar, Diego de Landa, arrived in the heartland of the Maya in 1549. The friar, unlike so many of his contemporaries, was deeply interested in the language and customs of the Mayas he encountered. He lived with the Maya, learned their language, and came to respect them for their temperance, quiet courage, and expression of mutual cooperation. He loved their occupation and preoccupation with tended gardens, planted fields, and cultivated rows of fruit trees. He admired their carefully built and well-kept houses. Landa visited their great cities and was in awe of the dazzling architectural achievements. He wrote back to the holy fathers in Spain that these were not savages, but people who displayed Christian virtues.

Landa became the guardian of a Catholic convent at the once important Mayan site of Izamal near Merida. There he continued to study the codices (hieroglyphic picture books) of the Maya. Of the pyramids Landa would later write (in *Relación de las Cosas de Yucatán*) "there are in Yucatán many edifices of great beauty, this being the most outstanding of all things discovered in the Indies; they are all built of stone and finely ornamented, though there is no metal found in the country for this cutting."

We may safely surmise that it was not the Indians' penchant for idol worship or even for sacrifice that so disturbed the Holy Office. It was astonishing reports, such as those by Landa, of great cities, ancient temples, beautiful gardens, lush vegetation—in short, all that Plato had described as part of the Atlantis and the Golden Age. It was not worship of the Serpent that the Church feared, it was the knowledge that the Serpent God, Quetzalcoatl, represented that shook the Church to its foundation.

If the existence of heretical thought and the worship of idols were perceived as a threat by the Church how much more so was the information that in a distant land there may be vestiges of a distinct civilization that was far older and, possibly, far more advanced than any found the bible? Could the Holy Fathers appreciate the brilliance of a civilization that pre-dated their authority?

"The Grand Inquisitor"

WILLING SACRIFICE is not anti-Christian unless you consider Jesus Christ anti-Christian. The Inquisitors probably did. In one of the most poignant chapters of one the greatest works of this century, *The Brothers Karamazov,* Fyodor Dostoyevsky describes what would happen if Jesus returned to Earth. In the chapter titled, "The Grand Inquisitor," Jesus returns and appears in Spain during the Inquisition. At first His presence is doubted. But His acts reveal His true identity. He appears before the Grand Inquisitor who is sympathetic and compassionate but cannot understand why Jesus has come back. The Grand Inquisitor decides, regretfully, that there isn't room on Earth for both the Church and Jesus Christ. Jesus is again condemned to his original fate.

Would knowledge then of the nature of Quetzalcoatl have changed the Church's outlook on the Americans? Could it in any way have altered the savage treatment, the destruction? It seems unlikely. If Dostoyevsky's view is correct, even Christ himself could not have changed the aims or conduct of the Inquisition. In fact, knowledge of the nature of Quetzalcoatl only intensified the Church's antagonism.

What the Church faced was the realization that the legend of Quetzalcoatl was part of the fabric of all ancient myths that had preceded Christianity, from the creation tales, the deluge myths, Tower of Babel parallels, the partaking of the flesh and blood of the one who sacrifices himself, to descriptions of his journeys, and his promise to return.

But the Church was accustomed to dealing with infidels. With the help of the mercenary, El Cid, they had overthrown the civil Moors in Spain. Throughout the long Inquisition (1252-1834 A.D.) they had persecuted the infidels, burned their books of science, astronomy, and mathematics. And then they had taken their land. But in the case of the Plumed Serpent, the threat occurred in a part of the world over which the Church had no control. An advanced civilization on a far continent was a serious problem for the Church. The real fear was that the Serpent God was not some easily dismissed terror in the garden of Eden, but the symbol of an ancient way of knowledge, reining over the peoples of the Earth for thousands of years.

The Church met this challenge swiftly and decisively. Sahagun's writings were burned, and Teotihuacan, which like Alexandria, had been subject to much destruction and many burnings, was razed again. But some knowledge of the old ways remained hidden from authorities. From these tales Sahagun recorded the legends of Tollan, the legendary city of the Toltecs, with its beautiful temples, gardens, and palaces. The great city had been deserted, at the urging of Quetzalcoatl, and left to decay and face destruction at the hands of its enemies, who toppled the monuments, and desecrated its temples. Tollan has never been found, but its legend and memory have never been completely erased.

Sahagun was effectively censored (somehow one copy of Sahagun's observations survived the attacks). And somewhere in his complicated life Frey de Landa, changed his views and decided that the great monuments had been built by the devil, and that the books of the Maya contained the devils teaching. He stripped the pyramids of their fine ornamentation. He publicly destroyed over 5,000 idols and thirteen great stone altars, then had the pyramid at Izamal dismantled. With its stones he built a fortress-cathedral for his monks. Landa then systematically gathered all the Mayan books in the Yucatán, which he burned in the public square of Mani, south of Merida.[18]

For his efforts Landa was made Bishop of the Yucatán. There is little doubt that orders from the Church in Spain, and possibly offers of a position he eventually assumed, had changed Landa's opinion of the Mayan culture.

Likewise, Juan de Zumarraga, Bishop of Mexico, was under orders from the Church to exterminate witches, works of witches, idols, and temples of evil (fig. 8K). Zumarraga "boasted of having destroyed 500 Indian temples and 20,000 idols. On Sunday, November 30, 1530, Zumarraga had Don Carlo

8.K THE GREAT CENOTE AT CHICHEN ITZA. In 1890, Edward Thompson, backed by meat processor Allison Armour, acquired (for the equivalent of $75) and began excavation of one hundred square miles of Mayan ruins, including the rich site of Chichen Itza and its nearby cenote, the source of the Mayan city's water supply. Thompson had long been fascinated by Bishop de Landa's reports of the sacred cenote as the scene of sacrifices by the Maya of hundreds, perhaps thousands, of young virgins, as a means of divining the prospects for the coming year. De Landa claimed that the practice of virgin sacrifice was still going on during his tenure in the Yucatán. Thompson received a grant from Harvard's Peabody Museum. From 1903 to 1907 he oversaw an extensive dredging of the forty feet of mud that lay at the bottom of the cenote's 180 foot wide base. His team was able to discover a vast array of jade, copper, and gold artifacts, more than enough to satisfy his sponsors. These ended up in the Peabody museum and in the hands of wealthy private collectors. But excavations in the cenote at Chichen Itza revealed that fewer than fifty human skeletons were found. Most of these were children, who, we can presume, played too close to the steep sided walls, fell in, and could not escape. Later excavations by divers with current equipment, in the 1970s and 1980s, including those of adventurer, Robert Marx, resulted in the discovery of more artifacts, but no more skeletons. The discovery of only fifty skeletons of children from a culture that contained as many as 50,000 inhabitants and existed for almost two thousand years means that the children must have been, as a rule, very careful around the cenote. But what happened to the skeletal remains of all those virgins? Were they a figment of de Landa's imagination, or just an excuse, a rational for the destruction of a culture?[20]

Ometochtzín, lord of Texcoco, publicly burned at the stake in Mexico City's Plaza Mayor, accused of having worshipped the god of rain. In the market place of Texcoco, Zumarraga had a pyramid formed of the documents of Aztec history, knowledge, and literature, their paintings, manuscripts, and hieroglyphic writings, all of which he committed to the flames while the natives cried and prayed.

"Into the holocaust went the codified laws of Texcoco's King Netzahualcoyotl, who had reigned in Texcoco a century before the arrival of Cortes and had acquired the reputation of a Solomon distinguished for his courage, wisdom, and virtue, a reined astronomer and lover of plants and animals, who had composed sixty hymns in praise of the creator of heaven."[21] Codices, books, inscribed artifacts, all were melted down for their gold, or burned to ash.

Justified by tales of pagan sacrifice, the extracting of the human heart from a live, and probably young, and innocent victim—often peppered with stories of Aztec priests dining on the warm, severed hearts of children—the Church began a systematic destruction of not only a people, but of the history and memory of that people. The Church did not rule out the possibility of an Atlantis and of a Golden Age. They simply sought to eradicate all possible memory of such an age.

Inexorably the Church and Spanish state pressed on in their destruction of the Aztec capital of Tenochtitlán. The city was torn to pieces by captured Indian slaves so that no stones of the once magnificent citadel were left standing. Peter Tompkins describes the events in *Mysteries of the Mexican Pyramids*. "Palaces, columns, and gods were buried in the mud. To avoid the stench of the dead, the Spaniards set up camp in the nearby village of Coyoacan. Groups of captive Indians razed every last building of the Aztec capital and filled in the canals till not a stone was standing. On the leveled ground Cortes founded his own great capital, Mexico City, patterned on a feudal model already dying in Europe.

"Mexican slaves by the thousands, many of them highly skilled as sculptors, carpenters, masons, and gardeners, hauled stone and timber from the debris of Tenochtitlán. Iron chisels and iron hammers enabled them to cut the porous red stones of the valley into palatial European houses, over the doors of which the new hidalgos could place their carved escutcheons. Where Indian palaces and pyramids had stood, Churches and monasteries sprang up complete with battlements, and heavy grilled windows against the Indians who had built them.

"Surviving on drinking water and a few tortillas, the Indians, at their own expense, supplied all the work and al the material. Brought up from childhood to a Spartan life, trained to endure pain, they worked long hours without showing fatigue, constantly subjected to unbelievable savagery by the Spaniards.

"Individuals were torn from their families to work as slaves in gold and silver mines, branded on their faces each time they changed masters. The prettier women were raped and infected with the pox, smallpox, leprosy, and all manner of plagues. By 1545, in Tlaxcala alone, a quarter of a million had died of the plague; altogether 3 million were to die as the disease spread to Tabasco and Yucatán. As a result of the Spanish conquest, the population of Mexico was reduced to one-tenth of its pre-conquest size. Indians, formerly in good health, were weakened by hunger and fatigue and became easy prey to disease."[21]

Scenes of brutality repeated themselves throughout the Americas. Mass genocide was the rule. Civilizations and their records were destroyed, slaughtered, diseased, and in the end, simply erased. Sahagun related how he had witnessed the introduction of the plague by the Spanish and how he had personally buried more than 10,000 victims, all Indian, often in great trenches 100 at a time."[22] The Caribes of the Antilles died out as a race. In Costa Rica the population was decimated. Today, only a few scattered indigenous people remain on widely scattered reservations.

Of course it has always been necessary for conquering nations to impose their customs, laws, and religions on the peoples conquered. Authority has been predicated on complete submission to new government. Torture and death of those who rebel has only been part of the story. Ruthless eradication of the memory of prior cultures has been the rule.

As noted earlier, it took the Catholic Church forty years to decide whether the Indians of the New World were humans or not. But, as unimpressed as they were with the natives of the Americas, they were amazed at the impressive architecture their conquistadors had found. They concluded that the Indians had not built the pyramids and temples and that they were the work of the devil himself. Since the official justification for the conquest of the Americas was the spread of Christianity it was more than convenient for the Spanish to discover the natives were involved with the works of Satan. No cruel or abominable act on their part could be questioned when combating such evil. Certainly not by a controlling Church that sought not only to destroy, but to eradicate the memories and the vestiges of wisdom of all rivals.

The evidence of myth, however compelling, was heresy and was therefore destroyed. Velikovsky spoke of mankind in amnesia—a simple interpretation is that man somehow forgot who he once was, and who he could be again. But mankind did not simply fall into amnesia, *he was pushed*. And on that fallen body of forgotten thought and truth, the figurative backs of ancient man, the fingerprints of the Church of Rome have stood out in temporary triumph over the expression of human memory.

Sacrifice existed to be sure. Otherwise Quetzalcoatl's admonition against human sacrifice, and his decree that sacrifice should be made with butterflies and flowers, not humans, would have been unnecessary. Even the revered Quetzalcoatl was ignored in his pleas.

The truth is sacrifice occurred. But all the evidence indicates that until MesoAmerican cultures were in full decline, human sacrifice was rare, occurring in times of a celestial or terrestrial crisis so great that acts in defiance of Quetzalcoatl, the Serpent God, were enacted. Even then sacrifice was most likely performed with the willing participation of the victims—their path to reunion with the gods. There is much ballyhoo about how the losers of the celestial ballgames at the great Mayan sites of Chichen Itza and Tikal were

8.L. THE BURNING OF THE LIBRARY AT ALEXANDRIA. The famous teacher and philosopher, Hypatia, is seized by Christian mobs near the library at Alexandria. She was stripped naked, dragged into a church, and scrapped to death with oyster shells. Her crime was to have written books on mathematics. Her writings disappeared in the burning of the library in 389 A.D.

It is known that Alexander's maps were kept in the great Library of Alexandria. The library, said to contain over a million individual volumes, was believed to embrace not only the literature but the entire technological and scientific knowledge of the western world. It was partially destroyed by fire when Julius Caesar captured the city. Caesar is reported to have lamented the tragic loss and to have gathered the Egyptians and lectured them harshly on the fruits of their resistance to his conquest. But the Romans had a poor record in such matters, having burned the great library at Carthage to the ground in 146 B.C. and in the process destroying the record of the greatest sea-faring people of the time as well as the roots of the Phonetic language to which we owe our written script. The library at Alexandria was rebuilt only to be totally destroyed by fire four centuries later by mobs following the orders of the Christian emperor Theodosius.[9]

A fading Roman Empire dealt another blow to the record of man in 415 A.D. when Archbishop Cyril ordered that the scholars of the great library at Alexandria were to be flayed alive to the bone with oyster shells. Their remains were then publicly burned with their works and most of the books of the great library. It has been estimated by some scholars that perhaps ninety percent of the knowledge of the ancient world was destroyed in that great fire. Later, the Roman Catholic Church saw fit to make Archbishop Cyril a saint.[23]

Islamic scholars were able to hand copy the few books that survived the burning of the library at Alexandria. Among those preserved were books on Greek and Roman architecture, Euclidean geometry, and instructions for building mechanical ear shifts, steam engines, and water-powered devices. These works enabled the Arabs to build great cities like Cordoba in Spain which had lighted streets, sophisticated plumbing and sewage systems, and great universities while the rest of Europe floundered in the Dark Ages.[24]

punished by having their hearts torn out. But certain readings of these events reveal that it was the *victors* in these games who were sacrificed.

The history of our world is, unfortunately, one long tale of migrations, invasions, war, and inflicted cruelty. In interpreting an understanding of the history of man and his cultures we must distinguish between those who merely conquested and assimilated, later claiming the accomplishments of a defeated culture as their own, and those who tried to obliterate and destroy all vestiges of a defeated culture.

When the soldiers of the Roman Empire, then rising to its peak of power, finally sacked Carthage in 162 B.C., they not only leveled the city and burned every record and every trace of the Phoenician civilization found there, they salted the Earth so that nothing could grow there again. The records of a great seafaring civilization were lost forever. Only their alphabet survives, borrowed by others, to prove that they ever wrote at all. The records of the knowledge of that civilization, one that spanned the globe in trade and intelligent contact, are lost forever.

The burning of libraries and obliteration of knowledge is not an exclusively Christian pastime (fig. 8L). Chinese emperors regularly had the works of past dynasties burned and the memory of any past civilization desecrated and destroyed. The most vigilant of the book burners was Emperor Qi, best known for having commanded the building of the Great Wall, and for having thousands of Terra Cotta soldiers, as well as the soldiers they were patterned after, buried with him at Xian. Now the Great Wall is a marvel—but it is only a *wall*, and the emperor who commanded its building also destroyed the collective record of his people. The present government of China seems equally determined that whatever knowledge is contained in the great pyramids of China should remain locked within. Which legacy would we really rather have? One of rule, or one of reason and knowledge?

The cruelty of the conquistadors was terrible and immense. But what they inflicted on the peoples of the Americas in the name of the sword was but only a continuation of the decimation that had long taken place in the name of Rome and later of the Cross. It was the Serpent gods of the Americans that had been the target of the Church. And the Church successfully crushed both the believers and the belief. What had been ruthlessness under Cortez and other conquistadors, became a systematic eradication under the Church.

The indigenous Americans were so degraded and demoralized in the process that men reportedly would no longer sleep with their wives for fear of bringing children into the world to serve in slavery under the Christians. What had once been both a diverse and a unified culture at Mayan sites and at Teotihuacan, and had later been dispersed into grand warring cities under the

Toltecs and the Aztecs, was now again reunited by their encounter with the Spaniards. They were now united in despair.

The triumph of the Cross over the Serpent in Mesoamerica has resulted in a lost culture, closely linked to a lost science, and a lost way of being human. When we can shed ourselves of the anthropologist's notion that these were illiterate, primitive people, and of the Church's notion that they were pagans and savages, we may begin to learn the nature of the people of the Serpent God.

9 Calendars and Star Temples: *Watchers of the Night Sky*

Astronomy compels the soul to look upwards, and leads us from this world to another.

—PLATO, *The Republic*

The architects of Pre-Columbian America were more fortunate than most of those of Europe. Their masterpieces were never condemned to invisibility, but stood magnificently isolated, displaying their three dimensions to all beholders. European cathedrals were built within the walls of cities: the temples of the aboriginal American seem, in most cases, to have stood outside.

—ALDOUS HUXLEY, *Beyond The Mexique Bay*

What manner of people were the Mayas, to build cities without walls, roads without curves, and numbers without an end?

SEVEN RABBIT *watched the women weaving their cloth of red, yellow, white and his favorite, blue, which was bordered by a thin strip of black. The yellow symbolized the east where the sun rose and where the rabbits and the deer lived in harmony. The red stood for the south, and the white symbolized the north. Each told a story that Seven Rabbit both remembered and anticipated, for they were both past and future and Seven Rabbit was close to both. As close as he was to the sky and the stars. How close he was, he suddenly thought. He could reach out, no, he could leap and touch them. A great leap, but possible. And in doing so he could touch his long lost ancestors. Yes, it was possible.*

A slight earthquake shook the pyramid. Seven Rabbit laughed! He knew his world could not be shaken, because he shared it with the stars who were his gods and his friends. And then Seven Rabbit laughed at that realization. He had once feared the gods, and he had once been angry at them. He had feared them in his youth, that they might take his life, or worse, take those of his family and loved ones, or even worse than that, he later realized, they would somehow find him inadequate while taking his life, or the life of his loved ones. So he had been, and he was, bold and indifferent, so that even if they took his life, they could not touch his spirit. And despite his recklessness and his defiance of the gods, what others called valor, in long sea journeys to the far sides of the world, and in battle, the gods had looked favorably on him. He fared well.

Seven Rabbit had never given any blessing to the gods for his survival. He had only accepted it. But when his parents and his older friends, and some younger, fell to illness and mishap, never to rise again, he became angry at the gods. It had all happened so quickly in his life, that his mother and father and older brother and younger sister had so suddenly been taken from him. For no reason!

Now Seven Rabbit was sitting on top of the pyramid, his honor and privilege, on a calm and warm and clear night far above the women at their weaving, far above the tradesmen, negotiating their wares, and even above the priests and astronomers, engaged in their esoteric conversations. It was also his honor and privilege to receive the sacred mushrooms, as he had this night, and to feel the unity with the oneness of all. Seven Rabbit no longer felt the distinction of his being separate from all else. In fact, he felt invisible, unknown even to himself, but aware of every thing. He could focus clearly on everything about him, without being in himself a focusing point. He was just there, or was he something greater, not just there, not just Seven Rabbit?

Again he regarded his people. They moved as ants below him but he loved them. He loved them in every detail of their existence, he loved them in every expression, and he knew that they would live forever, just as they were now, no matter what ever happened with earthquakes or ships or pyramids because they were fixed under the stars, each with a star as a god, identical yet, so free, just as he was temporarily free, for this moment, and he now realized, for this lifetime . . . so free, so blessed.

And just as Seven Rabbit realized how blessed he'd been, he knew that his blessing was only an ordinary experience of his people. An experience he was now remembering, exalting in! He was living, he realized, in the center of the world, and in that center, under the stars, the person he had been, with demands unsatisfied, with love lost, with grief, inconsolable, he no longer was. He was invisible, a conduit of knowledge, that had always been there, a slacking of thirst, that had always been there. He was part of a million, million stars, and he, forgetting who he'd been and forgetting what he'd feared, felt the warmth of the night and ecstasy of existence and knew that he'd live for a million-million years.

He looked down again at the women weaving. One of them must have told a funny story for, suddenly, they all laughed and hugged each other. How lucky he was to witness this! How great was his very existence! How great was the god that conceived and provided it all!

He laughed at his great fortune. An angry warrior, named Seven Rabbit, had climbed to the top of the pyramid above the priests, in disdain or the priests, and the priests had made no protest. And that warrior had, at that great height, communed with the gods, and he had found ecstasy. And when he had come down as one of them—finally—there was an unexpected rejoicing and celebration. It was the winter solstice—Christmas as it would later be called—but the idea of gift giving had not arrived, the realization of gift receiving was too powerful.

•

Astronomy has been described as the first science, giving rise to mathematics, geometry, architecture, and all the other known sciences. In truth, science, both as theory, and its ancient implementation, as city and temple building, arose from myth, which stands as the foundation of the great building period of the ancient world![1] Myth predates science and survives in an enduring form in the stone architecture of the ancients. Myth predates megaliths, but by how long?

Previously we've discussed the existence and destruction of Atlantis; in this chapter we shall look closely at the only surviving traces of that civilization—the megaliths found throughout the Americas. The civilization of the Atlanteans, and other great navigational cultures, had been destroyed by the deluge that occurred at the end of the last Ice Age. The few survivors, remnants of that civilization, had lost their cities, lost their ships, and lost their technological know-how. After the deluge destroyed Poseidon, killed a majority of the people, and wiped out the mammoths, horses and most of the large mammals of the Americas, Atlantis no longer existed.

These scattered survivors returned to what had once been their homeland to find their coastal cites submerged, their gardens and fields flooded, their forests devastated. They had lost their astronomer-priests, their architects, craftsmen, and philosophers. Most of those who survived moved inland, the higher into the mountains the better, to become simple farmers.

Flavio Barbiero in *Una Civilta Sotto Ghiaccio* makes the case that Neolithic cultures were not the much ballyhooed first stages of civilization but instead a regression to a more primitive state, occasioned by a worldwide cataclysm. Barbiero sees the establishment of simple farming communities in scattered river valleys of the world as the settlements of survivors of Atlantis who had lost their original know how.[2]

If Barbiero is right, how many years did it take the survivors of a great cataclysm to retrace the vestiges and rebuild the monuments of their Golden Age? The answer is not counted in years but in centuries and millennia (fig. 9A).

In the Middle East and Egypt we have an historical record, though far from complete, of a stone age from 10,000 B.C. and of a Bronze Age from 3000 B.C. to the time of Ancient Greece. The latter is recorded in the hieroglyphs of Egypt and cuneiform of Mesopotamia. In Mesoamerica, thanks mainly to the destruction of texts by Spanish priests, we have no written record, except for a few scattered codices, and no Bronze Age. What we do have is the most magnificent stone images that have ever existed.

In the Americas, we have been told, the pyramids, observatories, and astronomical gardens left by the Mayans, Olmecs, and Toltecs are "interesting," but Americanist archaeologists have insisted that they lack the antiquity to support theories of a civilization linked to a Golden Age. Americanists, anxious to emphasize native American ingenuity, have also dared anyone to show that there were obvious connections between Sumer, Egypt, India, and the Americas. They have called those who point to contacts, racists. In the

9.A. ALTUN HA, BELIZE. Deja Vu? This photograph of a star temple at Altun Ha is not likely, by itself, to inspire it. But a visit to the actual site will engender something very akin to a renewal of past recollections, even to multitudes of tourists who had never read nor heard of the astronomical or mythical implications of the site. But why not? Harmony between man and the cosmos has been built in. The observer need not be Mayan to have a connection. In fact evidence of Semitic, Europeans, Chinese, Japanese, Polynesians, and Negroids abound throughout this site and others in Mesoamerica. If a Jungian memory of racial archetypes exists it is no wonder that it is felt most strongly at sites that connected the astronomers and navigators of the ancient world.

9.B. TEMPLE OF KUKULCAN, CHICHEN ITZA. This structure is more commonly called "The Castillo" –- the Spanish dubbed it the castle although the site has no walls.

process they have obscured what we now must regard as the likely source of all these civilizations.

If we look at the constructions themselves and at the mathematical rules and cosmological implications we can begin to understand their true nature and their antiquity.

So we may ask again, how long had myth and tales of ancient deluge and destruction from the heavens been at the heart of MesoAmerican temple building? Mayan thought, and that of pre-scientific cultures throughout the world, reaches back to ages we have forgotten. Ancient harmonic communion with the heavens was little troubled by the passing centuries. In the first century A.D. the Mayans were still rebuilding Atlantis. They had been doing so for millennia.

At Chichen Itza, the Temple of Kukulcan (fig. 9B) has ninety-one steps on each of its fours sides. With the top platform added to the sum of the steps the pyramid totals 365, representing the days of the year. Viewed from each side, the nine tiers of the step pyramid have eighteen corners, symbolic of the eighteen months in the Mayan years (each month having twenty days). Calendrical information is built into every aspect of its superb construction, and the Temple of Kukulcan has been called "an enormous timepiece."

Balustrades frame the stairway of the north face of the pyramid and at their base become two enormous heads of Kukulcan, the Plumed Serpent. On March 21 and September 21, between 3 and 5 P.M., sunlight striking the northwest side of the temple creates a startling and singular effect. The balustrade seemingly begins to undulate—a wave like motion appears to descend the length of the side of the pyramid leading to Kukulcan's head—in a manner that makes the serpent appear to come "alive." As the sun drops lower in the sky seven distinct isosceles triangles are formed on the body of the serpent, which measures more than 34 meters in length.[3]

This spectacular event, which demonstrates the harmony of astronomy and architecture, occurred only twice a year for many centuries. Now it occurs every night. The Mexican government, using special-effect lighting has found a way to duplicate the phenomenon. Kukulcan (Quetzalcoatl), the kind god that the Church of Spain sought to eradicate all memory of, appears nightly before hundreds, sometimes thousands, of witnesses.

Maize and the Caste War.

DESCENDANTS of the Maya in the Yucatán suffered not only under Spain's rule, but under Spanish use of the land. The Spanish seized Mayan land and used it to grow tobacco and sugarcane. These prized crops of the Spanish, planted yearly, soon wore out the soil the Maya had used to grow their life-sustaining corn. In the 1840s the Maya staged a surprising and bloody uprising and soon had Merida, the Spanish capital of the Yucatán, surrounded. But with decisive victory eminent, the Maya noticed the appearance of the winged ant, a sign that the rains were coming. Military and political victory then held no significance for them. They walked away from certain military victory at Merida to return to their fields and plant corn. In the aftermath of that decision they suffered greatly, as the Spanish, with the assistance of a thousand mercenaries from the United States, regrouped, attacked their villages, beheaded the soldiers, raped the women, and sold what was left to Cuba as slaves. The Maya decision to quit the uprising to plant corn proved disastrous. But the Maya, had always had a different approach to life. Both mythical and mystical they also had an ear to the ground, and to what the Earth's creatures said to them. The gods, through the winged ants, were telling them it was time to return to their fields. Their ancestors had built great astronomical temples, but a precise calendar, and a precise astronomy were never needed for religious ceremonies, or to tell farmers when to plant their crops. Farmers do not plant their crops on a specific day but wait, generally, for the first rains of Spring. Like all good farmers the Maya had other ways of knowing the land and its needs.[4]

Traditional archaeologists have told us that the purpose of the Temple of Kukulcan, and all star temples and pyramids that equate their dimensions to the solstices, were built to remind primitive men when to plant corn (see facing page, "Maize and the Caste War"). Mayan sources tell us it was built to represent the symbolic descent of the Plumed Serpent to our Earth.

Which version is more likely to be true? We know that Mayan obsession with calendars and star temples verged on the fanatical. Why watch the skies so closely? Precise knowledge of the solstices isn't needed to tell a person when the days begin to lengthen. Nor is precise knowledge of the equinoxes necessary to tell a farmer when to plant his crops. Farmers know when its spring and when to plant. They know when fall is approaching and they know when to harvest.

An unusual structure at Chichen Itza, now dubbed the "Caracol," resembles a modern observatory.[5] The Caracol, a circular building sitting on a square base, is markedly different from the other star temples at Chichen Itza in that the facing sides of its base do not correspond to the cardinal directions. Nor do the sight lines of its observatory relate to the equinoxes, nor to any relationship between the Earth and the seasons. Instead they seem to have been used to trace the movements of the Moon, Venus, and to other planets, and star constellations. *Astronomical temples, aligned to face Venus, were not needed for simple farming.*

The Caracol (fig. 9D) has been dated as having been constructed around 900 A.D., making it one of the newest structures at Chichen Itza. Recently, however, it has been discovered that only the outer shell is a recent construction. The winding circular stairway in the center of the observatory is part of

9.D. THE "CARACOL" at Chichen Itza.

a much older structure, itself a circular observatory which may be significantly older than the other temples at Chichen Itza.

At it's inception in 4 A.D., Chichen Itza, in its construction and design, expressed an archaic pattern of thought that had already been in existence in the Americas for thousands of years. If Chichen Itza is itself only two thousand years old, and there is good reason to doubt this, we know that it was part of a culture that was much older. Chichen Itza was, in many aspects, a replica of the more ancient Toltec city-state of Tula. The Temple of the Warriors at Chichen Itza is almost a twin of Pyramid B at Tula, except on a larger scale, and it reflects Tula's lasting motif—that of Atlanteans holding up the sky (figs. 9E, 9F). The concept of Atlas (Atlantis's first king) or Atlanteans as supporting the heavens was a key tenet of Greek myth, but nowhere in the world, except in the Americas, did it find so eloquent and so repeated expression.[6]

If Chichen Itza is a relatively new site, it reveals very ancient ways of thinking. Who were the Itzas that settled there and why did they build pyramids along astronomical lines similar to those expressed by Sumerians and Egyptians 3,000 years earlier.[7] In North Africa, and in the Middle East the knowledge of pyramid building and astronomical observatories had been long forgotten . . . or so we are told. Why do the constructions of the Itza exhibit the geometry and concern with man's place in the stars that character-

9.E. TULA. Another view of the remains of a temple at Tula, exhibiting Atlanteans. Just as Atlas, the first King of Atlanta, was said to have held up the sky these Atlanteans probably held up a roof to a temple. Unlike the small stones and rocks, held together by mortar, that the Toltecs used in building their last temples around 1300 A.D., these fifteen-foot tall Atlanteans were each carved from a single block of basalt rock. They were discovered at an older and lower level and later placed atop the inferior construction.

ized more ancient peoples? What manner of people lived in cities without walls?

To find out we must return to Plato. Plato's concept of an ideal state was based on what he knew (and what Socrates, Homer and Pythagoras had known) of the nature of the Golden Age.

Earlier we presented excerpts from the *Timaeus* and the *Critias* that revealed some characteristics of Plato's Atlantis. Included were general descriptions of Atlantis as an immense island-continent of "god-like lavishness," endowed with lush tropical fruits, exotic animals (including elephants), and "trees of marvelous height and beauty." This continent was divided by its original king, Poseidon, and his bride, Cleito, among their five sets of twins— all ten to become kings of their share of Atlantis. The eldest child, Atlas, governed the central portion of Atlantis, and its capital, Poseidon.

Plato also wrote a more definitive description of Poseidon, built "with concentric rings of sea and land," and of the lands immediately surrounding the capital of Atlantis:

From the *Critias*: "This then was the island's natural endowment and the inhabitants proceeded to build temples, palaces, harbors and docks, and to organize the country as a whole in the following manner. Their first work was to bridge the rings of water round their mother's original home, so forming a road to and from their palace. This palace they proceeded to build at once in

9.F. Note the small stones held together with mortar at the 1,300 A.D. level of this site while at a lower level large megalithic stones reveal far earlier construction at Tula. Stone quarries about a mile downstream indicate where the megalithic construction blocks came from, but do not indicate the source of the Atlanteans themselves.

9.G. "**THE TREE AT THE CENTER OF THE WORLD.**" The Ceiba tree of Mesoamerica (drawing by Frederick Catherwood). Plato described trees of marvelous height and beauty as a mark of Atlantis. The Ceiba tree was sacred to the Maya. Indeed, it was called the Tree of Life, with roots reaching the underworld and soaring branches embracing the stars.[8] The presence of a great Ceiba, which unified heaven and Earth, marked the spot on which the Maya would build their star temples. Celtic mythology embraced a similar font of life. It was the Ash Tree, *yg drasail,* which contained all being and from which all life derived. A basic tenant of mythologies throughout the world has been that of monism, the belief that life is all pervasive and forms an essential unity, and that only ignorance separates the eternal from the material and ephemeral existence we now call individual lives and individual deaths. Hindu history attributes its origins to Aryan invaders of India, but the warring, land-based Aryans must also have incorporated beliefs of conquered Indus valley civilizations whose origins came from a sea-going age. Hindu philosophy continues to express mythic concepts today in its traditional acceptance of the Vedanta and the writings of the Upanishad which relate the message of TAT TWAM ASI (Thou Art That), the famous response of the philosopher Aruni to the question of his student Shvetaketu, who had asked him, "What is the absolute?" Essentially it is no different in its implications than a Cree Indian's belief in an ancestor's reincarnation as an owl, or a Maya's belief that an aspect of the planet Venus could affect his or her life - life was perceived as a unity. Transformation from one expression of being to another marked the beliefs of primitive myths. Our current belief of life as arbitrary and temporal, was as alien to their thinking as their belief that spirits could reappear in any form, as a coyote, tree, or as an owl, is to ours.

the place where the god and their ancestors had lived, and each successive king added to its beauties, doing his best to surpass his predecessors, until they had made a residence whose size and beauty were astonishing to see. They began by digging a canal three hundred feet wide, a hundred feet deep and fifty stades long from the sea to the outermost ring, thus making it accessible from the sea like a harbour; and they made the entrance to it large enough to admit the largest ships. At the bridges they made channels through the ring of land which separated those of water, large enough to admit the passage of a single trireme, and roofed over to make an underground tunnel; for the rims of the rings were of some height above sea-level."

The outlines of the city described, Plato goes on to describe the rest of the immediate area surrounding Poseidon:

"To begin with, the region as a whole was said to be high above the level of the sea, from which it rose precipitously: the city was surrounded by a uniformly flat plain, which was in turn enclosed by mountains which came right down to the sea. This plain was rectangular in shape, measuring three thousand stades in length and at its midpoint two thousand stades in breadth from the coast. This whole area of the island faced south, and was sheltered from the north winds. . . . Over a long period of time the work of a number of kings had effected certain modifications in the natural features of the plain. It was naturally a long, regular rectangle; and any defects in its shape were corrected by means of a ditch dug around it. . . . The rivers which flowed down from the mountains emptied into it, and it made a complete circuit of the plain, running round to the city from both directions, and there discharging into the sea. . . . They cut cross channels between them and also to the city, and used the whole complex to float timber down from the mountains and transport seasonal produce by boat. They had two harvests a year, a winter one for which they relied on rainfall, and a summer one for which the channels, fed by the rivers, provided irrigation."[9]

Plato was giving Atlantis the description of the ideal city-state, which Plato based on myth and a knowledge of form preserved from ancient times. Plato's cosmology was obsessed with the concept of the ideal state, that the divine harmony of the heavens could be recreated on Earth. If Plato's Atlantis was in Central America, at the heart of a great continent, then it is there that we would expect to find the expression of the harmonic state (fig. 9G).

In Plato's Ideal State, described in Book V of *Laws*, the number 12,960 represents sacred marriage and the union of the square and the circle. The number is derived thusly: Plato's ideal city is circular and based on a secret canon of numbers that apply universally to all aspects of human behavior. 31,680 miles equal the perimeter of a square containing the Earth's terrestrial

9.H. THE PYRAMID OF THE SUN, TEOTIHUACAN. The face of the huge Sun pyramid faces due west. Sixty-five meters in height it is angled in its construction so that, from the ground, it appears to disappear into the heavens. No one yet knows who the builders of these pyramids were, except that they were definitely pre-Aztec and pre-Toltec. The three large pyramids, the lessor pyramids, and the grand houses were all covered by stucco and painted in brilliant colors—mainly red. Red is also the color associated with the Atlanteans. Teotihuacan had a probable population of over 100,000 inhabitants when Rome was a small city. There is evidence of substantial racial diversity, including an Olmec (Negroid) enclave that produced lapidaries of greenstone, obsidian and jade. Vessels with volutes (wave designs) showed a definite gulf coast influence in this area. Although most of the Sun Pyramid is now made up of smaller stones, megalithic stones can be seen at it base, probably indicating an earlier, and more sophisticated, construction.

sphere and also equals the circumference of a circle drawn on the combined diameters of the Earth and the moon (the mean perimeter of the Stonehenge Sarsen circle is 316.8 feet). The number 5040, the recommended number of households in Plato's ideal city, is the radius of a circle with the circumference of 31,680. It is also the sum of $1\times2\times3\times4\times5\times6\times7$, and it is divisible by the entire decad, numbers 1-10. The number 7,920 is equal to a side of a square city that would hold the circular city and is also the product of $8\times9\times10\times11$. 5,040 combined with 7,920 represent the union of the circle and square, equaling the harmonic and sacred number, 12,960, the half-life (or mirror) of the "Great Year."[10]

How does current "logical science" account for Plato's number of harmonic unity on earth, 12,960? The integral number for the construction of the ideal state, plus its reflection in the heavens, 12,960, would exactly total the number 25,920—the recently, computer-enhanced determination of the number of years that it takes the Earth to complete a "Great Year." The "Great Year" is the time it takes for the Earth in its stately wobble through space and time through the Precession of the Equinoxes and the signs of the Zodiac, to come full circle and to reappear under the (almost) identical stars and constellations it had faced 25,920 years before.

25,920 was also a sacred number in Sumer and in India where it is expressed in geometric forms in the laws of Yoga.[22] Could this number have been divined independently in India, Sumer, Egypt, Mexico, and Central America? If so, why would it have been so revered that it would be built into the megalithic structures of these diverse people? If contact between peoples of the ancient world was made only occasionally and accidentally, on one-way voyages of lost sailors, would esoteric knowledge of essential numbers likely to have been exchanged? It is not likely.

Scholars have portrayed Plato as looking backward toward illogical thought and myth, and Aristotle as looking forward toward logical thought and science. Yet science itself, through the advanced use of computers has recently confirmed the chaotic model of the seemingly most fixed corner of the universe . . . the solar system. How could Plato, or anyone lacking sophisticated computer models, have known of the half-life of the Precession of the Equinoxes without a source of information based on actual observation? They could not. Thus we are faced with the realization that either sophisticated computers where known at or before Plato's time or that astronomical observation was an exact science for at least 26,000 years, and that Plato had access to a knowledge of both science and myth that was lost to "logical thought" and could not be re-confirmed until the invention of the super-computer and the launching of the Hubble telescope.

The people who built the Pyramid of the Sun at Teotihuacan (fig. 9H) used a base measure called a "finger," ten of which make a bema (comparable to. 706 meters).[11] The perimeter of the Pyramid of the Sun is 12,960 bemas. The number 12,960 is significant not only because it reflects Plato's number expressing harmony of the construction of the ideal state, but also because it is a key in deciphering the mathematical information of the pyramid at Giza. It also represented a number of harmonic balance to the Maya who incorporated it into construction of stelae at Tikal commemorating the Nine Lords of Time. The Maya began construction of this temple on their date 9.0.0.0.0 (our date 435 A.D.) which equals 1,296,000 kin or days that had elapsed since 3113, B.C., day zero of the current age of the Maya.[12]

If Plato's god (like Einstein's) was a mathematician, so was the god of the builders of the pyramids at Teotihuacan, Chichen Itza, and throughout Mesoamerica.

Plato only knew the ideal city-state through myth. But structures that

Plato could only envision were, in Plato's time, before his time, and even after, constructed in stone, a sea and an ocean away, in Mesoamerica.

At Teotihuacan, Hugh Harleston, Jr. used hunabs, the Mayan word for "unified measure" to arrive at the boundary markers that appeared to define the what the Spanish called the "Way of the Dead." This great causeway— which locals in the time of Father Sahagun (1529 A.D.) called the "Road of the Gods" because the "Lords therein buried, after deaths, did not perish but turned into gods,"—runs perpendicular to the Pyramid of the Sun (fig. 9I). The boundary runs 378 hunabs both ways, totaling 756 units, doubling the width of the citadel, and equal to the distance from the center of the Sun Pyramid to the center of the Moon pyramid. Harleston noted that the hunab multiplied by 100,000 gave an accurate figure for the circumference of the Earth. He then found that the 60 unit base of the Pyramid multiplied by 100,000 gave the polar radius of the earth.[13] In other words the pyramid was based on pi, and *built on a scale commensurate to the diameter of the Earth.*

Pi, a mathematical concept supposedly unknown before Pythagoras, is one of the "true equations" of our known universe. Without its assigned value we would be unable to measure anything from atoms to movements of the stars.[14] Further, Harleston found that not only were the sun and the moon represented at Teotihuacan, representation of all the planets could as well be found in unexcavated ruins along the "Way of the Dead (fig. 9J)."

9.I. THE WAY OF THE DEAD, TEOTIHUACAN. Leading to the Pyramid of the Moon, the Spanish called it the way of the dead because the Aztecs told them that the small pyramids that lined the great avenue between the massive Pyramid of the Sun and the Pyramid of the Moon were burial chambers. But the Aztecs were mistaken. The small pyramids contain no tombs. Instead they are part of a grand cosmic layout that describes the progression of the visible planets. Teotihuacan is an astronomical garden on a grand scale. Although vast, only about a mile-and-a-half of the Avenue of the Dead, known to extend for at least 17 miles, and possibly for forty miles, has been excavated and reconstructed.

9.J. ESCAPORES. Called circular "scrapers" (escapores) by the Spanish, could objects like this jade disc have had another purpose? Did the early astronomers have knowledge of the telescope? Mayan and Pre-Mayan knowledge of the heavens, including planets and moons that were not discovered until the last few hundred years has long intrigued investigators. Undoubtedly they had sharper vision than most of us now enjoy. Their skies, except after a volcanic explosion, were markedly less polluted, and the great diffusion of electric light was unknown. Yet all of this cannot account for their apparent knowledge of Uranus and Neptune, two planets "discovered" only with the help of telescopes in 1787 and 1846. In myth, the Mayans always described Earth as the seventh planet, and of Venus the eighth, showing that they, like the astronomers of Sumer, counted the planets from the outside in. But what could account for their knowledge of Pluto, a tiny and distant planet only "discovered" in 1930 by our modern methods?

Hugh Harleston has argued that the temples along the "Way of the Dead" at Teotihuacan–both those excavated and the majority that have not been excavated–have, in their distance from the Quetzalcoatl Pyramid, corresponded to astronomical units of the planets' distance from the Sun (an astronomical unit is the mean distance of the Earth from the Sun in its orbit). Thus Uranus appears at as an unexcavated pyramid 19.2 astronomical units (AU) from the Sun, and Neptune is defined by a mound 30 AU from the Sun. At a distance equivalent to 75 AU north of the Quetzalcoatl Pyramid the remains of an ancient pyramid, called the Temple of Xochitl "Flower Pyramid" are still discernible despite razing by looters. Harleston believes that this temple depicted the position of a planet twice the circumference of the Earth and at twice the distance of Pluto's orbit. The possible existence of this planet conforms to the now widely held view among astro-physicists that the solar system would have been formed symmetrically, with an equivalent mass of rocky hard planets lying both inside and outside and the gaseous inner planets of Jupiter, Saturn and Uranus and Neptune. This logical equation has never been satisfied by the discovery of tiny Pluto, but could in part be solved by the discovery of Planet X, which Harleston calls Xiknalkan (Mayan for "Flying Serpent").[15] This tenth planet may no longer exist! Myth has recorded its spectacular destruction, and the discovery of the multitude of comets, some 1,000 miles in diameter, in this region testifies to the possibility of an enormous celestial collision that turned the "Flying Serpent" into millions of specks of cometary debris. But the mass of this object still must exist, either as an undiscovered planet or in its diverse parts. How did the astronomers of Tula and Teotihuacan know that it was there? How did they know that it disappeared, and made Earth the seventh planet, not the eighth? A reassessment of the function of circular "escrapores" (scrapers) may be in order. These circular objects, found in abundance from Tula and Teotihuacan, in Mexico's central valley, to southern Costa Rica, could have held obsidian lenses. Focused through a long tube they would have made an effective simple refracting telescope. Further, we know that the Olmecs at La Venta had concave mirrors of obsidian, and of highly polished iron. The combination of a convex lens and a concave primary mirror, and a small, flat secondary mirror, contained in a sighting device, could have been an earlier version of the Newtonian reflecting telescope.

Mesoamerica is not unique in "harmonic" construction of its temples. In Egypt, where a sudden transition from Neolithic culture to full fledged civilization was supposed to have occurred at about 3100 B.C., there are almost eighty known pyramids, ruins of pyramids, and pyramid-shaped structures. Almost all of Egypt's pyramids were built as burial tombs, almost all contained hieroglyphs. But three appear to have been built in a different manner and for a different purpose. At Giza, the Great pyramid of Khufu (Cheops), and its companion, Khafre (Cephren), as well as the smaller (and seemingly out-of-alignment) Mykerinos, have no burial chambers, no hieroglyphs, and seem to have been built much earlier than those constructed at the behest of the Pharaohs. The Great Pyramid is not only much larger and of far superior in workmanship to all the pyramids that followed it–it contains an amazing amount of mathematical and geometrical information. The height of the Khufu pyramid is exactly equal to the radius of a circle whose circumference is equal to the circumference of the pyramid. Again pi, the formula for the temples at Teotihuacan, was found to be built into the Great pyramid at Giza (fig. 9K).

It is apparent that the Great Pyramid, unlike any of its later imitations in Egypt, was built as a scientific measurement and replica of the Earth, designed to be in perfect harmony with the dimensions and mathematical model of the Earth. Studies of the geometrical dimensions have concluded that the builders of the Great Pyramid had solved the great unsolved problem of mathematics—that of squaring the circle.[21]

Among the similarities between the Great Pyramid at Giza and the Pyramid of the Sun at Teotihuacan in their dimensions is the fact that they have almost identical bases; the sides of the Khufu pyramid are 754 feet in length, at Teotihuacan the sides of the Pyramid of the Sun measure 745 feet. This lone fact could be coincidental. However, the mathematical probability that pi could be expressed exactly and by chance in the formation of both pyramids has been calculated at one in 26 zillion. That's a one with 26 zeros behind it. The probability that by chance or independent discovery and sophisticated implementation pi could have been used at Teotihuacan, and also be described in the building of pyramids at Egypt and at Sumer would run off this and several succeeding pages. Suffice it to say that the number exceeds the fractional description of one year over the entirety of all the years that the universe has existed.

It has only been in the past thirty years that science has been able to appreciate the sophisticated mathematical interconnectedness of the dimensions, facing, and seeming purpose of these great pyramids in Sumer, Egypt and Mesoamerica. These similarities can hardly be attributed to coincidence. They had to result from a common source of information. In all three cases the peoples who lived with these pyramids for millennia described that source as a gift from navigators and survivors from an earlier and greater civilization. For evolutionists, intent on the concept of the American pyramid builders as "inspired savages," the complexity of the earliest pyramids has been a bitter pill to swallow—the mathematical precision evidenced in these structures exceeds the architectural evidence of any other age known to man.

As John Michell writes in *City Of Revelation* (fig. 9L), "Man, temple, and cosmos were therefore seen to be identical, and on this understanding the entire philosophy and science of the ancient world was founded. Moreover, the existence of the ancient canon . . . with its complement of cosmic numbers and measurements, reveals a higher level of astronomical skill in the remote past than in any period known to history . . . Whereas we are now asked to regard ourselves as irrelevant particles in infinite space, the ancient

9.K. THE GREAT PYRAMID AT GIZA. Like Chichen Itza in the Yucatán, the Pyramid of the Sun at Teotihuacan in the Valley of Mexico, and possibly thousands of other structures in the Americas, the Great Pyramid is a perfect equinoctial marker. Its north face is off line to true north by three minutes of one degree; the most precise structure of the twentieth century—the Paris Observatory—is off line by six minutes. Like Teotihuacan its construction is based on pi—the height of the pyramid is equal to the radius of a circle whose circumference is equal to the circumference of the pyramid (even though pi itself was historically not discovered until the sixth century A.D. by the Hindu scholar, Arya-Bhata.) The Pyramid of Cheops is in fact an exact scale model of the northern hemisphere, with its base as the equator, its apex as the north pole and its perimeter equal to one-half minute of arc.[18] With its east side pointing true east and the west side pointing true west and a facing of highly polished limestone (now long gone) whose reflection would have been visible from outer space, the Great Pyramid must have occasioned some spectacular sunrises and sunsets.[20]

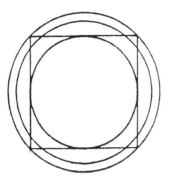 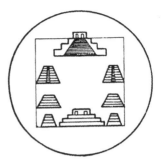

9.L. THE SQUARE CONTAINED IN A CIRCLE in cosmology and in the lay-out of MesoAmerican city-states (usually with a canal forming the circle as at Cerros, Belize). In *City of Revelation* John Michell points out that Plato's theory of education, based on ancient precepts, was founded on "the belief that the citizens of the perfect state should be exposed throughout their lives to the best possible influences, those of divine harmony; for which reason every manufactured object, every building and artifact as well as every form of social organization was formerly designed in accordance with the canon of proportion, said to have been given to the first men by the gods themselves. "The medium by which all the knowledge of the past has been transmitted into the present is the language of symbolism, and the particular cipher that represents and contains the secrets of the canon is the figure of the square in conjunction with the circle. The outer circle contains the square, the inner is contained within it and the intermediary circle has a circumference equal to the perimeter of the square measured round its four sides. This is . . . the symbol of the transcendental union of irreconcilable opposites, formerly conceived as a temple or city, which is both a plan of the universe and a model of each one its inhabitants."[23]

---

philosophers were concerned with the relationship between men and their environment, with the individual at the center of his own universe."[24]

Mathematics, astronomy, astrology, and architecture in harmonious balance provided a lingua franca, a universal language of the ancient world. Can coincidences alone explain why the great pyramid builders of widely separated places on the globe were also astronomers, mathematicians, and believers in a unified, living cosmos? Could similar myths arise throughout the world in isolation? Or did they have a founding source, deep in our long lost, and almost forgotten, antiquity? Surely part of the answer was mechanical and physical—since they knew that cataclysms had visited the Earth from the heavens they had to be concerned with a repeat performance. But in most part the answer was spiritual and political.

Like the Maya, Plato's perception of time and space was circular and definite, a common source in which past and future flow equally, meeting and uniting in the present. The Maya called this perception "Hunab Ku" meaning "cosmic consciousness." In the *Republic* Plato describes the travels of Er, the Armenian, who travels with a group of souls seeking rebirth through the other world until they come to, " . . . a straight shaft of light, like a pillar, stretching from above throughout the heavens and earth, and there, at the middle of the light, they saw stretching from heaven the extremities of its chains; for this light binds the heavens, holding together all the revolving firmament like the under girths of a ship of war. And from the extremities stretched the Spindle of Necessity, by means of which all the circles revolve."[25]

Plato's cosmology is similar to the Mayan Kuxan Suum, the resonant pathway between man and the universe, which has the literal meaning of "the Road to the Sky Leading to the Umbilical Cord of the Universe."[26] So similar that one might think they have a common source. The similarities are no less startling than those between the Kuxan Suum and its interconnecting planetary, solar, and galactic circuits and the interconnecting spheres of the Hindus (who also had a kind and loving serpent god, Garuda).

Plato called space a "receptacle" and spoke of astronomers as "men close to the Gods," witnesses to the "dance of the stars."[27] Pythagoras, founder of the Greek school of mathematics, told of the "music of the spheres." The Egyptian god Thoth (later borrowed as the Greek god Hermes) was regarded as "the reckoner of the heavens, counter of stars, and measurer of the Earth."[28] To Mayan astronomers it was the interplay between the heavenly bodies and the direct connection to the earthly plane that mattered.

For the Maya, the Hindus—Maya being one of their chief gods and their name for an ancient navigational tribe—and mythical man in general, time did not move as it does for us with yesterday, today and tomorrow proceeding in a straight line. Whereas our time is horizontal, theirs was vertical, ascending to the stars and returning according to a celestial axis. Cause and effect existed, not as isolated events, but as necessary communication with a totality we now find missing. Similarly, numbers did not progress according to our definition with two twice one, three greater, four more, and twelve, twenty, three hundred, and so on regarded as greater numbers. Actually the number seven was regarded, in most respects, as the greatest number in a diverse world, but the number one held the greatest original power.

Their concepts of numbering were not applied to the division of wealth, consumerism or accounting of goods at all, but to understanding unity. One and seven could not be divided and therein, beyond all other indivisible numbers, they retained their strength. Thus eight was not greater than seven, but less, unless you're counting beans or ears of corn. In the language of symbolism the square is solid matter, finite and definable, the circle is the infinite spirit, and the union of the two reconciles the contradictory aspects of nature and reveals the true image of the cosmos. In ancient city-temples of Sumer, Egypt, and Mesoamerica as well as Stonehenge, the answer to the problem of squaring the circle (the circle squared) is presented daily (or nightly) to the public view of its citizens.[29] Mayans would hopefully laugh at our mundane concept of numbers as a way to record our gains, they used them to understand the nature of the cosmos.

Of course, numbers, beyond their individual power, had a cumulative purpose as well—they were used to record the passage of time between irregularities in the cycles of the sun and moon. This use of numbers was sacred in their world but the consecutive sequence of the numbers, outside of recording time, held no particular value.

Knowledge of Plato's mathematics is not necessary to understand the parallels between the concept of Atlantis and the constructions of Mesoamerica. The circle in the square may be the ultimate defining concept of the Golden Age, and the squaring of the circle, a mathematical problem that cannot be solved today, may have been the source of their unusual power. But the chronicle of Atlantis in America exists on many levels.

Although a conquering ideology could destroy the literature, the writings, the people, it could not totally destroy the harmony of star temples left behind. In seeking Atlantis from that record we must look not only for calendars and knowledge of mathematics, but from expressions of pyramids, and observatories. We must recognize the traces of world-wide navigation, the significance of circular canals, encompassing cities, but also connected to the sea, the significance of twin motifs, and their antiquity in thought and expression that reach back through time. And we must put it all in the context of a lush and fruitful climate that existed 11,500 years ago.

The similarities between MesoAmerican culture and Plato's description of Atlantis abound:

On entering the Aztec capital of Tenochtitlán, Cortez and his men marveled at the concentric canals surrounding the Aztec capital, and at the floating gardens (chinampas) that supplied exotic fruits, vegetables and flowers to the city. The Aztecs were only the last in a long line of highly civilized people who inhabited Tenochtitlán in the Valley of Mexico. Like the Incas in Peru, they were recent dwellers in a megalithic empire far more ancient than themselves. Toltec history goes back much further than it has been given credit for. It is possibly as old as the Olmecs. The city of Tenochtitlán—the ruins now lie directly under Mexico City—actually predated both the Aztecs, who came to rule there, and the Toltecs. The city the Aztecs inherited from the Toltecs was situated on an island surrounded by concentric rings of canals, just as Plato described Poseidon (fig. 9M), the capital of Atlantis, in the *Critias*.[31]

The extensive canals at Tenochtitlán have been known for some time. But the extent of canal building in the rest of Mesoamerica was largely unknown.

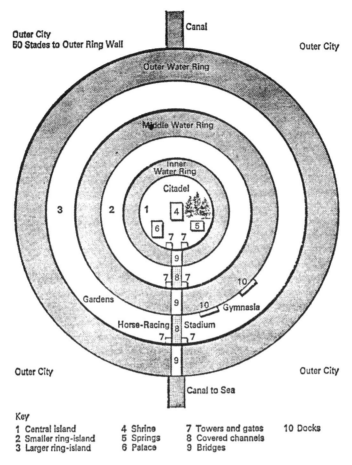

Outer City
50 Stades to Outer Ring Wall

Canal

Outer City

Outer Water Ring

Middle Water Ring

Inner Water Ring

Citadel

3 2 1

4

6 5

7 7

9

7 8 7

10

Gardens

9

10 Gymnasia

Horse-Racing Stadium

7 8 7

9

Outer City

Outer City

Canal to Sea

Key
1 Central island
2 Smaller ring-island
3 Larger ring-island
4 Shrine
5 Springs
6 Palace
7 Towers and gates
8 Covered channels
9 Bridges
10 Docks

9.M. PLATO'S CONCEPT OF THE INNER CITY OF POSEIDON. In the *Critius* Plato described Atlantis as the ideal city-state, which Plato based on myth and a knowledge of form preserved from ancient times. Plato's cosmology was obsessed with the concept of the ideal state, that the divine harmony of the heavens could be recreated on Earth. Compare the inner city of Poseidon with Tenochtitlán.[30] Tenochtitlán was rediscovered in the 1970s during preparations for a subway system that has now been built beneath present-day Mexico City. Aztecs took credit for construction of Tenochtitlán around 1300 AD. However, the Aztecs built very little, content to rebuild or build upon the temples and pyramids of their Toltec predecessors. Many levels of temple building must lie under the Aztec version of Tenochtitlán, but to fully understand the city it would be necessary to gut the heart of the largest city, in terms of population, in the world. Cortez and his chronicler described the city they encountered, and its circular canals, in terms similar to what we know of Plato's city, and to the city-states in Lubaantun, Cerros Maya, and hundreds of others in Mesoamerica as well as the circular city of Cuzco in pre-Inca Peru. Although it is now dry, the ancient city of Teotihuacan, site of the Pyramid of the Sun and the Pyramid of the Moon was apparently once a city of canals which encircled the vast city of 200,000 occupants three thousand years ago.

In the jungles of the Peten region of Guatemala lies the site of El Ceibal. El Ceibal takes its name from the sacred Ceiba trees of the Mayans. But the deeply and precisely chiseled stelae here reveal few Mayans. Instead the site is dominated by thickly mustachioed and bearded figures. It also has a perfectly circular platform, about 20 feet high and 60 feet in diameter. A spiral staircase circles the entire structure, which is perfectly flat on top. It is probably the base of a circular observatory that, over centuries of looting, has been dismantled. How did bearded sailors get to the middle of the Peten jungle in Guatemala? The presence of the eastern Mediterranean types in the central jungles of ancient Guatemala has led a few of us to understand the obvious navigational implications of this culture. El Ceibal, situated next to the Rio de la Pasion, was linked to other sites on the Pasion, the Rio Petexbutan, and the Usumacinta, which flowed to the open sea. Although rapids in the Rio Usumacinta would have made it difficult, open sea navigators could have reached El Ceibal.

Recent NASA radar imaging photography has shown such riverine travel was unnecessary, revealing a network of ancient canals that could not have been guessed at. Canals interconnected hundreds, even thousands of sites.

Again we can compare a layout of the canals surrounding the greater city-state of Atlantis (see fig. 6G.)[32] with a recent NASA radar imagery photograph that reveals a complexity of canals in the jungles of Guatemala(fig. 9N)[33] with an aerial view of the same Peten jungle with normal photography (fig 9O).

9.N. NASA radar imagery photograph of Guatemala.

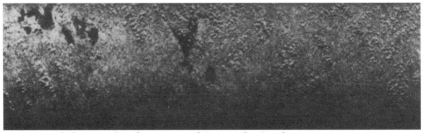

9.O. Normal photography of same area of Guatemalan jungle.

9.P. Side view of Aztec calendar. (See also fig. 2D).

The NASA radar imaging photography reveals a startling naval sophistication to Mesoamerica that linked, not just a few river based cultures, but tens of thousands of sites throughout present day Guatemala, Chiapas, Yucatán, Quintana Roo, and Belize.

An equally startling find was made at Mexico City (in the ancient canals of Tenochtitlán) in 1790—although few, at that time, understood its implications. While re-paving the Plaza Mayor, workmen uncovered a huge flat stone, buried under several feet of mud. When they had cleared the area around it they found it to be perfectly circular in shape. When they were able to right it they found that its underside was intricately carved and designed. It was a star calendar (fig. 9P, see also fig. 2D). When measured it was found to be a single slab of basalt twelve feet across, over three feet thick, and weighing over twenty tons. Rumors and legends of such a monumental astronomical clock had been known for centuries.

First hand accounts by chroniclers and emissaries accompanying Pizarro wrote of a great calendar disk made of gold at Cuzco, in Peru. But Pizarro had the great golden disk melted down into ingots. Cortez, and subsequent soldiers and priests had all "pagan" calendars, and objects of idolatry destroyed. But apparently the great calendar was simply too immense to be broken up, and Cortez's men, around 1522, buried it face down in the shallow waters of

Tenochtitlán. Over two and half centuries later, when the drained lakes of Tenochtitlán had become part of Mexico City, the great calendar reemerged.

Now called the Aztec calendar, this elaborate device is actually pre-Toltec, and could even be Pre-Mayan. An early investigator of its functions, Stonehenge expert Sir Norman Lockyer, has called it "an achievement which has never been surpassed in primitive astronomy."[34] Although all the functions of Mayan and Olmec calendars have not yet been discovered, we know that they reckoned time in three ways, all based on the vigesimal ("times twenty") system. A religious year consisted of 260 days, divided into thirteen months of twenty days each. (There are thirteen months because the Mayan firmament is based on thirteen levels. There are twenty days because twenty is the basis of their numerical system). A solar year had eighteen months of twenty days, to which an "unlucky" period of five days were added. Every fourth year (leap year) six days were added. The Mayans apparently noticed that even this system, similar to the Julian calendar, would result in the seasons arriving at a slightly later date every four years. So they devised a system by which thirteen days were removed at the end of fifty-two years period.[36] The result was a calendar, that over long periods of time, was more accurate than the Julian calendar (365.2500 days) and more accurate than the Gregorian (365.2425 days) we still use today. It's accuracy (365.2420 days) is only slightly exceeded by the atomic calendar (365.2422 days). Which brings up the question—how long had the devisors of this calendar observe, and tinker with the calendar before writing it in stone two thousand years ago?

A third Maya-Olmec calendar has come to be known as the Long Count. The "Long Count" measures time linearly, as we now do. But it could measure times into millions of years, as Europeans, until the nineteenth century, could not. That is because the Mayans had the concept of zero thousands of years before the Europeans. The main purpose of the Long Count, however, was to trace any one date or event in an age back to the first day of that age. Day one of the current age is generally believed to be August 13, 3113, B.C.[36]

For centuries the doctrine of the Church was reiterated in the dogma of academia which assured us that the star temples of Mesoamerica were "ceremonial centers" largely engaged in human sacrifice, and that ancient calendars were sacrificial altars. Only recent investigation has confirmed Lockyer's belief that the Great Calendar and the astronomical centers of Mesoamerica described not only the annual rotation of the Sun, but it's apparent journey, seen from our perspective, through the heavens.

As mentioned earlier, through their observations the Mayans understood the "Great Year," the time taken by Earth to complete a circle around the "pole of the ecliptic"—the sun's path among the stars. This precession of the equinoxes has been attributed to Hipparchus (134 B.C.) but was known to Pythagoras, Plato, ancient Sumerians, Egyptians, and MesoAmericans thousands of years before. The concept was not totally foreign to the Eurocentric world, it survived in occult readings of the signs of the Zodiac, but officially it was "forgotten" for two thousand years (see below, "Precession of the Equinoxes").

The Precession of the Equinoxes is for many a difficult concept. Due to influences of the other planets, most notably Jupiter, or possibly as result of the formation of the moon, the earth's axis wobbles as the earth spins, just as a spinning top wobbles. But the Earth's wobble is very slow, indeed. The base ellipse of the Earth's orbit gradually rotates at the current rate of 0.3 degrees per century. As a result the earth's axis traces out a huge curve in the sky over a 25,920 year period.[38] We have lived under the ascendancy of both the zodiacal sign and the constellation of Pisces for the past two thousand years. That is, it is the constellation Pisces which arises in the eastern sky just before the sun rises, creating the effect that the sun is residing in the zodiacal house of Pisces. But we are slowly precessing (backward, if you perceive the sun's journey as forward) toward the ascendancy of Aquarius. Within one hundred and fifty years or so, we will have entered a new celestial age. Today our pole star is Polaris. We must remember Plato's number of celestial unity, 12,960. Because

---

Precession of the Equinoxes

I N Hamlet's Mill Giorgio Santillana puts Precession in perspective. "The Precession of the Equinoxes has lost relevance for our affairs; whereas once it was the only majestic secular motion that our ancestors could keep in mind when they looked for a great cycle which could affect humanity as a whole. But then our ancestors were astronomers and astrologers. They believed that the sliding of the sun along the equinoctial point affected the frame of the cosmos and determined a succession of world-ages under different zodiacal signs. The had found a large peg on which to hang their thoughts about cosmic time, which brought all things in fateful order. Today, that order has lapsed, like the idea of a living cosmos itself. There is only history, which has been felicitously defined as 'one damn thing after another.'"[37]

9.R. OUR MOON. A solar eclipse. Why did astronomers watch the sky so closely? The action of the heavens are now considered to be so distant that they could not really have affected primitive existence. Or is there some relationship that the ancients knew, and of which we are unaware? What can explain the orbit of our own moon? Why is it circular rather than elliptical, as a captured body most likely would be? Why does the circumference of the moon at eclipse exactly equal the circumference of the body of the sun? It does so at only one perspective, from that of us who are on Earth. What is the mathematical probability that a captured body in space would form a perfectly circular orbit so that at any time its path crossed the sun it would reveal that great body's limitations precisely to an observer on earth?

12,960 years from now we will be under the ascendancy of Leo, as we were 12,960 years ago, and Vega will be the North Star.

The ancient astronomers of Mesoamerica, Egypt, and Sumer seemed to have been aware of the concept of precession and to have calculated it into their astrological predictions (see 6F). (Astronomy and astrology were not separate then, and astrology was then a true science—not the gobbledygook of today.)

Why watch the skies so closely (fig. 9R)? Why were these calendars and star temples built? The purpose of any linear calendar is to reckon time in *advance*, by measuring the units of time that must elapse before an anticipated event will take place. But the Mayans, Olmecs, and ancient Peruvians were equally concerned with time past.

For ancient astronomers time did not move in static circles, simply repeating itself every 25,920 years, but in a dynamic spiral—cycles within cycles, resembling the configurations of DNA. For Plato and the Mayans alike the primary reason why astronomers watched the sky was to maintain the link between the galaxy and the human mind. Portents of irregularity in the heavens signified an imbalance on Earth and in man's thought. And the information ran both ways. If man could correct his faults on Earth he still had a chance of influencing the heavens and of setting things right.

Neither ceremonial sacrifice nor the need to know when to plant crops would have made it necessary for the MesoAmericans to continually rebuild the pyramids and other astronomical structures. It was in response to the slow shifting of the Earth's position in the heaven in the 25,920 year cycle (the "Great Year") that the Olmecs, Mayans and Toltecs repeatedly built new structures using the stones of the old or by placing new stones over the older structures. In the later years of MesoAmerican culture, the Aztecs were building one pyramid atop one another, usually in an inferior fashion, as often as every fifty-two years. But by then they had, in most cases, lost the knowledge of the purpose of the star temples.

Cuneiform writings from Sumer reveal that the concept the Scorpion, Bull, and Lion were used to describe constellations in 4,000 B.C. Similar names were used in Egypt and Mesoamerica to describe the same constellations at dates most archaeologists call much later but that could in fact be earlier.

How did a similar manner of tracking the heavens through similar constellations (similarly named) come about in such geographically disparate regions of the world? How long had these ancient astronomers been tracking the stars and passing their knowledge in order to arrive at the concepts of Precession, and the circular and repeating form of the cosmos? The answer is simply that it could not be described without being observed. If man has knowledge of the full circle of the precession, he has been observing and recording the movement of the Earth through the heavens for at least 26,000 years!

The ancient astronomers of both the Middle East and Mesoamerica assigned ages to their divisions of the Heavens and believed that the passing from one age to another, or the culmination of each age, was marked by periodic, and predictable, cataclysms.

Sir Norman Lockyer, whose publication of *The Dawn of Astronomy* in 1894, also marked the dawn of the science of archeoastronomy, was among the first to realize that the great archeological sites of England were astronomical temples. In Sumer and Egypt he further discovered that the ziggurats and pyramids were of two types. Sun temples were oriented to the cardinal points and the defining of equinoxes. More complicated star temples were not oriented to the sun but to stars and constellations, often toward Sirius, then the brightest star in the sky. At the great pyramid at Giza and at Karnak in Upper Egypt, Lockyer found that the temples combined information that described both the movement of the sun and the equinoxes, and the movement of the stellar background due to the precession of the equinoxes.

The Great Temple to Amon-Ra at Karnak has two immense structures built so that a corridor of light will pass the entire length of the two structures and illuminate Amon-Ra precisely at the winter solstice. At least at one time this illumination was precise. A diminution in the extent of the sun's apparent yearly wandering (which is actually a diminishing of the extremes of the Earth's tilt which varies over millennia of from under 21 degrees to an excess of 24 degrees) has gradually thrown the beam of light at the Karnak Temple slightly off.

Lockyer then realized that knowledge of the precise angle of the sun needed for illumination, combined with a concomitant knowledge of the angle of the sun at that time, could reveal, within centuries, the date of the temple's construction. Working back through his calculations, he determined that the sighting lines of the Temple of Karnak corresponded to a date of about 3,200 B.C. This date, at least in its solar implications, has been confirmed by current mathematical models of the Earth's tilt.

Lockyer had already discovered that at Stonehenge and throughout England from the earliest shrines to the greatest temples, all were oriented astronomically, *and that the older the temples were, the more sophisticated their astronomy had been.*[41] And although he may not have fully understood the implications of the dates his method of archeoastronomy had found in Egypt, Cyrus Gordon did. In *Before Columbus,* Gordon wrote, "Hebrew, Greek, Mesopotamian, Egyptian and other literature of antiquity refer to a golden age in the distant past. Actually if we look at the monuments of bygone ages, we note something striking. The most impressive monuments of Egypt are the great pyramids going back to the early Bronze Age."[42]

What this points to is a progressive loss of the purpose of astronomy and astrology even within those times we call ancient. The ability to build megaliths did not immediately decline, it continued for two thousand years in Egypt. But the *purpose* was gradually lost.

The pharaohs of Egypt that ruled after the period from 3100 B.C. to 2500 B.C. obviously had no understanding of the mathematics of the building of the more ancient Great Pyramid of Khufu. That is evidenced from their inferior design and lack of universal knowledge of earth- commensurate geometry. Neither did their subjects who toiled, for the most part, not as slaves, but as well paid and generally content craftsmen. The priests were something else. Protecting a power that rivaled that of the ruling families they preserved knowledge that was kept from the pharaohs and their architects. Perhaps they hid it too well. In Egypt, by 900 B.C., even crude astronomical gardens were no longer being built. By the time of the Greek ascendancy in history, only the esoteric schools of Pythagoras and Plato understood man's mathematical relationship to the stars. By the time of the Romans, and the subsequent Dark Ages, all had been "forgotten."

Lockyer, although familiar with the so-called Aztec calendar, had little knowledge of the astronomical gardens of Mesoamerica—most had not even been discovered, let alone excavated, at the time of his research. But, increasingly, the vast number of archeological sites in Mesoamerica are beginning to be appreciated as astronomical and mathematical time pieces, carved in stone. Yet a similar progression to what he observed at Stonehenge and at

Karnak, took place in the Americas—a progression from sophisticated star temples combined with equally sophisticated sun temples, to knowledge only of sun temples, and then to knowledge only of pyramid building, with little understanding of the what, and less of the why.

Egypt really has only four structures that are true astrological gardens, oriented to both the sun and the stars and planets. Mesoamerica has thousands, most of them unexcavated. The search for the link to the age when man was the geometer of the heavens must begin to concentrate on the astrological gardens of the ancient civilizations of Anahuac, the indigenous Nahuatl name for Mexico and Central America meaning, "The Place Between the Waters" . . . that lay on the strip of land at the heart of the great American continent, just where Plato said it would be.

At Chichen Itza the Temple of Kukulcan had to have been built within the past two thousand years or less, otherwise the illumination of Quetzalcoatl at the vernal and autumnal equinoxes would not occur. But the Caracol observatory, as mentioned earlier, appears to be much older. Its sighting lines, ostensibly devised to observe Venus, do not agree with Venus's positions in the past several thousand years. But traveling back along the movement of the Precession of the Equinoxes we find that in a far more ancient time, at least 7,500 B.C., the sightlines agree with the reappearance of Venus, after an absence of seventy days, as the morning star. Is this Caracol the same Caracol that measured the appearance of Venus 9,500 years ago? No it is not. The Caracol, like the pyramids of Chichen Itza and all the star temples of Mesoamerica, has been rebuilt many times. But even the most recent of these have been built with ancient mathematical and symbolic knowledge incorporated into their design. At some pint the symbolic knowledge and purpose was forgotten, and ritual sacrifice, probably as rare as the eight year cycle of the reappearance of Venus, degraded into warfare and mass sacrifice. But the last few centuries of a culture cannot erase the millennia that preceded it.

At Uxmal, in the Yucatán, most the structures are oriented towards the cardinal position. Included among the "sun" structures, the Pyramid of the Magician is renowned for its unusual oval shape—myth holds that a dwarf, hatched from an egg, erected the pyramid in a single night—but which also has recently revealed five levels of previous construction. One magnificent structure, now called the Governor's Palace, has no relationship with the other structures or with the cardinal points. It's central doorway, however, is in perfect alignment with Venus.

In present day Honduras, at Copan, called the "Paris of the ancient Mayan world" the beauty of its artistic motifs, and what is understood of its astronomical sightlines and temples tell a story of harmonic convergence with the heavens. Yet its hieroglyphs, tell a very different story—that of a dramatic conquest and reinvention of history. Lord Quetzal Macaw rose to power around 435 A.D. Building new structures on top of existing ones, he soon proclaimed himself Great Sun Lord Quetzal Macaw and represented himself as a divine being, descended from the sun (remember Seven Macaw and the Flood). Under the line of kings established by Quetzal Macaw the purpose and expression of Copan's art shifted from cosmological motifs to that of elaborate portrayals of the supremacy of Copan's rulers (fig. 9S). By the time of the twelfth ruler in this new line, Smoke Jaguar (628-695 A.D.), warfare and conquest were the principal activities of the once peaceful city-state. When Smoke Jaguar's successor, 18 Rabbit (695-738 A.D.) was beheaded in a war with nearby Quirigua, the entire region fell into chaos and turmoil. Although marvelous construction and art works would continue for centuries, Copan's link with its ancient past was already in decline eight hundred years before Columbus's arrival.

9.S. Ivar Zapp points to a stela at Copán with a sphere implanted in its mid-section. Is this evidence that the erectors of the stela understood a more ancient tradition?

At the same time that medieval kings huddled in dank castles in Europe and exacted feudal allegiances from their inferiors, Mayan warlords, operating under a bright sun, and under a new creed, finally began to mirror their European counterparts. Navigation was forgotten, trade and interaction ceased. Wars, retribution, and forceful acquisition of adjacent lands prevailed. At a time that later would be described as the "Classic period" Mayan civilization was in full decline.

Recent advances in the ability to read the hieroglyphs on MesoAmerican bas-reliefs and stelae has lead some investigators to conclude that they have uncovered the true history of the Mayans and of their constructions. Accepting the dates given on the stelae accompanying pyramids and star temples as an indication of when the pyramids were constructed could be very misleading—the stelae most likely were erected hundreds or thousands of years *after* the pyramids themselves, probably by a different people than those who erected the pyramids. The apparent reason for the erection of the stelae was to celebrate victories in war. Warfare was not a dominant way of life until late in the Mayan Classic Period although, surely, over the centuries it had occurred.

Conquering armies have always had a habit of looting the riches of the vanquished, sometimes removing their treasures from older burial vaults and incorporating them into their current valuables. Conquerors also have a habit of rewriting history. They would hardly tell the true story of warring upon a city, of whose origins they knew little or nothing, of slaughtering its people, and then of occupying and claiming that city's temples as their own. The story they would tell would be that *they* built the great temples.

At first it was thought that Tikal was about 1,700 years old because accompanying hieroglyphs carved into stele identified fourteen rulers who had ruled at Tikal from 292 A.D. to 869 A.D. Commencing with a leader known as Jaguar Paw, who sired a lineage that would last 270 years, Tikal dominated much of Mesoamerica, or so we have been told, until an army led by Lord Water, the ruler of Caracol in the Maya mountains of Belize, conquered Tikal in 562 A.D. Since no mention was made of rulers before 292 A.D., it was assumed that Tikal didn't exist prior to that date, as if, somehow the entire site with its great ceremonial sites and possible population of 100,000 people had suddenly sprung into being. Then layer after layer of ruins were found beneath the original ruins including an interior burial chamber, which leading archaeologists have repeatedly told us did not exist in Mayan ruins. Radio-carbon testing of some these tombs has now dated Tikal to 600 B.C. But deeper layers are yet to be fully excavated or dated (fig. 9T).

It now appears that the hieroglyphic history of Tikal may have been com-

9.T. LOWER LEVELS AT TIKAL. Photos at new excavation levels at Tikal, below established dates of construction, reveal giant carving similar to Kohunlich and to carvings found in Czechoslovakia dated to 22,000 B.C.

missioned by Jaguar Paw to portray his rule as the founding reign while the city-state had in fact existed for centuries, if not millennia, before. If so, the process of rewriting history to favor the rule of a particular lineage of rulers did not begin with Shakespeare's history of the good King, Henry V, and the rise of the Tudor family. This process has been going on for thousands of years.

If, as it appears, the erecting of stelae at the astronomical gardens of the great sites of Mesoamerica had little or nothing to do with the mathematical or astronomical information contained in the site themselves, what relevance can we give to the information they give us?

As in Egypt, it appears that the stories on the stelae of Mesoamerica were told by a people who had lost the original knowledge of why the star temples were constructed.

What manner of people lived in the city-states of the star temples? John Michell wrote, "The existence in prehistoric times of closely linked, intercommunicating centers, engaged in the same scientific program from one end of the country to the other, can only indicate that the various communities lived together in a state of peaceful cooperation where elaborate fortifications would be wholly unnecessary" Was Michell commenting on ancient Mesoamerica? He could have been. In fact, however, his commentary concerned the interconnecting ley lines of the monuments of Celtic Britain. But they hearkened back to a more harmonic time when cities were built without walls, and roads were built to facilitate the interaction of knowledge.

These civilizations were prehistoric not just in context but in spiritual content. In the entire context of historic time, from Troy, to the castles of Medieval Europe, to China and to Berlin, the theme of walled cities, walled countries, gates, moats, and breaches in the walls have resounded throughout our history. Yet there was a time, and a place in time, when walls weren't even considered—not from lack of a means to build them, but from a lack of motive. Jericho, the most ancient "historical" city, whose twenty excavated layers date back 9,000 years, wasn't walled until 1200 B.C.

When did civilization make a left or U-turn? When did walls become a necessity? The date varies around the world. The walls of Jericho were built at least 5,000 years after the establishment of a civilized city-state at that site. The builders of the great astrological gardens of Sumer, Egypt, India, and in the British Isles, were still in touch with a cosmological constant five millennia ago. Why did they wait so long to build walls? The answer is that they simply did not need walls. No walls were ever built around Giza or Luxor in Egypt, nor around Stonehenge in England. Then around 1000 B.C., with the coming of the age of iron and the demise of navigation, a new age of warfare commenced. Walls quickly followed, and the memory and purpose of a common meeting of harmonic people was lost.

In the Americas (once Atlantis), inter-communicating centers possessed a remarkable number of similarities, the most remarkable of which are their common myths of deluge, and their advanced knowledge of mathematics, astronomy and architecture. They covered a vast area stretching from Tiahuanacu (Lake Titicaca) in present day Peru and Chile, to Teotihuacan and Tula in the valley of Mexico. Construction of these great sites, construction of canals to connect them by sea, and construction even of roads continued in the Americas for fifteen hundred years after the Celts, Egyptians and Sumerians had forgotten their purpose.

We may never know the true extent of their roads but there are glimpses in sacbeob still intact (fig. 9U). "Sacbe" was the Mayan term for the ancient roads that radiated out from the major city states. Usually made of surface limestone these roads were invariably perfectly straight and often very wide (the Mayan word "sac" means "white," "be" means "road"). The Sacbeob (plural of sacbe) were well constructed, and were capable of handling repeated use by great weights. Unlike our modern highways, these sacbeob never swerved to conform to the contours of the land, and were never turned from their course by low hills, or by thick swamps. They pursued another course. Seemingly, they followed the paths of stars!

At Dzibilchaltun, a vast site in the far northern Yucatán, twelve known sacbeob radiate out from the site's center, including a wide limestone causeway that extends on an east-west axis for almost a mile before disappearing into the jungle. Dzibilchaltun, is now known to have flourished a early as 2000 B.C. and to have had over eight thousands buildings. It now appears as mostly a pile of rubble, although it is distinguished as the only known Mayan site with windows. Most of the limestone blocks from the temples and from the causeway have been, over centuries, removed. The site is known to have a minimum of five levels of construction and even the most recent has not been fully excavated. But the axis of what remains of the causeway, dubbed "The Great White Way" corresponds to the axis of the Peten sites of El Mirador and

9.U. SACBEOB. Ancient roads of the Maya(detail of Catherwood drawing). The ancient roadways were filled with stone, solidified with lime, and covered with a smooth plaster cement. They were actually causeways, raised at least six feet above the surrounding, often swampy, ground. Culverts were used in wet areas, and protective walls were built where seasonal runoffs could have inundated the roadways. The sacbeob varied from nine feet to sixty feet in width, the wider dimensions occurred in centers, or junctures, with out-lying city-states, and at these junctures circular ramps were built. We have been repeatedly told that the Mayas and Pre-Mayans did not have knowledge of the wheel, but the existence of ramps and the strength of the construction of these ancient roads, far beyond what would be need for foot traffic, brings that assessment into considerable question.

Nakbe several hundred kilometers to the south.[43] Dzibilchaltun shares similarly decorated stucco masks with El Mirador, Lamanai, and Altar de Sacrificios, all in Guatemala's Peten.

At El Mirador, in Guatemala, now called the pre-eminent site of the Formative Maya, causeways extended in several directions, radiating out twenty-one kilometers southwest to Tintal, twelve kilometers southeast to the earlier dated site of Nakbe, and in directions that even traditional archaeologists admit, "seem to be aligned to astronomical positions."[44]

Traditional anthropologists, such as Michael Coe and Sylvanus Morley, who have given dates of 100 A.D. for sites like Tikal and Coba, have recently admitted that El Mirador flourished at least 300 years earlier and that Nakbe had evolved into a major Maya site by 630 B.C. They have accounted for the discrepancy in dates by repeating the assumption that as one city-state disintegrated, its people moved on and founded a new site. They had simply not found, and were therefore justifiably unaware of, the preceding city-state. But the evidence of connecting roads, the sacbeob, and evidence of interconnecting canals, show that many of the great city-states coexisted over long periods of time. Can we now appreciate, that if you establish a date for one city-state that predates another by several hundred years, yet has interconnecting canals with the later dated site, that the established dates could be very wrong?

The sites are also aligned with one another. At Calukmul, a recently excavated site in southeastern Mexico, excavator William Folan has uncovered a city-state of over 6,250 structures that held an estimated population of at least 50,000 people. The 114 engraved stelae discovered so far, outnumber those of any other Maya site. The Mexican government guidebook at Becan states that carved stelae at Calukmul, discovered in 1993, give a calendar date of 1500 B.C. More significantly, Folan has found evidence of sacbeob connecting this site to El Mirador, twenty-six miles to the south, in Guatemala, and to Nakbe, seven miles beyond. Although the roads themselves no longer exist, Folan has learned from Landsat satellite imagery that variations in vegetation, notably chlorophyll content, and elevation, can distinguish man-made objects from natural vegetation. The results of the Landsat imagery indicate a pattern of lines, corresponding to the dimensions of sacbeob, radiating out of Calukmul, and probably extending to Coba, about 186 aerial miles to the northeast. Folan, under the auspices of the Universidad Automa de Campeche, is now in the process of hacking through the jungle to find definitive evidence of the remains of the actual roads.[45]

Folan has found jade and pearl ornaments at Calukmul, in an area where there is no jade and no pearls. The presence in abundance of precious materials not native to the area indicates that this city-state was a major trade center.

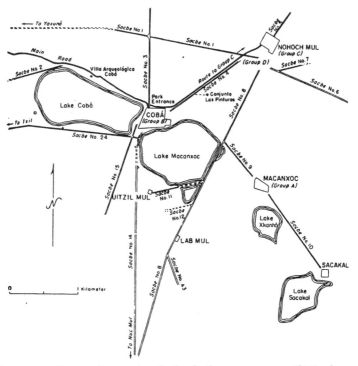

9.V. SACBEOB AT COBA radiate out hundreds of miles to seaports, to El Mirador and, possibly, to Tikal and Teotihuacan. Only partially excavated, the importance of this site in the Yucatán jungle was virtually ignored until very recently. Coba boasts the largest pyramids in the Yucatán and it was a center of interconnecting sacbeob—great roadways, that united Mayan sites over a great expanse, revealing the true nature of the pre-degenerative culture. The great Maya were united in purpose, united by roads, united by canals, united by astronomical temples, and undivided by walls.

At Coba sacbeob radiate like star paths from the center of a city-state of over fifty square kilometers that may have once held a population of over 100,000 (fig. 9V). From the top of the pyramid Nohoch Mul, the Yucatán's highest structure at forty-one meters, slight indentations in the jungle canopy below indicate the paths of a few of the more than thirty confirmed sacbeob. One perfectly straight sacbe runs one hundred kilometers to Yaxuna, near Chichen Itza. At Coba it is speculated that another twenty or more sacbeob once existed (the total equaling the Mayan holy number of fifty-two). Traces of a wide sacbe linking Coba to Tulum on the Caribbean coast thirty miles away suggest a sea link for this inland metropolis. The excavation at Coba has been rudimentary. Only a few of the known murals and hieroglyphs have been fully studied. Yet what is known reveals a story of fresh seafood delivered daily from the ports on the Caribbean. The means of delivery are not described but the hieroglyphs reveal that catches made in the morning were delivered to the plates of the royalty by noon! Ancient remains of conch shells, sea urchin spines, shark's teeth, and sailfish bills confirm the glyphs.[46]

In Chile and in Peru giant road systems radiate out in a manner similar to Coba. One extends in a straight line from the Nazca desert in Chile all the way to the ancient megalithic site of Tiahuanacu in Bolivia. At Nazca, however, the lines also take on curves, forming figures resembling constellations of the stars, as well as a wide variety of earthbound animals including birds, spiders and reptiles (fig. 9W). One imaginative scholar, Zecharia Sitchin, an undeniable expert on the ancient Sumerians, has described these earthbound cosmic layouts as landing strips for the Anunnaki, gods from another planet. Presumably these gods arrived to enslave earthlings for the purpose of mining gold. However, Sitchin does not convincingly explain why these gods needed gold, nor, with all their powers, they needed earthlings as slaves.[48]

In 1952, a significant tomb was discovered beneath the Temple of Inscriptions at Palenque, a vast astronomical garden, now mostly restored from ruin. The tomb, rivaling any found in Egypt's Valley of the Kings, was built for Pacal Votan, a warring Mayan ruler, who reigned, according to accompanying

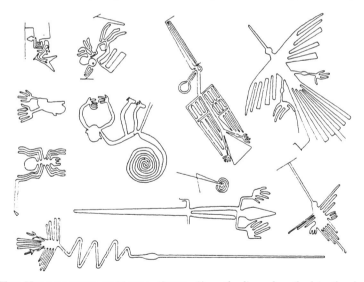

9.W. The Hummingbird at Nazca, Chile. Since the lines described in the desert at Nazca can only be seen from the air, some imaginative writers (i.e. Erik Von Daniken) have suggested that the lines marked "spaceports" for travelers from distant star systems. Would sophisticated spacemen have needed landing strips? Our view is that the straight lines were part of a cosmic and navigational university that extend from Chile to the Californias. (Similar giant land figures have been found near Blythe, in southern California. Were they man's attempt to duplicate harmony with the heavens?)[47]

hieroglyphs, from 615 to 683 A.D. A monolithic slab, twelve feet in length, covered the sarcophagus that contains Pacal Votan's bones.

The intricate carving on the face of the lid describes, by some accounts, the lowering of Pacal into the underworld. Yet Pacal Votan is seated and is gazing up at figures representing the sun, moon, and the Serpent God. What's more, Pacal's hands seem to be manipulating a mechanical device. One could speculate that Pacal, in seeking the Serpent God, is gazing through an ancient telescope or some other sighting device (fig. 9X).

Of course, one can speculate anything. In the late 1960s Erich von Daniken made a case for travel between star systems by describing the lid as a portrait of an ancient astronaut sitting at his command module. Von Daniken described comparisons between the stylized relief carving and Gemini spacecraft which were then first taking men to the moon by emphasizing the apparent presence of rockets beneath the seated Pacal Votan.

Gemini space modules as intergalactic vessels? Aliens did not arrive here using an identical (and primitive) technology to that used on our moon missions. Man will not travel to other star systems with 1960s Apollo rocketry. Alien gods, bent on enslaving, but also teaching, a primitive humanity in the way of the heavens? Not likely.

The wide appeal that books like those by Van Daniken and Sitchin have generated only signifies an impatience with traditional archaeology, and a perception that an essential understanding of the ancients of Mesoamerica is lacking. Among traditional archaeologists that understanding is unlikely to come without a new paradigm, one this book is attempting to define by focusing on the realization that the "ancients" were master mariners, astronomers, and great builders. The sophistication of the Mayan road system, the extent of trade in goods and concepts, and the interconnection of cultural traits, all within the framework of cities without walls, cities open to each other in trade and in ideas, point to a great and ancient civilization, such as the one described by Plato.

We have suggested that most Americanists and archaeologists must not have be sailors. They may not be mathematicians either. For they have failed to understand the purpose or appreciate the knowledge of astronomy and harmony of thought that had to have existed among ancient Americans. Traditional archaeologists have followed the trail of potsherds, relics, hieroglyphs and, when available, human remains. But they have ignored the trail of human thought—expressed in a common astronomy, expressed in mathematics, expressed in stone. That trail is found in Myth and in man's wonder of and knowledge of the stars. And it is found in his construction of star temples.

In defense of the academics we can only offer that the parameters of their

9.X. PACAL VOTAN'S SARCOPHAGUS. Palenque, Chiapas, Mexico.The lid of Pacal Votan's sarcophagus has led to much speculation, including the ideas that he was an astronomer looking through a "seeing device", that he was using a "bong" pipe for inhaling cocaine, and that he was an alien who had arrived in a space capsule, powered by rockets very similar to our own in the 1970s. The first notion is very possible–notice that the thimble-shaped attachment lines up with the tip of the nose, not the nostril. The third speculation is highly doubtful because, in our time, the early Apollo craft was barely able to take astronauts to our own moon—such a craft powered by such primitive rockets could not have taken any voyager from or to distant planets or other solar systems.

The ruler Pacal Votan was, in terms of the history of the Maya, one of the most recent rulers. But he had taken his name from Votan, a mythic figure who had been ordered to leave his homeland. In his travels, recounted in the Odyssey of Votan, Votan came upon a tower that was destroyed due to a confusion of tongues among its builders. Votan escaped that confusion by discovering a subterranean passage.49 It was Votan's destiny, in Mayan myth, to await the return of the Serpent God. In doing so Pacal Votan laid his claim to being an initiate of the greater cosmos.50

orthodox science were part of an institution described by Einstein as "a collection of prejudices which are fed to us with a porridge spoon before our eighteenth year." Based on their own limited knowledge, our academic tutors simply couldn't expect that ancients knew a great deal more about mathematics or geometry than what these academics themselves had been taught. Nor could they conceive that any civilization could have been more advanced, politically and socially, than the founders of our Eurocentric world in Greece and Rome. But the ancients of the Americas did indeed know a great deal more.51 Until their much heralded decline they knew how to live in peace and harmony for thousands of years.

Through the analysis of evidence from many sources that we present in this book, we emphatically repeat that the notion that the cultures and temples of the Americas were the work of "inspired" primitives, who may have had only chance encounters with more advanced peoples from the Mediterranean, *must be reevaluated.* The "conspiracy of ignorance" that has maintained wrong dates about the antiquity of the Americas must be abandoned. As excavations proceed throughout Mesoamerica, accepted dates are being pushed back, by hundreds of years in Mexico and Guatemala, by thousands in Belize and Costa Rica. But even more enlightened dating will shed little light on our ignorance if we fail to grasp the *nature* of the civilization that flourished there.

What we are now beginning to appreciate is that for hundreds and thousands of years before the dated and excavated sites from Mexico to Peru, there existed in the Americas a vast interaction of peoples and cultures. For millennia city-states, numbering in the tens of thousands, and governed by a common calendar, and a common understanding of astronomy, cosmology and mathematics, formed an interconnecting civilization that stretched from the high plains of Chile to the valley of Mexico. In seeking Atlantis we must look for expressions of ingenuity and divine harmony in the minds of the people who created the Golden Age.

In sum, the memory of Atlantis and a Golden Age has survived in the star temples of Mesoamerica. The record of its people is written in stone. Atlantis, preserved by myth, was rebuilt again and again where it had once flourished. Why else would we find Olmecs at La Venta, and Mayas at Tikal and Copan, erecting great star temples and pyramids in geographical areas that have become, over the past 4,000 years, terribly hot and humid climates? It is because myth, and the record of the true "ancients" were there. They had returned to the coordinates of the star temples, and to man's place in the cosmos. At Chichen Itza, the Mayas, like countless generations of their ancestors, were still rebuilding Atlantis in the first century A.D.

10 Pyramids & Megaliths: *Older than you think*

EIGHTEEN RABBIT had never understood what the observatories were for. None of his people had. His father had told him that at one time his people knew their function and the great mysteries they revealed but that they had forgotten them. Once these things are forgotten, his father had told him, it is very hard to remember. Three Rabbit's father used this lesson over and over again in his instructions to Three Rabbit. "Remember your trail back," he would tell him. "Once it is forgotten you will find the way difficult." Or, "Remember what your mother tells you about oiling your sandals. Once they've dried out you'll never get them to work properly again." The theme seemed endless. Everyone talked about how much they'd forgotten. Eighteen Rabbit knew it was because of the megaliths that surrounded them, the great and ageless stones of Sacsayhuaman. No one knew how they were built, or why, or when.

Once, in a time his people could remember, they had tried to duplicate the building. His ancestors had gone to the quarry where they knew the rocks Had come from. Rock cutters had to work for years before they had cut a boulder that looked like it could fit in with the great boulders at Sacsayhuaman. They had gathered the people. Twenty thousand Indians had pulled the great stone from the front with great ropes. Four thousand more had gone behind the stone, pushing and holding, afraid that the stone might break loose and tumble back the steep slopes they'd worked so hard to climb. Then, part way up the slope, disaster had occurred. First one rope had broken, then another, then the great boulder had begun to slide. The Incas who had held the remaining ropes felt them burning their hands, pulling them down. Some had held on and had been pulled to their deaths down the mountainside. Most had let go and had saved themselves. But those behind the boulder had had no choice. They were crushed as the great stone tumbled down to the plain below.

In all over 4,500 men had died that day. The great stone lay on the plain, unmolested. It was thereafter called "The Weeping Stone" and it was said that the stone wept tears of blood because it could not attain a place on the edifice at Sacsayhuaman.1

Eighteen Rabbit climbed out on the rocks above his city. The sacred rocks of Sacsayhuaman. He looked down on the Coricancha, the City of Gold. His people did not know how to build great cities but they did know how to smelter the gold. And they'd dressed everything they had inherited in the brilliance of that metal. It was their contribution, their way of paying respect to something they no longer understood. But for all its brilliance they knew it meant nothing.

His people were weak, and they knew it. And they had once been so strong. But it was now all forgotten. They lived without hope of knowing who they were. Maybe that was why there was so much tension, so much fear. Maybe that was why civil war had broken out among the Inca! But now word had reached them of the return of gods to their lands. As prophesied they had come from the sea! These gods had actually been seen. They had white skin and true beards growing from their faces. And they were coming to Cuzco. Atahualpa himself, the great ruler, was making ready to welcome them. As reckoned by a very different people it was the year 1532 A.D. It was to be a great day and a great year for the Inca. At least, that is what Eighteen Rabbit thought.

•

In the early 1900s William Niven, a Scot geologist, found evidence of cataclysmic tidal waves that had overwhelmed the Valley of Mexico on several occasions between 11,500 years ago, and 50,000 years ago. Investigating hundreds of sand and clay pits between Texcoco and Haluepantla, Niven found indications of not only a vast cataclysm—a strata of strewn rocks, pebbles, sand, and boulders—but indications of ancient ruins and prehistoric cities beneath them. Beneath the 9,500 year old layer Niven found thousands of stone houses filled with ashes and debris but cemented together with a material harder than the stone itself. He also discovered hundreds of terra-cotta figures, one sitting cross-legged, similar to Olmec figures, and others that represented in Niven's account, "all the races of southern Asia." At this ancient level Niven also found thousands of carved stones that revealed pictographs that have never been fully deciphered.[2]

To many of us today at the close of the twentieth century, Niven's finds were not so astonishing. But by the established standards of the early twentieth century they were declared "out of context," and "impossible." What made it worse for Niven was the fact that he sent reports of his findings to James Churchward, who incorporated Niven's discoveries into his theory of the lost Continent of Mu. Churchward claimed that the stone figure and tablets that

Niven showed him were identical to the Nacaal tablets he had found in a monastery in Tibet.

Although Niven's credibility was never challenged by authorities—his obituary in the *New York Times* described him as a distinguished mineralogist who had discovered several new minerals, including cytrialite, thorogon, and nivenite—the association of his finds with Churchward's fanciful Mu brought Niven's considerable work to easy ridicule by American archaeological authorities.

Peter Tompkins, who has detailed Niven's discoveries in *Mysteries of The Mexican Pyramids*, noted that by linking Niven's finds to Churchward's theories, the scientific world threw out, "along with Churchward's Lemurian bath water, some living, screaming babies."[3]

Niven's site has been bulldozed over to make way for the suburbs of present day Mexico City. It's exact location can only be guessed at. Niven sold some of the artifacts he found to finance his explorations, but much of it was donated to the Museum of Natural History in New York. Although the museum admits to having received the artifacts, the curator of Mexican Archaeology, Gordon F. Eckholm, issued a statement in 1976 that he did not know what had become of the famous Niven tablets.

Niven's find only confirms those of Darwin and Eiseley, previously discussed—traces of a vast cataclysm in the Americas—except that Darwin and Eiseley's were associated with the extinction of many species of mega-fauna, while Niven found traces of a human civilization now lost.

Recently, a rapidly accelerating knowledge of the sites of repopulation after the deluge have been discovered. Around 5500 B.C., agriculture and domestication of animals began in Mesopotamia, the much heralded "birthplace of civilization."[4] What has not been appreciated, until very recently, are *older* agricultural cultures in the Americas. Investigation of cultures at the Guila Naquitz Cave in the Valley of Oaxaca, originally excavated and dated by archaeologist Kent Flannery of the University of Michigan indicate that squash cultivation was present as early as 8000 B.C., and perhaps earlier.[5] Flannery's dates were hotly disputed by traditionalists. But Smithsonian archaeologist, Bruce Smith, using accelerator mass spectrometer radiocarbon dating recently (1997) confirmed the deliberate cultivation of the *Cucurbita pepo* (a pumpkin) at least 10,000 years ago.[6] This would place the redevelopment of agriculture at a minimum of fifteen hundred years after the deluge. The possibility of the existence of slash-and-burn agriculture in Belize is now tentatively dated to 9000 B.C., a date that rivals the earliest known plantings in Asia. This by no way means that agriculture did not exist earlier. Corn, always the preferred crop of Americans, may have been planted earlier. There are indications that deliberate cultivation existed 32,000 years ago in Brazil. But the findings at Guila Naquitz do indicate that the agricultural knowledge that was virtually wiped out at the time of the deluge took very little time in finding its resettlement.

What knowledge was lost and what was retained by these ancient settlers and re-settlers of Mesopotamia and Mesoamerica? If they had the knowledge of how to build step-pyramids and erect astronomical observatories why did it take so long for them to build them? The answer may lie partly in the extent of devastation. Knowledge of pyramids was retained but the knowledge of how to build them may have been closely held by a priest-architect-astronomer class that had no survivors. Certainly the infrastructure required to build them was destroyed. It may have taken millennia to regain the extent of civilization and division of labor necessary to undertake such construction. During that time myth alone had to have held the knowledge intact. The exact skills required had to be learned anew.

It is also possible that it didn't take millennia and that the megalithic constructions, and their unfound, buried predecessors are simply much older than they have been given credit as being. We have cited accepted dates for the astronomical constructions of Mesoamerica. And we have also noted that even the accepted dates keep slipping back. We will soon find them slipping back further, into a more distant past.

According to conventional theory we should find earlier constructions cruder, and less defined in terms of astronomy and celestial observation. Later structures then would be more sophisticated. Megaliths would be progressively bigger and better.

However, this progressive theory encounters considerable obstacles when it comes to explaining the ancient and mysterious cities of the Pre-Incans from Cuzco and Machu Picchu, in Peru, to Tiahuanacu, near Lake Titicaca in Bolivia.

Cuzco, the capital of the Inca Empire, contained 100,000 houses, perhaps half a million people at the time the Spanish arrived in 1533 A.D. Its narrow streets and high altitude, 11,500 feet above sea level, can still leave a novice visitor confused at first encounter. Altitude sickness, a condition far more severe than the average "turista" problem can severely limit the intent of any investigator. But the splendor of what has been called both "the celestial city" and "the navel of the Earth," would have been more dazzling to the Spanish conquistadors—most of the city, particularly the inner area of Coricancha, was covered in gold.[7]

Sacsayhuaman

Cuzco was laid out in an oval of twelve wards, believed by some investigators to represent the twelve signs of the zodiac. Cuzco (fig. 10-A), like Coba in the Yucatán, lay at the hub of a vast network of paved roads that stretched out in all directions and totaled over 30,000 kilometers in length. The roads were cut through the many steep passes and deep chasms of the Andes. Chiseled steps were cut into the hard bedrock lining many gorges, suspension bridges of braided twigs and vine hung thousands of feet over raging rivers.[8] This remarkable engineering feat was rivaled by the intricate underground system of tunnels that linked Cuzco and the golden enclosure of Coricancha to the nearby megalithic structure of Sacsayhuaman.[9]

But it is the site of Sacsayhuaman (fig.10-B) that is the true wonder. There, huge stone blocks, some weighing as much as 300 tons (600,000 pounds!), and standing fifteen feet high have been precisely fitted together to form massive walls. These great blocks are so perfectly carved, and where they are still standing, so perfectly fitted, that you cannot pass a knife between them. The enormous stones are polygonal in shape, some with as many as 30 sides, yet they have been cut, faced, and fitted precisely.[10]

How were they built? The Spanish chroniclers who took their eyes off the gold of Cuzco long enough to realize the spectacle of the great stones asked this question of the Inca.

The Inca responded that they had no idea. The megaliths, they told the Spanish, had been built by an earlier people, a race of giants, and after their

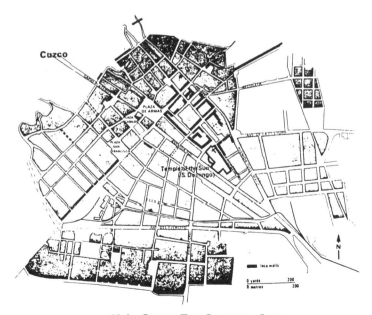

10.A. Cuzco, The Celestial City.

10.B. MEGALITHIC CONSTRUCTION of Sacsayhuaman near Cuzco, Peru. These are not surface cuts on a stone mountain. They are individual boulders, many of different origin, and weighing up to 300 tons, (one hundred times as heavy as the surface blocks at the Great Pyramid in Egypt), yet fitted precisely together. How was this accomplished? The Pre-Inca builders of the great walls remain unknown.[11]

departure had been left as a gift to the Inca people. Later it was theorized that the stones were local in origin, perhaps a single monolith, carved to look like individual stones. But every geologist who has investigated the site has concluded that the stones are not only individual, but they are also separate in origin. Some of the boulders used are believed to come from quarries twenty miles away, some forty miles distant, while others came from quarries over seventy miles away. In fact some are believed to have come from Ecuador, several hundreds of miles distant.[12]

The constructions have been compared to the pyramids in Egypt. But the Egyptian pyramid builders working with precisely shaped cubes, weighing at most three tons, did not possess a comparable technology. The Egyptian megaliths were built along the banks of the Nile, benefiting from river transportation. Any visitor to the Cuzco–Machu Picchu–Tiahuanacu region will marvel at the towering Andes. Even the relatively flat plains were over 10,000 feet in height and they are cut through with steep green valleys, and white-water rivers rushing through gorges up to 4,000 feet deep. How do you transport huge boulders in this country? And once the stones were moved, how could the individual boulders be so precisely fitted together?

Some interesting solutions have been proposed. Garcilaso de la Vega, an emissary of the Church, wrote about these structures in 1601. "How can we explain the fact that these Peruvian Indians were able to split, carve, lift, carry, hoist, and lower such enormous blocks of stone, which are more like pieces of mountains than building stones, and that they accomplished this . . . without the help of a single machine or instrument? An enigma such as this one cannot be easily solved without seeking the help of magic, particularly when one recalls the great familiarity of these people with devils."[13] Of course, this "solution" was just another justification for genocide.

Sound as a force of neutralizing gravity has been proposed for the erection of structures in the Middle East. Music and repeated and harmonious chants have been cited by the legendary priest of On in Chaldea as the instrument by which the great stones of Baalbek was raised. Today Sufis in Poona, India, continue to raise 120 pound spheres by three words chanted in unison and the touch of eleven index fingers.[14] But grander implications of this idea, on the scale needed to elevate the great stones of Sacsayhuaman, continue to elude even the Sufis.

Stone softening agents from an unknown plant have been proposed by explorers such as Hiram Bingham, the white "discover" of Machu Picchu, and Colonel Brian Fawcett who had described a red plant that grows to a foot in height and whose sap will melt stone.[15]

But this plant has still not been independently found.

A *Scientific American* article (February, 1986) by French investigator Jean-Pierre Protzen proposes that the colossal stones could have been pulled along specially built ramps by a minimum of 2,400 men. But since the terrain permitted ramps of 8 meters at most (and in the case of Machu Picchu a much narrower passage) the questions arises—where did all these men stand? After many months of study Protzen begins his article by claiming duplication of the procedure is relatively easy. However, he concludes by admitting that he doesn't' have all the answers—proving that sometimes attempts at rational explanations only deepen the mystery.

As to the precision fitting of the polygonal stones, some with as many as thirty-two facets, Protzen proposes that the feat of exact fitting could easily be accomplished by a continual raising and lowering of the boulders, chipping away at that which didn't fit, and eventually making the greatest jigsaw fit known to man. Has Protzen ever visited a dentist to have a new crown fitted? Working with all the latest devices of modern technology including precise molds (of what substance could the megalith builders have made a mold of a 150 ton boulder?) the dentist must still spend a great deal of energy in polishing and grinding to make the new artificial tooth fit in with a precision equal to these megaliths. Yet the giant boulders of Machu Picchu, Ollantaytambu and Tiahuanacu, like the spheres of Costa Rica, show no evidence of grinding or polishing or even chipping. And even if they did, the vision of a repeated lifting, chipping, and lowering of 150 ton boulders boggles the mind. With what devices would they have been raised and lowered massive stones so many times? With what material could they have been fashioned that would leave no trace of alteration? The Incas' only metal was gold, with which they later decorated many of these megaliths. But gold is simply too soft a metal to accomplish such an undertaking.[16]

How were they built? Sound, plants that melt stone, the use of immense manpower, and even the Devil himself do not provide satisfactory answers. The megaliths at Sacsayhuaman may have been built by giants, but it is more likely that they were built by scientific and mathematical "giants" rather than actual men who could hoist 200 ton boulders!

Why were the great walls at Sacsayhuaman built? At first glance the asymmetrical blocks at Sacsayhuaman and the megaliths of Three Windows at Machu Picchu seem cruder than the more recent and highly uniform rectangular blocks subsequently built on top of them by the Incas. But the Inca blocks, on close inspection, prove to be made of small split stones, adobe bricks, mud, and a rough finishing of masonry.[17] The polygonal fitting of huge blocks seems logical, until you consider how much more difficult it is to build a wall in this fashion. But why build them this way?

One answer is earthquake resistance. Huge earthquakes have demolished Inca walls of three hundred pound to half-ton boulders, scattering the boulders much like a moderate earthquake destroys a brick fireplace. Earthquakes have leveled stone cathedrals in Cuzco three times in the past four centuries. But no earthquake can budge the monoliths at Sacsayhuaman. Even today, in

10.C. CIRCULAR OBSERVATORY in square at Sacsayhuaman.

the earthquake prone Pacific Rim of Fire, no other structure in the world is built to the earthquake resistance of these structures.

What did the megalithic walls of Sacsayhuaman protect? Sacsayhuaman has been called a fortress. But there was no city behind these walls. There was no palace. Even if there had been one to protect against enemy tribes, a higher wall of smaller stones would serve as a fortress just as well, or better. Excavations behind the walls does, however, reveal the past existence of several small rectangular buildings that surrounded a perfectly circular building (fig. 10-C). This is now just a sunken area, but it is perfectly circular, suggesting links to the semi-circular observatories at Machu Picchu, the Caracol at Chichen Itza, the half-sunken city at Cerros in Belize, and with dozens of other circular star temples in South and Mesoamerica!

The gigantic walls of Sacsayhuaman could withstand the force of any earthquake. There was no force known to ancient man that could have dislodged these massive fortresses of stone. Except, possibly, the force of a giant tidal wave that could inundate the world. Because it now appears a good possibility that this is why the walls were built—to protect a sacred observatory from an immense tidal wave.

But why fear a tidal wave at altitudes in excess of 10,000 feet? To understand the implications of such a fear we need to go some two hundred miles, by air, south of Cuzco and Sacsayhuaman, to Tiahuanacu.

Tiahuanacu

The ruins of Tiahuanacu stand on a high plain in the Andes near the borders of present day Bolivia and Peru and within twenty miles of Lake Titicaca, whose reed boat builders fashioned the *Ra II* that Thor Heyerdahl's party used to sail across the Atlantic. Built on a now desolate area of the Altiplano, a 13,000 foot high plain surrounded by snow-covered mountains that tower to heights above 20,000 feet, the Tiahuanacu site, like Sacsayhuaman, is composed of great megaliths, some weighing up to 200 tons and measuring 27 feet in length.

The region is covered with a layer of seashells, which prompted Le Plongeon to surmise that it may once have been at sea level and was later uplifted by some cataclysm to its present height. We know that the actions of plate tectonics in South America are intense. The subduction of the Pacific plate under the Peruvian and Nazca plates is one the most dramatic upheavals of our geologic epoch. Only 5,000 years ago a series of severe earthquakes and uplifting along the Peruvian coast destroyed canals that had been in place for thousands of years. Canals that once ran gradually downstream were suddenly encountered by a new ridge of land near the coast that rose up breaking the

10.D. PUMA PUNKU, TIAHUANACU. Keystone cuts in massive blocks weighing up to 200 tons. What pains were taken to secure these megaliths, as protectors of the sky temples, from ruin? At Puma Punku and Ollantaytambu T-shapes have been cut into the giant stone blocks at the point where one block corners another. Obviously a metal clasp was once fashioned at these points to hold the stone blocks together. Again, it could not have been a gold clasp, it would have been to weak to have any effect, (and we know the megalith builders were effective!) and it could not have been put there by the Incas at some later date.

flow. The rise in land at that time is now calculated to be over sixty feet in a century. The Andes in this region may have risen 600 feet in the past 1,000 years. If they have risen at a constant rate that means they been uplifted by 6,000 feet in the last 10,000 years. But if in times of great stress, these upliftings occur at an even greater rate, the idea that Tiahuanacu was a coastal city, within the memory of man, is highly plausible. Whether such an upheaval could have occurred in the memory of man is debatable but the purpose in building such enormous monoliths and so great a city in the middle of so high and desolate a place remains a mystery.

D.E. Ibarra Grasso (*The Ruins Of Tiahuanacu*) investigated the nearby port of Puma-Punku which is connected to Tiahuanacu by tunnels and canals. There he found evidence of retaining walls and deep water piers. While the statues and megaliths of Tiahuanacu stand intact—except for the smaller blocks carted off to build La Paz—the megaliths of Puma Punku, some weighing 300 tons, lie strewn in disarray as if tossed about by some tremendous force.[19] The accepted theory is that Puma Punku was destroyed by an earthquake. But the sheer size of these boulders, weighing 100 times as much as the stones at the Great Pyramid at Giza, and the fact they, like the colossal stones at Ollantaytambu, were held together by large metal clamps (fig. 10-D) show that if an earthquake caused the destruction it must have been an earthquake of an unparalleled force.[20]

Are the ruins of Puma Punku the remains of the great flood of myth, while Tiahuanacu is just what the Incas told the Spanish it was, a new city erected near the ruins of the old, shortly after the deluge?

As at Sacsayhuaman, the Incas who lived there quickly told arriving Spanish that they had had nothing to do with Tiahuanacu's construction. They related a tale in which Tiahuanacu was built in a single night, immediately after the great flood, by a race of giants. The giants later disregarded a prophecy of the coming of the sun and were annihilated by its rays, and their city was reduced to rubble.[21] By *coincidence* Nahuatl myth tells that the Pyramids of the Sun and Moon at Teotihuacan in the Valley of Mexico were built by giants before a cataclysmic event turned day into night. A biblical parallel can found in Genesis (6:4), which describes a cataclysmic change in which the sun did not come forth, also stating that "there were giants on the Earth in those days."[22]

If Tiahuanacu was built in a single night it wasn't any recent night. Archaeologist Arthur Posnansky, who spent thirty years excavating the site, came to believe that the city was built between 10,000 and 12,000 years ago. Posnansky based this dating upon his discovery that the astronomical sight

10.E. STAFF GOD, GATEWAY OF THE SUN, TIAHUANACU. These stiff, rectilinear figures appear at Tiahuanacu in Bolivia, and throughout Peru. The are attributed to the "Chavin" style of artistic expression after the navigational Chavin de Huantar site in northern Peru. Their style also echoes the stiff Atlanteans figures of Tula, in the valley of Mexico, and Chichen Itza in the Yucatán. The need to portray figures holding up the sky was a repeated motif in ancient art. The only explanation for it is that they knew the sky sometimes fell on them! The Staff god is invariably depicted with tears beneath his eyes. According to Quechua myth he is weeping for the "sunken Red Land." Atlantis is often referred to as the Red Land.[18]

lines of the Kalasasaya Temple, Tiahuanacu's celestial observatory, were not based on the present day 23.5 obliquity of the Earth to the Sun but rather on an angle of 23 8' 48."[23] Since the angle of the obliquity changes slowly, less than 1 degree every 6,000 years it is relatively easy to determine when a structure measuring the obliquity was constructed (fig. 10-E).

Of course, traditional archaeologists balked at his date, dismissing archaeoastronomy as unproved pseudo-science. They preferred to believe Tiahuanacu and Kalasasaya were built in the first century B.C., while conceding that Puma Punku might be a little older. In 1926 the German Astronomical Commission sent an expedition to Bolivia to investigate Posnansky's dating. Their conclusions, after nearly three years of intensive study, was that the correct angle of obliquity could have been used in the formula to build Kalasasaya in either of two dates: 10,150 B.C. or 4050 B.C.[24]

When it became available radiocarbon techniques were used to date artifacts and organic matter found at the site. The official results of Bolivia's National Archaeological Institute report dates of 1580 to 1700 B.C. Although these dates do not fit the traditionalist's paradigm they were welcomed as proof that Posnansky was wildly wrong. Actually they only prove that Tiahuanacu was occupied around 3600 years ago. We know that the Spanish found the site occupied by the Inca a little less than 500 years ago. But neither of these dates tells us how long Tiahuanacu might have been occupied before these dates, nor does it give us any indication as to when it was built (fig. 10-F).

Now that we can reconstruct the ancient skies over Peru, by use of com-

10.F. SQUARE AND ROUND CHULPAS, LAKE TITICACA.

10.G. Mummy and accompanying woven cloth. These mummies, found wrapped in woven textiles, were discovered in the Altiplano of Bolivia. They have been dated to 8,000 B.C., over 3,000 years earlier than the entombed mummies in Egypt. Why are so many evidences of early man found in caves or on the driest plains of the Earth? The answer is simple—climate control. If we could really see into the past and see the diversity of the ancient world we would realize that most of the advanced cultures and great cities were situated on what is now either jungle-clad swamps or continental shelves laying in up to 500 feet of water. But these sites are not available. What is available can only be found at high elevations or in the driest deserts or in a combination of both. And in these places the record of civilized man goes back tens of thousands of years.

puters, and because the Precession of the Equinoxes occurs at a constant rate, we can confirm that Posnansky's dating of the site as 10,500 B.C., during the heliacal rising of the constellation Leo, was absolutely correct.

An indication of the age of Tiahuanacu may be inferred from a recent discovery of well-preserved mummies in nearby Arica in the Atacama desert of Northern Chile. A team of archaeologists headed by Dr. Marvin Allison, a pathologist, excavated ninety-six mummies, believed to be the remains of noblemen and priests. The mummies (fig. 10-G) were found buried in sacks, in fetal positions, accompanied by articles of gold and jewelry. They were wrapped in linen bandages and clothed in fine woven cloths of brilliant colors that were embroidered with cosmological symbols. Dr. Allison carbon dated the occupant of Tomb 761 as 7,810 years old, 2,500 years older than the oldest Egyptian mummy, and pronounced the Arica mummies as the oldest in the world. Subsequently similar subterranean vaults and burial chambers have been discovered at Nazca, Paracas, Ica, and at other sites in the northern deserts of Chile, some radio carbon dated as being over 9,000 years old.

Chilean Professor Ivan Munoz who heads the anthropological and archeological laboratories at the University of Tarapaca has dated mummies of men, women and children found in the desert sands surrounding Arica as being at least 8,000 years old. The elaborate process of mummification and preparation for the life beyond included not only removal of only the eyes and organs (including the genitals) but the skin of the deceased as well. All of

10.H. NEW DISCOVERIES IN THE TOMBS OF RAMSES II AT THEBES. In ancient Thebes, in the Valley of the Kings, across the Nile from the Egyptian city of Luxor, a new tomb was recently uncovered. In February of 1995 Kent Weeks entered what *USA Today* calls "the largest and most complicated mausoleum yet uncovered in Egypt's legendary Valley of the Kings." Weeks had found a passage to a vast tomb that contained the burial chambers of the more than fifty sons of Ramses II. Hieroglyphs in front of the tomb of Amen-hir-khopshef, the first-born son of Ramses II, indicate that the mummy is inside, and may prove, or disprove, the biblical story of Exodus. Ramses II is believed to have been the Pharaoh at the time Moses led the Israelites out of Egypt, after a scourge had brought death to all firsts-born sons of the Egyptians. If excavation shows that Amen-hir-khopshef met an early death it would confirm the Old Testament story. But another question would remain. Why would an old tomb that had been entered many times before, and that lies in one the most famous, and most extensively excavated, archeological sites in the world suddenly seem capable of such startling revelations? The answer is that the early entries were by looters who had no interest in archaeological revelations. Later discoverers were simply careless or looking for something other than what they found. Further excavation of the site was brushed aside as unimportant or fruitless. We now find that even in Egypt's Valley of the Kings the archeological record is far from complete. What does this mean for the vast number of archeological sites in Mesoamerica where less than 10 percent have been excavated, and where excavation has been partial and often misguided?[36]

these were treated with preservatives, then charred over a hot fire to remove all moisture. The organs, genitals, eyes and skin were then put back into the body. A final dressing was applied, and the facial features were expertly reconstructed. After treating the body with a final dressing it was wrapped in cotton. Munoz has reports of finds of over 300 mummies and his team has thoroughly examined over two dozen of them. Munoz believes that such an elaborate system of mummification, far more sophisticated than the later Egyptian mummies, would have required a school of embalming to train them in the necessary techniques.[25]

Examinations of Chinchorro culture, named after a beach near Arica, by Bernardo Arriaza, now Professor of physical anthropology at the University of Nevada in Las Vegas, have uncovered mummified skulls that may date back 10,000 years from a culture that derived 75 percent of its sustenance from the sea.[26] The diet of the of Chinchorros also included wild tomatoes, and mint, found in the bowels of several mummies, among other standard grains of early corn. But most of the Chinchorro diet was derived from the sea. This sustenance, from a people described as "masters of the ocean," by Virgilio Schiappacasse of the National Museum in Santiago, points toward a culture that truly never relied on migratory hunting of big land-based game nor on intensive agriculture.[27]

But is 9,000 years really so ancient? The Atacama desert is the world's driest with average annual rainfall of less than a half an inch a year. In some areas there has been no recorded rainfall at all within the last hundred years! Conditions therefore are perfect for the preservation of mummies, just as they have been in Egypt for the last 6,000 years, and where many more ancient finds await our discovery (fig. 10-H). It seems quite plausible that if it were not for the decomposing effect of the humid climates of Central and Mesoamerica we would find mummies there just as old, if not older.

Did astronomy and astrology really have their beginnings 6,500 years ago in Sumer? It would appear that an ocean and a continent away man had already been watching, measuring and recording the heavens. In the late nineteenth century, writer Ephraim George Squirer dubbed Tiahuanacu as "the Baalbek of the New World" in reference to their similarity to the ruins of colossal megaliths found in Lebanon. But since Tiahuanacu was probably built millennia before Baalbek perhaps the latter should be called the "Tiahuanacu of the Old World." The discovery that Tiahuanacu was a rectangle of megaliths constructed over an oval of canals and the probability that these canals ran all the way to Cuzco, and much further, hearkens back to Plato's description of Atlantis in the *Critias*.

Malta

The fallen structures at Puma Punku remind one of similar megaliths at Malta. Recently, excavations at Bahrain and at Malta (whose letters read right to left, as was the custom at that time, spelled Atlam) have uncovered sites older than those of Sumer and Egypt. At Malta the evidence is that a great wave overcame the site.

Just as at Stonehenge, the positioning of the sight lines of the temples at Malta were astronomical, geometrical, and numerical. The Temples at Hagar Qim contain various stones marking the vernal and autumnal equinoxes, solstice stones, and stones facing due north and due south. Entrances to the temples also faced major positions of the rising moon and positions of the rising planets of Mercury, Venus, Mars, Jupiter, and Saturn.[29] The similarities to Stonehenge are striking, including the horseshoe shape, the size and style of the megaliths, the astronomical evidence that they were essentially observatories, and the spiral inscriptions on the monuments, including the double spiral carving on the Second Tarxien Temple.[30] Organic material found at both sites has been radiocarbon dated to 3,000 B.C. (But, again, these may be evidence of peoples who worshiped the site thousands of years after its construction, not the builders themselves).

The unmistakable similarities to Stonehenge do not stand alone. The spiral forms of the zodiac both at Malta and at Stonehenge closely resemble those of early dynastic Egypt (3,000 B.C.).[31] And pottery techniques at Malta including "impressed decorations," rockering, and the use of cardium shells, and depictions of mammiform feet, have all been found in pottery in Mexico and Guatemala with datings as recent as 1500 B.C.[32]

Since there is no evidence of inhabitation of the Temples at Malta after 3,000 B.C., one could easily speculate that the cultures of Stonehenge, Guatemala, and even Egypt were a continuation of a culture that had, for some reason, been abandoned. And the logical cause for abandonment would be the cataclysm that hurled its huge megalithic stones, through air or water, to the ground.

In Malta megalithic ruins have long been considered a mystery because of the enormous size of some of the stone blocks used in construction (one measuring twenty-three feet in length, nine feet in height, and over two feet in thickness) and because of the horseshoe shape of the ruin, reminiscent of Stonehenge. But the greatest mystery has been the manner in which huge blocks of stone, some over 9 feet in length have been "blown off" of what we now know their original position to have been by a distance of fifteen to thirty feet. All of the great slabs that formed a north-to-south line, and therefore had there broad sides facing west, were moved by some great force in a direct line from west to east. One great slab measuring nine feet by nine feet by two feet, that obviously had been the horizontal lintel of the main entrance (the horizontal piece across the top of the entrance that carried the weight of the structure above it) was moved more than twenty feet to the east and broken in its fall.[28]

No earthquake could have moved all these huge blocks such a distance nor would it have moved them all in one direction. The only viable explanation is that a huge wave of water, moving from west to east caused the incredible destruction. The question that arises is what could have caused a wave of water of this magnitude? If it was the great flood then the ruins at Malta would have had to have been antediluvian and originally constructed over 11,500 years ago. Could the ruins of Malta be that old?

At Malta, comparison of the violently dislodged westward facing stones to those on the west-to-east running south wall that stood intact, and therefore were not subject to erosion, reveal that the stones hurled by the cataclysm have endured an extra 5,000 to 6,000 years of erosion and weathering. Since the power of that inundation was immense, we can only speculate that something extraordinary happened at that time. Has the dating of the weathering been incorrect, or is it possible that a subsequent worldwide cataclysm and inundation occurred around 5,000 years ago? While the current evidence now indicates that the Temple of Hagar Qim was destroyed at that time, it appears that it was constructed from 5,000 to 7,000 years before that, making Malta a contemporary culture of Atlantis. Why Malta was abandoned shortly before the time that Sumer, Egypt and Mesoamerica began a new age is still a mystery. But they must be related.

If, outside of Malta, we have insufficient physical evidence of an "event" 5,000 to 6,000 years ago, we do have sufficient evidence in legend. Based on myth, and the Mayan long count, it is apparent that a great event, with worldwide implications, occurred around the year 3110 B.C. If the event was in the form of a disaster it must have been very minor as cataclysms go—certainly it was nothing compared to the disaster six millennia earlier, because it left no record of extinguished species.

How else can we account for Malta's "demise," the sudden emergence of dynastic civilization in Egypt, a great expansion of pyramid building in Sumer, the rise of civilization in China, and the beginnings of the Stonehenge culture in England—all coinciding with the Mayan calendar's reckoning of the year zero (of the fifth and current Mayan age) in 3113 B.C.? Conventional science has long suggested that this date was mythical (read "untrustworthy"), but some extraordinary event must have happened. And it must have happened in the heavens, to have so influenced sky watchers around the world that it acted as a catharsis for a new age.

In *City of Revelation* John Michell points out that the decisive moments in history have always been believed to be attended by strange celestial phenomena. Michell cites the glowing cross recorded by Josephus at the fall of Jerusalem and the comet over the battlefield of Hastings as examples.[35] But celestial portents of doom, as we have seen, have occurred universally. Mere coincidence could not account for these occurrences, not for the "mythical mind," where correspondences between upheaval in the heavens and upheavals on Earth were intrinsically connected.

Could the year 3113 B.C. been attended by a near miss by a comet without the mass destruction that befell Atlantis but rather, with a short period of upheaval followed by a new resolve to rebuild? It is at least a possibility. All great moments in history seem to have been attended by celestial upheavals or signs—including the birth of Christ.

If we know that this date, 3113 B.C., marked a new beginning for diverse cultures around the world why not regard it as the time of Atlantis? There are two reasons: One, the sinking of Atlantis was attended by world-wide destruction, and not an event that synchronized with immediate rebuilding. Secondly, the great megalithic constructions of the world all appear to have been built near to, or prior to, 9500 B.C. In the archaic world, 9500 and 3100 B.C., are really not that far apart. Little needed to change, and little was likely to have changed in the basic structure of civilization during that period. Mankind was in "dream-time" prior to the inception of great wars in the Mediterranean (1000 B.C.) and later in the Americas (around 600 A.D.) Time was measured by the movements of the celestial universe, not by man's acts on land. Yet building skills deteriorated, particularly those needed to erect great megaliths with exact measurements. When civilization itself finally deteriorated to warfare, time itself came to be defined by the acts of conquerors, the length of their rule, and the extent of their acquisitions. Today we behave like the material manikins the *Popol Vuh* once portrayed in describing a failed earlier attempt to create man. Are we about to encounter a disaster that will wipe meaningless conquest out, or a near disaster that will put us back into a more enlightened and meaningful relationship with the cosmos?

Egypt

There are two types of pyramids in Egypt (fig. 10-I). Those built during the times of the Pharaohs and those built before the Pharaohs. We think we know the dates of the Pharaonic pyramids because we've been able to decipher their accompanying hieroglyphics. (We also know that history, both recent and ancient, can be revised). We know the dates of Sumerian ziggurats because of the cuneiform writing that accompanied them. And we think we

10.I. THE GREAT PYRAMID OF KHUFU (CHEOPS). Seen from above (see also 9K). The yardstick of the Great Pyramid is the sacred cubit and the base of the pyramid is 500 cubits. The cubit, described by Pharoanic Egyptians to be the measurement of a man's arm from the elbow to the tip of the middle finger, is in fact a much more precise measurement, apparently based on precise knowledge of the size of the earth. The sacred cubit, we now know, is exactly one-ten millionth of the radius of the earth taken from the center of the earth to either of the poles. The radius of the Earth is 3,949.89 miles or ten million sacred units.[37] Thus the cubit, unlike the foot, yard, or meter used today, accurately describes that essential and irrational equation of pi. Coincidentally (we use that word in its ironic sense), there are 86,400,000 cubits in the circumference of the Earth and 86,400 seconds in one twenty-four hour day. Could a cubit be both a measure of time and space, or space-time?

In addition the estimated weight of the Great pyramid is 5.3×10^6 tons. The weight of the Earth has been calculated to be 5.3×10^{20} tons, making the pyramid an earth-commensurate one thousand-trillionth of the Earth's weight. Many other precise dimensions reflecting the Great Pyramid as an exact model of the Earth have been recorded. No other Egyptian burial pyramids match any of this precise construction. Hieroglyphs depicting the majesty of the Pharaohs grace the lessor pyramids. No hieroglyphs accompany the Great Pyramid.

know the dates of construction of some of the most recent of the Meso-american pyramids because of the hieroglyphs on accompanying stelae . . . although there is evidence in each case that the stelae and accompanying records could have been erected and written by a later conquering people who wanted to claim earlier constructions as their own. But of the unadorned MesoAmerican and the pre-Pharaonic pyramids we really know little in terms of dating. The Great Pyramid of Khufu (Cheops), the world's greatest astronomical measuring device, could be anywhere from 5,000 to 12,000 years old.

The Great Sphinx (fig. 10-J) which seemingly accompanies it, may be as old, or older than the Great Pyramid. Long attributed to the pharaoh Khafre (Chephren), hieroglyphs on the stela of Tuthmosis IV reveal that the Sphinx had already been long in existence at the time of the pharaoh Khufu, long before Khafre's rule.

Recently archeoastronomer, John Anthony West, geophysicist, Dr. Thomas Dobecki and geologist, Professor Robert Schoch of Boston University, working on theories first put forth by the brilliant mathematician, R.A. Schwaller de Lubicz, have placed the construction of the Sphinx in the same time frame as the Great Pyramid at Giza—- around 12,500 years ago—at a time when its leonine body (and probable lion's head) would have faced the constellation Leo rising in the east (fig. 10-K).

The combined efforts of these three scholars, including seismic surveying of subsurface rocks and studies of weathering indicate that the Sphinx was carved at time when the climate in Egypt was much wetter than it was in the time of the dynasties of the Pharaohs. Paleoclimatology has placed the dates for a wet environment in Egypt at from 7,000 to 15,000 years ago.

Most Egyptologists, defending the traditional paradigm, have insisted that the Sphinx shows great erosion only because it was carved from inferior stone and was subjected to centuries of sand blasting from desert winds. But the main body of the Sphinx was hard rock that had for millennia been buried in sand, protected from wind for most of its existence. A team from Stanford University found that the limestone of the Sphinx is every bit as hard and durable as the limestone used in the construction of all the great (and unprotected) structures in Egypt. The Sphinx should appear much younger and less eroded than the dynastic monuments. Its extreme weathering, particularly in deep fissures that have long been buried under sand, and reflect erosion by

10.J. THE GREAT SPHINX. What riddle has the Sphinx? The Sphinx, carved out of a single ridge of rock, lay buried up to its neck when Napoleon arrived in Egypt. Since the rock from which the Sphinx was carved was in a hollow this natural burial process occurred every twenty to thirty years if the monument was left untended. Thus the body, protected by covering sand for millennia, should show the least erosion. Instead it shows the most. Why? Under Napoleon's direction the Sphinx was excavated in 1816. (The great pock marks on the nose of the Sphinx are the result of artillery practice by Napoleon's bored troops).

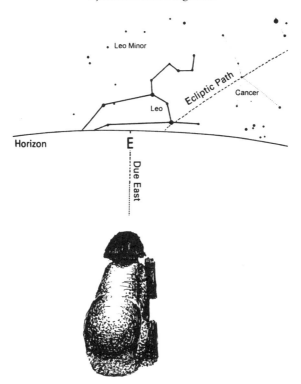

10.K. LEONINE SPHINX. All but the head is lion. But since the head is proportionally smaller than the rest of the Sphinx it may well be that it was once all lion and later modified to resemble the head of the pharaoh Khafre (Chephren). The Sphinx faces due east, toward the rising of the sun and, over millennia, gazes at the heliacal precession of constellations that "house" the signs of the zodiac. If the zodiac house had been in Taurus at the time of its construction you would expect the builders of the Sphinx to have erected a bull to reflect the harmony of earth with the heavens. In fact it is the bull that is celebrated by ancient Minoans and very early Greeks, indicating that that their sciences of astronomy and astrology dated from at least 2500 B.C. But if the builders of the Sphinx were sky-watchers–they were–it is obvious that they celebrated a constellation 6,600 years older than Taurus, in an age when Leo marked the rising of the sun.[40]

---

water rather than by wind, points to the conclusion that the Sphinx not only predates the lesser pyramids and colossi of Egypt by thousands of years, but to the possibility that it was constructed *prior* to the time of the great flood of 12,500 B.P.[39]

In fact the erosion of the Sphinx is now believed by geologist Schoch, and geophysicist Dobecki to be due not only to the work of water, instead of sand or wind, but to a particular kind of water erosion—precipitation (fig. 10-L). Although the erosion corresponds to the time of the melting of the ice sheets from the last great Ice Age, Nile floods could not account for kind of erosion the Sphinx now displays. Erosion by floods would have undercut the layers of limestone rock indenting the weaker layers of limestone in a horizontal direction—working very much like wind erosion in cutting out softer layers. But the erosion at all levels of the Sphinx form an undulating profile of vertical fissures that could only have been formed by water constantly cascading down the sides of the Sphinx. That condition would require great and extended rainfall! Since by the time of the first pharaohs—5,000 years ago—the climate in Egypt was already quite dry, and since the pre-Pharoanic period on the Nile is generally considered to have been populated by a simple farming people, the builders of the Sphinx must have come from a far earlier age.

Were they Atlanteans? Quite possibly. Although the outer shell of the great Pyramid was fitted with mere two-and-a-half ton granite blocks, the interior blocks, laid out at precise angles, were immense, with some weighing over seventy tons each. Granite blocks at the base of the Sphinx measure 30x12x10 feet and weigh approximately 200 tons. Precisely fitted megaliths of that size can only be found at very few places, including Stonehenge in England, Sacsayhuaman in Peru, and as the legacy of the builders of the spheres of Costa Rica. The builders of the greatest megaliths all came from an age far earlier than that commonly accorded to the rise of civilization. And they had means of construction that, in some cases, were beyond our present abilities.

10.L. EROSION OF SPHINX. Geologist Robert Schoch of Boston University found that erosion has cut more deeply into the higher rock layers of the base of the Sphinx even though the rock at higher levels is composed of harder and more durable rock. Why? Because rain comes from the top. If the Sphinx had been eroded by flood waters there would have been an undercutting, with the softer, lower levels receding more significantly than the upper levels. This is not the case. Persistent rainfall is the only explanation for the erosion of the Sphinx.[38]

Could civilization in Egypt be 12,000 years old? Could it have been much older? The Egyptians thought so. Although no artifact of comparable merit or age to the artistic masterpieces of Lascaux and Chauvet (France), or to earlier art in the Americas and Australia, has yet been found in Egypt, chronological tables of the Egyptians place the founding of that civilization at a minimum of 23,000 B.C. Herodotus quotes Egyptian historians as saying that during the long rule of the Neters and the Shemsu Hor "the sun has twice risen where it now sets, and twice set where it now rises." In *Serpent In The Sky* John A. West repeats Schwaller de Lubicz' interpretation of this remark as depicting the passage of one and a half precessional cycles, or "great years." That would push Egypt's foundation back to 36,000 B.C., a date that corresponds with the sudden arrival of Cro-Magnon man in the Mediterranean region.[40]

In myth the sun god, Ra, created Seb, the Earth-god, and Nut, the sky-god. Nut was also Ra's wife, but Ra believed that she betrayed him by cohabiting with her brother Seb.[41] In Frazer's rendition in *The Golden Bough*, taken from Plutarch, the sun God decreed as a curse that Nut should be delivered of a child "in no month and in no year" under his rule.[42] At that time the Earth was believed to have twelve months of thirty days, all under Ra's domain. But Nut called on the god of wisdom, Thoth, for assistance. Thoth, in Frazer's words, played "at draughts with the moon (and) won from her a seventy-second part of every day, and having compounded five whole days out of these parts he added them to the Egyptian year of three hundred and sixty days." The extra five days lay outside Ra's curse and Osiris was born on the first of them, the elder Horus on the second, Set on the third, and they were followed by Isis and Nephthys.

Osiris and Isis were wed, and were believed to have ruled Egypt in this "First Time," in a Golden Age without strife or warfare, that endured for a long time. But Set became jealous of his older brother and one day slew him and cut his body into fourteen parts. Isis discovered her slain husband and wrapped his dismembered parts together with cloth, creating a mummy. Her devotion brought Osiris to life again for one moment, enough time for Osiris to impregnate her with their son, Horus the younger. Horus later avenged his father's death, and became the first of the Pharaohs, and from Horus all pharaohs traced their descent and their divinity.

After his moment of rebirth Osiris left the Earth and was reborn as the brightest of the three stars of the Orion belt. At her death Isis became the bright star the Greeks called Sirius, which forever follows Orion (Osiris) through the heavens. Frazer: "In the resurrection of Osiris the Egyptians saw the pledge of a life everlasting for themselves beyond the grave. They believed that every man would live eternally in the other world if only . . . there was enacted a representation of the divine mystery which had been performed of old over Osiris."[43]

Parallels can be drawn between the Egyptian myth of Osiris and the biblical story of Cain and Abel, and even in the resurrection of Christ. But an even more poignant parallel can be found in the myths of the Quiche Maya of Guatemala, preserved in their book of creation, the *Popol Vuh*. In the *Popol Vuh* we are told that there was Golden Age when gods lived as men on Earth. One of these was Hunahpu, who with his twin brother, Xbalanque, was adept at playing ball. One day, in a fierce game against the sky-gods at the brink of Xibalba (the underworld), Hunahpu was beheaded, his heart was torn from his chest, and his body was dismembered. But Hunahpu was resurrected and he ascended to the heavens to become the evening star, Venus, and a symbol of the everlasting nature of courage.[45]

Thereafter warriors playing in the god-given game in the ball courts of Mesoamerica, reenacted Hunahpu's battle, just as the ritual of Osiris had been replayed in dramas throughout the pharaonic dynasties of Egypt, usually at the winter solstice.[46] Mayan ballplayers gladly gave their lives at the end of the game in the belief that they would join Hunahpu in the heavens. Archaeologists have maintained that it was always the losers who met a brutal end. But there is also evidence that it was the winners who were ceremoniously sacrificed.

In our model, myth predates and precedes the construction of megaliths and star temples. In the recently well-received book *The Message of The Sphinx,* authors Hancock and Bauval, make a strong case that the construction of the Sphinx and of the pyramids at Giza, were inspired by the myth of Osiris. Their presentation, based on an examination of Egyptian myth and the newly developed science of archeoastronomy dates these megalithic structures to about 10,500 years B.C., predating the later and inferior burial pyramids of the pharaonic Egyptians by over 7,000 years.

Hancock and Bauval have pointed out that the angle of the three pyramids at Giza exactly replicates the alignment of the "belt" of the constellation Orion to which Osiris is believed to have ascended. Except that Orion is today "out of kilter" with the pyramids, as if the sky has rotated away from the line drawn by the pyramids. Of course that is what the entire sky has done, from Earth's perspective, due to the Earth's wobble and full precession of 25,920 years. Even at 2500 B.C., when the myth of Osiris was reputedly written down, Orion was out of alignment with the pyramids which had been built to reflect and imitate the Egyptian myth (fig. 10-M).[47] If Osiris ascended at the "first time," the time that the three great pyramids would have exactly mimicked the three stars of Orion, that date would have been 12,500 years ago, at the

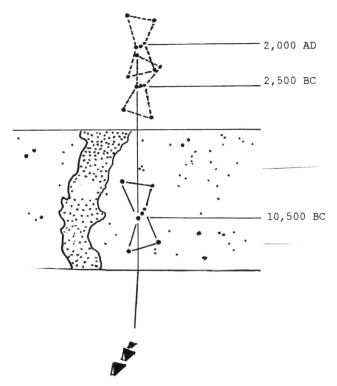

10.M. CONSTELLATION ORION with Osiris and Isis and its configuration in the sky over the past 12,500 years. The same constellation appears as a repeated motif in Maya art with the three bright stars of Orion's "belt" appearing as the back of a turtle. The Maya hieroglyph of the turtle constellation was associated with the 584-day orbit of Venus and was used to signify the reappearance of Venus as the "morning Star" once every eight Earth years. (Actually the Maya knew that Venus's orbital year was completed in 583.92 Earth days proving once again that Maya observations were sustained over a very long period of time).[44]

beginning of Orion's precessional cycle at the heliacal rising of the constellation Leo.[48]

The myth of the god-man dismembered and resurrected as a star, moon, or planet, mummification as a means of preserving the body in its journey to the after-life, and presentation of creation and foundation myth in immense stone structures, all occur in antiquity on both sides of the Atlantic. The huge Aztec stone wheel demonstrates that as late as the twelfth century A.D. the myth endured and was recreated in stone. since we know the Egyptians and the Maya held virtually identical myths expressed in stone thousands of years earlier we also know that the more recent Aztecs did not originally fashion their myth of Coyolxauhqui (fig. 10-N). However, in constructing their temples they repeated elements of an older and more sophisticated culture that had long been in decline. The Egyptians, through all the years of the dynasties of the great pharaohs, never duplicated the mathematical and astronomical knowledge found at the earliest pyramids at Giza. The later pyramids were not built in accordance with myth, nor in harmony with the heavens—they were simply tombs for pharaohs, built by a people who had forgotten why the original pyramids were built. Yet both cultures, in the display of beliefs carved in great stone, hearken back to a Golden Age of mankind, that can be found to be an international, if not universal, belief in man's harmony with the heavens.

Can the fact that step pyramids, based on knowledge of pi, are duplicated in Sumer, Egypt, and the great pyramids of the Americas, be coincidence? Can the nearly identical telling of foundation myths, such as the Quiche Maya

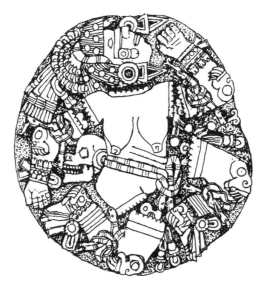

10.N. COYOLXAUHQUI, TEMPLO MAYOR, MEXICO CITY (TENOCHTITLÁN). In 1978 workmen digging next to the National Cathedral in Mexico City uncovered what was described as a huge stone wheel engraved with the dismembered body of Coyolxauhqui, the moon-goddess. Eventually archaeologists unearthed much of Tenochtitlán, the vast Aztec capital encountered by the conquistadors. The legend of Coyolxauhqui, the Aztec version of the Mayan myth of Hunahpu, relates that she was dismembered by her brother, Xiuhcoatl, the god-serpent of fire. Thereafter she became the evening star, ruling the night only to be dismembered again each morning at the rising of the sun. The "wheel" on which Coyolxauhqui is engraved is more likely a depiction of the moon into which she is transformed. It is of little consequence that Coyolxauhqui is female while Osiris and Hunahpu are male. The Aztecs were recent invaders of the Valley of Mexico who had been there only several hundred years before the Spanish arrived. We must remember that, by their own admission, the Aztecs did not originally construct the great temples of their city nor did they invent the myths that accompanied them—both were borrowed from the great Toltec-Mayan cultures that had long preceded them.[49]

Hunahpu myth of Guatemala, in its complex, yet succinct depiction of man's origins, travails, and final destiny, be the product of parallel evolution? Can the celestial orientation of star temples in Egypt, that point to constellation positions that existed 8,000 to 12,500 years ago, find a similar orientation in Costa Rica, Peru, and Bolivia—where mummification was practiced over 8,000 years ago—only by some wild chance? Or did significant and repeated contact exist in a time that Plato and his Egyptian sources could still remember, at least have access to, but that we have forgotten?

Of course, dating the Sphinx to nine thousand years before the accepted dates for monument building in Egypt places it "out of context," just as the spheres of Costa Rica have been similarly judged with apparent dates dismissed as "preposterous." The same goes for many of the sites we've discussed, be they in Mexico, Peru, or in the "Old World": "out of context" has been the response of the authorities of academia.

Cuicuilco

Off the road between Mexico City and Cuernavaca, flanked by central Mexico's towering volcanoes, lies the site of Cuicuilco (fig. 10-O). Cuicuilco is unique among ancient pyramids in that it is circular, often described as a truncated cone, and in that it has four internal galleries and a central staircase leading to the summit. Discovered and first excavated by Manuel Gamio in 1917, Cuicuilco is unusual in another way; it is partially covered by pre-historic lava streams. Commenting on this fact David Hatcher Childress writes in *Lost Cities of North and Central America,* "Cuicuilco is said to be one of the oldest structures in the Valley of Mexico, and traditional archaeologists, with their conservative ways, usually say that Cuicuilco is the forerunner of Teotihuacan. (But) the amazing thing about the Cuicuilco pyramid is the dating that it is given. The site is dated at being built in the first century of the Christian era. Yet, incredibly, the lava flow, which covers a portion of the structure, is dated as being 8,000 years old."

It occurred to Childress, as it has to others, that a pyramid that has been covered by a lava flow must have been built sometime before the date of the lava flow. Childress comments, "This fact is apparently lost on traditional archaeologists who continue to maintain that Cuicuilco is about 2,000 years old."

Actually, Cuicuilco *was* blanketed by a volcanic eruption in 300 A.D. But lava from that eruption was only the last of a series of lava flows that covered parts of the pyramid. In 1922 geologist George E. Hyde had estimated the age of the flow that covered the pyramid, called the Pedregal lava flow, as being 7,000 years old.

10.O. PYRAMID OF CUICUILCO. The top view is of the entire pyramid. The inset view is of the encroachment of lava that, in ancient times, repeatedly covered the pyramid. This site, accepted as among the oldest in the Valley of Mexico is dominated by a massive circular pyramid with a base 387 feet in diameter and a height of 75 feet.[50] Although parts of the large and complex site are buried by ash from volcanoes as recently as 300 A.D., other parts are buried under volcanic ash that has been dated as 7,000 years old. (Despite this evidence Cuicuilco is still officially dated as from 2,000 to 4,000 years old).

Archaeologist, Byron Cummings, became interested in the site when he learned of Hyde's findings. In his excavations Cummings found eighteen feet of sediment and ashes between the bottom of the Pedregal lava layer and the pavement surrounding the pyramid. He estimated the accretion time of these layers to be 6,500 years. Later, carbon 14 tests came up with dates of 4161 B.P. for organic material on the pyramid and surrounding pavement. This would give it a calibrated date of around 5,000 B.P.. Since the organic material could have been deposited at any time subsequent to the building of the pyramid but could not have been deposited prior to its construction, and since a 7,000-year-old lava flow covers one corner of the pyramid, the structure must have been built at least 7,000 years ago but it more likely was built centuries or millennia before that.

Despite this evidence archaeologists continued, until very recently, to date Cuicuilco as about 2,000 years old. But after dates for Cuicuilco's "step-child," Teotihuacan, have been "officially" pushed back to 900 B.C., traditional archaeologists began to admit a date of 1800 B.C. for Cuicuilco's construction. Childress observes, "Though Cummings' discoveries and assertions created something of a stir at the time, archaeologists have conveniently ignored the fantastically ancient date . . . the 'experts' do not like to be confused by the facts. Cuicuilco is perhaps a good example of how the current dating of ruins in Mexico and over much of the world is spurious, at best. Arbitrary dates, usually conforming to preconceived opinions on the age of structures, are given to stone structures, and these dates are final ... science has spoken, and history books need not be rewritten."[51]

Mitla & Monte Alban

In the Valley of Oaxaca two great megalithic sites reveal patterns identical to ancient sites in the Andes and in the Mediterranean. At Mitla, where entire walls are covered by mosaics of geometric stonework, and at Monte Alban, where intricate underground tunnels and canals rival Cuzco and Tiahuanacu, the megalithic pattern again asserts itself. The deepest and oldest levels are graced by huge megaliths, precisely carved, like those at "Three Windows" at Machu Picchu (fig. 10-P). The more recent levels, those that conform to archaeologists dating of the sites as circa 500 B.C., are both smaller, and cruder, revealing a very different construction phase, and a much more recent evolution.

At Monte Alban (the Spanish called it "White Mountain" but its Zapotec name has been lost), gold masks and intricately carved jade stones have been found, and have been systematically looted. The jade found there is not native to the Valley of Oaxaca, but had come from Guatemala, cacao had come from Panama, tin from Bolivia, copper from Lake Superior, all indicating extensive

10.P. ONE OF THE "THREE WINDOWS" AT MACHU PICCHU. Compare this site with Lubaantun (fig 3K.), with Tiahuanacu (below) and other sites where stones are fitted perfectly together and where no mortar is used. Traditional archaeology has called this site at Machu Picchu as recent as 1400 A.D. Archaeoastronomy has dated "Three Windows" to 2500 B.C. Incas have always told of a more ancient people who built the megaliths. Whom are we to believe?

trade. It has also been found that this deep valley, isolated from the seas by high mountains, had considerable contact with the sea, both by astronomical and navigational guidelines left written in the megaliths but also by the presence of many sting ray spines and sharks jaws, and an almost endless number of sea-turtle shells.[52] But a much more interesting tale has been told by the stone carvings that remain etched in the cyclopean rocks. Called *danzantes*, dancers, these figures have a Negroid appearance with flat noses, round faces, and thick lips (fig. 10-Q). At first appraisal they were thought to be swimmers, acrobats, and dancers. Then the traditionalists arrived and pointed to a darker aspect: they argued that the dancing figures appeared to be victims of some form of sacrifice. At one stone carving a heart seems to have been torn out, at another a brain has been extracted.

In the tradition of archeological stereotypes it was soon established that the depiction of these danzantes tell a horrible story of torture and human sacrifice. But recent rereading of the murals and their instructions, as well depiction of pregnant women helped through childbirth, have revealed a *different* nature to this center of ancient activity. It now appears that Monte Alban was in part a medical university, teaching methods in child delivery, bone repair, and brain surgery.[53]

10.Q. DANZANTES, MONTE ALBAN. These figures, called *danzantes*, or dancers, have been depicted as captured and tortured warriors. Actually, they were more likely to have been portraits of ailing patients at an ancient medical university.

The Web of Knowledge

What knowledge of the ancient world has been lost due to our inability to see MesoAmerican cultures as comprised of nothing more than gifted, but blood-thirsty savages? Ancient star temples, aligned with the heavens, have been depicted as "ceremonial centers" of human sacrifice. Ancient calendars, intricate in their depiction of time and in their mythological depictions of celestial eras, have been called sacrificial slabs. Apparent ancient medical universities have been depicted as scenes where prisoners of war were humiliated, tortured and then mutilated.[54]

What do all of these similarities in construction, from Monte Alban and Tenoctitlan to Cuzco and Tiahuanacu, and from Stonehenge to Malta and Egypt—reflecting similarities in myth as well—point to? They point to a remembrance of a past glory of mankind and to cataclysms that destroyed their culture.

The evidence also points to ancient survivors of the great cataclysm of 9500 B.C. A people whose memory was obsessed by a great deluge and who still possessed the rudiments of a technology which we no longer understand. It may be inferior to late twentieth century technology but if we suffered a similar cataclysm and a subsequent "nuclear winter" in its aftermath, we would do well to repeat this performance.

Why were mathematical equations built into the pyramids and other

10.R, 10.S. GLYPHS FROM THE GROLIER CODEX describe the movements of Venus. 10.R (left) shows the winged Venus as it bisects a sightline of a temple. Fig. 10.S (right) shows Venus directly above a ball court. Since half the court is dark this may indicate a rising at dawn at the equinox.

The Dresden Codex, like the Grolier Codex, is basically a 400-year calendar of the cycles of Venus, a planet of endless fascination to the ancient Maya. More recently another Venus calendar has been found in the form of the Grolier Codex, so named because its anonymous owner permitted its unveiling at the Grolier Club in New York in 1971. The Grolier codex, which now can be described as a highly complex astronomical computer, predicts a cyclical reappearance of Venus, in which it returns to its original position in the sky, every 1247 years.[57] In fact, the codex is the "world's first and only perpetual calendar of Venus." How long had the Maya been observing the movements of Venus before realizing the repetition of its synodical revolutions?

ancient megaliths of Sumer, Egypt, and the Americas? Did the builders expect a computer would come along some day to read the numbers contained in their constructions (figs. 10-R, 10-S)? Or did mathematics once have a significance later lost and only recently rediscovered?

The mathematical sophistication of the Great Pyramid at Giza was never duplicated in the later, historic pyramids constructed by the pharaohs. The precision of the thirty-two-faceted megaliths at Sacsayhuaman were never duplicated by the latter Inca builders. The precision of the spheres of Costa Rica stands in stark contrast to the relatively primitive cultural sites that have been excavated in that country, and which date thousands of years later. Under the simplistic paradigm that views history as a gradual, but ever more sophisticated, advance through time we have no way of accounting for the building of harmonic and astronomically complex structures. Yet, in each of the above cases, evidence points to a once highly sophisticated mathematical culture being replaced by a less sophisticated culture, able to mimic, but unable to revitalize the celestial knowledge that were the integral aspect of the original building.

The most monumental structures of what we have called the Stone Age and of the Bronze Age appear to be the oldest. Commenting on the megalithic temples of Malta and pre-Roman Britain Cyrus Gordon wrote . . . "Such achievements can not be the work of primitive men starting from scratch with nothing but independent invention to raise them from barbarism. Their structures are masterpieces of architecture and engineering that reflect long scientific and technological development. Moreover, the technical interrelations among early builders in various parts of the world point to some common background, rooted in a great, earlier culture on which they all drew."[55]

According to Herodotus, Thales of Miletus predicted an eclipse which occurred on May 28, of the year 585 B.C. Saint Augustine states that Thales was able to predict solar and lunar eclipses through his knowledge of astronomical calculations. If scientists, by Thales' time, had established the cycle of eclipses through observation, they must have done so on the basis of global coverage. The minimal coverage required for establishing the cycle is at three longitudinal bands, 120 degrees apart, splitting the Earth's surface into thirds. Ancients, in order to determine eclipses and other significant would have had to have known of solar events from a very wide perspective. Did they?

Was Cuzco Poseidon, the central capital of Atlantis? It was old enough, large enough, advanced enough, and it fit Plato's physical description of a circular city with concentric rings, even down to the worship of bulls, although they (like the horse and camel) were not supposed to have been in the Americas.

Both Cuzco or Tiahuanacu as the *center* of Atlantis share a central flaw, but it is a great one indeed. They do not lie at the *center* of a great continent and they aren't seaports. Probably Tiahuanacu is just what the Incas said it was, a great city, an Atlantean city, built high above sea level but also closer to the visible stars that held man's destiny. Or was it built shortly *after* the last deluge, and set high in the Andes as a retreat from the ocean where great waves from another Deluge was unlikely to destroy it?

If Tiahuanacu and Cuzco are close, but still not the real thing, where should we look for Atlantis's heart and center, the destroyed city of Poseidon? One path to the answer can be found by dividing the Earth into longitudinal thirds. If we regard the Near East as one center of ancient science, and took the area of ancient Baalbek and Jericho as one point (approximately 35 degrees east longitude), and moved to a point 120 degrees to the west, we would find ourselves on a longitudinal line that bisects the west coast of Cuba, the east coast of Nicaragua, and runs directly through the plains of the Diquis Delta, where the great spheres are found (at 85 degrees west longitude.)

If we place the Near East center in Sumer (southern Iraq) at 47 degrees east longitude, and traveled 120 degrees west, we would find ourselves at 73 degrees west longitude, at Cuzco and Machu Picchu. From Karnak and Giza in Egypt (at 31-32 degrees east longitude) it is 120 degrees west to a longitudinal line that runs past or through Chichen Itza and Coba in the Yucatán, Santa Rita, Caracol, Nim Li Punit and Lubaantun in Belize, and Copan in Honduras–all great areas of astronomical observation and development. In each case the third longitudinal coordinate lies in the western Pacific, in the ancient navigational centers of the Carolinas, the Solomons, and the Samoan Islands. And in each case the great astronomical centers of the Middle East had counterparts in the Americas—and vice-versa. If you believe this to be the result of coincidence, consider that the megaliths of Malta lie at 15 degrees east longitude, and the megaliths of Easter Island lie at 105 degrees west longitude—120 degrees apart.[56]

Diogenes Laertius, in the third century A.D., stated that ancient Egyptian astronomers had recorded 373 solar eclipses and 832 lunar eclipses. Given the perspective of Egypt and accounting for the periodicity of eclipses in a region of known star temples, it would have taken 10,000 years for these astronomers, recording the heavens from 2,000 years B.C., to have observed that number of eclipses.[58]

The Mayans recorded thousands of eclipses. It has recently been determined that the Mayan hieroglyphs of the so-called Dresden Codex, are believed to have been compiled near Chichen Itza, described 77 eclipses in a thirty-three year period from 755 A.D. to 788 A.D. Computer recreations of the past paths of the moon have now confirmed that all 77 eclipses did occur during those years. But all these eclipses did not fall on the line of observatories from South America to Mesoamerica. They occurred randomly, all over the Earth. In fact, during that period, only four of the eclipses fell on the star temples of eastern Mexico; many could only have been witnessed from vantage points in Siberia, Africa, Antarctica, and from points in the oceans where astronomers and their devices were supposedly absent.[59]

Observation of these eclipses, by itself, required communication from all points of the globe. And that information had to have been conveyed in terms that understood the key tenets of Mayan mathematics. Prediction of the eclipses would require not only a worldwide network of information, but some knowledge by the Mayans that we simply do not yet understand. This much is clear, a world-wide "web" of information was needed for the Mayans to have attained a 100 percent accuracy in describing solar eclipses and a 98 percent accuracy in predicting lunar eclipses on a world-wide basis. That information could not have come from migrating peoples, or sailors blown off course. It could only have come from navigators and astronomers working under a single mathematical system, and regularly reporting their observations to a central cosmic university. That university had to be at the center of the world's sea lanes. It had to be where the Pacific and the Atlantic met in Mesoamerica. It had to be at Atlantis.

Curiously, during repeated CNN broadcasts of a solar eclipse in the Caribbean region on February 27, 1998, reporters stressed a story of how Columbus was faced with violence by native Americans but quelled their aggressiveness by predicting a solar eclipse, an event that reportedly occurred almost immediately after the prediction. Columbus must have known of eclipses and much more than the average European of his time, but there is no evidence to suggest Columbus knew when and where they would occur. There is a great deal of evidence, written in hieroglyphs of the native Americans, that they knew when and where solar eclipses would occur. How did this story get "turned around?" Why is it still repeated?

•

Eighteen Rabbit could only cry for the people that had been vanquished at Cuzco. His people had put up so little resistance that not even a sword was raised in their defense! But he thought of what a great city it once was, and of the knowledge that had been destroyed? He vowed that the knowledge of his ancestors would become his knowledge. It would not die. It would live for an eternity. They were so great. Why were they not fighters! Why had they not protected their great city?

11 Ancient Navigators: *Man Across the Seas*

THREE RABBIT watched as Smoke Monkey pushed the balsa log out into the river current. As usual Smoke Monkey got to the biggest log first and he seemed sure to be the one to ride it out into the crashing surf. But to Three Rabbit it only meant that Smoke Monkey would be the first to be turned over in the heavy surf and drubbed into the sand bar. Three Rabbit had a different idea. He had been working on it in secret for weeks. He'd been taking long strips of vine off the trees and been lashing two logs together, just as he'd learned to lash his ax to its handle.

Three Rabbit wondered why no one in the village had ever thought of it before. But he hadn't actually thought of it either. He'd discovered it just the week before when he and Smoke Monkey had been racing toward the mouth of the river. As they got to the surf Three Rabbit had begun to pull ahead and Smoke Monkey had steered his log to crash into Three Rabbit's. Just as the logs had come together they were hit by the first wave and Smoke Monkey was thrown clear. Three Rabbit had waited for his log to roll over taking him with it. But somehow, for a moment, his log and Smoke Monkey's had been pinned together. Three Rabbit threw his arms around both logs. Another wave hit. For an instant the union held and Three Rabbit rose, triumphantly, over the crest of the wave. Then the logs rolled apart and Three Rabbit had slipped between them, still trying to hold on. When the next wave hit the logs came back together. They had almost smashed Three Rabbit like a caterpillar, but he dove under the water and he had escaped with some minor scrapes and bruises. Afterward Three Rabbit kept thinking how wonderful it was when he had seemingly held the two logs together. If only his arms had been strong enough!

Now he had a better idea. He would let the vines be his strength! He worked secretly on this new idea for weeks. Then Three Rabbit lashed a final short vine near the front of the logs. He pushed them out through the lily pads into the swift *current. As he jumped on the logs he brushed off the scabs on his scraped chest, but he felt no pain, only the tingle of anticipation.*

Smoke Monkey was far ahead and the gap was widening. Three Monkey didn't know why but the two logs together moved more slowly than a single log. He didn't care about Smoke Monkey but he knew he had to be moving faster when he hit the surf. He paddled furiously and found the current where it rippled. Slowly he was gaining speed! As they hit the first wave he hung on and the logs plowed through. A second wave knocked them almost sideways but now he could feel the undertow beneath him pulling him out. A third wave was smaller than the first two, barely cresting, and the bound logs slid easily over them. Three Rabbit had reached the open sea and he still had his logs beneath him!

Smoke Monkey watched, waist deep in the water, as Three Rabbit glided effortlessly on his logs, almost parallel to the beach, but angling out slowly into the blue sea. Three Rabbit shouted at Smoke Monkey. He waved. He was almost tempted to try to stand up on the logs. He was in ecstasy. The year would someday be reckoned as 9000 B.C. and Three Rabbit, to the best of his knowledge, had invented the raft.

Three Rabbit lay back on his raft gazing toward the hot blue sky. He felt the ocean moving under him. He closed his eyes and laughed. When he opened them again he realized that the current was sweeping him up the coast away from his village and toward the People of the Moon. He thought of jumping off and trying to swim to shore. Was he already too far out? He didn't know. He'd never been this far out in the sea before. He turned himself around on the logs and started paddling furiously. After several minutes his arms ached too much, so he stopped. He dared to glance at the shore. It had moved further away!

Three Rabbit had never actually seen the People of the Moon. He had lied once and told Smoke Monkey and some of the other young men that he had seen them at a distance in the forest. But, in fact, he had been frightened by some monkeys that had surprised him, and he'd run back to the village. He'd only said that he'd seen People of the Moon to explain his fast-beating heart. He'd never seen them but he had, once, while hunting with his uncle, come across the bones of members of his own tribe. He'd seen the crushed skulls of his kinsfolk and heard his uncle softly tell him, "They only eat the brains and, sometimes, the nose. I think they like to chew on it. The rest they leave for the buzzards."

Now Three Rabbit lay face down on his raft and sobbed. If the sea monsters didn't eat him, then he would surely come ashore in the realm of the People of the Moon and they would dine heartily on his inquisitive and misguided brain! But just then he felt a bump, felt his raft stop, and saw a shadow above him. When he dared look up, he saw people—not brown skinned people like himself, not ashen-skinned people like the People of the Moon, but red people, so red they reflected a bronze glow off the deflection of the sun. They even shone a deep red in the shadows of the sun! They were huge—giants beyond his wildest dreams! And they were on a raft, like his, only much larger, with many, many logs, and with a great animal skin (was it one skin?) held aloft by a tall, slender tree trunk in the center of the raft. Was he dreaming? Who were these oddly-attired people smiling down at him? Three Rabbit did not know what to make of them. Many of the men had hair on their faces and on the backs of their hands—like a monkey! Yet they had such large heads with eyes like hawks, yet so much gentler! Three Rabbit smiled back. Best to meet the Gods with a happy face.

Gradually Three Rabbit realized they were towing him back toward the shore, back toward his village. There was something about this huge craft that enabled them to move against the current! They were taking him home.

Three Rabbit was the first of his tribe to meet the Cro-Magnon.

The Decline of Navigation

In the millennium-and-a-half before Columbus, Europe, and all the world governed by the Catholic Church, suffered a great loss of learning. Among other significant losses, knowledge of the geometry of the Earth was replaced with abject ignorance that the earth was a sphere, of Earth's place in the Cosmos, and of any mathematical order to the universe itself. Though not yet dead—that decree would await the new "science" of the last three centuries—the action of the celestial universe was no longer tied harmoniously with the activities of man, nor was man, once the geometer of the universe, even vaguely tied to the celestial spheres. Reverence for the celestial bodies was condemned by the reigning Church as idolatry. Suggestions that the Earth was a circular body were ridiculed and condemned, not that many would make such an absurd assertion.

What were the causal events that stilled the philosophy of thought and brought about the Dark Ages? One plausible theory is that the demise of navigation was to blame. This demise itself had several causes. Early Egyptians were, from depictions of their reed-bundle rafts, considerable navigators. But as the pharaohs became obsessed with their sarcophagi-pyramids, their interest in sea-going rafts was replaced by the need for long riverine barges that could carry huge blocks of granite down the Nile, but were useless in the open seas. The Greek notion that death at sea would deprive them of an afterlife was probably borrowed from Egyptian predecessors who believed ritual mummification was necessary to carry them to the next life. Whatever fear the Greeks held, the truth is that they had no motivation for exploration by sea beyond the Aegean. Like the Egyptians and the Sumerians, they understood that their culture was derivative and had been introduced from another culture from across the seas. Yet, with the exception of Homer, Plato, Socrates, Pythagoras, and a few other philosophers, they had little interest in outside cultures, branding them all "barbarian."

The Romans were more practical in their disdain of navigation. Amassing a great army, they chose land routes for conquest, and by successful conquests they could thus snub their noses at the hated Carthaginians, admittedly their superiors at sea, but destined to become the last of the ancient seafarers of the Eurocentric-Mediterranean world. The war-like tribes from Germany who succeeded these civilizations simply had no concept of navigation. Indeed, in medieval Europe, from all reports, a simple dunking in a large bathtub brought on fear of a watery grave.

A possibly more important factor in the demise of navigation, as crucial and as simple as the fear of death at sea, was the discovery of iron. Much of the purpose of navigation in the warring Mediterranean was predicated on the need to find great sources of copper and tin, which had abundant supplies only in the Americas, in Lake Superior in the case of copper, in Bolivia in the case of tin. Once iron was found to be superior to bronze, the need for long-range navigation was supplanted by easy access to the iron fields found everywhere in Europe! The Eurocentric world, around 1,000 B.C. became obsessed with iron as the new instrument of warfare.

While MesoAmericans were building great star temples and observing and predicting eclipses from information gathered from around the world, and while Polynesians were settling virtually all the islands of the vast Pacific, a large part of the world settled into cosmological and navigational darkness. Unfortunately it is from that half of the world that we have inherited our historical perspective.

But even if the will to navigate was lost, how did historic knowledge of the sea become lost for over two thousand years? How did knowledge that the earth was a sphere, let alone any idea of its dimensions, vanish? The simple answer is that all knowledge during those times had come under the vigilant control of the Church of Rome. Any information, any world view that did not fit in the direct line from the Old Testament of the near east to The Greco-Romans, from whom the Church inherited its power, was heretical. Any world view that did not place the earth at the center of the Universe and Rome at the center of the world was antithetical to the word of the Church.

Even before the Christian era the state of navigation in the Mediterranean can only be described by as in decline. During the several centuries that preceded Christ many cultures of the world retained their legends of the lost continent of Atlantis but, particularly in Europe and the Mediterranean, seemed to have lost the ability and knowledge to make transoceanic voyages. The Basques, claiming descent from Atlanteans became over millennia both isolated by their ancient language and geographically landlocked. The Etruscans, also citing Atlantis as their culture's wellspring, were swept over by the Romans. The record of their civilization, with the exception of some exquisite art works has sadly been lost.

From Europe to Africa only those cultures that remained outside the influence of the Greco-Roman tradition maintained a strong relationship with the sea.

The Celts sailed in curraghs (fig. 11A), a short boat of sewn animal hides coated with grease, for thousands of years before the Romans arrived in Britain in the first century B.C. By that time the Celts had also developed wooden planked, flat-bottomed ships that, still utilizing sewn-skins as sails, confronted Julius Caesar in a great sea battle in 55 B.C. Historians have made much of Caesar's description of the Celts as "half-naked" savages, while ignoring his description of the 220 Celtic ships he encountered as, "all larger than and superior in construction" to those of the Roman navy under Admiral Brutus. Caesar further described the ships as capable of outriding tempestuous or contrary winds and sailing across "the vast open sea." The Romans won the battle despite sustaining heavy losses by using the same technique they had successfully used against the superior boats of the Phoenicians. They used grappling hooks to secure the Celtic boats close in and then sent their superior numbers of armed men swarming onto the Celtic ships, thus reducing the engagement to a land battle.[2]

11.A. SEWN-SKIN BOATS. A Curragh. In 1976 Tim Severin duplicated St. Brendan's feat of crossing the North Atlantic in a 36-foot boat similar in construction to the legendary craft of the Irish saint. Historians, like anthropologists, have rarely been "small boat people." So it would probably surprise them that Celtic voyages to the New World were most likely carried out in the sewn-skin curraghs, not in the larger, faster, and more maneuverable wooden planked ships they used to battle Caesar. The small and slow *curraghs* were able to ride with and over the waves. Larger ships, whether flat bottomed or heavily keeled, were required to cut through the waves. In heavy seas this could mean capsizing, and when a heavy boat capsizes it sinks. The curraghs would not only be less likely to capsize but if they did they would not sink.[1]

While the Polynesians were completing the task of populating the greatest ranges of the Pacific, the self-absorbed Greeks rarely ventured from the Aegean, and the Romans were intent on a land based empire. They had destroyed the Phoenicians at Carthage in 146 B.C., killing an estimated 500,000 people and enslaving 50,000 more. When Caesar subdued the Celts, at Brittany in 55 B.C., the last navigational culture was stilled. The Romans did not bother to rebuild their navy after the losses sustained defeating Mark Anthony and Cleopatra (fig. 13L) at the battle of Actium in 31 B.C. They never fully developed a merchant fleet. The Romans simply had more interest in building roads than they did in following sea lanes. Except for Viking forays, it would be over fifteen hundred years before Europeans returned to the open seas.

While the official right hand of Rome ruled out navigation, the unofficial left hand seemed to condone some exploration, as witnessed by a discovery made by American underwater archaeologist, Robert Marx, near Rio de Janeiro in 1976. Two intact long-necked storage jars, or amphorae, of the type used on long ocean voyages, were found in the muddy bottom of Guanabara Bay. These jars, and hundreds of fragments found since, were identical in design and firing to those used by Roman sailors in the second century B.C., when the Romans were still interested in voyaging.[3]

Subsequently in 1982 scuba divers located an entire Roman shipwreck at Rio de Janeiro. Hundreds of the amphorae, dated to the first century B.C., were found contained in the wreckage. Another wreck, undoubtedly a Roman ship with a Roman cargo, was found off Venezuela in 1987.[4]

However, the decline of Greco-Roman navigation did not mark the end of long-range navigation. Some vestige of oceanic travel endured into the sixth century A.D., even among the defeated Celts.

St. Brendan, a sixth-century Irish monk sailed from Ireland to Newfoundland in a leather-and-wood vessel.[6] The Vikings, notably Erik the Red and his son, Lief Eriksson, established colonies in Iceland, Greenland, and on the coasts of North America around 1000 A.D. Arab contemporaries of the Christian empire had a flourishing sea trade, while Europe floundered. Arab books contained instructions on ancient ship building and navigation which may have included the maps on which the Piri Reis map of 1513 were based. Certainly the voyages of Sinbad the Sailor described in the thirteenth century classic, *The Thousand And One Nights* were based on real voyages by real sailors (fig. 11B). Included in the legendary trips to Africa and India was the record of a voyage down India's Malabar coast, to Ceylon, Sumatra, and on to China. Descriptions of a parade of royal elephants in Ceylon (now Sri Lanka) and ledgers of trade for silk and porcelain in China leave little doubt that the

11.B. THE "SOHAR." Designed by Colin Mudie and built to the exact specifications of a fourteenth-century Arab ship, not a single nail was used in its construction. Tim Severin has also retraced the route Ibn Battata (perhaps the legendary "Sinbad") followed in sailing from Oman to China. Severin's journey, aboard the "Sohar" spanned 6,000 of the 75,000 miles of journeys covered by Battata in the 14th century (1325-1354). Battata's adventures included voyages of several thousands of miles along established trade routes and were well known in the Arab world. Copies of his journeys were available at the great Moorish library at Cordoba in Spain in the Fifteenth century. If Columbus had wanted a short route to China he should have asked the Moors.[5]

Arabs, in wooden ships with sewn keels, actually made Sinbad's famed voyages, in the sixth century A.D., and probably much earlier.

But from the time of the First Crusade, which ended in Jerusalem's fall in 1099, to the inception of the Spanish Inquisition in Spain in 1478, to the forced conversion of the Moors in Spain in 1499, the navigators of the Arab world, once free roamers of the Mediterranean and beyond, had to spend most of their time and energy fighting off the Crusades launched on the Holy Lands. Eventually, inexorably, libraries were burned, and a civilization was altered in its purpose. Boats rotted in their harbors.

Similar religious and political disasters befell China and India. Some Chinese history has managed to survive the reign of Emperor Qi, the builder of the Great Wall, but also the burner of Chinese libraries, and other emperors who executed astronomers, historians, and philosophers if their words were found displeasing. According to surviving records Han dynasty Chinese in the first millennium B.C. had four-masted ocean going vessels equipped with fore and aft lug sails that could carry up to 7000 people and 260 tons of cargo.[7] Buddhist monks who accompanied the voyages specifically mentioned a mountainous land, called Fu-sang, that had no iron but that was rich in gold and silver. Henrietta Mertz in her book, Pale Ink, and other historians, have identified this land as present day Mexico, and believe that there are specific references to Chichen Itza, although conventional archaeology insists Chichen Itza was built well after these voyages occurred. There is definite evidence of Chinese figures, including sculptures of elephants at Copan and other Mayan sites although the "classic" dates for these sites are well after the Chinese had ceased most long range voyaging (fig. 11C).

Long before these voyages, however, there is a substantial record of Chinese voyages to America, compiled in the Classic of Mountains And Seas,

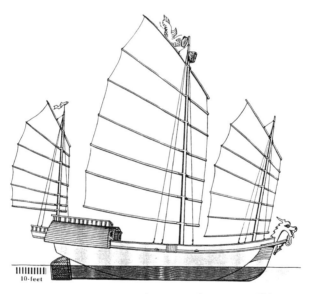

10-feet

11.C. Nu Sun. In *Nu Sun* Gunnar Thompson documents Chinese voyages to the Americas in ships like this ancestor to the sea-going junk. Chinese emperors, three centuries before Christ, had regularly sent out expeditions to the "land below the eastern horizon". They were sent to discover the mountain paradise where the drug that could prevent death with the illusion of immortality could be found. The drug was known to be a hallucinogenic mushroom, known only in the eastern barrier to the great ocean.[9] The *Shih Chi*, oldest of the known and un-destroyed dynastic histories records these voyages, but doesn't say if they were successful. In the Americas, descendants of the Mayans, the Mazatecs of the state of Oaxaca, still use the psylosibic mushroom, also known as The Divine Mushroom of Immortality. One of the last of the legendary curanderos (shaman-priests), Maria Sabina, died only recently at the age of ninety-two.

in 2250 B.C. Also called the Shan Hai King, this great geographical work, gathered from centuries of previous explorations, describes a series of peaks that in their vivid and precise detail could only be a 2,200-mile span of the Rocky Mountain chain, stretching from Manitoba, Canada to Mazatlan, Mexico.[8]

The Chinese classic somehow survived repeated burnings of libraries, most at the command of petulant emperors. But the political and navigational history of China went through a fate similar to the decline of navigation in the Mediterranean, and this decline happened at a matching time, in the two centuries before Christ.

Despite the exceptional voyages of St. Brendan and the Vikings, and some possible forays by the Romans and Greeks, deliberate and sustained worldwide trade seemed to have ended with the demise of the Phoenicians. Who were they?

Historians have repeatedly portrayed the Phoenicians as among the first of the ancient navigators. Actually they were among the last. We know well what followed the Phoenicians. But we know little about the Phoenicians themselves. What we do know about them has been occasioned because they were based in the Mediterranean, from which our view of world history originated, and because they (as Carthaginians) fought a great war with the land-based Roman Empire.

We've known about the Phoenicians since Herodotus, the Greek historian, wrote of their arrival from the Red Sea, probably around 1200 B.C. We know they dominated trade in the eastern Mediterranean for several hundred years, devised a simplified alphabet, which you are now reading, and wrote great volumes of their deeds, of which none survive. We know that their settlements were all coastal, they lived off the sea and had little interest in agriculture, none in land acquisition, and that they hired themselves out to the large empires, notably the Egyptians.

We know the Phoenicians were long involved in worldwide trade. During the Bronze Age, they brought copper and tin to the Mediterranean region. When the Iron age, and its wars, obviated the need for bronze they traded in gold, incense, spices, and the royal purple dye which has come to be associated with them. And we know from other sources that they were long intent in keeping secret an island of great wealth, which they called Antilla.

Records indicate that the Tyrrhenians (Etruscans) learned of the discovery and intended to dispatch a colony to that land, but were prevented from doing so by a large Phoenician naval force. Thereafter the Phoenicians took great pains to keep their knowledge a secret. Throughout the Mediterranean the Phoenicians spread the word, already expressed in legend, that the rich island-continent had been destroyed by a cataclysm and had sunk under a sea of mud.[10] Many, including the Greeks and Romans, actually took the Phoenicians at their word.

Can we still hear echoes of Phoenician laughter at the idea that Atlantis was forever lost? Can we imagine that the "bare bones of the lost continent," the islands of the Antilles, were, in fact, Carthage's gateway to the Old World, which today we call the New World?

For the Phoenician peoples of Carthage keeping the Antilles secret promised not only a domination of its riches, but respite from the constant warfare that was encompassing the Mediterranean. Persia, under Cyrus the Great, had conquered all of Asia Minor by 539 B.C. The eastern Phoenicians were made vassals of Cyrus and forced to war against their cousins in Carthage. Soon, Carthage, once a colony of the Phoenicians, was its only Mediterranean base. Rome, Carthage's mortal enemy, was on the ascendancy. Egypt, in decline, still treated the Carthaginians and the few remaining eastern Phoenicians as servants.

By the fifth century B.C., Carthage itself was becoming destabilized and depopulated. Carthaginians were

leaving in great numbers to sail to the "new island." Few returned and those few who did had fantastic stories of a lush and verdant land. To prevent a general exodus the governors of Carthage announced that there would be no more sailings out through the Pillars of Hercules. They invoked the death penalty for any who disobeyed the edict and put to death all those who subsequently returned from the "island."

Was the Phoenician "island" Atlantis? In reporting Phoenician explorer Hanno's journey in about 500 B.C., Herodotus wrote that sixty ships took part in the expedition, with 30,000 men and women on board. They were equipped with sufficient provisions to sail through the Pillars of Hercules and another 3,500 miles beyond without taking on further supplies. These provisions, with a substantial lift from the currents which would effectively shorten the voyage by over a thousand miles, made a voyage to Atlantis relatively simple.[11] This undertaking, many times larger than Pilgrim voyages to America over two thousand years later, more resembles a migration than an expedition.[12] We know some small colonies were planted along the upper west coast of Africa, but the destination of the majority of the fleet was never known. Phoenician artifacts found throughout the New World, however, provide substantial clues to Hanno's destination (fig. 11D).

An important find was made on the shores of the Paraiba River in Brazil in 1872. Slaves working on a plantation uncovered four pieces of a stone tablet inscribed with a curious and unknown text. A copy of the text found its way to Ladislau Netto, Director of the Museu Nacional in Rio de Janeiro, who,

11.D. Phoenician ship of the fifth century b.c. engraved in stone. Where had the Phoenicians come from? A common misperception holds that the Phoenicians were the sons and daughters of desert nomads. This view holds that some climatic change in the deserts of the Middle East, which had not always been deserts, forced the nomads out of the open deserts and into settlements on the sea. Once at the sea the Phoenicians, still motivated by nomadic urges naturally started wandering restlessly across the seas.

What isn't explained is how they suddenly had the necessary naval technology to sail throughout the Mediterranean and Red Seas, becoming the dominant sea power in that realm, and to explore the Indian and Atlantic oceans and circumnavigate Africa, presumably before anyone else had done so. Had the Phoenicians, one could speculate, actually been navigators of the Arabian and Libyan deserts, possessing a great store of knowledge of the configurations of the heavens, later applied to knowledge of the sea? Or, we think more reasonably, one could wonder if the Phoenicians were in fact themselves descendants of other sea people, astronomer-navigators, whose knowledge of the sea and the stars stretched back over millennia? If so, who had preceded them?

---

after much study declared it to be the work of Phoenician navigators centuries before Christ.

What followed was a classic example of establishment bias to outsiders meddling in the affairs of experts. Netto had ventured into a field not of his own specialization. In eager anticipation of confirmation, Netto sent portions of the text to the leading authority on Caananite texts, Ernest Renan, in Paris. Renan promptly pronounced it a fake. As a result Netto was ridiculed and scorned, even in his native Brazil. Netto finally sent a letter of apology, professing that he was the innocent victim of some forger's hand. The "Paraiba Stone" controversy was laid to rest. The stone itself disappeared without a trace. Netto died in shame.

Almost a century after the Paraiba Stone's original discovery, Cyrus Gordon, Head of the Department of Mediterranean Studies at Brandeis

University, entered into the controversy. Dr. Gordon, an unquestioned authority on Caananite texts, reexamined the content of the stones in 1967, working from a copy acquired at a rummage sale in Providence, Rhode Island, by an associate, Dr. Jules Piccus. Gordon found Netto's reading to be accurate and Renan's to be filled with errors, some understandable, some careless. He concluded that if forgers had created the text, they had created it with Phoenician characters and readings unknown to experts in 1872, but later authenticated by inscriptions discovered and deciphered in the twentieth century. Gordon found the text to be authentic and translated it as follows:

> We are Sidonian Canaanites from the city of the Merchant King. We were cast up on this distant island, a land of mountains. We sacrificed a youth to the celestial gods and goddesses in the nineteenth year of our might King Hiram and embarked from Ezion-geber in the Red Sea. We voyaged with ten ships and were at sea together for two years around Africa. Then we were separated by the hand of Baal and were no longer with our companions. So we have come here, twelve men and three women, into [Barzel], the 'Island of Iron.' Am I, the Admiral, a man who would flee? Nay! May the celestial gods and goddesses favor us well![13]

The authors of the Paraiba Stone, probably sailing in the reign of Hiram III in the year 534 B.C., may have been blown off course. It was an easy thing to have happened if a storm separated them from the other vessels in their fleet, and if they were in some way crippled. The currents would simply have carried them away from Africa and to South America's shores. But why did they identify their landfall as the "island of iron"? Did they find mines? And who was mining iron ore?

By the same token why would the Phoenician term for the land from which they acquired iron, Barzel, so closely resemble the name of the country now known to be richest in iron, Brazil? It appears that this is a case of sailors blown off course to an unintended and distant landfall, but not to an unknown land.

Just as significant are the Phoenician inscriptions recorded by Harvard Professor Barry Fell. Fell reviewed 4,000 fired bricks from the ancient Mayan port city of Comalcalco, excavated from 1976 to 1978 by archaeologist, Pancio Salazar, under the direction of Mexico's National Institute of Anthropology. A majority of the bricks were inscribed with markings that proved to be Mayan glyphs, but several hundred, about seventeen percent of the total, carried inscriptions that had come from the Old World. Fell determined that a calendar of twelve months and fifty weeks was lettered by Neopunic letters, a degenerate last phase of Phoenician script. Fell also detected Libyan script on a plaque that featured a Semitic looking figure. Some of the bricks contained inscriptions of elephants.[14]

Comalcalco, located on the coast of Mexico's state of Tabasco, within a few miles of the mouth of the Usumacinta River, suggests contacts with El Ceibal, where bearded and mustachioed figures, very Phoenician in appearance, dominate the carved stelae (11E). El Ceibal is located on the Rio Pasion which flows into the Usumacinta. Archaeologists have generally given dates of 700 to 900 A.D., "Classic Maya" dates, for the Comalcalco site, and they have given similar, though slightly earlier dates for El Ceibal. It is curious, however, how sites with definite Phoenician facial depictions and definite Phoenician script can be attributed to dates almost a thousand years after the known end to the Phoenician and Carthaginian culture. As usual, in dating the sites archaeologists have only looked at the most recent construction, forgetting the Mayan, and later Aztec, Toltec, and Christian habit of taking the bricks or stones of one civilization and rebuilding another atop it.

Dr. Fell has also discovered Celtic Ogam script at various sites in New England, dated from 435 B.C. to 1200 B.C., and at Saint Vincent Island, in the West Indies, dated at around 800 B.C.[15] Phoenician coins and inscriptions have been found in abundance from Brazil to New England. If Phoenician presence in the New World were a matter of chance encounters, resulting from African trading vessels blown off course and shipwrecked on the

11.E. Phoenician features on a clay head found under a ninth century A.D. ruin in Mexico City.

11.F. RED HAIRED MUMMY. Speculation that the death masks of Mesoamerica were placed on the remains of mummified bodies has been confirmed by bits of red cloth wrapping attached to eroded bones in the crypt of Pacal Votan at Palenque (Chiapas). But just who was mummified? The coarse black-haired, short-statured, round-headed, descendants of a Beringia migration are absent in examination of mummies found in South America. These intact mummies, which predate Egyptian mummies by three thousand years, all have large bodies, long heads, and fine hair that still retain their colors, from light to dark brown. Some of the hair is almost blond, and most of it is definitely curled.[17] If a mixed race existed in the Americas prior to, or even concurrent with Beringia migrations, how did they get there? The answer is navigation.

Americas, how can so many sites, over such a great distance and over several hundreds of years be explained?

Besides the discovery of inscribed stones, there are the carved figures to be explained. The skull shape of Mayans, Olmecs, and Incas are all extremely round-headed. Yet figures of bearded Semites, exhibiting the dolichocephalic ("long-headed") features of the Northwest Semite have been found, not only at El Ceibal, but at the Mayan site of Iximche (Chimaltenango, Guatemala) and in the states of Guerrero, Veracruz in association with Olmec sculptors, and at Palenque, in Chiapas, Mexico. Most have been conventionally dated prior to the Maya Classic period (from 300 A.D.), but some go back to 900 B.C., by sources that agree with late Phoenician navigation, and to 1400 B.C. by others.[16]

They may be much older. The "long-headed" feature has been found throughout Peru and Bolivia, this time in actual skulls. Long-headed skulls predominated among burials at Paracas, where mummy skulls have now been dated to 9,000 B.P. (fig. 11F). However, these have been judged unreliable because some mummies showed flattening at the back of the skull, a custom among ancient Peruvians. But investigators working on the Early Chimu in northern coastal Peru reported a predominance of the long-headed skull shape, even where cranial flattening was not practiced. At the great ancient center at Tiahuanacu cranial shapes varied from extremely round-headed to very long-headed, indicating that the ancient navigator-astronomers of this region were of a mixed racial bag, unlike their historic successors, the Inca.[18]

The Phoenicians kept "hands-on" knowledge of Atlantis alive from at least 1,500 B.C. until the Romans destroyed, burned, leveled the city of Carthage and "salted the earth" of the Phoenician city so that no record could survive, no people could survive, and no resurgence of the city was possible.

Curiously, despite all the evidence, historians and academic archaeologists have continued to call Phoenician knowledge of the Americas either "unlikely" or "impossible."

Since we know that the Phoenicians circumnavigated Africa, enduring difficult seas and currents, particularly at the stormy Cape of Good Hope, in 600 B.C., why would a deliberate voyage across the Atlantic, and a return, be so forbidding? We also know that the Phoenicians had mastered the Mediterranean for hundreds, if not thousands, of years before that. The land-locked Mediterranean is full of unpredictable winds, and odd currents. Seafaring at any time of the year can be difficult. The coasts of Africa are beset with a multitude of problems, as any coasts are. By contrast the open waters of the Atlantic are blessed with steady and highly predictable winds and currents. It is only during the brief hurricane season (August-October) that any difficulties are likely to be encountered. How could the tropical Atlantic have been judged more difficult?

As we've mentioned previously, a key error historians have made is the assumption that open-ocean navigation is treacherous, while navigation along the coasts of continents is simpler and less dangerous. Actually the opposite is true. Coastal navigation is beset with a host of problems: storms can run a ship aground, fog can hide rocky outcroppings, currents can be swift and treacherous, and unpredictable winds, born inland, can run suddenly offshore. Even steady sea winds can suddenly clash with continental air masses causing turbulence in both the air and sea.

For a landlubber it is comforting to always be within sight of land. For an experienced seaman comfort comes only when the dangers of coastal sailing are left far behind. The open ocean promises greater comfort, often expressed as "steady as she goes, mate."

The ability of small ships to cross the Atlantic was dramatically demonstrated by Dr. Alain Bombard in 1952 when he climbed aboard a fifteen foot life raft and, without any stored water or food, set off from Casablanca to cross the Atlantic via the Canary Islands. Equipped only with two lee boards, a cloth net, a fishing line and hook, two harpoons, and a dinghy sail, set so far forward that the raft could not have sailed into the wind, Bombard floated along the warm mid-Atlantic trade winds in his rubber inflatable for sixty-five days before arriving at Barbados. Both the raft and Dr. Bombard arrived in the Caribbean in good shape.

Six years later, Dr. Hannes Lindemann successfully repeated Bombard's crossing twice, first in an African dugout canoe and later in an Aerius folding boat. Eric Peters sailed from the Canary Islands to the Caribbean in forty-seven days in a six-foot plastic barrel equipped with a sail. In 1993, Tom McNally sailed from Portugal to Florida in a bathtub-sized boat that measured just under five-feet, five inches in length. Months later Hugo Vilhen sailed from Canada to Britain in a craft that was five-feet, four inches long, establishing a new record in navigational down-sizing.[19] The number of crossings on "unlikely" craft since Thor Heyerdahl's groundbreaking voyages on the *Kon-Tiki* and the *Ra* Expeditions is now legion. Since Heyerdahl proved the feasibility of inter-ocean voyages on balsa rafts and reed boats any number of voyages on almost any description of small vessel have been successfully achieved. The stability of the vessel is the deciding factor, not its size. Bathtubs and barrels are not particularly stable, but a good boat of less than thirty feet in length is now considered the optimum size to withstand rough seas in the open ocean. Historians for generations have missed this simple fact.

Just how difficult is open-sea sailing? The adventures of young Tania Aebi, recounted in her book, Maiden Voyage, throws considerable light on the subject. In the late summer of 1983, Tania, then seventeen, and her younger brother and sister, none of whom had any sailing experience flew to England to join their father on a proposed sailing from England to the Canary Islands via Spain, Portugal, and Morocco. Tania's father hadn't much more experience than his children. Having decided, on a middle-aged whim, to buy a sailboat, he took a one-week course in sailing in Florida, then a correspondence course in celestial navigation and, within a month, went off to England to buy the 38-foot *Pathfinder of Percuil*. After three days of practice they set out on a month-long journey in which the children regularly overtrimmed the sails, manhandled the wheel, and sent booms and sails flying across the cockpit, while the father spent most of his time below trying to figure out the ship's navigational equipment. The *Pathfinder,* however, showed great patience with the novice's many mistakes and delivered them to the Canary Islands without incident. Two months later Tania and her father and two sea-fearing novices who replaced her school-bound siblings successfully sailed from the Canaries to the Caribbean and up the Atlantic seaboard to New York, a voyage by novice sailors and outright landlubbers of 4,500 miles.

But Tania wasn't done yet. At her father's urging she set sail a year and a half later, at the age of eighteen, to circumnavigate the globe, alone. Because she and her father feared she had not developed the skills to handle a larger boat, Tania set out on a used twenty-six-foot sloop, the *Varuna,* on May 30, 1985.

Tania truly did not know how to sail alone. Spending her first night at Sandy Hook she put out only five feet of chain in fifteen feet of water and thus failed to secure her anchor. Her small engine quit completely ten miles out into the Atlantic shipping lanes. She soon discovered her new factory-fitted water tanks were contaminated with fiberglass—she had no drinking water. She didn't discover a gaping hole where the anchor chain passed through the deck until her boat was swamped with six inches of water and the main bilge pump seized. Violently seasick, Tania could not remember whether bad weather made a barometer go up or down. She soon found out as howling winds and high seas rocked her tiny boat, but as depressions approached she complicated her problems by heading directly into the middle of the depressions instead of skirting the sides and using the winds to her advantage. With half her navigation equipment down (Tania did not even understand that two lines of position are needed for a fix), and having failed a course in celestial navigation, Tania somehow completed the first leg of her voyage and landed at Bermuda on June 12, 1985.

Two-and-a-half years and twenty-seven thousand miles later, having long since become, of necessity, a very good sailor, Tania became the first woman, and the youngest person of modern record, to complete a solo circumnavigation of the globe. Throughout the journey she remembered her father's advice to the effect that, "It's really very easy. Sailing is just common sense."

We must ask again, how difficult is open-sea navigation? Without a doubt it can be very difficult, dangerous, and even deadly. But compare it to what was asked of those who, according to Beringia theory, trekked over three thousand miles over a glacier several miles high without food, game, or the hope of either. It seems obvious, that even treacherous coastal navigation would be easier and wiser.

In 1933 Dana and Ginger Lamb proved this. As recorded in their book, *Enchanted Vagabonds,* they paddled a dugout canoe, hewn from a large tree trunk, from San Diego to Panama.

In 1987 Ed Gillette paddled a kayak from California to Hawaii. Of course he had considerable help from the currents. Tania Aebi, Dr. Alain Bombard and thousands of others who have made significant ocean crossings, solo, in the past fifty years faced great difficulties. Included among them is a solo voyage in a converted Indian dugout canoe that sailed from Vancouver to the Cook Islands, some 5,500 miles, in fifty-six days. We can add William Verity's journey, from Florida to Ireland, in a home-built twelve-foot sloop. There are many other examples of solo ventures across the oceans. And after most of these ventures, often harrowing, when the sailor finally reached the safety of land, they almost invariably had one ambition—to return to the sea (fig. 11G).

Please remember, leading American archaeologists have said of Thor Heyerdahl's voyages on the *Kon-Tiki* and the *Ra II*, "All that he has proved is that he is a good sailor, and that he has courage." Their view is that the combination of seamanship and courage could not have occurred before Heyerdahl, much less as a common occurrence both before and after his exploits. In fact, the Pacific drifts of Eric de Bisschop were more spectacular. One voyage, from Tahiti to Cannes, drifting toward the south pole, and then east in a double canoe for 264 days, brought them to landfall in Chile over five thousand miles later. This was followed by another in which de Bisschop and a few companions, drifted north and west from southern Chile for some six moths and seven thousand miles until they wrecked on Manihiki some six months and seven thousand miles later.[20] Heyerdahl and De Bisschop are capable sailors, but Tania Aebi proved that you need not even begin as a good sailor, as long as you have a good boat and courage. The Lambs, Ed Gillette, Eric Peters, and Drs. Bombard and Lindemann, among many others, proved that you don't even need a good boat.

11.G. "AUSSIE SAILOR" GREG BROOKS. At fourteen, when his parents' marriage broke up, Greg Brooks started "wagging school" and sailing "Hobie cats" on the Swan River and

in the Indian Ocean near his home town of Perth. By eighteen, after crewing on various ships that sailed to Malaysia and Indonesia, he joined skipper Tom Brady on a two-year journey around the world on the 70-foot teak schooner, the *Attu*. Along the way they suffered a broken topmast in heavy seas off the Cape of Good Hope, were shot at in Mozambique, and, pushed by Force 6 and 7 winds that began off the volcanic island of Krakatua, covered 2,100 miles in thirteen days of hard sailing. Afterwards, Greg became the first mate on the 70-foot junk rig, *Zubinubi*, and sailed from Thailand to the U.S. across a storm-tossed North Pacific. After some years of sailing off Mexico's west coast, Greg and a buddy sailed a two-man 32-foot catamaran from Costa Rica to Australia. Despite "rest stops" in the Tahitian and Samoan islands, the two men covered the entire Pacific in just twenty-four days, often reaching sustained speeds of over 26 knots. After a ten-year absence, most spent on the sea, Greg returned to Perth, became a crane operator, married, and fathered two boys, now three and five years old. Greg, like many experienced sailors, maintains that a 32-foot-vessel is superior to larger craft in open seas. Greg is saving his money, hoping that in five years he can buy a boat, quit his job, and introduce his children to the oceans.

In another age, Columbus "discovered" America in an awkward ship that defies any present-day knowledgeable mariner's concept of a good boat. The Age of Discovery included not only the discovery of a "New World," inhabited by barbarians, but also encounters with methods of navigation very unlike those used by the explorers of his day and the later Conquistadors. As usual, these encountered vessels, and the techniques which allowed their captains to orient themselves in the vast expanse of the Atlantic and Pacific ocean were, in the Eurocentric view, disdained, downgraded, and scorned.

Evidence of encounters by the conquistadors with advanced naval cultures was widespread. Juan de Saamanos, a chronicler of the Pizarro expedition, reported to Charles V, in 1526, an episode off Panama involving Pizarro's' pilot, Bartolomeo Ruiz. Ruiz was sailing ahead of Pizzaro exploring the coast to the south when he encountered another sailing vessel of almost equal size coming in the opposite direction. The northbound ship, later proved to be Peruvian, was a balsa raft,(similar to but far larger than the one Heyerdahl later constructed to cross the Pacific.) This vessel was laden with cargo, estimated by the Spaniards to exceed thirty-six tons, and had a crew of twenty men and women.

Saamanos wrote of the vessel as a "wash-through" raft with an underbody of partially submerged balsa logs and a raised cane deck that kept the crew and cargo dry. Saamanos described the rigging and masts as follows: "It carried masts and yards of very fine wood, and cotton sails in the same shape and manner of our own ships. It had very good rigging of hennequen, which is like hemp, and some mooring stones for anchors formed like grindstones."

As mentioned earlier Pizarro and his men were told of balsa journeys along the coasts of South America and were given directions on how to sail to Easter Island, and Polynesia. He paid no heed. But Spanish navigator and historian Sarmiento de Gamboa, who followed Pizarro in 1567, was interested. During the several years he stayed in Peru he was repeatedly told by Inca sailors of inhabited islands that lay far out in the Pacific. Gamboa recorded their tales noting that they knew about these islands because their fathers and grandfathers had sailed to them, and returned. Subsequently, Spanish explorer Alvaro de Mendana following the instructions given to Sarmiento, successfully navigated to the Marquesa Islands in 1595. Following a Mercator map he missed Easter Island but a century-and-a-half later, in 1722, following the manuscript records of Sarmiento's interview with Inca navigators, Dutch Admiral Roggeveen discovered Easter Island, exactly where the Incas had told the Spanish it would be.[23]

Sarmiento also learned from several sources of a voyage by the Tupac Inca, twenty years before Pizarro's arrival in Peru. Tupac embarked on an immense

11.H THE RA II. An amazing continuity of culture is evidenced in the ability of the descendants of pre-Inca people—the Aymara of Lake Titicaca—to still build bundle-reed rafts 5,000 years after construction of similar craft ceased in Egypt. Thor Heyerdahl sailed the *Ra II* from Europe to the Americas in 1970. He had previously proven the possibility of raft voyages across the Pacific when he sailed the balsa raft *Kon-Tiki* from Peru to Raroia in the eastern Pacific in 1947.

number of balsas carrying 20,000 men. When he returned a year later he brought back considerable booty and had "black people" with him. Sarmiento visited the Cuzco fortress that had housed the treasures from this journey before the Spanish under Pizarro arrived and looted them. He even interviewed the custodian of the fortress who attested to the existence of the treasure.[24]

Despite the implications of Sarmiento's discoveries, and of Pizarro's observations that the Incas were a great sea-faring people, influential Americanist S.K. Lothrop, the first archaeologist of widespread influence to see the spheres of the Diquis Delta, provided the definitive answer to the question of ancient navigators in Peru: Balsa rafts were incapable of long range navigation. (See Chapter 1).

We've stated this earlier and, because it is a crucial error of navigational judgment, we must repeat it—Lothrop's misunderstanding of the capabilities of these ships reflects a bias against balsa craft in favor of displacement-hulled ships of large dimensions. In the view of terrestrial-based archaeologists, and in the view of Mediterranean and European ship-builders going back almost 5,000 years, ships were meant to defend their occupants from the sea, thus long and tall ships with water-proof planking were devised. Unfortunately, these ship-builders underestimated the power and size of the seas. "Tall ships," meant to keep the sea outside, repeatedly found the sea inside their water-tight hulls. Because tall also meant awkward, the ships would often lay side-by-side with a raging sea—a position and predicament that spelled certain disaster.

Thor Heyerdahl (fig. 11H) paid little heed to Lothrop and other established anthropologists. Heyerdahl, like most visionaries also had insight into the past. He marveled at the "ingenious wash-through construction" of the balsa rafts which "allowed all entering water to disappear as through a sieve."[25] These ships ran in close harmony with the sea, often riding under fierce crests of great waves, escaping unharmed. No bailing of unwanted waters was necessary.

Navigation in Antiquity

We've discussed the decline of navigation in our known historical era—now let us look at navigational history as recorded in myth and lore as well as other "hard" evidence for Old and New World contacts that came before the standard record. In doing so we will connect the dots between ancient Sumer, Mesoamerica, and the shores of Lake Superior.

Before the great star temples, pyramids, and megaliths were built, myths preceded them. Before the cataclysms that afflicted him, destroying his temples and great cities, man plied the seas. And after the deluge, as soon as he was able, man returned to the sea. In warm latitudes, under steady winds, man traded in both goods and ideas, freely throughout the world. Long before Columbus, and long before the Phoenicians, ancient navigators roamed the seas in canoes, and in reed and balsa rafts. From their base at the center of the great island continent, now called the Americas, these men drifted, and navigated, on unfailing ocean currents, and followed a host of star columns, fixed in the overhead sky. These people were once Atlanteans. Their memory is both more recent, and far more ancient, than Plato's tale.

The descendants of Atlantis, as myth informs, us, lost their common culture, and lost their common language. Probably, since ancient Atlantis itself was a melting pot of the cultures and races of the world, some survivors of the cataclysm were able to return to former colonies and to cultures that resembled their own.

In the Indus valley, the third century sage-historian, Valmiki, who recorded the epic Ramayana, described sea people from across the ocean who in India's remote antiquity conquered Indochina and from there spread their culture throughout the Indian Ocean settling in the Indus Valley. These people were known as great navigators, fierce warriors, learned architects, and were famous for their beautiful women and inexhaustible treasures. They were called the "Nagas," and were also known as "the educators of the world."[26] (The Indus Valley civilization, fell victim to earthquakes and aggressive migrations of a land-based peoples, the Aryans, around 2,000 B.C. The Aryans rewrote history, claiming to be the eternal people of the Indus valley and the rightful heirs to all of India.)[27]

In America, The Fourth Dimension Natalia Rosi de Tariffi, describes the same Naga peoples as the founders of Etrusca, a civilization eventually vanquished from Italia by the Romans. She links the Etruscan language with

Giants

URRY HOPE in her comprehensive an enlightened study of the question, *Atlantis: Myth Or Reality?*, thoroughly examines the precursors of Mediterranean cultures. Hope quotes Professor W.B. Emery as follows: ". . . towards the end of the fourth millennium B.C. we find the people known traditionally as 'The Followers of Horus' apparently forming a civilized aristocracy or master race ruling over the whole of Egypt. The theory of the existence of this master race is supported by the discovery that graves of the late pre-dynastic period in the northern part of Upper Egypt were found to contain the anatomical remains of a people whose skulls were of a greater size and whose bodies were larger than those of the natives, the difference being so marked that any suggestion that these people derived from the earlier stock is impossible. . . . The racial origin of these invaders is not known and the route they took in their penetration of Egypt is equally obscure."[32] Actually that arrival has only been dated by Professor Emery as the end of the fourth millennium BC because it fits the traditionalist viewpoint. Speculation of graves of giants has also occurred throughout Mesoamerica. (James E. Brady has found bones of individuals that averaged 5'9" in height and who produced dramatic cave paintings dated as 1400 B.C. in the Cave of Glowing Skulls near Catacamas in Honduras). If giants, precursors of Osiris and Isis, had arrived in Egypt, they would most likely been Cro-Magnon, and their arrival would have been about 33,000 years before present, not the fourth millennium B.C.!

11.J. MINOANS SHIPS. Until a hundred years ago legends of King Minos and his empire were considered "legendary" but without historic merit. But in the early years of the twentieth century excavations on Crete revealed a civilization that rivaled the glory of ancient Greece, except that at it's height it was at least 1,000 years older.[37] Greek authors often wrote of the thalassocracy of Minos, in reference to their navigational way of life (Thalassocrats meant "sea-lords" in Greek).[38] Interestingly, "Thallassophobia" is a recent coinage meaning "those who fear knowledge of ancient sea-lords."

Peruvian origins.[28] Easter Island scripts, which Heyerdahl claims are Peruvian in origin, and Indus valley scripts are also very similar.[29]

Diodorus wrote of the peoples who came to settle the Nile valley, "The Egyptians were strangers, who, in remote times, settled on the banks of the Nile, bringing with them the civilization of their mother country, the art of writing, and a polished language (see facing page, "Giants"). They had come from the direction of the setting sun and were the most ancient of men."[30]

Similarities between rafts from divergent parts of the world point, unmistakably, to deliberate and sustained contact in millennia past (fig. 11J). While there was no one worldwide culture, astronomy and rafts were part of one worldwide tradition and network of communication.[31]

Early Egyptians were very aware of the Atlantic. They described mysterious "sea peoples," (who, like the Mayans, wore a feathered headdress), as ruthless raiders of the coasts of the Mediterranean, occasionally advancing up the Nile to threaten Egypt's great cities.[33] Since the Minoans traded regularly with Egypt, and the Phoenicians served as the merchant marine for Egyptian rulers the fear and dread the Egyptians held for the "sea people" indicates that it was a separate and alien culture altogether.

Who were the "sea people"? Some have suggested that they might be Etruscans, a mysterious people that dominated the coasts of the Iberian peninsula before the rise of the Roman Empire. It is known that they practiced the custom of ceremonially reddening their likenesses on statues, a custom also practiced in Egypt and in Mesoamerica.34 An Etruscan rhyton from

303

the fourth century B.C. depicts a Classic European face on one side and a Mongolian from the Far East on the opposite side.[35]

Others have speculated that the "sea peoples" were an early navigational people called the Dans (also Danites), described in the Bible as a Semitic people, who aligned themselves with the Philistines in a thirteenth century B.C. assault on Egypt. They were known to sail outside the Straits on trips to the British Isles and are credited by some in founding Danmark (Denmark), the land of the Dans.

But navigation undeniably goes back much further than the dates attributed to Minoans, Dans, and Etruscans. The Sumerian hero of legend Gilgamesh, is associated with navigation, as are most of the Greek gods, including Hercules. Three of Israel's tribes described as navigational (Genesis 49:13; Judges 5:17). But even before the time of Gilgamesh, frescoes and papyrus art in Ur depicted their gods as reed boat navigators. Their founding god, ENKI, the equivalent of the Greeks Poseidon, was the god of the sea, said to have arrived from a distant land on a reed boat to found the Sumerian civilization.

Depictions of ships under sail date back to before 3100 B.C. in pre-dynastic Egypt and ceramic boat models in Sumer (southern Iraq) date back to 4000 B.C. At that time Sumer's sea merchants were known to have been in contact with the civilization of the Indus valley, and there is evidence of Sumerian presence at Lake Titicaca in Bolivia.[54]

But little attention has ever been paid to the naval aspects of Sumerian civilization, probably because they sailed on reed boats, their makings gathered from the river valleys of the Tigris and Euphrates. Such boats were very early on dismissed as incapable of ocean travel. Even Thor Heyerdahl's crossing of the Atlantic in *Ra II* (fig. 11K) in 1970, a ship almost identical to those the Sumerians sailed, has oddly done little to change historians' minds.

In seeking early navigators the traditional land-based paradigm has looked for sea peoples who built and sailed in wooden planked ships.[38] Reed and balsa rafts have been ignored. Yet it is of the raft to which history extends back to the formative years of the great cultures of the Americas and of both Mesopotamia and Egypt. Anthropologists' ignorance of primitive navigation has led them to adopt a condescending attitude about the reed wash-through boats of this era, convinced that only displacement-hulled boats were capable of sailing the open seas. The first wooden planked ships date back to 2800 B.C., and are attributed to the Hittites who had access to the hard cedars of Lebanon. Eventually they replaced sailing rafts in Sumer and Egypt. But for thousands of years both rafts and planked ships were in use from the Mediterranean to the Indian Ocean and from the Americas to the Pacific islands. Egyptian murals of 1500 B.C. show both types sailing into the headwa-

11.K. THOR HEYERDAHL AND THE REED RAFT. In *Early Man and The Ocean* Heyerdahl notes that, whereas the later Hebrew myth of the deluge had Noah and his ark landing on Mount Ararat, at the source of the Tigris and Euphrates rivers, the Sumerians believed Ziusudra landed on the island of Bahrain. From there Enki himself, depicted in illustrations by the Sumerians as arriving on board his divine reed ship, with a "high and gracefully curved bow and stern . . . carrying a sacred altar and sphinx . . ." arrived in Mesopotamia to found the Sumerian people.[41]

ters of the Nile. But it is the single-masted, square-sailed reed boats of the "sea peoples" that are depicted on Egyptian pottery as entering the open sea of the Mediterranean as early 3100 B.C. The larger Egyptian hulled ships are depicted navigating only the protected waters of the Nile.[39] Evidence of the remains of the reed ships from pre-dynastic Egypt are now being excavated in dried-up wadis between the Nile and the Red Sea.[40]

Wooden-hulled boats kept their occupants comfortably dry, may have carried more cargo, and could travel faster in calm seas. This latter consideration must have been a compelling reason for their use in waters where warfare or piracy was a factor. In fact, it probably accounted for the eventual demise of the raft in the Mediterranean region.

Sumerian civilization itself cannot be explained as a product of agricultural Sumer, whereby a nation of farmers lifted themselves by their bootstraps to excel in the arts. Either the Sumerians themselves were "sea peoples," or the

Sumerian civilization was established from the outside, because Sumer (southern Iraq) did not produce the metals and stones upon which their civilization was founded. Sumer excelled in the arts of lapidary, copper-, gold- and silversmithing, and, particularly, in the making of bronze. The materials used by the Sumerians from the beginnings of their civilization came from many directions and from great distances.[42] For example the lapis lazuli was imported from Afghanistan. When archaeologists found Sumerian-type clay tablets in Romanian Transylvania, from about 2700 B.C., many a savant was completely mystified. Actually there is no mystery about it. Transylvania is full of minerals, including gold, which the Sumerians needed to import because there was none available in Sumer.

The most vital element in the rise of Sumerian culture, however, came not from Europe, but from a continent-and-an-ocean away. At the incipient and all stages of the Bronze Age, Sumerian contacts had to go far beyond Transsylvania and Afghanistan. Bronze requires both copper and tin. Although limited amounts of tin could be found in the British Isles (once called the Cassiderides), dominance in a Mediterranean world suddenly turned to warfare—and the need for hard bronze weapons—required a great supply of tin. And that supply could only be found in Asia and high in the

11.L. A POSSIBLE ROUTE TO ISLE ROYALE, LAKE SUPERIOR. There are about 5,000 ancient copper mines located around the northern shore of Lake Superior and on adjacent Isle Royale. Radio-carbon dates indicate that the mines were in operation between 6,000 and 1,000 B.C., corresponding to dates for the Bronze Age in Europe and the Near East. The shores of Lake Superior have always been the only place in the world where large amounts

of native could be found. And huge amounts of this native copper, up to 750,000 tons, were removed from these mines in ancient times.[43] Yet no large numbers of copper artifacts have ever been recovered from American sites."[44] The carcass of a mastodon, apparently killed by miners and found with their remains, indicate that the mining sites may be much older. The Mastodon disappeared at the end of the last Ice Age, 11,500 B.P. After the year 1,000 B.C., corresponding to the birth of the Iron age in the Mediterranean, copper mining in that region declined sharply.

Andes mountains in Bolivia. Copper, ninety percent of the tin-copper alloy that is fired to make bronze, was even more limited in its worldwide distribution. In one place native copper was unlimited: That place was Lake Superior.

Thus the great sailors of the Bronze Age sought tin and copper. How, in the quest to obtain copper, did ancient explorers find the shores of Lake Superior from the Mediterranean. How, to obtain tin, would Sumerian rafts get to Peru and Bolivia? In each case they would have started out on the same route—the Canary current. And voyagers from Sumer could have easily reached the shores of the Americas, once they had made the more difficult voyage across the Mediterranean. But upon reaching the region of the Caribbean how could they have known which way to turn.

In seeking tin how would Sumerians know where to cross the isthmus of the Americas? Having crossed, how would they know to sail south to Peru, and then to somehow transverse the Andes to discover the rich tin mines of Bolivia?

In seeking copper, it is easy to envision how they could have discovered the mouth of the Mississippi River (fig. 11L). But how could they have known that by sailing over 2,000 miles up that river, and making a right turn at the Illinois River, one of hundreds of lesser rivers that joins the Mississippi, and that by following the Illinois upstream until it became nothing more than a creek, that they could reach a short portage to Lake Michigan? How could they have known that by sailing northward the length of Lake Michigan, then passing through the Mackinaw Straits, then through the narrow De Tour passage to reach Potaganissing Bay of the North Channel of Georgian Bay, then to Munuscong Lake, then a narrow passage to Lake Nicolet, and then passage up the St. Mary's River into Whitefish Bay, that they would then find themselves in the open waters of Lake Superior? How could they have then known that by traversing Lake Superior—whose rough waters would make the Mediterranean seem child's play, and, by comparison, the open ocean of the Atlantic a dream—that they would find the world's richest deposit of native copper at the other end?

An exploratory journey up the St. Lawrence seaway, with its many twists and turns, and with no idea of what to expect, is just as unlikely. Yet vast amounts of copper were mined from the northwest shores of Lake Superior and from Isle Royale at least five thousand years ago, and possibly much earlier. Copper artifacts are found in the Americas but nowhere in the amounts that could account for the mining at Lake Superior. Vast amounts of tin were mined from Bolivia in the same period. But tin, by itself, had very limited use, and the copper-tin alloy, bronze, was rarely used in either area of America, but was extensively used in the eastern Mediterranean, where neither tin nor copper, in any credible supply, have ever been found.

The implications are clear. Either the Sumerian expeditions made improbable finds in the Americas, against all odds, requiring extraordinary intuition and luck, or they made contact with a sophisticated navigational people who were fully aware of the resources and trade routes of their own continent.

By the traditional paradigm, early Americans have never been considered maritime people. Yet reed rafts in Peru, similar to those used in Sumer (around 4000 B.C.) are depicted on ceramics, tapestry, and wood carvings in the oldest tombs in Peru, which antedated the founding of Sumer by thousands of years.[45] Maritime "Red Paint" cultures flourished in North America from 4,000 to 7,500 years ago (see facing page). In the context of worldwide trade, copper disappeared from Lake Superior just as jade left Guatemala, tin left Bolivia, and distinctly Japanese (Jomon) pottery showed up in Ecuador in 2500 B.C. Standard explanations of land migrations cannot account for any of the "movements" of these precious goods; but they very certainly were moved and they were moved great distances.

Comparisons of boat-building techniques and of the Sumerian language with the Aymara language of the ancient Peruvians, including the use of the Peruvian term Uru as the "olden people," has led to repeated speculations that Sumerian colonists from Ur founded the Andean peoples. However, could the migration have been the other way around, with the Uru from Peru traveling east to establish Sumer and Ur? To believe that, you would also have to believe the Sumerian legend of Oannes' arrival by sea, and believe that they knew of their own origins.

The Neo-Darwinian concept that each widely accepted change in technology reflects unbridled human progress simply does not permit such an idea. Yet the increased use of wooden-hulled boats, less ably suited to oceanic voyaging, and the arrival of the Iron Age, were the two principal factors in the demise of world-wide cultural contact. The discovery of the method to smelt iron ore, at high temperatures, into an early form of steel, meant the end of the need for bronze. This early steel was in no way superior to bronze, but it was far more common. No longer were voyages of several months required. Iron ore, once its significance was determined, was found to be readily available throughout the "Old World." And the speed with which new weapons of iron could be forged was reflected in the rapidity of warfare in the Mediterranean. The eventual great demise of navigation in the Mediterranean, and eventually Europe and the entire "Old World" was brought on by so-called technological progress.

"Red Paint" Culture

Examination of the "Red Paint," or Maritime Archaic, cultures in Maine show that a seafaring culture flourished there between 4,000 years ago and 7,500 years ago. Remains of swordfish and other deep sea fish, plummets, gouges, slate lance points and toggling harpoons confirm that these were seafarers of considerable skill.[46] Images of whales, and other marine species, as well as stylized bird heads appeared on decorated objects, such as combs and pendants, and funeral sites revealed the use of red ochre at burial sites. The cemeteries were inevitably placed on high hills overlooking the sea.

James Tuck and Robert Mcgee of St. John's Memorial University uncovered a rectangular stone chamber of upright stones on the coast of Labrador that closely resembled similar stones found on the island of Teviec just off the coast of France.[47] Both were burial sites where the dead were covered with red ochre, and dating of charcoal pieces from ceremonial burnings at these sites have been carbon dated as being 7,500 years old. The graves, like pyramids built in Mesoamerica, were oriented to reflect light at the time of the rising sun on one day only, at the time of the summer solstice. And instead of a red ochre burial we find at these sites an urn containing cremated ashes, obviously a special treatment for a unusual person, a shaman or tribal chief.

The use of ground slate, a material inferior only to metal, in harpoons and bayonets in both northern Scandinavia and the northern shores of the Americas may not by itself reveal a shared maritime culture 7,500 years ago. But the use of red ochre, the similarity of designs and engravings, the use of bamboo in tools, and a similar use of oil lamps, all point to a shared culture across the North Atlantic.

What had become of "New World" navigation? Did it meet a similar, isolationist fate? In fact, it flourished. It merely turned in a different direction—toward the Pacific. Some contact with the Africans whose realms existed outside of Mediterranean contact, and some contact with the Phoenicians, remained. Some contact by voyages from America to Europe must have persisted. But given the general state of upheaval and warfare in that region the Americans must have limited those voyages. When you notice that your trade ships do not return, you grow reluctant to send others out in that direction.

Despite the academic establishment's dismissal of the possibility of long range voyaging by reed and balsa rafts, and by canoes, such transoceanic voyages certainly occurred, and not haphazardly or "luckily." Early navigators of the Pacific substantiate our claims. Magellan had marveled at the speed and maneuverability of the flying proas when he "discovered" the Marianas in 1521.[48] Captain James Cook and other explorers of the Pacific were at first amazed that virtually every inhabitable island in the Pacific was in fact inhabited, and that within great regions they were inhabited by people who looked the same, had the same customs, similar languages, and similar craft. The expanse of Polynesia is twice as wide as the entire Atlantic. Yet Polynesia, with the exception of New Zealand, is less than two-thousandths part land, more than 998-thousandths part open water. How had these people found one another? The accidental drift of an occasional storm-driven fisherman could not account for the uniformity of culture. Nor could they account for the tales the Polynesians related of deliberate voyages in pursuit of trade, war, and just to escape their own island for awhile.

How did these people cover these great distances of open ocean with so little probability of making an intended landfall when Europeans before Columbus dared not venture beyond the sight of land into the Atlantic? If the Europeans had ventured out to sea, as Columbus eventually did, they could not help but be carried by the currents to America, even if they didn't know it existed. The continent, from north to south, is over 9,000 miles long. They couldn't miss it!

How did the Polynesian people, long before contact with the "superior technology" of the Europeans had touched them, populate these tiny islands in this vast ocean?

There are several answers: First, they had superior vessels. Captain Cook himself admitted that the Tahitian pahis (large ocean going outriggers) could sail much faster than his ship, could travel as far, and gave his opinion that they could sailing "with ease 40 leagues (120 miles) a day or more." (figs 11N(a-c).

Secondly, they had a different attitude toward the sea. In *We, The Navigators,*

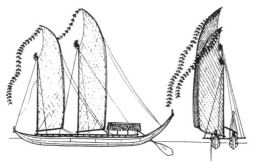

11.N(a). A TAHITIAN PAHI (*from Neygret,* 1967)

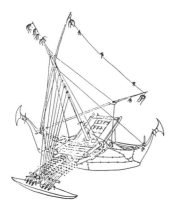

11.N(b). MARSHALLESE CANOE
(*from Alexander,* 1902)

11.N(c). FIJIAN NDRUA
(**from Williams,* 1858)

David Lewis describes his exploration of indigenous navigational techniques in Micronesia and Polynesia. With the help of native navigators, Hippour and Tevake, Lewis retraced traditional sea routes without a compass, relying on the navigators to direct them to landfall, based on "what their fathers and grandfathers knew." Although the navigators admitted that much information had been forgotten since the arrival of the white man they still were able, using traditional methods, to make voyages of up 450 miles and make landfall exactly as predicted. These islanders, Lewis discovered, not only had no fear of the sea, they felt completely at home with it. Among the Tikopians the loss of a man at sea was regarded as a "sweet burial." In the Carolinas a Puluwat captain was more likely to beat 150 miles to windward for five days to Truk Lagoon to obtain cigarettes than to wait a short time for the administration's motor vessel to bring them.[49] The 100-mile passage from Puluwat to a tiny islet called Pikelot was considered so simple that the Carolinians frequently set out in their canoes "on the spur of the moment, and when drunk on palm toddy. They always arrived."[50]

Third, they had superior technology. Lacking the magnetic compass, they developed a surer way to tell where they were and where they were going. They learned to read the stars: Sailing west they used steering stars and followed them until they set beyond the horizon. Sailing east they would first use horizon stars, following them until they were too far overhead, by which time they were already on the path of a new horizon star. Sailing north they used the pole star, or they used any combination of the above.

How can we possibly fit all this information together? Under the current authoritarian paradigm we cannot—the information doesn't "fit." Yet at one time navigational man knew how to read zenith stars, a method no longer in use. The ability to read zenith stars, or star pillars, was nothing less than the ability to determine latitude anywhere in the Pacific, or anywhere in the world. The declination or pathway of a star across the sky will reach its zenith

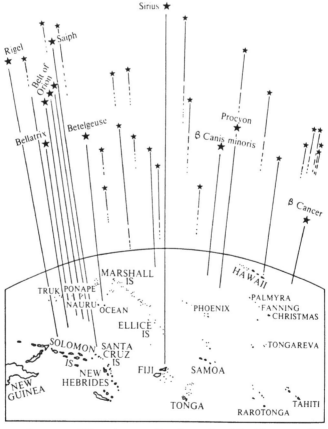

11.0. ZENITH STAR MAP. When they are directly overhead Zenith stars indicate the latitude of an island of the observer at sea.[53]

at midnight. If the zenith of the arc, as it passes east to west across the sky, reaches the same latitude as a known island then that star will become a pillar star for that particular island. Navigators who observe that a star has come "overhead," effectively splitting the sky in halves at midnight, will know that they have arrived at the correct latitude for the island. If they observe it to the south, they will know they are too far north, and vice versa.

Because the stars in the night sky were vast and possibly disorienting in a heaving sea, reflective sighting devices were required to focus in on the sought after star. Lewis's scholarship has shown that Caroline ocean-going canoes used a cane filled with water to indicate when a star had reached its zenith. Hawaiians once used a calabash (gourd) filled with water as a sextant, although the curator of the British Museum, which possesses the artifact, explains it as "a modern replica of one of the indigenous clothing containers."[52]

In Tahiti all notions of zenith star navigation (fig. 11-O) has been lost except the record left by a chant recited in 1818 at Bora Bora by an old woman named Rua-Nui. The chant describes a declination of zenith stars that indicated the eastern extremes of Polynesia, including New Zealand (with Phact as the overhead star), and the southward extreme of the Tubuai archipelago, and Hawaii to the north. The sky was said to be propped up from the earth (islands) by the star pillars. The star names were given by a navigator named Paora'i. The zeniths described did not refer to any star positions existing in the nineteenth century, but research has proved they accurately portray, without exception, those of 1,000 A.D. Rua-Nui's chant was an accurate portrayal of celestial navigation over eight hundred years old![54]

At the time the first Europeans were exploring the Pacific the navigator-priests of Micronesia and Polynesia knew thousands of zenith stars. By the time anyone was curious enough to discover and record the knowledge of these astronomer-navigators, most of it had been forgotten. Samoans, interviewed in this century, stress that a group of three stars that form the pillar must be known, but they cannot satisfactorily explain why.[55] They also stress that the zenith star, "the star on top," is of no use for steering by, but that when it is directly above, they know that they are near the land they are seeking. They seem to have forgotten that zenith stars can be observed from a great distance, and that by steering one's course to arrive beneath them one will find the sought after island.

Zenith star navigation is no longer in use anywhere in the world. Electronic equipment has obviated its use. Soon it will be completely forgotten, and, like raft navigation of millennia past, it will fall victim to technological progress. But if one decided to get rid of our current gadgetry and sail the seven seas the old way one would come to understand the complexity and depth of knowledge required. Unlike horizon star, or directional star navigation, zenith star navigation was only practical if you knew many stars. The significance of the ability to read zenith stars through sighting devices, long ignored, should no longer be discounted.

The Polynesians of just a few centuries ago, the MesoAmericans of a few millennia ago, and the Sumerians of a forgotten time, all knew hundreds of stars, perhaps thousands. They knew the time they arose and set, they knew what seasons they could be used, and they knew the arcs of their progression across the sky. They knew enough about the stars that, even if most of the sky was overcast, and they could only glimpse a few stars, briefly, in one part of the sky, they knew what direction they were going and where they had come from.

Of course they knew other things. They could read the clouds that formed over unseen distant islands, they could recognize the birds that ventured tens of miles out from those islands, they could read ocean swell patterns, and deep phosphorescence and its meaning. But all of these matters required only a generation or two of learning, maybe a few centuries. The knowledge of the stars that they possessed, the precise movements, gravitating over seasons, required much more time, millennia of time, millennia of observation, millennia of communication. And knowledge of the stars was passed on to only a few. For the ways of the stars were secret to the navigator-priests. But every navigator knew them.

These were sea peoples! Children who grew up with the sea could have been no different than the children of today, who reaching the age of sixteen, finally able to legally drive a car, will venture far out at night, often at breakneck speeds, just to prove their mettle, and will return, perhaps just before dawn, exhausted but exhilarated at their independent adventure. So it must have been with teenagers who first took to the seas without the guidance of their mentors. The whole vast ocean before them, Sirius was the lucky star to guide them. The world was theirs!

Only the first Europeans to reach these people, the true navigators, Magellan and Cook, could stand in wonder at their craft and skills, because only they could appreciate what was before them. Those who came after them, blinded by the scientific dogma and prejudice of their day, could only see dumb savages.

Throughout Polynesia there is no separate word for astronomer or stargazer. If you want to find an astronomer you ask for a navigator. Captain Cook learned a great deal from an a navigator-priest of Raiatea, who sailed with Cook to Batavia on the Endeavour, and despite a circuitous route that ranged between 48 degrees south and 4 degrees north, "was never at a loss to point to Tahiti, at whatever place he came." Cook concludes these people sail in those seas from island to island for several hundred leagues, the Sun serving them for a compass by day, and the Moon and stars by night. When this comes to be proved, which I have now not the least doubt of, we Shall no longer be at a loss to know how the Islands lying in those Seas came to be people'd, we may trace them from Island to Island quite to the East Indies."[56]

But subsequent investigators had no interest in talking to the navigators or in learning from them, content instead to measure the islanders and their craft by the standards of European technology. Banning of inter-island canoe travel by English, Dutch, and Japanese administration in latter centuries contributed to a decline in navigation throughout Oceania and led to another curious phenomena; whenever native navigators made landfall on an island forbidden to them they claimed to have arrived by accident.

Since the knowledge of astronomy and navigation was passed on orally, and only among a select few, we have to regret that the knowledge "my grandfather knew" has now been lost. And in appreciating just how much has been lost we must lament that it is only recently that the peoples of the Pacific have lost the ability to learn from past generations.

Some evidence remains. In the Gilbert Islands sighting stones, discussed in Chapter I, point to other islands. But in fact, the stones do not point to the islands at all, but give a bearing generally 5 to 8 degrees off in the windward direction of each island. This fact has led Lewis to surmise that the sighting stones were used to align canoes on the star paths they would need to follow to make landfall (the prevailing currents and winds making up for the 5 to 8 percent). Although the stones invariably face outside the local groupings of island, a very large basalt stone in the old village of Niuafo'ou, a mile from the coast of Butaritari, leaves little doubt about its significance. It's name means, "Facing Uvea," an island some 132 miles away.

The "sighting stones" do not now agree with zenith or horizon star positions, their positions have changed over time, but we can deduce that at one time they must have been commensurate. Since we know that star courses were still being taught among the Gilbertese well into this century we can only assume that these islands were the site of an astronomical garden, and a school of navigation. The physical sighting stones provided a method of passing on valuable information that could not be taught by myth and legend alone. Ward's informant, an old man in 1946 said that "his father" had known how to use the stones.

Today, Polynesians still use a reticulated grid, implied in their reed mats, to design navigational charts with current directions, wind directions and the position of islands that surrounds their naval courses. We believe that at their historic first meeting Montezuma's offer to Hernan Cortez of a reed mat to sit on while they talked was meant to honor Cortez as a navigator. But Cortez, not knowing the symbolic meaning of the reed mat, asked instead for cloth to sit on.

If in primitive cultures like the Carolinian, and others found in Polynesia, it is only recently that the people have lost the ability to learn from past generations, when did the Greeks lose this ability? As our original "moderns," those who thought the past had nothing to teach them, they were already disavowing the "old ways' before Plato's time.

Evidence of devices for reading zenith stars and star pillars, still practiced in the Pacific at the beginning of the twentieth century, are reflected in the megaliths of almost every known astronomically advanced ancient culture, including the Sumerians, early Egyptians, Maltese, and the builders of Stonehenge. But they are most particularly revealed by the builders of the great star temples of Mesoamerica where sighting devices for zenith stars are a constant and dominant motif.

How long has deliberate transoceanic contact been going on? We have only to consult known maps for an idea. Charles Hapgood, in his Maps of The Ancient Sea Kings (fig. 6D) clearly shows the continent of Antarctica although that continent was not officially discovered until the nineteenth century.

The last time the map could have been drawn, the time Antarctica was free of overhanging icecaps that would have hid the outline of the continent was at least 7,000 years ago. We stress the words "at least" because it is impossible to believe that Antarctica was correctly mapped by ancient navigators just as storms were creating a new ice cap during "the little Ice Age" that began at that time. The most likely date for the mapping was in the period from 8,000 to 9,000 years ago (facing page, "Lake Vostoc, Antarctica").

Could the map be a forgery? Scholars have authenticated it's parchment as being from the early sixteenth century. But even if it was forged prior to its rediscovery in 1929 the correct detail of the outline of Antarctica's coastline, long hidden under massive ice sheets, was not fully known until it was confirmed, in precise detail, by space age satellites that were not in use in 1929.

Hapgood concluded that: "It becomes clear that ancient voyagers traveled from pole to pole. Unbelievable as it may appear, the evidence nevertheless indicates that some ancient people explored Antarctica when its coasts were free of ice. It is clear, too, that they had an instrument of navigation for accurately determining longitudes that was far superior to anything possessed by the peoples of ancient, medieval, or modern times until the second half of the 18th century." The evidence presented by the ancient maps is further evidence of the existence in ancient times of an advanced civilization, capable of world-wide navigation.

A multitude of sites in Australia, confirm that the arrival of Asian boats to that continent were neither instances of marooned traders nor fishing ships

Lake Vostoc, Antarctica.

In June, 1996 research scientists from the Scott Polar Research Institute At Cambridge University and the Russian Academy of Sciences announced the discovery of up to seventy fresh water lakes two and half miles under the ice sheet that covers Antarctica. The largest of the lakes is 124 miles long, averages 400 feet in depth and has an average temperature of slightly above freezing—even though the temperatures on top of the ice sheet that covers average 90 degrees below zero. The lake is warmed by either the tremendous pressure of the ice sheet or by geothermal causes, and is believed to contain ancient living bacteria, viruses, and simple plant life. Since It is believed that even at the time the Piri Reis map described the ice-free coasts of Antarctica, about 8 to 9,000 years ago, the interior must have retained large ice sheets. But the discovery of Lee Vostok shows how little we understand about that vast continent.[58]

blown off course, but rather a deliberate mass movement of peoples out of southeast Asia. Evidence has now been established that a series of navigational migrations took place from Asia to Australia 80,000 to 58,000 B.C. We know that the migrations were by boat because there has been no land bridge to Australia within the last 100 million years.

Skeletons at these sites have been determined to be those of modern Homo sapiens, sharers in the chromosomes found in a female in Africa, dated to 270,000 years ago, and now called "Eve." The chromosome evidence refutes previously accepted theory that peoples in Asia, far distant from Africa, would be descendants of Homo Erectus, a more primitive man known to have been in Asia for over a million years. No chromosomes from Homo Erectus were found at the sites in Australia. How did "Eve's" descendants get to Australia?

Recently, the discovery of "Adam" and "Eve" chromosomes in virtually every part of the globe seems at first glance to bolster "out of Africa" theories that place man's origin in Africa and his presence elsewhere as a one-way migration from that continent. But on closer inspection this discovery refutes that theory. Since we know that the predecessors of Homo sapiens, including Anthropopithecus erectus (Java Man) and Peking Man, as well as Homo erectus, must have left Africa at least 1.8 million years ago and evolved into a separate species, then why is there no evidence of their chromosomes found in any part of the world today? The only explanation that supports "out of Africa" theory is that the children of "Adam" and "Eve" in their subsequent migration as Homo sapiens wiped out every living member of Homo erectus in the world without any instances of interbreeding and without a trace of their chromosomes entering the genetic picture any where in the world. That simply, given man's proven penchant for interbreeding, is not possible.

One answer to this problem is found in the "Multi-regional hypothesis" which states that Homo sapiens did not arise in any single location but in many regions of the world as the result of many complex movements and migrations. In a very small time frame these "back and forth" migrations resulted in the dominance of Homo sapiens, as evidenced by the proliferation everywhere of his genetic material.

One of the leading proponents of Multi-regional theory, Alan Thorne of the Australian National University, explains that populations, even from 270,000 to 100,000 years ago, did not evolve in isolation but in concert, trading genetic material as the result of two-way and even more complicated migrations and interbreeding between people. Homo Erectus existed throughout the world, the result of migrations at least a million years ago. Thorne believes that evolution from Homo Erectus to Homo sapiens occurred independently in many places throughout the world without the need for a second wave of Homo sapiens "out of Africa." He states, "Today human genes flow between Johannesburg and Beijing, and Paris and Melbourne. Apart from interruptions from Ice Ages, they have probably been doing this through the entire span of Homo sapiens' evolution."[60]

Thorne's argument is the ultimate in a long list of "no contact is necessary theories," an argument that stresses that no matter where evolution occurs or has occurred it will not only result in man, but probably will result in a culturally similar man, possibly in a Wall Street executive, wearing a three-piece suit, driving a BMW, and exulting in his position as the science-driven inheritor of the Earth. Little is known of the culture or tools of these people, probably, Thorne theorizes, because they didn't use stone tools, preferring more versatile, but also more perishable, bamboo tools.

If man moved out of southeast Asia and navigated to Australia 80,000 years ago, as we now know he did, how much longer did he wait before using this superior means of transportation to travel to Melanesia, Micronesia, and beyond? And since in the multi-regional hypothesis evolution in isolation would have possibly led to a distinctly different genetic makeup, but did not in Australia, we must assume that the voyage to that continent was not a single one-way event, but was followed by a series of two-way contacts.

How could the DNA make-up of every human who exists today be so sim-

Polynesians and Cro-Magnon

Until 32,000 years ago Neanderthals dominated Europe. Then a very different type of human, taller, slimmer, and more intelligent, suddenly appeared. The Neanderthal disappeared entirely. Cro-Magnon displaced the Neanderthal and left sophisticated paintings as evidence of his large brain. But was this artistic and intelligent giant truly a unique race? Genetic evidence now points to a common ancestor for Cro-Magnon and for the early man who sailed from Asia to Australia. Sites at Pedra Furada and Monte Verde suggest that Cro-Magnon navigated across the Pacific to the Americas and to Europe around 32,000 years ago. At that time he displaced the last species of humans other than Homo sapiens (Homo Erectus had, reportedly, disappeared from Asia a 100,000 years earlier). By DNA evidence humans, at this time, despite differences in skin pigment and hair and eye color, any one member of Homo sapiens is far less differentiated than even one closely related dog species is to another. We appear, genetically, to be not only one race but one family. A common mother, dubbed "Eve," is believed to be the genetic mother of all of us humans who currently inhabit the planet. Recently studies of the Y chromosome in men from thirty-eight countries around the world found that they all descended from a common male ancestor who lived about 270,000 years ago.[57]

ilar to each other. We can pretend differences among ourselves, different skin color, different hair, but really we are remarkable in our precise DNA relationships—almost perfectly exact. We speak of clones, we fear clones, but genetically we—your white, black and yellow neighbor—are almost perfect clones. Humans (Homo sapiens) are genetically the most perfect homogenous race to have ever existed(see above, "Polynesians and Cro-Magnon").

But what if we weren't genetically the same race, the same peoples? How did this interregional contact occur? Some of it could have been by land migration. But at least 80,000 years ago most of the migration had to have been by sea. Thorne theorizes that complex movements and migrations would have been interrupted by Ice Ages. Actually, the opposite is very likely true. Ice sheets moving down the Asian continent would have inspired man to enter the warmer waters of the Pacific—as he surely did in migrating to

Australia—and having, from necessity, found a far simpler means of travel, man would venture out from Australia.

Man the navigator may not have been born in southeast Asia and Australia, but certainly he was well established there 80,000 years ago. It stands to reason that, in an interacting world, man the navigator was everywhere on the face of the Earth within several thousand years of that time.

Pleistocene (Ice Age) occupation of Pacific isles is now known to have extended well beyond Australia to truly oceanic islands by, at least, 33,000 years ago. Radiocarbon dating of the Matenkupkum Cave site on New Ireland in the Admiralty group has confirmed the site as between 31,000 and 33,000 B.P.. Occupation at a rock shelter on Buka Island in the Solomon Islands has been confirmed as 28,000 B.P.[61] Pleistocene occupation in the western Pacific expanded to the island of Manus which lay some 100 kilometers beyond sight of the nearest island. But since no sites dating before 4000 B.P. have been confirmed in the Pacific east of the Solomons, a case has been made that this wave of migration resulted in a "voyaging nursery" in the western Pacific. There, the powerful academic doubters of navigation hold, an aggressive and adventurous navigational culture supposedly lingered for four to forty thousand years until it developed the temerity to sail out to the other islands of the Pacific.

This notion of a "pause" in human navigational exploration could explain, to Eurocentric historians, the seeming gap in known migration in the western Pacific until the arrival of the Europeans 400 years ago. But it cannot explain the exploits of the Lapita culture, known to have spread plants and fauna throughout the Pacific from at least 3,500 years ago. It cannot explain the spread of the coconut from the Americas to the Pacific at least 12,000 years ago, or the introduction of the sweet potato or "kumara" with its name intact from pre-Inca Peru, or the mutual existence of identically tuned musical instruments such as the pan-pipe in the Solomon Islands and in Peru.[62]

What happened in the intervening four to forty thousand years? The "voyaging nursery" theory holds that these sea people had made their migration and subsequently had lost interest in adventures in a vast sea that promised so little contact with land.

But what would the effect have been if an adventurous man had become attuned to, and at home with discovery by sea. Man left Asian tigers, apes, squirrels, weak-flying birds, such as woodpeckers, and a wild variety of flora behind as he crossed the Indonesian archipelago 60,000 to 80,000 years ago. They had followed him, probably preceded him in migration, until they met the "Wallace line" and a series of deep ocean trenches separating Bali from Lombok, Lombok from Borneo, and all non-navigational species from Australia.[63] In the Pleistocene ice ages all creatures could cross lines between islands where the present ocean bottom lays less than 75 fathoms (450 feet) deep. None but a sea-faring man could cross depths of thousands of feet during that time. Yet man did, sailing from one island to another, many more than a hundred kilometers distant, until he reached out to thousands of miles beyond his original home on the Asian mainland. With a confidence born of the mastery of the seas, with successful excursions from one distant island to another, why would sea-faring man suddenly stop and contemplate his naval accomplishments for from 40,000 to 40,000 years?

In fact, significantly reduced sea levels in this period made western Pacific islands many times larger, and far easier to "hit" with random sailing. There is no reason to believe that experienced sailors, able to read both the stars and the ocean waves, would have become timid and remained that way for 40,000 years. Moreover, we believe these navigators did not engage in "random sailing," but depended on a body of navigation and astronomical knowledge that made voyaging then, as it is today, relatively easy—especially when it is compared to migration over ice-laden continents. The records of all navigators show that knowledge of stars, currents, wave and winds, with some skills, play a greater part in discovery than the size of islands.

If so, why is there little proof of human occupation throughout the Pacific from 43,000 to 12,000 years ago? The answer literally lies buried in the sea. Our history is truly submerged. During the late Pleistocene the ocean, drained by the creation of the ice sheets, was as much as 480 feet lower. All of the coastal sites of that time are now submerged under up to 400 feet of water or have been destroyed by rising sea levels that at least once rose cataclysmically. We must remember that navigational man was a coastal man—he would not have built his cities in the high interiors of either islands or continents. We can remind ourselves that even today, man, by preference, gathers to live and trade by the sea. In the Pleistocene this natural inclination would have been greatly magnified. The interiors of all continents were very cold and very dry. They were inhospitable to plant life, and to munchers of plant life, and to man. Follow the food chain. Unlike the australopithecines, who arose on the lush though drying African continent four million years ago, and, unlike Homo Erectus, Homo sapiens, (a Pleistocene mammal), has lived and flourished in the Ice Ages—a time of significantly lesser temperatures, and significantly less moisture. He has long been by necessity a coastal creature drawing his existence from the sea (fig. 11R).

E. James Dixon believes that the significant migration to the Americas had to have come long ago, most likely via the same navigators that migrated to Australia and the Solomon Islands. But he doubts that navigators languished in the western Pacific more than a few thousand years. Dixon points out that

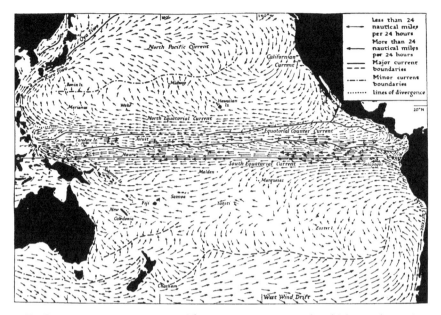

11.R. CIRCULAR OCEAN CURRENTS. The ocean currents served as highways for ancient man. Use of rafts in Micronesia goes back to at least 60,000 B.C. America, as a melting pot of sea-faring peoples, must be at least that old. No 60,000-year-old rafts have never been found in the Americas or in Europe. But there is no other explanation for man's presence, recorded in artistic expression, and in stone, throughout the world, at a minimum of 32,000 B.P.

30,000 years, at a minimum, is an incredibly long time for modern man to have sat in this "voyaging nursery" and watched the breezes, waiting for a favorable wind. If only two or three expeditions set out each decade, or even each century, in search of new islands, new adventures, or in simple escape from tyrants, poverty, or unhappy wives, landfall in the Americas could have been achieved forty thousand years ago. If so, we might expect that archeological remains from the oldest levels at Monte Verde and Pedra Furada would look more like Pleistocene Austronesia than like Clovis and other Paleo-Indian sites in North America. And they do.

Pedra Furada, in Brazil, and Monte Alegre, in southern Chile, boast some of the earliest known dates for wall art in the world. Pedra Furada also contains stone tools similar to those found at the oldest level at Monte Verde (32,000 B.P.). These widely separated sites confirm one another. An artistic and diversified agricultural society existed, actually flourished, in the Americas over twenty thousand years before the more primitive Clovis man supposedly migrated across Beringia.

That advanced civilizations existed 12,000 or even 20,000 years ago can no longer be denied. Picasso's comment on the "sophisticated" cave paintings at Lascaux, the artistic sculptures at Vosni, in what is now the Czech Republic, the harmonic designs of the "great pyramids" at Teotihuacan and Cheops, the antiquity of the Sphinx, the precise construction of the spheres of Costa Rica, and the intricate megaliths at Sacsayhuaman and star-temples throughout the world all attest to ancient artistic, astronomical and building skills that flourished long before the traditional dating for the rise of civilization. The conclusion is as simple as the subject is complex: Civilization has occurred more than once but rarely, if ever, in complete isolation. Navigational contact between peoples has been the cathartic instrument of civilization's rise, and that contact has been going on for at least 36,000 to 80,000 years. The avenues of contact have been the constant winds and currents of the oceans, rivers of civilized contact, in ages now all but lost to memory.

12 The Parrot & the Coconut: Diffusion & Migration

Said the mariner to the isolationist, "We will speak of many things, of coconuts and parrot's wings, of pottery and Quepu strings, and of an ocean current and the bounty it brings, like sailing ships and the seals of kings."
(Apologies to Lewis Carroll)

AT COPAN, once believed to be a recent Mayan site, but now known to be much older, stela B (fig. 12A) portrays an Asiatic face, possibly Mandarin, flanked by what appears to be two intricately carved elephant heads. America's leading archaeologist of the 1930s, Sylvanus Morley, dismissed any notion that these figures could represent elephants. Morley declared that the figures were "blue macaws" and the American school of anthropology was not only quick to agree with him, they have continued to support his odd assessment sixty years later. After all, if knowledge of elephants existed in Copan in 300 A.D., as traditionalists have dated this site, six hundred years earlier or even six hundred years later, their concept of "no contact" would be in serious jeopardy. "No contact" has remained an edict crucial to the view that American cultures arose isolated from the "known" ancient civilizations of the Eastern Mediterranean as well as to the general theory that cultures would rise and take shape in accordance with neo-Darwinian principles.

Investigators working at the edge of demonstrable science, like Thor Heyerdahl, have questioned academic dogma in its entirety. Heyerdahl's journeys proved that one-way contact from the Americas to the western Pacific, Australia and Asia were really not so difficult. Sea journeys from the Mediterranean to the Americas were just as easy. Heyerdahl recreated the means of deliberate contact between ancient civilizations, but his proven

12.A. STELA B, COPAN, HONDURAS. Elephants and Chinese figure.
(Catherwood drawing).

routes of sea contact have been dismissed by authorities as lucky sailings by an uninformed navigator. "No contact" has been the virtual religion of Neo-Darwinism philosophy.

The isolationists have long held the high ground in this dispute by virtue of their control of America's universities and institutions. They have insisted that confirmation of their theories must dominate any actual evidence that contradicts them. Therefore, to the isolationists, the questioned sculptures at Copan *are* "blue macaws" even if they don't resemble birds at all.

Diffusionists, mainly scientists from other fields such as botany, astronomy, and mathematics, have raised significant challenges to the isolationist view. In the case of the stele at Copan, they have pointed out that the rounded snout (characteristically tucked in), the proportions and position of the eyes (faced directly ahead), the presence of tusks (not usually found on macaws), and the symmetry of the broad head, all say otherwise. If the accompanying photograph does not convince you, we invite you to come to Copan. Anyone who even glances at this ancient depiction will appreciate that this is a portrayal of an elephant! Molars of mastodons have been found in a cave near Oxkutzcab south of Merida in the Yucatán in association with bison and American horses dated, with fires from American Indians, to 11,000 B.C. But Mastodons, though related, were not elephants, and having become extinct over 11,000 years ago, Mastodons were not around when Copan was built.[1] These elephants appear to be wearing turbans, similar to those worn by Hindu elephant drivers.

How could the artist, who created this decoration so elegantly, portray an elephant? Certainly not from a chance description by a marooned fisherman from Asia, and probably not from copying art brought across the seas. The depiction is too lifelike.[2] Only an artist who had experienced an elephant first hand could have recreated it.

Did Chinese or Indic voyagers carry elephants on their rafts as Hannibal had transported them across the Mediterranean? It's highly unlikely. The only logical answer, sacrilege to the Americanist view, is that the artist who sculpted this stela visited southeast Asia or India and brought back a rare and wonderful image, a unique contribution to a great sculpture.

Only long-range sea voyages, with extended stays and safe returns could account for an artist's precise mimicry of the works of another culture. Thus panpipes in the Solomon Islands that are identical to panpipes in Bolivia would have required extensive contact between peoples over 4,000 miles distant from one another (fig. 12B).[3] The fact that the base of the sarcophagus at Palenque is broadened in the same manner as the sarcophagi of the Egyptians

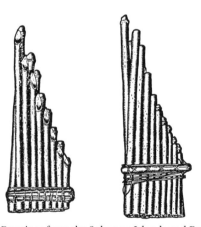

12.B. Panpipes from the Solomon Islands and Bolivia.

required similar long-range contact, even though the broad base of the tomb at Palenque was unnecessary. The Maya, unlike Egyptians, did not stand their sarcophagi on end. Portrayal of the Asian-like lotus at Chichen Itza, with the rhizome, or root-like stalk at its base, is identical with the depictions of Buddhist art at Amaravati on the east coast of India and could not have occurred without cultural contact.[4]

At Chichen Itza, important finds were made recently by divers exploring the bottom of the site's sacred well (cenote). Thousands of clay objects were found with bearded men resembling those depicted throughout the columns and walls of the temples of Chichen Itza. Many other objects, made of silver, gold, copper, copper alloys, and tin were removed from the waters of the cenote. The metallurgical sophistication of these latter objects has been all the more puzzling to traditional scholars because the Yucatán region is virtually devoid of metals. The jade would have had to have come from Guatemala. The tin could only have come from thousands of miles away, either from the high Andes of Bolivia or from the British Isles. The copper would have to have come from even a greater distance—from Isle Royale in Lake Superior. But where did the bearded warriors come from?

Chichen Itza's frescoes themselves depict seashore battles, with bearded Semitic-featured men arriving in reed boats resembling those from Sumer.[5] Chichen Itza has been dated to the first century after Christ. Reed boat navigation in the Mediterranean was almost totally discontinued with the advent of wooden planked boats three thousand years ago and with the arrival of the "terrible Age of Iron" and universal warfare among Mediterranean states. Since reed raft construction was effectively forgotten a millennium before Christ, these frescoes must represent contact with Mediterranean navigators at dates that far precede our standard dating of civilization in Mesoamerica.

Although the Maya themselves had no facial hair, beards and mustaches are common at Maya sites throughout Mesoamerica. At El Ceibal in Guatemala mustached warriors dominate the stelae. At Kohunlich in the southern Yucatán giant stucco masks two to three meters tall clearly display mustaches.

In 1992 and 1993 a team lead by Mary Miller, Chairwoman of the Department of Art History at Yale University, used standard and infrared photography and computer reconstruction to enhance the large murals at Bonampak. The enhancement only confirmed what was already apparent to the naked eye. The depiction of Bonampak's ruler, Chaan Muan, revealed he wore a distinct black beard. The murals describe events of 790 and 791 A.D. when outside influence from the Mediterranean world was unlikely, due to the decline of navigation long before Bonampak's dates. However, the depiction of a beard on the face of Bonampak's ruler probably demonstrates a reverence for beards by the Maya, that undoubtedly dates back centuries or even millennia.[7]

The dominant American anthropological theories of the twentieth century have stressed independent inventions and independent evolutions. Similar inventions can be argued to be responses by a people to similar problems, and man is renowned as the problem-solving animal. But could man have temporarily evolved facial hair in the first century A.D. on a continent where it was (seemingly) previously unknown and where, in a tropical climate, it could have served no purpose? Would man have subsequently discarded this facial hair before the arrival of the Europeans in the sixteenth century?

If man could control his growth of facial hair could he have also recreated the genetics of a variety of plant life?

As the noted plant geographer G.F. Carter once observed, "Any fool can make an arrow-point, but only God can make a sweet potato."[8] Carter was referring to the diffusion throughout the Pacific, by 12,000 B.C., of the genetically wholly American sweet potato. But he could as easily referred to the spread of the American coconut, American cotton, or to many other plants and animals.

Nigel Davies, in *Voyagers to the New World*, maintains that early migrations by sea were impossible by man but that diffusion by natural organisms were not only possible but the likely answer for migration of plant life. Davies has voiced the isolationist's view that birds carried cotton and other seeds and that the ocean currents carried floating coconuts across the vast seas.

If so, how did the banana (plantain) arrive in the Americas? Because it was found from Mexico to Brazil when the Spanish explorers arrived, and later found in Peruvian tombs dated to over 8000 B.C., the Spanish assumed that it was native to the Americas. Botanists have now determined that the banana is a wholly Asian plant, with no American genetic history, and they have determined that, from investigation of stratigraphic layers of undisturbed soil, it must have been introduced throughout the tropical Americas sometime between 11,000 and 15,000 years ago. No flying bird nor swimming fish could have carried this seedless plant across the seas, nor could the entire plant of this fruit or any part of it have survived such a journey on a twist of logs journeying between continents without rotting. The banana had to have been deliberately introduced by man, specifically by a seaman. For no wanderers across Beringia, taking generations to complete such a trek, could have kept a banana plant alive.[9]

The banana proves navigational migration of plant life to the Americas but there is also considerable proof of migration *out of* the Americas. The problem of the diffusion of the coconut has long baffled those who doubted man's worth on the seas. Genetically an American fruit the coconut has been cultivated for thousands of years in the Pacific and in Asia. Once assumed to have arrived in the opposite direction, from Asia to Polynesia, then to America, the coconut is now acknowledged by biologists to have gone the opposite route. Any understanding of ocean currents will confirm this, but isolationists have seized on this idea to claim that the ocean currents themselves dispersed the coconut throughout the world. Unlike the banana, the coconut's solid shell, in theory, would have protected it on an extended ocean voyage and allowed it to regenerate on some distant shore. However, in experiments first conducted from Hawaii in 1941, it was demonstrated that on any extended drift of coconuts, fouling organisms would, without exception, first eat out the eyes of the coconut and then eat out the meat. In fact every attempt to float coconuts across the Pacific has met a disastrous outcome—the sea water softens the coconuts' eyes, and micro-organisms enter the nut and destroy its meat and its ability to regerminate. Only unregenerate husks could possibly reach distant shores . . . that is, unless the fruit was carried by human voyagers.[10]

Yet Plato knew of the coconut, describing it in the *Critius* as a large "fruit with a hard rind" that flourished in Atlantis and provided meat, drink, and ointment. How could Plato have so precisely described the attributes of this unique fruit, a fruit that was unknown in the Greece of his time and unknown in Egypt in Solon's time?[11] Can we still give credence for an argument for Atlantis in the very cold climate of the North Atlantic or the equally chilly Mediterranean 11,500 years ago? The tree of the coconut palm only flourishes in tropical climates.

As mentioned before, if a bird carried the sweet potato from the Americas to distant islands in the Pacific it must have been a parrot. And, as we mentioned before (fig. 2G), this parrot must have been squawking the name of its burden as it flew, because the original name for the sweet potato in ancient Peru, kumara, was identical in pronunciation to its name throughout Polynesia. From Easter Island to New Zealand, thousands of years before European ships arrived, this edible root, with an exclusive genetic history that rested solely in the Americas, was called kumara. Another edible rhizome, the lotus of India, is called *kumari* in Sanskrit.[12]

Then there is the question of the parrot itself. Genetically solely American, a favorite of Pre-Inca Peruvians (to judge from its appearance in ancient tombs), and too poor a flyer to have transversed oceans on its own (parrots have almost no gliding ability but depend on constant wing flapping in flight), chance migration theory would have a difficult time in explaining its appearance throughout Polynesia, Micronesia, and Melanesia as well as its introduction into Asia and the Indian sub-continent, probably around 15,000 years ago. The parrot must have gone by ship, where its occasional squawking could be tolerated by people who cared for it. No other circumstance could account for its migration.

The question of long-linted, spinnable cotton is equally fascinating. Cotton weaving in the Americas and in ancient Egypt are both dependent on the long-linted form, which have thirteen large and thirteen small chromosomes. But in the Americas wild cotton had only thirteen small chromosomes. Some hybrid had to have been introduced to create the thirteen small and thirteen large chromosome pattern that became the long-linted American cotton. Again the idea that a bird carried the seed in his beak in a long flight across the ocean is preposterous. Somewhere in the bird's flight he would have swallowed the seed, or dropped it. Even if he had not the cross-fertilization with American wild cotton required the help and skills of a botanist. Spinable cotton was a deliberate invention in the Americas, and an ancient invention.

The bottle-gourd, native to India and East Africa, has recently been found in settlements in coastal Peru dating to 7,000 B.C. Pre-Inca Peruvians were already cultivating a variety of other squashes, as well as peppers and avocados. Yet cultivation of the less tasty bottle-gourd was widely adopted. It also came into cultivation in Mexico and in Thailand at around the same time. Why? It likely was because the bottle-gourd had a use its more tasty rivals lacked—it was literally used as a bottle—a sturdy, light-weight vessel that navigators could use to carry water and other life-giving liquids on long voyages.[13] Like the coconut the bottle-gourd cannot withstand saltwater and boring organisms on its own. Its appearance, world-wide–at least 9,000 years ago–shows that it must have been carried and used by navigators undertaking deliberate voyages.

Fruits and vegetables may be mundane and unexciting evidence to any but the specialist. But they are a reconfirmation of everything that myth and the great physical relics of MesoAmerican have been telling us: Man was not only an ancient and efficient navigator, he was a bold communicator with little fear of death and persecution from far-flung peoples, no matter how foreign their cultures may have been. The present authors, both of whom have roamed the world in search of ancient beginnings have had similar experiences. If you arrive with good will and keep your head about you there is no more likelihood of experiencing anything more than minor inconveniences than if you stayed in your own city, which in America these days is likely to be overrun with guns and violence.

Could a small edible object such as a gourd or a sweet potato root drift across an ocean unmolested by fish and boring organisms such as the shipworm (teredo), while a man on a raft could not?[14] Could a bird fly 6,000 miles with a root or seed in its beak or claws while a man could not sail that distance? Could cotton seeds remain fertile after months of exposure to salt water?[15] Probability demands other answers.

Related ideas and means of expression of these ideas are known to have existed and shared between the Americas and the rest of the world for many thousands of years. Ideas, concepts, even entire mythological and mathematical systems could arise independently, according to isolationists. But even the most obdurate isolationists must now admit that neither a banana nor a sweet potato could negotiate the oceans on their own.

If seamen, venturing out from the Americas, brought the banana back to their home continent why did they not also bring back wheat? They surely must have encountered it. The likely answer is that wheat *was* brought back and that the explorers probably did try to introduce it to their own cultures. But wheat simply did not do well in tropical and marshy environments. The grain probably failed in competition with the preferred corn, while the banana, with no real competitor, took root and flourished.

As we have investigated throughout this study, evidence of a world-wide navigational culture that goes back in time for hundreds and even thousands of years before Columbus abounds in the Americas.

If the nature of the most sophisticated cultures of the pre-Columbian and pre-Christian era of civilization was not navigational and if there was "no contact" how do we explain any of the following?

- The American pineapple depicted in murals in the Roman ruins of Pompeii.[16]
- Evidence that the American peanut was cultivated in what are now the Jiangxu and Zhejiang provinces of China as early as 3,200 B.C.[17]
- The presence of Hibiscus rosasinensis, the bright flower that every Polynesian girl wears behind her ear, throughout Oceania for thousands of years before European explorers reached these distant islands. Ornithologists, as well as the noted plant expert, George F. Carter, have established that the Hibiscus can only be pollinated by the Hummingbird, a strictly American species. Neither the Hummingbird nor the Hibiscus could have migrated across the Pacific on their own.[18]
- The use of the *atlatl*, the Nahuatl (Mexica) name for spearthrowers, conservatively dated to 8500 B.C. in the Americas and coincidentally found at Magdalenian sites in France dated to 13,000 B.C.[19]
- As mentioned, the presence in Australia of the bones of Asians who had

migrated there at least 80,000 years ago (fig. 12C). These "anatomically *modern humans* appeared in Australia before they did in Europe.[20] And they did not arrive by land migration. Even at the lowest sea levels of the deepest Ice-Age there was no land bridge to Australia.

- Pleistocene (Ice Age) occupation of the Admiralty and Solomon Islands in the Pacific, at a minimum of 12,000 years before present.
- Ice Age occupation of the Channel Islands (off California), together with the charred remains of mastodons. (Again across waters too deep to have been connected by a land bridge).
- The fact that the Maya, like the Hindus, attributed a different color to each of the four cardinal directions.[21]
- The fact that the four-sided Maltese Cross was represented in ancient India, Persia, and in the Americas at dates that preceded Christ, and that it appeared again on the ships of Columbus in his venture to the new World.
- The fact that the ancient Hindu game of *pachisi* (Parcheesi) and the pre-Columbian Mexican *patolli* were both played on a schematic that resembled a four-sided cross whose arms depicted steps leading to an interior summit. It is a mathematical game whose exact coincidental duplication, in separate cultures, has been described mathematically as 7x10 to the twenty-seconded power, that is a probability of 7x10 multiplied by the number 1,000,000,000,000,000,000,000 over one.[22] There are considerable odds against such a coincidence–equivalent to the likelihood that a penny thrust from an orbiting satellite in space will drop precisely on *your* head.

12.C. "THE MOUTHLESS ONES." Found in the Kimberly region of Australia where cave painting, as in America and Europe, go back at least 32,000 years.

- The existence of mummies, similarly embalmed, found in widely separated sites of today's Egypt and Peru, dating to 5,000 years before present in Egypt and to 8,000 years B.P. in Peru. The odds of independent origins of identical means of embalming mummies go off the chart reaching a number that does not exist in the physical description of our universe.

- The recently discovered (1992) presence of both cocaine and nicotine, derivatives of wholly American plants, in Egyptian mummies dating to 3000 B.C. in Egypt (their presence had been detected in far earlier mummies in the Americas). This discovery created a storm of protests from traditional scientists who insisted the discovery was either the result of a contaminated investigation or a hoax. Yet the discover, noted toxicologist Dr. Snejana Balabanova, repeated her tests on several mummies and found that over half of them contained cocaine and that almost all contained nicotine. To test contamination Dr. Balabanova subjected mummy hair shafts to an unreproachable test. She placed them in alcohol for several hours, then removed them. If the cocaine had been introduced any time after death the alcohol would dissolve the cocaine into the solution and the hair shafts would test negative. However, the hair shafts continued to test positive for cocaine and nicotine. The alcohol showed no trace of either substance. There was no outside contamination of the mummies. They had ingested both cocaine and nicotine.

If not contaminated was there a hoax? Had someone somehow switched Peruvian mummies for what Dr. Balabanova had accepted as Egyptian mummies. The tests were repeated by Dr. Rosalie David, Keeper of the Manchester Museum, on mummies known to have been removed from Egyptian tombs decades before. The majority of Dr. David's mummies tested positive for cocaine and tobacco. And there was no contamination. Subsequently, in 134 separate tests of verified mummies from Egypt and the Sudan, by many scientists, most of them doubters, cocaine and nicotine have been found. Since no botanist has ever found evidence of either the coca plant or the tobacco plant to have grown anywhere outside the Americas the evidence is unmistakable—coca and tobacco were exported from the Americas over 5,000 years ago.

Could all of this evidence—including, of course, all that we've mentioned earlier, (similar myths, similar means of building step-pyramids, similar attributions to the configurations of the stars)—be coincidence? Could African, Semitic, Nordic and Asian faces appear on Mayan and Olmec sculptures in ages preceding Columbus without any actual contact of their cultures?

Isolationists argue that there could not have been contact between the Old

World and the New World prior to Columbus because the Americans had shown no resistance to the smallpox, measles, influenza, and other diseases the Spanish introduced to the Americas. Since infectious diseases, pestilence, and typhus were believed to be the result of humans living in too close proximity without sufficient means of disposing waste a further argument was made that while the Old World had flourishing dense urban populations the New World must have been a series of small villages.

In answer to the first argument we would point out that the first known smallpox epidemic, the disease that later virtually wiped out many millions of native Americans, did not occur in the Mediterranean region until the third century A.D. Before that the disease was unknown. Hundreds and thousands of years of contact between Mediterraneans and American could have preceded that date without any adverse effect on anyone. Contacts with Asia and Africa could have continued even past the third century A.D. since smallpox was still unknown on those continents at that time. In fact, sporadic contact with Europeans and Mediterraneans could have occurred as long as there were no infected persons involved. Even contact with Mediterraneans would have resulted in no damage unless an infected person was encountered and that probability was slight among trading sea cultures. It was only after the Spanish domination brought thousands of people to the New World that a chance diseased human carrier was able to introduce this new deadly strain. It is even possible that smallpox and influenza had been introduced in America at some earlier time and that they had previously developed an immunity to them. Only a few generations of no contact would have had to have ensued for these immunities to have been lost.[23] Just as today we're seeing a loss of immunity to tuberculosis, polio, smallpox, and a return of these and other diseases to many regions of the world.

In answer to the second question the Americas had dense population centers for thousands of years before any recent contact with the peoples of the Mediterranean or Europe. Teotihuacan supported a population of over 150,000 diverse people, including a large settlement of Negroid Olmecs when Rome was little more than a village. However, no diseases had resulted because the ancient Americans did not domesticate the pig or the cow. Influenza, like the common cold, did not develop in the crowded confines of humanity. Instead it developed in the crowded confines of the pig's environment, the sty.

The pig is still one of the filthiest animals known to man, and it's environment, including the ingestion of its own excrement, is a perfect situation for development of endemic disease. Once introduced, disease among pigs, sharing many characteristics with man, could later to be passed on to humanity.

Smallpox developed from cowpox, and from similar crowding of beef cattle, plagues and Black Death from inadequate means of treating sewage—common in medieval Europe but not a problem in the canaled cities of the Americas. Americans had to have known of pigs and cows but rejected them, probably from a cultural imperative, without knowing the deadly diseases they would eventually carry.

Ancient Americans domesticated only the dog, the cat, the parrot, and, in Peru, the llama—creatures that transmit no deadly diseases. These animals had been domesticated for thousands of years before the massive contact that followed Columbus's voyages. In urban communities that numbered over one hundred thousand residents—including Tikal in Guatemala, El Mirador and Teotihuacan in Mexico, and Caracol in Belize—these domesticated animals had lived in close proximity with man, all with no proven adverse affect on the Americans.[24]

If there was no contact how do we account for a diverse navigational culture at Monte Verde, 500 miles south of present day Santiago, Chile, that is now indisputably dated to a minimum of 12,800 years ago? How do we account for Chan Chan in Ecuador and Moseley's description of a maritime culture that goes back 9,000 years? Jomon pottery from Japan has been compared to Valdivia pottery found on the other side of the Pacific among the Chan Chan cultures of Ecuador and Peru.[25] The Jomon style of pottery, with its highly decorated red-clay incised vessels, often with unusual castellated or peaked rims, braid impressions, zigzag cross-hatching, and parallel line patterns can be traced back at least 9,000 years in Japan.[26] The same pottery, identically fired and designed, has been found at Valdivia, the site of an ancient maritime culture in Ecuador. Valdivia pottery, in fact, has more similarities in its decorative designs to the Jomon pottery of western Kyushu than those shared by Kyushu and Honshu Jomon styles within Japan.[27] Valdivia pottery has been carbon dated to 3,200 B.C. Earlier pottery in Ecuador, dated to 4,000 B.C. and dubbed San Pedro, bears no stylistic connection to the Jomon-Valdivia style.[28]

New pottery finds in the Amazon have pushed the dates on pottery in America to over 12,000 years before present.[29] Older finds only await discovery. But nothing found to date in the Americas, prior to Valdivia resembles the Jomon style. The Valdivia style was not developed in the Americas. It was obviously imported. How did this occur?

Theories have been advanced that hearty Jomon seamen sailing the waters south of Japan were one day blown off their fishing grounds by a typhoon and were swept by the Japanese and California currents to America, and eventually to Ecuador.[30] Such theories make some rather dubious assumptions. The ship would have to have been at least partially disabled. Otherwise the fishermen would have simply sailed home after the effects of the typhoon had passed by. The seamen would had to have had the foresight to carry enough water to sustain them in a disabled drift of possibly several months to make landfall in the Americas. Upon making initial landfall, most probably along the coast of what is now British Columbia, the seaman would had to have been unable to make sufficient repairs to their craft to sail home, but would have decided instead to continue their drift down the west coast of the North American continent. They would further have had to choose not to enter the North Equatorial current off Mexico or Central America, but instead continue drifting southeast, and away from home until they reached Ecuador. And they would have had to have encountered friendly people who welcomed them and their mode and style of pottery making and duplicated it.

It is a highly dubious story. Chance introductions, in the ancient world were not likely to result in immediate acceptance and duplication among whole and completely self-sufficient societies that believed in their own integrity. Today, it is easy to introduce any foreign and unusual object into our Eurocentric and oddly eclectic culture. We seem to have no intrinsic culture to defend from outside forces. Being materially minded, any unique or even vaguely different matter is greatly welcomed as long as we can put our label of ownership, or consumerism, on it.

Our ancestors didn't think that way. Chance introductions of foreign objects, foods, and concepts would probably have been viewed as alien, laughable, or threatening to ancient man's harmonious existence with his greater concepts of existence. These ancient societies were culturally conservative. In Mayan cultures of the Yucatán intricate bowls were carved and marked "cacao," because nothing other than this ancestor of chocolate was to be put into these vessels.31 Where primitive cultures still exist they retain a similar resistance to outsiders and their goods and their beliefs.

Then as now there was a natural resistance to the adoption of new ideas. Only then it was stronger. A few starving Jomon fishermen are unlikely to have successfully introduced a new style of pottery to South America. If in fact, they arrived in this manner and stayed for any length of time they would have been more likely forced to adopt the ways of the resident Americans than to start teaching their crafts to the natives.

How did Jomon pottery become not only acceptable in Peru, but a source for imitation? Probably only by its introduction by prominent members of ancient Peru's own culture, and not by contact with lost and forlorn Japanese fishermen. Logically, that would mean contact initiated by Americans who set sail along warm sea currents, pressed on by constant trade winds, rather than initial contact by Asians forced into the North Pacific, then crippled by typhoons. Chance landfalls by disabled ships blown off course were not responsible for the introduction of Jomon pottery techniques in South America. Deliberate, planned voyages by able ships, sufficiently stocked with provisions make much more sense. And the contact must have been over a long period, long enough for one culture to study and appreciate and finally to adopt the accomplishments of the other. The voyages need not to have been East to West. They were more likely both ways, with the initiation from the Americas to the Orient and the Mediterranean realms more likely. Why? Warm waters entice seafarers. On the Pacific side the warm oceanic waters of the central regions of America are pushed eastward by steady trade winds. Owing to its unique configuration the warm waters of the Atlantic side of the Americas are carried to the northeast by the unfailing Gulf Stream. On either side of this narrow heart of a continent the currents move away from the land and lure the adventurous. Once bound on a great adventure, with all the elements in his favor, the worthy voyager can be lulled into a sense of omnipotence, forgetting that the return voyage may not be so easy. Thus navigators from America could easily have reached southern Asia and made their way north to Japan. There, as throughout their journey, they would had to have been open to foreign ways of thinking, learned how the Jomon made pottery, and adopted their designs. At the same time the bounty of the Americas, where the largest numbers of useful domesticated plants first occurred—including the potato, maize (corn), tomatoes, sweet potato, cotton, tobacco, and cocaine—were diffused throughout the navigational cities of the ancient world.

Marco Polo's discoveries and their acceptance by most of his people undoubtedly holds true for many other adventurers. The lesson of Marco Polo's adventures, in his land-based journeys, reflects the sea journeys of Arabic Sinbad, undoubtedly a "representative archetypal hero." For Italians and Arabs alike, the introduction of new but foreign ideas by a native explorer—one of their own people—was acceptable, but the introduction of foreign ideas by a foreigner, without outright conquest and imposition, would not have been.

The replication of Jomon pottery of Japan at Valdivia in Ecuador over 5,000 years ago is only one example, and one further evidence of intense cultural contact thousands of years before Columbus. The fact that Chinese dragon motifs (fig. 8B), worked in jade among the Shang civilization in the Yellow River area in the eighteenth century B.C., found almost exact repetition among Olmec cultures of Costa Rica, identically worked in jade and dated to 1100 B.C., is another proof. Both cultures interred their highly regarded dead with these jade pendants.[32]

Still isolationists have claimed to have the upper hand. If there was repeated cultural contact between the peoples of the Americas and other advanced civilization why did the Americans lack all knowledge of the wheel? The wheeled Olmec dog found at a grave site at Tres Zapotes (dated at about 1500 B.C.) answers this prominent isolationist objection to diffusionist theory. The wheeled pottery animals prove that ancient Americans knew both the wheel and the axle and how to use them. Apparently, except for toys, they simply chose not to use the wheel.

Why disdain the use of the wheel? One argument that has been advanced is that the Olmecs lived in swamps and jungles that would make the wheel more of a hindrance than a help. But subsequent Mayan cultures built incredibly straight and wide and elevated limestone roads called sacbeob that traversed the jungles, and ancient Peruvians built similar roads in high and dry mountain plateaus. They lacked draught animals such as the oxen but any visitor to China or India will marvel at how much one man can pull on a wheeled cart. Yet even today Peruvians and Lancandons, descendants of the Maya, prefer to travel on foot carrying their heavy loads on their shoulders or on the sides of pack animals like the llama. The wheel may not have been used because of cultural bias.

It is even likely that the ancient Americans did once use the wheel for transport and that we have just not found the evidence. They may have fashioned wheels from wood. In tropical climates wood rots. Because the archeological record is so far from complete we can only speculate about its use, but we now know for certain that the wheel was known to them.

Our own cultural bias compels us to read intellectual inferiority into peoples who do not, or did not, share in our technological advances. Could Mayans and Pre-Mayans have really been intellectually advanced if they did not use the wheel? It seems to have been forgotten that the entire pyramid building era of Ancient Egypt existed without the use of the wheel. The wheel is thought to have only been introduced to Egypt around 2000 B.C., at the end of the great dynastic achievements. Can we call the builders of the Egyptian pyramids, the Sphinx, the Temple of Karnak, and the tombs of Thebes, intellectually inferior to their successors, who built nothing of lasting value?

If anything, the introduction of the wheel coincided with an extended period of intellectual decline in Egypt. Was there a connection? A substantial argument could be made that the introduction of rural electrification—bringing radio, television, and a host of games and gadgets to every corner of the current American culture—has resulted in a similar decline in intellectual activity in the United States. The art of conversation, of tales of discovery, and Abraham Lincoln's fastidious reading of the classics by oil-lamp has been replaced with TV's sitcoms—virtual morality plays that are empty of any meaning, including morality. While depicted as humor they are essentially very sad statements about our present culture.

Ancients had no TV, no pressure to accept mass, uninformed, and unintelligent culture. They could not have foreseen the ridiculous renderings of human conduct that television has forced upon us, but they did have the integrity to refuse almost all offerings from other cultures. The same cultural bias probably played a role in the perceived omission of other traits and objects. The pig was known to have been domesticated in China by 5000 B.C. in association with settled village life, cultivation and grinding of millet, and the manufacture of sophisticated pottery.[33] If sea voyages from China to America, or from America to China, or both, were ongoing, why would some traits be adopted and others ignored. Pottery techniques, concepts of astronomy, astrology, and numbering, dragon motifs, depictions of elephants, and even an intriguing list of place names were exchanged between these cultures. Yet there is no evidence of cultivation of millet or rice in the Americas, disputable evidence of corn in Asia, and no evidence of pigs in America prior to Columbus.

The absence of these later foodstuffs can simply be viewed as cultural bias. Undoubtedly Asians introduced millet to the Americans, but the Americans preferred their own corn. Probably Asians introduced pigs throughout the Pacific but while the Polynesians and various island peoples welcomed the domesticated swine ancient Americans, for some reason, did not. Pork lovers may find this astonishing but, again, even today, hundreds of millions of Muslims and Jews shun pork as disgusting and "unholy," and cringe at the idea of domesticated swine.

For millennia the Chinese have been exposed to a world of people who regularly milk their livestock making cheese, butter and other dairy products. Yet until very recently the Chinese rejected this simple means of obtaining needed fat and protein. Southern Chinese cuisine (Cantonese) lacks any form of bread, even though bread is a staple throughout virtually the rest of the world.[34] Hindus will not eat beef products, Orthodox Jews will not eat any food that is not kosher, and the list goes on. Absence of any particular food or trait from a cultural pattern does not mean lack of knowledge, it is and has been merely a matter of cultural bias or choice.

Every aspect of a culture need not be assimilated to prove significant contact. Probably the ancient navigators, mostly astronomer-priests, carried their own foods and made little attempt to impose their scarce resources on other appetites. And, regarding their own food as sacred, they were likely less than happy to partake of the food of foreigners except when in dire need. A few certain goods, like jade and gold, were not only welcomed, but coveted; others were simply shunned. Ancient Chinese visitors to the Americas may have quietly reviled in disgust at the Americans penchant for eating small beans. The Americans were equally appalled at the idea of eating the meat of a pig. It is only in the past few hundred years that native Americans have admitted pork and rice into their diet (though now both are staples). Europeans still disdain corn except as feed for livestock. The list of taboos and prejudices goes on and on. No one is right on these matters. It is simply a question of cultural preferences.

Even among cooperating people of high intelligence different preferences in food may provoke cultural conflicts. On the *Mir* space station Russian cosmonauts breakfast on jellied pike or perch and on a buckwheat gruel that turns the stomachs of American astronauts. Meanwhile the American penchant for steamed plain vegetables, like carrots and green beans, cause the Russians to wonder if they've taken true aliens aboard.[35] In the confined quarters of a space station, where several men and women must live in the confines of a small mobile home for many months without the benefit of a refreshing walk to town or to a nearby stream, these are not insignificant matters, even among scientists.

Was there Pre-Columbian, Pre-Christian, and even Pre-Mesopotamian contact between ancient civilizations? The implications are clear–there was. We have previously described the "Red Paint" cultures of the Americas and their use of ochre to cover their buried dead 7,500 years ago. Patrick Huyghe in *Columbus Was Last* reports that, "In 1975, archaeologists from the Danish National Museum discovered the remains of a maritime culture at a site called Vedbaek. They uncovered nineteen burials there, including one of a woman bearing a large necklace of teeth and with a small child at her side. Both were covered with red ochre, an iron ore used as a pigment. Radiocarbon dates indicate an age of more than 7,000 B.P. for this site. If access by Europeans was this old, can access to America's riches in copper and tin be doubted? In millennia past, just as today, trade and exploitation in the name of trade were the rule.[36]

How extensive was this trade? A fourteenth-century B.C. trading ship that sunk off the Turkish coast at Ulu Burun has recently been explored. Because the ship held a virtual international cargo, Canaanite and Mycenaiean (Greek) swords side-by-side, Syrian pottery and gold pendants, Assyrian tablets, Mesopotamian seals, Egyptian glass and solid gold scarabs, and a wealth of other goods, investigators have concluded that it is impossible to know exactly what country the ship sailed from.[37]

Why has the idea of ancient cultural contact been so strongly denied?

American archaeology has long argued against the worldwide diffusion of ideas. They have based their view on a prejudice favoring isolated development of like ideas on separate continents. Pyramids, mummies, priestly orders, common artifacts, common language roots, similar hieroglyphic writings, sacrifice, observance and worship of similar heavenly objects, myths, cosmologies, even similar means of making pottery, *all* have been judged separate and *coincidental* achievements by the great laws governing Neo-Darwinian cultural evolution. In the Americanist view there was no need for cultures to have been interrelated or to have influenced one another in any manner, because, they theorized, civilization would happen in exactly the same linear pattern without outside influence. This notion itself is absurd. What are the mathematical chances that MesoAmerican culture and Mesopotamian cultures, to name only two, could have so precisely mimicked each other without contact? In the context of cultural transmission and interplay, with variables as great as the human mind can create, separate duplication takes on a probability number that is too vast to count.

Man has always been a great learner. The exchange of ideas, fruits, and even birds have provided the basis for the blossoming of cultures. Yet the prevailing academic prejudice implies that if contact can be demonstrated it must do so with the implication that the peoples of America were innately inferior to the ancient nations of the Middle East. This concept itself is out of balance. The majority of significant migrations of domesticated plant life was *from* the Americas to the other regions of the world. MesoAmerican culture may well have received information from the Middle East and the Far East, but they could as well have *supplied* vital mathematical and navigational information.

Which was the chicken and which was the egg? In a long lost naval civilization they were *both* the chicken and the egg. Intelligence and its diverse expressions have been with us too long and have been too varied to have arisen under one intelligence or one race, or one nation of beings. In one sense Atlantis symbolizes a single world culture, separate lands united by myth and mathematical and navigational knowledge long lost. But in the Golden Age the physical reality of Atlantis was only one part of an intelligence that circumscribed the known world. Civilization then existed in a narrow belt, restricted to the tropics by the effects of great ice sheets, but it was defined by navigators who freely traded precious goods, information, and ideas crucial to the building of ancient cultures—and Atlantis was at its very heart and center.

13 Ancient Ports & Colonies: *Realms of the Golden Age*

THREE RABBIT *wrapped his thin blanket tightly around his shoulders. He slid his uncovered sandals deep into the grass to try and find warmth but there was none to be found. In his young life he had never felt the air so cold or the ground so hard. Since he had turned twelve he had been allowed to follow his older brothers and uncles on the overland trading journey. But before this time he had only gone in summer. This time it was winter. Since they had left his seaside city the sun was getting smaller and lower in the sky each day. And often there was no sun at all, but only howling wind and constant rain, not the hard short rains of summer, but rain that lasted all the day.*

It had not been a successful trading mission. The ships from the east arrived with sparse gods and the trading was hard and bitter. The people from the east wanted too much jade for their meager spices and the odd, and utterly repulsive, animals that they had brought with them. Now returning through the mountain passes it was snowing, something marvelous to see, but hard to endure day after day. This day had a name, Saturnalia, given to it by traders from the east. These Greek pagan traders had given their week of December 18 to 25 to a tradition of festivals and gift giving, wherein masters, for a week, become slaves, in observance of the winter solstice. It had been interesting to watch them play out their roles. But Three Rabbit had no role other than to be first entertained, then disappointed in the trade that followed, and then to be very cold in the long trek back to his city. This date would later be reckoned as December 24, 11,553 B.C. Three Rabbit thought it would be the coldest and darkest day he would ever see.

•

From records of pollen in the soil, and from dust particles in mountain glaciers, we can paint a picture of what the world was like in the age of the Atlanteans, from 25,000 to 11,500 years ago. An understanding of the climate and geography of that age will reveal why civilization could not have been the product of land-based migrations but was instead the result of navigational migrations and of coastal cultures. These coastal cultures possibly flourished and endured for millennia before the apparent rise of river-based cultures, but now they survive, with a few exceptions, only in myth. Yet these exceptions—at Chan Chan in Peru, at the site of the spheres of Costa Rica, at Pedra Furada and Monte Allegro in Brazil, and at Monte Verde in Chile, represent an age of humanity that has been lost and awaits rediscovery by logical, unprejudiced investigation.

But first we must frame the context and climate of navigational cultures. It is well understood that, up to the very end of the Pleistocene, the global climate was much cooler. Even at equatorial latitudes snow lines and glaciation occurred at substantially lower altitudes. What is little understood, or appreciated, is that the world-wide climate was also *much dryer*. There were two principal reasons for this aridity: first, the atmosphere was much cooler than it is today, and cool air holds less moisture, and second, much of the world's fresh

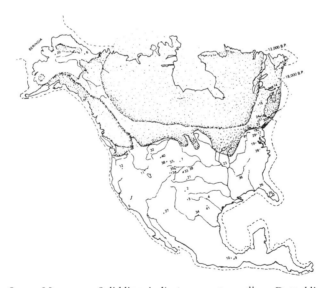

13.A. Ice Sheet Maximum. Solid lines indicate present coastlines. Dotted lines represent late Pleistocene coastlines. Poseidon and other seaports of Atlantis must lay somewhere in between these lines in the southern regions of this map. Ice Ages are often inaccurately portrayed as times of unrelenting winter storms and dark and threatening skies. Actually they were periods, ages, of continual blue skies and unrelenting cold. In most of the world these cold blue skies held little life-sustaining moisture, though somehow, primitive hunting bands were able to eke out an existence throughout much of America. Civilized, artistic, man on this continent could have only prevailed in a narrow band of land that lay close to the Ice Age tropical seas.

water supply was frozen in glaciers (fig. 13A). Even today over ninety-nine percent of the world's surface fresh water (about 7 million cubic miles) is contained in icecaps and glaciers, while less than one-half of one percent (33,000 cubic miles), is found in all the lakes and rivers of the world. One-tenth of that (3,100 cubic miles) can be found in the form of water vapor in the atmosphere. Yet our current atmosphere is literally drenched in water compared to the cold, dry atmosphere of the last Ice Age. Ice Ages are often depicted as cloud-shrouded ages of storms and mist. In fact, they were periods of unrelenting blue skies, virtual world-wide droughts that increased the world's mass of ice by an occasional twenty-year or hundred-year storm. But the unrelenting blue skies were accompanied by an unrelenting cold.

Recently a team from Ohio State University, led by Lonnie G. Thompson, took core samples from the Peruvian mountain glacier, Huascaran, from ice deposited at the close of the Pleistocene. The team chose Huascaran because it lay at the western end of the Amazon rain forest, believed to be a primeval jungle, unaffected by a series of Ice Ages, and virtually unchanged for millions of years. What they discovered was that atmospheric dustiness at that time (12,000 B.P.) was about 200 times above current levels. This glacier is on the eastward (wet) side of the Andes, and, unlike the normally dry regions of the Andes that lie west of the dominating peaks, it was downwind of the trade winds that have always carried, and uplifted, the dense moisture from the climate of Amazonia. The study shows that even this vast equatorial region felt the affects of a severely dry Earth. The ancient Amazon basin retained only enclaves of rain forest and jungle; much of this now lush land had to have been, in a distant past, very dry. Separate studies of the ice core reveal very low levels of dissolved nitrates, which will emanate from any wet rain forest, and they reveal a very slow trend toward the high levels that exist today, indicating that tropical rain forests took thousands of years to resume their current, though now embattled, condition. Results from studies by Paul A. Coinvaux of the Smithsonian Tropical Research Institute in Panama show that entrapped pollen in ice-age lake beds in the Amazon were populated by plant species that only now can be found thriving at higher, cooler, and dryer elevations.[1]

Biologists are now confirming the theory of geologist Jurgen Haffer—that the Amazon rain forest was apparently sparse, and limited to isolated "refugia." The idea of isolated patches of rain forest, separated from each other for a very long period of time is probably the only explanation we have for the enormous biodiversity of flora and fauna in the Amazon region.

If the Amazon was that dry and that cool what was the rest of the world like (see facing page, "Everygreen Forest in Central America")? Except for a few ancient lake beds, like Texcoco in the Valley of Mexico, and a few river val-

Evergreen Forests in Central America

Driving through the interior of Central America you would expect it to be jungle, as much of it is, but much more of this land has been montane evergreen forest. These forests have been largely destroyed. But driving through Honduras or Belize, where the destruction of forests has not been completed, with the air conditioner on, the high pine forests will startle you. You would swear your were in Canada, or at least in the Sierras of California. The realization that you are among the vestiges of a different age, an Ice Age, when proximity to the equator meant little, will quickly dawn, and pre-conceived notions of the jungles of Central America will be put into perspective. In the high plateaus of today's' Honduras and in the lowlands of Belize the flora of Atlantis survives, quite unexpectedly, in pine forests that have stood the test of vagaries of time and of human cultures.

leys, like the Nile and the Amazon, the interior of continents must have been very dry and desolate.

Our conventional historical perspective has told us that man, during the Pleistocene, was not agricultural because his conceptual mind was too primitive, and had not yet evolved to the *idea* of agriculture. It seems more likely that man was not agricultural because most of the world's climate was too dry to support agriculture. Mankind, not because of stupidity, but of necessity, relied on the sea.

Plato described the climate of Atlantis as subtropical, with a fertile plain protected from the north wind, and spoke of Atlanteans gathering two crops a year. Circular ocean currents, as today, had to have existed, but they also had to have been compacted into an area within twenty degrees of the equator. No Gulf Stream could have reached Gibraltar nor any part of Europe. An Atlantis outside Gibraltar's gate would more likely be a much dryer, and much colder, version of today's Iceland. Lush fruits, two crops a year? Not very likely! Surface warm water is highly active as a conveyor, cold water is sluggish and extremely slow moving. If Atlantis had been an island situated in the mid-Atlantic at the latitudes of Gibraltar, as it is commonly depicted, it would hardly have had the characteristics described by Plato nine thousand years later. If Plato's dates for Atlantis are correct only the narrow strip of land at the heart of the Americas, bathed on either side by warming seas, could have been Atlantis.

We have records that some primitive men eked out an existence as hunters and tool makers throughout the Pleistocene. We have been provided ample evidence of that from high and dry (and then very cold) Clovis sites in North America. What we lack is evidence of *civilized* man for the same period. Yet man not only prevailed during the Pleistocene, he flourished. When the Ice Age ended, in large numbers, throughout the globe, man began building (or rebuilding) cities, constructing (or reconstructing temples), and when warm moist air afforded it, he developed agriculture. There was nothing contained in the primitive hunting cultures of the Pleistocene that prepared man for this transformation. But there need not have been. Ancient man, non-

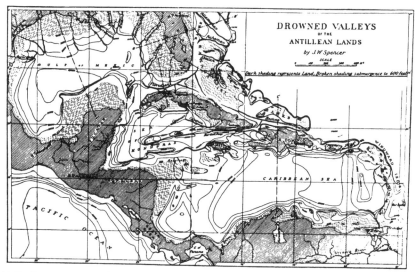

13.C. PLEISTOCENE COASTLINES AND ANTEDILUVIAN LANDS OF THE MIDDLE AMERICAS. Before the Earth's atmosphere had sufficiently warmed to carry the abundance of moisture it now enjoys, advanced civilizations and seafaring were both probably confined to a coastal belt extending less than twenty degrees in either direction from the equator. Worldwide temperatures were still substantially lower until 7,000 B.C. and local glaciers could still be found on the highest peaks of Mesoamerica. At about that time, with warming agriculture in inland valley regions, agriculture commenced in such place as Oaxaca. Did man develop agriculture at the precise moment in time when it was possible to realize fruitful crops? Or, as Plato's dates indicate, was there an ongoing agriculture that had been limited to coastal areas (that now lie under the oceans), but was transported to previously barren lands after the deluge? Myth has one version, history another. Both have been undeniably altered. But the body of scientific knowledge, as it becomes dislodged from church and historical dogma supports the version contained in myth!

primitive mankind, had already been living a fruitful existence on the coastlines of tropical seas for millennia.

Did we say "tropical seas?" Did they even exist in the Ice Ages? They did. Even during the Pleistocene, while gigantic ice sheets reflected most of the sun's heat, and dry, cloudless, continental skies lost, through night time radiation, most of the heat that had gathered during the day, the equatorial seas absorbed the sun's offerings. Analysis of tropical seas indicates that the same creatures, living among tropical reefs that today cannot stand temperatures less than 72 degrees, flourished during the Ice Age. Temperatures in tropical seas 12,000 years ago were not much lower than they are now! And the clash of cool continental air and moist warm air from tropical seas produced, locally, the life-enhancing phenomena so rare during the Ice Age: Rainfall! Rainfall meant crops, fruits, drinking water, perhaps plumbing, perhaps life itself. But it could occur only in the confines of a near equatorial coastal and tropical climate. Here only could fruits and vegetables grow. Here only, in a desolate world, do we find the ingredients for a Poseidon, capital of Atlantis, or for the Garden of Eden.

While a few bands of adaptable and transient men twelve thousand years ago, seemingly preferred severe cold and drought and managed to survive at the extremities of Clovis cultures from New Mexico to Maine, logic tells us that most of mankind, would have chosen to live along warm seas near a bounty of food supply. None would have chosen the straight of Beringia where there was no plant food, no pollen evidence of plant food, no Caribou to follow, not even any water because the cold was to dry to produce water or ice, and only extreme, debilitating cold. And the archeological record reflects this obvious preference. Beringia was settled much later, *after* the ice and cold abated.

Yet Americanist anthropologists continue to tell us otherwise. They insist they our American forefathers chose to migrate over desolate ice sheets. While there is no difficulty in proving their "logic" wrong, there is still a difficulty in proving the existence of an alternative navigational settlement of the Americas. A look at the probable coastlines at the end of the Pleistocene will tell us why we lack this certain proof. A drying up of the lakes and streams of the Pleistocene could not have yielded enough moisture to feed the growing ice caps. The ice sheets also, over thousands of years, drank from the saltwater oceans, lowering them to a depth of, perhaps, 400 feet below their present level.

A map of the tropical Americas (fig. 13C) that outlines the probable coastlines of the antediluvian world—the world as it existed before the great deluge that accompanied the end of the last Ice Age—shows that our coastlines were then very different, particularly in the Caribbean and the Gulf of Mexico. In that part of the world, great coastal city-states, if they existed, would now be

13.D-E. OLMEC PORTRAITS. In attempting to explain Negroid features at Olmec sites traditional archaeologists once asserted that Olmec sculptures were actually idealized and highly stylized Maya warriors. It is now recognized that each sculpture, whether found at La Venta, Tres Zapotes or at the more recently found sites at El Manati and El Azuzul, has an individual quality including different braid patterns in their hair. It appears as if each sculpture was modeled after a distinct individual ruler or leader. Can anyone still hold claim that these were stylized Mayas, who only coincidentally looked like Africans, a people, by isolationist theory, they could not have encountered?

---

hidden under debris, sediment, and under 400 feet of water. No attempt has been made to excavate these areas nor is any attempt likely in the foreseeable future. Why would one search under difficult and dangerous (and expensive) conditions in 300 to 500 feet of water when thousands of easily accessible land sites still lie untouched? Of the thousands of sites in Belize, only about twenty are under active excavation. Yet out of information contained in the few that have been excavated, the dates for Mayan culture have been pushed back thousands of years. With so much work to be done on above-water sites, so many paths to be followed, why would you search under so much water?

The answer is that by a simple shift of paradigms, from the ancient Americas as descendants of a terrestrial migrating culture, to ancient Americas as inheritors of a very ancient navigational culture, you may not need to search under water at all.

When traces of the Olmec culture were identified and dated to hundreds and thousand of years before accepted dates for the Maya they were called Pre-Maya. Olmec dates have been constantly pushed back since the discovery of Negroid heads at La Venta (13D, E). Scholars now prefer to call Olmecs "proto-Mayans" as if they had occupied Mesoamerica in an earlier period than the Mayans and stood as forefathers in a straight line descent or as if they had been an incipient stage of Maya development. Actually all the recent information is contrary. They existed contemporaneously with the Maya.

However, if traditional archaeologists acknowledged this, it would make all the textbook dates for Mayans hopelessly wrong.

But the case for Olmecs as pre- or proto-Mayan is hopelessly wrong on another count. Olmecs didn't just look Negroid, they *were* Negroid. Examinations of the crania (skulls) of the Olmecs have definitely confirmed that they were African in origin. They hadn't come through thousands of years of arduous treks across the unbearably dry and cold Bering straits. They had simply navigated to the Americas, from Africa, in voyages, that even without sails, could only have taken several weeks. At La Venta an Olmec lodestone compass, concave iron mirrors, and a variety of other gear that were of little use to non-navigators, have been found and dated, conservatively to 1000 B.C.

Little attention has been paid to the pyramids of the Olmecs. Although small in height (35 feet, generally, although a fluted mound at San Lorenzo reaches 110 feet above the base of associated structures), they were arranged in astronomical patterns. In fact their entire settlements were astronomically ordered.[2]

The San Lorenzo site consists of two hundred man-made mounds situated on a compact plateau that is cut into by several deep ravines. At first the ravines were thought to be natural formations but it is now known that they are man-made canals.[3] The "colossal heads" found here, some weighing as much as forty-four tons, were carved from basalt rock from the Cerro Cintepec, a volcanic flow fifty air miles to the northwest in the Tuxtla mountains. The stones were dragged down from the mountains to the nearest navigable river and transported on large rafts to the San Lorenzo site where they were somehow lifted up onto the plateau. Obsidian and iron ore for manufacture of concave mirrors had been imported to the site. Shells of sea turtles and swordfish remains indicate a sea-going culture.

Once called a "Gulf of Mexico culture" it is now known that there are as many Olmec sites (fig. 13F) on the Pacific coast, prominent among them

13.F. JADE BIRDMAN, COSTA RICA. The Olmecs were long believed to be limited to the Veracruz area, and possibly only a chance encounter of Africans with the Americas. But evidence of widely separated Olmec cultures, from central Mexico to Costa Rica, must finally dispel the notion of chance encounter. The Olmecs, obviously an African people, did not come to the Americas by way of Beringea. They were navigators who established a sub-culture at least 2,400 years B.C.

Izapa, La Blanca, and Abaj Takalik. Aided by great rivers, almost absent in the Yucatán, Olmec culture spanned the isthmus of Tehuantepec and linked the Atlantic to the Pacific. Trade routes of Olmec cultures at least 4,500 years old extended from Tres Zapotes (near present day Veracruz) to Tlatilco near Mexico City, to Chalchuapa in Salvador, and up to Cuello (fig. 5G) in northern Belize. And Olmec style pottery and jewelry has been discovered at Pre-Maya levels at Copan, traditionally believed to a classical Maya site.[4]

It is now certain that the Olmecs, a Negroid people, spanned Mesoamerica and Central America as late as 700 B.C. but undoubtedly much earlier. They rarely dominated any one area but rather lived side by side with the incipient Mayan, the still unknown people of Teotihuacan (fig. 9H), and, possibly, with other unidentified navigational cultures of Central America. Phoenicians, Hittites, and Chinese coexisted in the Americas at the same time. What brought them all to the narrowest, the hottest, the most humid, and most mosquito-infested stretch of the Americas? What compelled them, in these hot tropics, to arduously build enormous star temples that meticulously measured, recorded, and found harmony with the cosmos? The simple answer is that the currents brought them there. In the age of navigation, when bronze was king, long journeys to the tin mines of Bolivia and copper mines of Lake Superior, were both staged from the confluence of the ocean currents, in Mesoamerica.

It is hard for us to imagine now, but prior to the great surges in population, prior to the domination of agriculture as a way of life, prior to the Iron

13.G. "Candlestick of the Andes." It can best be seen in its entirety from the sea.

Age, land had very little value. We live now in an interglacial period within a two hundred thousand year glacial age. Modern man has evolved in this age, yet most of it has been marked by a very cold and very dry climate. Man's existence has both depended and has expanded by his reliance on the sea. The curiosity is how quickly this interaction has been forgotten.

Content with the concept of man as a solely terrestrial animal, with his migrations limited to land routes, historians and archaeologists have paid little attention to how much maritime knowledge was known to early man. Archaeologists have been fixed on the recent dates they give to their excavated sites. But looking and *seeing* are different matters. They have looked at these sites from only one dimension, that of a terrestrial and agricultural,(or a pre-agricultural hunter-gatherer) viewpoint. They have not looked for navigational sites, nor have they *seen* navigational implications in sites they have found.

In 1975 Michael Moseley, then an Associate Professor of Anthropology at Harvard, began to turn this limited view around. In *The Maritime Founda-*tions of Andean Civilization* Moseley published the results of his extensive work at the Chan Chan and El Paraiso sites, the centers of the Chavin culture in Peru. In describing a civilization that flourished between 3600 and 1500 B.C. in the Ancon-Chillon area, and an older continuous navigational culture at El Paraiso dating from 10,000 B.C., Moseley wrote, "It took me a decade to gradually shake traditional archeological preconceptions and come to grip with the blatant implications of the data. . . . The ancient Peruvians were not derived or descended from Sumerians or Egyptians, but were prior to either. Chavin culture exhibited a gradual development that cannot be found anywhere else in the world."[5]

Peruvians who were not derived or descended from Sumerians or Egyptians, but were prior to either? That meant that they possibly existed at the same time as the builders of Sacsayhuaman in the altiplano of Bolivia and of the spheres of Costa Rica!

Moseley's studies showed that the incipient stages of the great Peruvian culture were not based on subsistence farming but on a purely navigational culture (fig. 13G).

While admitting that Moseley's findings represented the nascent stage of a civilization that produced monumental structures, Stuart Fiedel, in *Prehistory of the Americas,* suggests that "coastal Peru would appear to be a *unique* case of civilization developing from a non-agricultural subsistence base." Coastal Peru could hardly have been unique. What is *unique* about coastal Peru is that it has been both violently and continually uplifted by unrelenting subduction of the Pacific plates under the Peruvian and Naca plates. Thus, instead of up to 400 feet *under* the sea, as most other ancient coastal cultures remain, the coastal Peruvian sites, because of uplifitngs of the Andes, stand today hundreds of feet *above* sea level, as indicators of a greater navigational culture that graced the Americas in times past.

The reason that they cannot be found anywhere else in the world is not that the builders existed only in "myth." Instead it simply reaffirms the fact that it is not easy to identify cultures that lie under the seas. Nor is it easy to find traces of wooden boats that have long since rotted away in humid jungles of Mesoamerica.

Except in stone, which cannot be dated, only in Peru can we find the geological and geographical situation—very high in the interior, and very dry along the coast due to the cold Peruvian current—where mummies, cities, and traces of ancient navigational civilizations have not totally crumbled and decomposed.

Yet navigational instruments and other traces of a navigational culture have also been found among the Olmecs, and Olmec sites have recently been found to contain evidence of mummification! Although no mummies have been found in humid coastal sites like La Venta, Olmec skeletal remains and sculptures have been found high in Mexico's interior at Oaxaca. These skeletons and sculptures depict the dead in an identical manner to Egyptian mummies—with their arms crossed on their chests, and with their fingers open.[7]

Navigationally based civilizations are not unique. They have simply, until very recently, not been looked for. That is changing. Anna Roosevelt discovered that the people of Monte Alegre, cited earlier, had a very distinct tool kit from Clovis man, one that like the peoples of Chan Chan, emphasized fishing and foraging from nearby waters—in their case the Amazon river. They also created sophisticated cave paintings.[7] Their world, carbon 14 dated to 11,200 was more diverse, and less desperate than that of Clovis man, a contemporary in New Mexico. But was this outpost on the Amazon the most sophisticated of that time? Probably not. It was likely a fringe culture that coexisted with Clovis man, but also coexisted with even more diverse and sophisticated cultures in the navigational regions of the greater Atlantean civilization.

Now that archaeologists are looking it is very likely they will find many sites like Monte Alegre. And they will be found to have arisen independently of the founding of agriculture or of terrestrial migrations.

The ports of ancient cities were all there when Columbus and the conquistadors arrived. They had been there for thousands of years before. Seemingly inland cities like Becan, and El Mirador were surrounded by circular canals that were part of a greater interconnecting web of canals, rivers, and lakes, that traversed what is now Guatemala, Belize, and the Mexican states of Chiapas, Yucatán, and Quintana Roo—all of the waterways led to the sea.[9]

El Mirador, whose 150 foot pyramids dwarf those of Tikal in both height and age, was not only surrounded by circular canals, but was linked by sacbeob to other major sites throughout Maya lands. Nakbe, El Mirador, El Ceibal, Palenque, Coba, and as many as a thousand other sites were all interconnected by ancient canals and rivers, and eventually all were connected to the Gulf of Mexico and to the Caribbean.[10]

Archaeologists have persisted in looking at Tikal and Chichen Itza as the earliest sites of Maya and Toltec culture in the Americas. Why? It is only because they were the first excavated and because their excavators wanted "their sites" to be the oldest, and therefore the most significant. Nakbe, a major center by 600 B.C., even by conventional dating, has a pyramid rising 150 feet, twice the height of Kukulcan at Chichen Itza with a gigantic stone head measuring 34 feet long and 16 feet wide.[11] Cuello, in Belize, has been dated to 2500 B.C. by its excavator, Norman Hammond.

We must begin to examine sites from their function, not from the egoistic needs of their excavators, and realize that function follows purpose, and that both relate to the sea.

Xicalango, on the Laguna de Terminos, sat at the eastern extreme of the Aztec empire and at the beginning of a sea trade route that stretched for over a thousand miles to Costa Rica and Panama. Goods traded included cacao beans, lime for making mortar, jade, basalt, obsidian, serpentine, pottery, gold, copper, alloys, cotton cloth, honey, vanilla, slaves, live iguanas and parrots, plumage of quetzal birds, tobacco, medicinal herbs, stone metates for grinding corn, resin of copal and rubber trees.[12]

Isla Cerritos served as a port for Chichen Itza. "Mexican archaeologist Tomas Gallareta of INAH and Anthony P. Andrews of the New College of the University of South Florida excavated there, finding "ruins of docks and piers, while on its south shore a sea wall more than 1,000 feet long encloses an artificial harbor that once offered refuge to a large number of canoes.

"Farther south the large town of Chetumal controlled an intersection of sea trade and overland commerce. In the southern extreme of the Gulf of Honduras the Chontal Maya traders reached their eastern destination: the busy ports of Nito (Guatemala) and Naco (Honduras)."[13] Large standing stones, similar to those in Polynesia, were found in the Bay Islands off Honduras by Mitchell-Hedges. Although photographs remain, the stones themselves have seemingly disappeared.14 Honduras has been ignored by archaeologists, yet unconfirmed tales circulate throughout Tegucigalpa of a great "white city," built from huge blocks of stone, by a civilization earlier than

13.H. SANTA RITA. Though small and unimposing the site of Santa Rita once continued colorful and beautiful wall paintings, photographed and published by Dr. Thomas Gann in 1900. Unfortunately most of the brilliant wall murals were destroyed when the site was dynamited by looters in 1920. This event was witnessed by the father of Roy Wilshire, who is now the guide-caretaker of Santa Rita, and heard by the surrounding Mayan population. But since the demolition of the site was conducted by an armed gang of about twenty members who had terrorized the local population for weeks, Roy's father (Roy is Mayan-Belizean, despite his English name) was helpless in preventing the destruction.

the Maya. The present authors, in fact, once stood ready to ride a government helicopter to this very site, only to have the mission arbitrarily canceled at the last moment, for reasons unexplained.

The ancient Mayan city of Chetumal, most archaeologists now agree, is not the current Mexican city of Chetumal, but lies some fifteen miles south near the Belizean city of Corozal at a site that has been renamed Santa Rita. Santa Rita has been graced by intricate stucco paintings reflecting its connection to the sea-going Chontal Maya, as well as paintings depicting Ecuadorian vessels from a far earlier era. Pottery remains at Santa Rita (fig. 13H) have been carbon-dated to 2,000 B.C. (a calibrated date of at least 2,200 B.C.).

Like Cuello, the dates at Santa Rita would make Mayan navigational culture at least as old as the Olmec culture. The position of Santa Rita points to an even older culture, that contained in the remains of Cerro Maya (fig. 13-I). Harriet Topsey, the chief Archaeologist of Belize until his untimely and suspicious death in 1995, believed that Santa Rita was a Maya site that was built on astronomical and navigational knowledge that earlier had been contained in the constructions of the nearby Cerro Maya site. Santa Rita has direct sightlines to Cerro Maya (Cerros), which lies across a narrow passage in the bay of Chetumal. Cerros is also surrounded by a canal in the shape of an arc around the southern, western and eastern boundaries of the site.[15] The canals themselves are known to be older than the pyramids that now dominate the site.

But they are probably not as old as the entire site, because at least half of Cerros lies under the waters of the bay. Like many Maya sites that have been rebuilt over the years Cerros seems to be one that was rebuilt next to, and partially covering, the site of older temples. In this case we can actually see that the older temples are well below our current coastlines!

Did a massive tidal wave, the result of some celestial collision, visit this region? The site of Nim Li Punit, with its magnificently carved stelae that measure up to thirty feet in length, now lay vertically among its ruins. What force could dislodge these great stelae? Nim Li Punit is considered to be an early classic Maya site by American archaeologists. That would make it several hundreds of years older than the ruins of nearby Lubaantun. But, as earlier presented, the resident archaeologist, Santiago Coc, who is a Maya and supervises both sites, judges both the Mayan site of Nim Li Punit and the Maya culture itself, to be more recent than Lubaantun, perhaps by several thousand years.

Puzzling? We must continue to seek other evidences of this long lost age. Where? We know that often the older sites lay buried under more recent sites. Sometimes the older sites are nearby. Tulum, located on a cliff side above the Caribbean sea has long been as photogenic as Tikal. If an older site lies beneath Tulum you can understand the reluctance to disturb a site that brings

13.I. CERROS. Reaching this site by boat from Corozal, in northern Belize, one gets the impression of approaching a low, wooded hill. But this is the impression one gets throughout Belize–the hill's almost invariably are pyramids thousands of years old.

355

13.J. **GREAT STONE BLOCKS OFF ANDROS ISLAND.** The psychic Edgar Cayce (1877-1945), dubbed "The Sleeping Prophet," believed in endless cycles of life, and the ability to 'read' the past while entranced. Cayce described many past catastrophes that have befallen our planet, including the deluge, and calmly predicted that such events were certain to happen in our future. Cayce, who has been prove wrong on some predictions but spectacularly predicted the rediscovery of the Qum-ran papers in Israel, and has predicted a shifting of the poles, interpreted the "past lives" of many of his patients and followers and determined that not only had Atlantis existed but that it had dominated the world from fifty thousand years ago until its destruction twelve thousand years ago.

Cayce believed Atlantis went down in the region of the Antilles at the eastern end of the Caribbean Sea. Yet he predicted in 1940 that its capital, Poseidon, would reappear in the Bahamas. "Expect it in 1968 or 1969; not so far away." By coincidence, or something extraordinary, airline pilots in looking down through the clear waters off Bimini were startled by what looked like an ancient city under the surface of the sea.

---

in thousands of tourists every week. Muyil, less photogenic, but at its surface excavation much older, lies twenty miles south of Tulum. Canals link Muyil to the Caribbean, nine miles to the east, at the Boca Paila cut in a peninsula that is now called Punta Allen. Extended sacbeob and vestiges of canals link Muyil to Coba and from Coba to all the great sites of the Yucatán and the Peten.

Underwater sites are not limited to the southern Caribbean. Since 1968 dramatic finds, perhaps traces of a highly developed civilization that existed before the flooding associated with the end of the last Ice Age, have been made in the shallow waters of the northern Caribbean and in the Bahaman banks (fig. 13J). Large standing stones have been found in the waters off the Bay Islands, a few dozen miles off Honduras. These have been compared to compass stones used in the Polynesian and Micronesian Islands.[17] They appear to

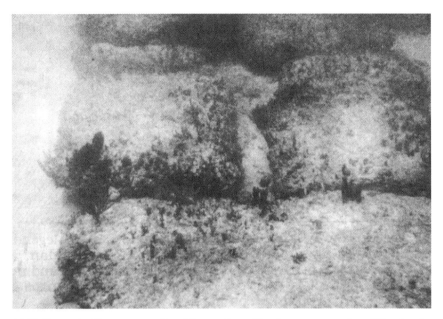

13.K. BIMINI'S UNDERWATER SEA WALLS. Rene Noorbergen states that, "Not far the Bimini sea wall, divers have uncovered a stone archway at a depth of 12 feet, a pyramid with a flattened top and base 140 by 180 feet, plus a huge circular stone construction, made of 20-foot blocks, that appears to have been a well-designed water reservoir when it existed above sea level. "Noorbergen cites other sunken structures in the Bahamas; "Andros Island, near Pine Key, possesses its share of submarine structures as well. In 1969 airline pilots photographed a 60-by 100-foot rectangular shape, clearly visible thorough the calm waters. The eastern side and the western corners were partitioned off. What is amazing is that this submerged rectangle is an almost exact copy in size and design of the Temple of the Turtles, an ancient Mayan sanctuary found at Uxmal in Yucatán, indicating that the survivors of the Caribbean civilization center may have influenced the development of the early Central American cultures and the culture of the Mound builders."[18]

Noorbergen also states, "Other sunken ruins in the Caribbean area include a sea wall 30 feet high, running in a straight line for miles off Venezuela, near the mouth of the Orinoco River; an acropolitan complex, complete with streets, covering five acres in six feet of water off the Cuban coast; remains of sunken buildings off Hispaniola, one measuring 240 by 80 feet; several stone causeways (sacbeob?), 30 to 100 feet below the surface, which leaves the shores of Quintana Roo, Mexico, and Belize, British Honduras, and continue out to sea for miles toward an unknown destination; a sea wall running along a submarine cliff near Cay Lobos; and huge stone squares, rectangles and crosses, clearly of human design, off the windward and leeward sides of al the keys down to Orange Key."

Noorbergen notes that, "These Caribbean ruins are perplexing to Archaeologists and to orthodox historians," because the architecture is far beyond anything the Spanish conquistadors found in the make-up of the Amerinds they encountered. But that series of encounters is relatively recent. The last time that the mysterious walls and temples could have been built was during the last Ice Age, over 12,000 years ago. That's not such an old date, considering man's presence on Earth for over 4 million years. But it's a date modern archaeologists and historians have been reluctant to accept.

be man-made but this notion has been vigorously disputed. If they were man-made it would indicate that not just a Pre-Columbian, but a pre-deluge naval culture was at work here. We must keep in mind that all of the shoal waters of the Bahamas and of the Caribbean were well above sea level 12,000 years ago.

In his book *Secrets of the Lost Races*, Rene Noorbergen states that finds, now called the "Bimini Wall" were made, ". . . at depths ranging from 6 to 100 feet." According to his account, "there are numerous giant stone constructions—walls, encrusted with fossilized shells and petrified mangrove roots, indicating their great age. Among the first finds made were stretches of a wall composed of blocks measuring as much as 18 by 20 by 10 feet and weighing approximately 25 tons each. The wall appears to have encircled the islands of North and South Bimini to form a dike. Along the sea wall, three-to-five-foot sections of fluted columns were also discovered, some still fixed in their original positions, while others were found lying in a jumble on the sea floor, covered with sand. Since the pillars appear at regular intervals along the sunken wall, it is believed they may have formed one continuous portico. Both the wall and pillars reveal a high level of engineering skill in their construction. Divers uncovered a pillar of worked marble and a stone artifact that revealed a fragment of tongue-and-groove masonry.[16]

More "Bermuda Triangle" folklore? Possibly. Much of what Noorbergen has reported has been disputed by American archaeologists, who claim the megaliths are natural formations. But further undersea explorations have revealed stone formations resembling wide cobbled roads on the seabed north of Bimini(fig. 13K).

More recent finds include a flight of stone steps off the northern coast of Puerto Rico and underwater roads in the Caribbean off the Yucatán peninsula, extensions of the sacbe roads that connected the ancient ceremonial sites of the Maya, indicating that there were man-made structures in a great expanse of the Caribbean prior to the rise in seas at the time of the melting of continental ice sheets around 11,500 B.C.[19]

What would the ancient ruins of a civilization that was submerged 11,500 years ago look like today? If visible at all they would likely appear as ridges in plains of sand and silt. More likely they would be hidden under coral reefs. Archaeology on land began only within the last 150 years and is still in its infancy. Marine Archaeology by comparison is embryonic. It is also difficult. Sediment and sand, lichens and coral growths likely cover virtually all of the seaports built during the last Ice Age. Moray eels and sharks guard their secrets. It's now another world, a marine habitat. But it's there that the physical secrets to our past reside. The spiritual record has survived, barely, but it too is in danger of being buried under a tide of neglect and ignorance.

In 1901 Greek divers working a shipwreck near the island of Antikythera in the Aegean Sea found a large bronze item associated with groups of smaller items that all appeared to resemble gears with teeth. The items were cleaned and later examined by Professor Derek de Sola Price of Yale university. In his book, *Gears From the Greeks*, Price describes the mechanism as consisting of several spherical rings, all interlocking, and producing a differential gearing similar to complicated Swiss watches. But what has confounded many scholars is the dating of the mechanism. The ship itself was built around 200 B.C. Foodstuffs such as wine and olive oil have been dated to around 100 B.C. Nothing at the site has been dated to less than 2,000 years old and there were no signs of tampering, nor any doubt that the bronze mechanism had been according for at least two millennia.

The gears have been likened to a complicated mechanical compass, but they also appear to be more than that. Models set in motion seem to demonstrate the movements of the Sun, the moon, Venus, and important stars and planets. Although its probable use was in navigation, the device appears to be a computer-like celestial observatory that shows the changes in star positions over great periods of time.[20]

Like the spheres of Costa Rica, the "Gears of the Greeks" appear to reveal a navigational sophistication and a knowledge of astronomy that traditional thought has deemed impossible—more relics from the Golden Age.

Herodotus has reported that after 1200 B.C. Phoenician colonies returned from the Red Sea to settle in the western Mediterranean. Historians have assumed that he was referring to the body of water that lay between Africa and Arabia. But it could easily have taken its name from the sea of the Red People, where the Phoenicians obtained their copper, and what we now call the Caribbean.[21]

In the late nineteenth century some English and Europeans were visited with a rare treat when Buffalo Bill and other famous cowboys brought their "Wild West Shows" across the ocean. In addition to riding and shooting stunts they also paraded several native Americans, "Red Men" as they were billed, before a gaping and gasping audience. To the European mind the sight of these savages marked the first appearance of native Americans in Europe. Their progressive concept of history could not have permitted them to appreciate the likely truth—that 3,000 years before red men, traders, primarily in bronze, had regularly visited their shores, and that they came at time when some of the ancestors of the gaping Europeans were wearing fur skins and painting themselves blue.[23]

Were ancient ports also established in the Mediterranean? Very definitely they were—navigation was world-wide. Caesaria, a navigational site in what is

13.L CLEOPATRA'S PALACE. In 1996 archaeologists located the foundation of the Pharos lighthouse. This site, once called one of the seven wonders of the ancient world, lies under only twenty feet of water in the Mediterranean, but it is water that has been made murky by the constant tons of silt washed down by the Nile. Also, in November of 1996, Franck Goddio, a French marine archaeologist, announced the discovery of what appears to be the ruins of Cleopatra's palace, and of ancient Alexandria. Again the discovery was made in only twenty feet of water, but it includes the palace, statues, paved streets, granite columns, piers, and a grid of city dimensions that suggests the location of the great library. All of these physical sites have been described in our history books, yet none of them were actually seen until this past year. Their discovery raises the question as to what we might possibly find at levels more than twenty feet below current sea level.[22]

now northern Israel has recently been excavated by marine archaeologists. It was built from large timbers set in a concrete that hardened under water. The density and strength of this undersea concrete in this harbor, used by the Romans 2,000 years ago, has only been duplicated in the past thirty years. The construction of the harbor, with a portal which allowed entry of tidal sea water at one end and departure at another, effectively removed all silt. The design of an angle that permitted this inflow and egress of waters is still a mystery to most modern harbor masters, as evidenced by the many harbors throughout America, such as the harbor at Santa Barbara which must be dredged of silt on a regular basis. In fact, the art of devising a shallow sea harbor that does not require dredging is almost unknown. This is the principal reason that deep harbors like those at San Francisco, New York and Long Beach, have created trade centers. Yet it is now obvious that trade centers can be created anywhere, as long as the technique of harbor building, as practiced by the ancients, is known.

The melting of the polar ice caps, and of the great lakes, at the end of the last Ice Age permanently raised the level of the seas by several hundred feet. Presumably all the naval cities of that time, in a navigation-based world, were permanently submerged either in gradually rising waters, or in a deluge as a result of a catastrophic event. Of course, "permanently" is a relative term. We have only to wait for the next Ice Age to lower the oceans 400 feet or so to find out if such cities really existed. Or we could listen to the voices of our past and pursue the traces of civilizations buried under the sea!

There are many reports of great cities and civilizations lost to the seas (13L). Strabo, who chronicled the Phoenicians' seafaring exploits, also reports tales from 2,600 years before his time of a rich and powerful city called Tartessos, a seaport on the southwest coast of Spain. The travelers cited by Strabo claimed the written records of Tartesso went back 7,000 years before their time which brings us back to the time of the deluge and the destruction of Atlantis![24] Since no physical evidence of Tartesso remains we might conclude that its ruins now lie crumbled under the sea.

Lixus, said by the Greeks to be the burial place of Hercules—also called the "Sun City" because its great megaliths were oriented according to the solstices of the sun—similarly disappeared under the sea. Although it had vanished long before, Romans of the first century B.C. continued to refer to Lixus as "The Eternal City."[25]

Dioscuria, a city in the Black Sea, now lies under hundreds of feet of water. Spina, a city built by Etruscans—who claim their descent from Atlantis—now resides under the waves of the Adriatic Sea.[26] Island cultures like Malta and Bahrain are indisputably older than pharonic Egypt (although so are the Sphinx and the Great Pyramid!) but early sites on these islands may have disappeared under the sea.

The present authors have received many reports of sunken cities and temples that lie off the Pacific coast of southern Costa Rica near Uvita, and off Costa Rica's Guanacaste coast near Papagayo. At both sites gold and jade objects have been recovered (and shown to the authors by proud private collectors). And at both sites divers have related tales of unusual mounds, resembling pyramids, and the existence of the outline of an underwater port city. Only the lack of time and money have prevented a diligent exploration of these sites by any authorized means—but the repeated insistence by veteran and reliable divers that these sites exist must soon be explored and verified— or dismissed. For any one site that may be easily dismissed there are hundreds more to be examined! We must always be aware that looters and private collectors, lacking neither the time nor money for such adventures, have always had a way of getting to treasures first. As their private riches have grown, the common knowledge of our collective history has diminished.

A significant discovery was recently made on the Costa Rican side of the San Juan river—a river that forms the eastern end of the ancient system that linked the great oceans (13M). Near the town of Upala, at the border of Costa Rica and Nicaragua, a Mediterranean vessel was dug out of riverbank mud.

The amphorae discovered on this vessel contained resin that has now been determined to have come from African trees with a carbon dating in excess of 1500 B.P..

The Egyptian *Book of the Dead* records that the birthplace of Thoth, god of literature and science, was in a city by the sea that stood between two active volcanoes in a land of "crossing waters" far to the west. Thoth was among a race of demi-gods who came from a super-civilization, a land amidst the seas, that guided the descendants of survivors of the cataclysm, and whose installation in the Egyptian "book of records" took place in 9850 B.C.[28] And it positions its founders as arriving from a land that lay between the great sea (the Atlantic) and a greater sea (the Pacific).[29]

The Egyptian myth of twin volcanoes finds its realization in Ometepe's great twins that are connected by a narrow isthmus. The "land of crossing

13.M. MAP OF NICARAGUA showing passages from the Atlantic to the Pacific. Thor Heyerdahl has proposed that a major center of maritime culture must have existed at either end of the isthmus of Panama.[27] Actually, Costa Rica was just as likely a place for the crossings, terminating on the Pacific side at the Diquis Delta, where many of the great spheres have been found. An even more likely candidate is present day Nicaragua, where the San Juan River links Lake Nicaragua to the Atlantic. For the last 11,5000 years a simple sail up the calm San Juan would deliver any sailor into what is now Lake Nicaragua. From the western shore of this lake it is about a 12-mile hike over low hills to the beaches of the Pacific. Evidence that Lake Nicaragua was once directly linked to the ocean still exists in the presence of many marine species including swordfish and 12-foot-long sharks, the only fresh water sharks in the world!

13.N. An Atlantean found on Ometepe Island, Lake Nicaragua. Hamilton Silva Monge, the curator of the museum at Altagracia (pictured with Sandra Erikson), relates that Nicaraguan archaeologists believe this statue is 12,000 years old.

waters" could refer to the San Juan River and Lake Nicaragua as continuous across all but a dozen or so miles of the isthmus. Wooden planked ships would have been stopped at this point. But reed rafts could have been taken apart, and easily carried to the Pacific to be reassembled.

Sewn boats of treated animal skins, like those used by the Irish Saint Brendan, could have also been dismantled, their wooden beams disassembled, and portaged by carriers over this short distance. On the Pacific shores they would have been reassembled, sewn together, and treated again with tree gum. The voyage across the Atlantic could quickly be followed by a voyage across the Pacific. Balsa logs, from pine timber available on both coasts, could have been assembled at both coasts. Then only the goods of trade would have needed to have been transported overland. Of course, the whole process would have required an established culture of high order.

Did it happen this way? In fact, most likely it did. Mesoamerica, as the connecting link of the oceans of the world, is marked both logically and geographically as a crossroads by the easy access to both oceans, but also by the diversity of Pre-Columbian peoples whose evidence is still written in stone and found throughout the Americas, as we have shown.

Only five hundred years ago hundreds of magnificent statues graced the two principal islands of Lake Nicaragua, now called Ometepe and Zapatera (fig. 13N). Most of these statues were destroyed by Spanish soldiers. However, several dozen remain, but only a few stand in their original sites. Seven-foot statues line the main square of Altagracia on Ometepe, an island dominated by the perfect cone of a 5,500-foot volcano. A few dozen more, these from Zapatera Island, can be found in a museum at the back of the main cathedral in the delightful, colonial city of Granada, Nicaragua (fig. 13-O). Others, *in situ*, are jealously guarded by Nicaraguan archaeologists, who have good reason to fear outside meddling. Observers have categorized the style of various of the statues, some reaching fifteen feet in height, as Sumerian, East Indian, Egyptian, and Mayan. Clearly, not all the carvings reveal the same style but rather a multiplicity of styles. Since the Chorotegan Indians inhabited the islands for at least a thousand years before the Spanish arrival it was thought that they might have some answer to who constructed the stone sculptures and when they were constructed. But the Chorotegans always disclaimed any knowledge simply saying that they were built by ancient gods.

Lake Nicaragua is unique in the world in that it contains the world's only freshwater sharks and a variety of water life normally only found in a marine environment. These "out of context" creatures are denizens of what was once a bay of the Pacific Ocean, but became separated from that larger body of water by a series of violent earthquakes and upheavals that formed a ridge of low hills, now about twelve miles across, between the newly formed lake and the great ocean. These low hills will continue to rise and someday, perhaps 10,000 years from now, perhaps 100,000 years in the future, will resemble the

13.O. ATLANTEANS from Zapatera Island, Lake Nicaragua.

364

13.P. OMETEPE ISLAND. Erikson examines a petroglyph that, dominated by a bird, also exhibits a left-handed spiral with a circle at its center. In the most ancient sites on Malta in the Mediterranean the same symbol is believed to represent the sun.[30]

13.Q, R, S. Similar spirals can be found throughout the navigational belts of the ancient world. Most often these symbols, like those from Crete, India and Tonga in the Pacific (below), are believed to represent infinity.[31]

coast range of mountains on the Pacific coast of California. And like the coast range, hikers to their heights will be amazed at the great quantities of seashells they will encounter. But a more pertinent question remains—how long have these low hills, effectively the shortest natural separation of the great oceans—been there (figs. 13P, Q, R, S, T)?

13.T. THE INWARD AND OUTWARD SPIRALS at New Grange, north of Dublin, Ireland, could represent the cyclical expansions and contractions of nature (and knowledge). They are situated at the end of a seventy-foot-long passage that is only illuminated at one date in the year—the winter solstice—when life is at its lowest ebb and poised for renewal.[32]

Until the selection of Panama as the site of a trans-isthmus canal the route of traders had always been to sail up the San Juan River into Lake Nicaragua and then transport goods overland to the Pacific. That route, rather than the swamps of central Panama, had been used for millennia, and the Spanish were only following suit when they constructed the elaborate city of Granada on the northwest shores of Lake Nicaragua as their trading center. But was there a day when sailing up the San Juan brought the navigator directly to the Pacific bay that is now Lake Nicaragua? Could there have once been a natural link between the great oceans? It seems likely there was not because Lake Nicaragua, unelevated by the push of plate tectonics would not have likely spilled as a continuous river to the Atlantic side. Instead there would have been low marshy areas more easily connected by man-made canals.

Gradualist geological theories, based on the idea that everything happens at a constant rate, judge that it would take 50,000 to 100,000 years for the uplifted plate that holds Lake Nicaragua to lift itself out of and above the diving Pacific plate, based on the current rate of subduction of the Pacific plate in that region. But we have been for the last few hundred years in a very quiet geologic period, internally. Subduction does not occur at a constant rate. Neither does mountain building. At times of great stress on the Earth's crust, cataclysmic times, changes can be violent, and very sudden. And repercussions of that initial violence can continue for a long period. Just as aftershocks of a great earthquake can continue for years after an initial event that lasted but minutes, geological upheavals can continue for centuries before reaching a state of relative quietude.

Navigation itself, the link between what the Gods did (move across the skies) and what man could do (move across the seas) survived the cataclysm. That story has been told in myth and in the records of star temples, megaliths (fig. 13U), and other navigational traces we've found. But there were no great journeys for the actual survivors of the deluge. First man would have to find a way to merely survive in a world suddenly turned menacing and bleak. Then he would have to provide for his children, and those for theirs. A slow reconstruction of the basics of survival would ensue. Centuries would pass with only stories of past glories and abilities to sustain those who hungered for more than sustenance. It would be millennia before man could put his celestial house in order.

In tracing man's history we should now be aware, and we should long ago have been aware, that most coastal sites are under water. Knowledge of the effects of the melting of the lands dominated by Ice Ages is not recent; it has been available to archaeologists throughout this century. We know that the inter-glacial warming we are presently experiencing has only happened rarely in the past 200,000 years. Thus we should know that records of man over the last 40,000 years will be limited to above water sites. And we should know that, if man was navigational, most sites of civilization constructed during that span of time will, at this moment in time, be under water. Why? Because man has always lived close to the sea. Man is the thinking animal, the tool making animal, but he is also the sea-faring animal. All intelligent mammals have returned to the sea for subsistence, and man is no different than the whales and porpoises.

13.U. ATLANTEAN FROM ZAPATERA ISLAND, LAKE NICARAGUA. Note the chakra dot on the forehead and the long beard.

Early man depended on the sea, traded from the sea, fished from the sea, and founded his communities near the sea. But for ninety percent of that time proximity to the sea was in very different places than our present seashores. The coastal cities of nine-tenths of our history all lay under our present seas, as much as 450 feet deep. And during the recent Ice Ages, extending back over that froze and denuded much of the available land, For 400,000 years man's existence was united with the sea. with game scarce, and agriculture limited, man most needed his traditional relationship with the sea, not just for trade, but for basic sustenance itself.

Atlantis existed throughout the Americas, but it's heart was at America's center. The remains of the Atlantean capital city of Poseidon may lay off either coast of Costa Rica or off the Caribbean coast of Honduras, Belize, or the Yucatán Peninsula. Poseidon must lay in 300 to 500 feet of water. But a diver at those depths is unlikely to encounter anything resembling the ruins of Atlantean civilization. The sea has a way of taking back and making its own anything left by man's endeavors, particularly in tropical waters. Even the remains of Japanese and American destroyers, battleships, and airships, buried for fifty years in the relatively shallow water off Pacific islands and atolls are difficult to find beneath the silt, sands, and coral growths that have covered them over the last fifty years. Remains that have been buried for over 12,500 years under coral growth, caprice of tides and sediment will be harder to identify. Their surrounding agricultural support system will be impossible to identify after all this time. So we live in ignorance. But it is not an irreparable ignorance.

Was Ometepe in Lake Nicaragua Poseidon, the ruling city of Atlantis (fig. 13U)? Or was it a few hundred miles south in the midst of the great spheres that grace the Diquis Delta? Or was it several hundred miles to the north among the thousands of sites in present day Belize, Guatemala's Peten, and Mexico's Yucatán peninsula? The answer is that it was *all* of these. The precise spot on which Poseidon, the capital of Atlantis stood may never be found, but we must continue to search. With advancements in diving equipment it may be found in the next few decades, as far south as Uvita in Costa Rica, or as far north as the Bahamas. But Atlantis, the island-continent of myth and Plato's' rendering surely existed. And it existed at a particular place and at a particular time. That memory and meaning of that "lost" continent can be found in the ruins of subsequent civilizations that long engaged themselves in the rebuilding of the harmonic purpose of Atlantis—on an island-continent that we now call the Americas.

14 A Summing Up: *Awaiting the New Paradigm*

W E LIVE AT A critical time in the history of human thought and endeavor. Mankind's cherished inventions have dramatically extended a common, aggressive ape's grasp of the world. They have brought us great riches: Jet-travel, nuclear energy, telecommunications, hair-spray, air-conditioning, and gasoline-guzzling SUVs, to name a few. They have also threatened our world's existence. When we are confronted with the knowledge that our marvelous inventions are killing our lakes, rivers, and seas, as well as the protective ozone layer of our atmosphere that has made life on Earth possible and fruitful, we seem to take the attitude that the same sciences that have made us materially rich will also furnish remedies to the destruction of our ecosystem.

When we see pictures of sharks consuming their prey, even striking and eating each other in a blind feeding frenzy, we gasp and shudder at their ferocity. When we learn that 50 percent of Indonesia's rain forests have been burned away in just the past thirty years to make way for the planting of industrial crops such as palm oil, we simply sigh. Worldwide, if present rates of deforestation continue, all tropical forests will be cleared in just 173 years. Over 60 percent of the 250,000 known plant species, the source of most of our known medicines, and innumerable insect and animal species will disappear with them. One view, perhaps the common one, holds that Man must reap his harvests, realize his profits, and assert his dominance. Another view realizes that we have become locked into our own heightened feeding frenzy—one that is consuming the bounty of the Earth that we only pretend to hold dear. While many view man's current place in history as a crest, others call our century of unprecedented warfare and genocide a mere episode in an extended trough of ignorance. Which view is most intelligent? What is the truth? How are we to know the way to proceed into an uncertain, if not terminal, future?

We suggest that man has not always behaved solely as the opportunistic descendant of an aggressive ape—that he has acted from motivations inspired by those lacking, even rejecting, the aggressive imperative as well. Could there have been a Golden Age when "higher" motivations were embraced? Told there was a more harmonious time on Earth most of us laugh. Hasn't survival of the fittest always been the rule? Are we not now at the pinnacle of achievement? A simplistic view would tell us so. And scientists and those in authority of church and state have insisted on it. But the truth appears to be that the history of life more resembles a complex, many-branched tree than a linear ladder of progress. In defiance of an interrelationship with the greater cosmos, and in a willful use and misuse of all other biological life, has mankind positioned himself out of the mainstream of cosmic purpose? Have we, through continual destruction of the ecosystem that sustains all life, ventured too far out on our particular and arrogant limb at the expense of the body of the tree of life?

Our work is, in part, about the Golden Age, an age first evident in expression of great art 33,000 years ago, and its apparent destruction around 12,000 years ago. In this long-enduring Golden Age, despite the limited availability of land, warfare was almost unknown. Ships, canoes, and rafts of many descriptions freely roamed the world, rarely encountering anything more than an occasional battle. Perhaps because the effects of the Ice Ages rendered much of the Earth frozen and most of the rest very dry and barely inhabitable, the occupation of territory may rarely have occurred to anyone. Thus what wars there were must have been occasioned by grudges, trade wars, or (if we believe Homer), the occasional abduction of women, and not in order to possess land.

Plato wrote of these more noble people of the Golden Age, whom he regarded as great lawgivers, architects, navigators and astronomers. He also wrote of their final destruction caused in part by their own arrogance, in part by the fine military defenses of his Grecian ancestors, but in most part by a catastrophe which was beyond remedy. In Plato's rendering, and in many other legendary tellings, these people were called Atlanteans. They were described as fruitful, intelligent, and capable of living in harmony with the Earth and with their perceived notion of the greater cosmos. Yet they became flawed. In Plato's words, "Atlantis became too proud and warred against the whole of the Mediterranean." If the Greek record is correct, the Atlanteans met a just end. They fell out of balance with the harmony of the universe. Atlantis, once the paradigm of Harmony, became a metaphor for all nations bent on subjugating other nations. They perished almost without an apparent trace, almost without a memory.

But, was the downfall of Atlantis brought on by its own arrogance, or was

Atlantis simply a victim of being in a particular place in geography and in a particular, and terribly fateful, time? Was Atlantis destroyed by the force of the arrival of another heavenly body? Was it coincidence that Atlantis disappeared in the same fashion and the same geologic moment that the mammoths, saber-toothed tigers, and American horse disappeared . . . just as the dinosaurs, millennia before had perished, in a sudden celestial event, beyond their power to withstand? We now have a record of only a few of these events of destruction over millennia. However, we can be certain there are many more records to be revealed, which recently interested minds are finding worthy of discovering. The search has only begun. We must finally discard the doctrine of a recent and pagan beginning to civilization—a dogmatic paradigm that has directed and controlled scholarship and, hence, the advancement of our understanding of ourselves and our past simply because it is the only view that has been acceptable to the Church, as well as to the traditional "authorities" in government and academia, who "oddly" have furthered Church dogma in the name of science. Further, we must renounce the Darwinian imperative that "catastrophism" was a myth devised by primitives, and that we now stand at the pinnacle of evolution. The mysteries of the ancients will remain "out of context" until we shed the stranglehold of religious dogma and Darwinian precepts and subsequent theories.

Why is knowledge of the Atlanteans and of the Golden Age important? It is our belief that the Golden Age did not end with the physical destruction of Atlantis nor with the deluge that engulfed the world 12,000 years ago. Mankind, though rendered few in numbers, survived, and slowly began to rebuild civilization. In this time man's reemergence had another friend—the Earth itself had become warm and moist. Corn, wheat, and plants of every nature could be sown and developed, not just on the thin coastlines of the equatorial belt but almost everywhere. For the first time in the history of man land, not the sea, was the giver of life. Sustained by myth, man's purpose found expression again in a new Golden Age that developed along inland river valleys in Sumer and Egypt and in the interconnected canals of Mesoamerica 5,000 years ago. In this more recent Golden Age pyramid builders in Egypt, Sumer and throughout the Americas reestablished culture, mathematics and pathways to the gods.

Our current academic renderings demand that dates for the reemergence of civilization fit a linear timetable. We have demonstrated that they do not. The limbs of the tree of all life have sprouted, prospered, and withered, by methods and causes we do not fully understand. Man's cultural history has taken a similar path. As we have seen, the dates archaeologists have assigned to "classic Maya" civilization—ranging from Copan in Honduras to Uxmal in the Yucatán—are surely *more recent* than the pyramids of Sumer and Egypt. We have also seen that significant sites in the Americas—the Kalasasaya Temple, Tiahuanacu's celestial observatory in Bolivia, Sacsayhuaman in Peru, and the spheres of Costa Rica—all *predate* Sumer and Egypt when measured by the newly found science of archaeoastronomy. Hancock and Bauval's investigation of ancient Egypt, by similar methods, place the construction of the Great Pyramid of Giza at twelve thousand years ago—a date that differs sharply with Egyptologist's version for the traditional rise of civilization in Egypt—but that corresponds to the earliest maritime sites in America.

What are we able to make and to understand of our temple building ancestors? They did not share the same culture, the same geographical location, nor always the same time-frame—some cultures arose millennia before others, some died out while others continued to flourish. Yet they were all inhabitants of a similar world of understanding. They shared a world view— they were believers of myth and meaning. And they were children, survivors, of disaster. It doesn't matter that their building efforts spanned thousands of years, continents and oceans apart. The world-view that created and sustained them was continuous. They clearly understood its mission that centered on a central theme—the rebuilding of Atlantis!

Like creation of step-pyramids, similar means of recreating and measuring heavenly movements through sighting stones and spheres and in vast stone temples, reflecting precise mathematical and geometric equations, did not occur by accident nor did they occur by Neo-Darwinian necessity for parallel development. When we look at their record the similarities go beyond coincidence. They had to have occurred by *contact*. Sumer, Egypt, and Mesoamerica could not have been connected by primitive hunting tribes that took hundreds or thousands of years to cross Beringia. (The "Beringia Paradigm" must be reassessed, *or simply discarded*). They had to have been connected by the warm and constant sea lanes.

When did this significant contact end? When did the Golden Age come to a close? How did a sophisticated mathematical world-view known to the ancient temple builders of Egypt and Sumer and later expressed by Plato and Pythagoras suddenly cease to exist? Again the dates elude a linear timetable. While an astronomical civilization flourished in the Americas and throughout the Pacific this knowledge died out in the Mediterranean and European world. The link to the recipient cultures of Atlantis ended, for the most part, 1,000 years B.C. with the dawning of the terrible Age of Iron. Around that time iron replaced bronze in tools of construction as well as tools of destruction. Carvings in stone, and the permanence it offered were replaced by the discovery and smelting of the new and harder metal. Iron, once discovered, was found everywhere. Commercially, excursions to the Americas, despite the Phoenicians and the occasional accidental Roman voyage, were no longer needed. Philosophically, a Mediterranean world-view that retained communication with the greater world, despite Pythagoras, despite Solon, and despite Plato, effectively came to an end.

The concept that civilization took root and hold only in the Mediterranean and only within the parameters of the Eurocentric view, must be abandoned. While the Mediterranean world rose in military power, but declined in ancient knowledge, its recipient cultures in Europe fell to feudal wars and to gross atrocities. Meanwhile, Mesoamerica city-states stood open to each other, built without walls, without protective barriers, so that any man or band of men could enter another city without having to overcome, moats, bastions, catapults, or burning oil. Yet it is the Eurocentric view of history, aided by conquests and the burning of libraries, that now dominates.

The message of true history is that Atlantis was recreated not once, but in response to myth, its recreation was attempted numerous times. So many experts over the last hundred years, bogged down in minuscule (yet important) diggings, have simply not gotten this vital point. When twentieth-century archaeologists encountered American sites that reflected the harmony in composition of the ideal cities Plato once described, they simply failed to grasp the message of what they were encountering. To truly rediscover our past, the light of civilization must turn its focus again on Mesoamerica and on that continuation of ideas, both astronomical and navigational, long forgotten in the "Old World."

Most of Mesoamerica itself was already long in decline when the fifteenth and sixteenth century Europeans brought a wave of warfare, disease, and ignorance. Yet traditional archaeologists have repeatedly focused their attention exclusively, on the most recent pre-Columbian cultures of Mesoamerica and their constructions, which, most often, are inferior repetitions of more ancient structures. They have misunderstood and even failed to question the *purpose and function* of these structures. *National Geographic Magazine* and a host of other periodicals seem content to call great astronomical structures "ceremonial centers" and to emphasize a tabloid-like glee in reporting pagan sacrifices and massive bloodletting. However, the bloodletting they so vividly and repeatedly describe had really only became widespread long *after* the original temple builders had been usurped by Toltecs, Aztecs, and decadent Maya, such as the painters of Bonampak—all very recent players in the long history and drama of the Americas. These scientists and their funding journals simply have not understood the message of history recorded in stone. The perpetuated message, as concocted by priests and historians of the

Spanish Inquisition, is that the Americans, despite their great achievements, must be viewed as "enlightened but savage pagans." What a natural cataclysm began, the physical destruction of the "Golden Age," the Church of the Inquisition and the Eurocentric mind sought to finish—through the destruction and suppression of the historic record of a civilization obviously far older than their own. This suppression continues today from some unlikely sources in a supposedly liberal and "enlightened" society.

Homo sapiens has long been an intelligent and inter-connected species. But why has the obvious so long escaped intelligent minds? It is not because he has not been looking, nor because he has been looking in the wrong places. Though most are still untouched, many of the known sites of Mesoamerica, with astronomical, archeological and calendrical implications, have been studied, but only in a manner biased to *land-based peoples*. Naval implications have been ignored. Their antiquity has been little understood.

It has only been in the past year (1997) that leading academics have acknowledged that Monte Verde in southern Chile significantly predates the impossible Inquisition-inspired theory of Beringia migration. The ivy walls of academic intransigence have begun to crack and tumble. But a host of early maritime cultures in the Americas, including the culture demonstrated by the great spheres of Costa Rica, are still regarded as "enigmas" or "out of context." We are only at the beginning of rediscovering our past. And if there is cause for optimism there is also considerable cause for alarm. Ancient sites are still being plundered, now at a rate that exceeds any time in the past. Others are being bulldozed over in the name of progress. Precious underwater sites are being dynamited, sometimes by relatively innocent and impoverished fishermen but just as often by looters. As the record of the past is destroyed so are the hopes for our future.

It is not a nostalgic desire to understand our past that drives us to discover the true history of a Golden Age, and its aftermath. The importance of the great sites of Mesoamerica lies in their displayed continuation of contact with the concepts of Atlantis. We are a product of our past, and that past has been written in stone. Atlantis began to fully flourish again in the Americas, over five thousand years ago. It is the certain knowledge that unless we rediscover this harmony with the universe we are fated to repeat true history's repeated lesson—that arrogance and abuse of power lead to destruction.

When was the Golden Age? Does the exact date matter if we know, intuitively, and from the evidence in stone, that builders and rebuilders of that era persisted and endured? Who shall we believe, the makers of myth whose tales stood unquestioned and unchanged for millenniums, or modern archaeology, forced yearly to redefine theories and recount dates? In understanding Atlantis we can begin to know that there were cultures advanced beyond our own, not in material achievements, but in a sense, and in a "technology" that reflected that sense, of a oneness with the universe. For their Serpent gods did fly in a place in time and beyond time, in concepts about which we can only marvel.

An understanding of the true relevance of the harmonizing astronomical and mathematical sites of the Americas continues to elude us. The true message of history is that from the time of the last great destruction to the still existent knowledge of the shamans of Mesoamerica, wise men have constantly viewed and recorded the movements of the stars. And they have believed that the stars described their destiny. The long held view that comets were omens of celestial disturbance, (anger of the gods), is no longer laughable. Chaos science and NASA observations have confirmed that myths of destruction were not only possible, they were likely to have been based on fact.

If Chaos science has rendered the world we live in more dangerous, less certain than previously thought by scholars and academicians, we do have some solace. Potential collisions of the comets with Earth must be regarded as terrible events. Undoubtedly they will kill most of us. But they can also be regarded as a possibility of renewal for an Earth that has lost its freshness and diversity and that has suddenly grown heavy with pollutants and old with unrelenting warfare. The lesson of the Atlanteans is that arrogance leads to death. But the lesson also is that renewal and rebirth will follow any such destruction.

However, should we welcome another celestial event of mass destruction, one that would cleanse the Earth of the greatest threat to life's diversity—mankind? We have an alternative: The metaphysics of the ancients and our own current metaphysics are drawing ever closer together. In place of the great rift that separated "primitive" magical man from modern empirical science we are experiencing a coming together of man's past and present. Our horizons are expanding both linearly and in directions we had not thought possible a few decades ago.

Many of us have begun to realize that we have recreated civilization in an arrogant and often ignorant manner. Our technological achievements are unrivaled in the history of our planet. They also threaten the very existence of many forms of life on this planet. We have relied on the accumulation of wealth and implements of sophisticated warfare—"smart-bombs" that may have recently destroyed underground Iraqi defense positions, but also ancient Sumerian ruins and texts with them—to defend our culture. But if there is some interrelationship between wealth, arms, and the wisdom we seek it is doubtful computers, or any form of technology, will be able to tell us what it is.

Only intuition, along with an accurate reading of the past can reveal our purpose. A trip to Peru for a harmonic convergence, by itself, will solve nothing. Chanting might help, if you do *nothing else*. We must learn to live more simply. Do we have time enough? According to the Mayan calendar the current age began in 3113 B.C. It will end on December 23, 2012. If their mathematics, observations, and their concept that great and terrible events mark the passing from one age to another are all correct we have some fourteen years to rediscover our past and to prepare for our imminent future. Are we intelligent enough? Courageous enough?

Atlantis existed. However, we cannot presume the folly, advanced by pseudo-science, that the Atlanteans had helicopters, televisions, and atomic bombs. Such an Atlantis never existed on this planet—until now. Nor should we accept the sensationalists' view that Atlanteans and all ancient builders were influenced by aliens from another solar system or galaxy. It is unlikely such an advanced civilization would so greatly interfere with an unstable world. Besides, the idea that we are unable to advance technologically without outside help really is not so sensational. But, an Atlantis in a Golden Age of worldwide communication and trade, with city-states and nations, built without fortresses or walls, *did exist*. The important quest for us is to rediscover the nature of a civilization, made up of humans like ourselves, that lived for millennia in harmony with itself, with its neighbors, and with a practical knowledge of the celestial universe—a civilization now lost.

Yet, how do we know, truly, that an Atlantis and a Golden Age ever existed? Myth has told us so. We must realize that despite all our previous attempts to destroy and alter our past, as described in myth, we still have *all* the possibilities myth itself has proposed, and that myth has retained for us—an undeniable link to the true intelligence of the universe. As long as the imagination of humans survives, civilization can occur many times, but only in a harmonic interaction with the fabric of all life, and with a greater universe we now so mistakenly perceive as distant, and impossible to comprehend.

A narrow, linear view of history has disregarded myth as the container of truth and replaced it with the notion, now imperative dogma, of myth as primitive and unreliable fable, while Darwinian evolution and material progress is reliable fact. By seeing our past as analogous to a ladder, history has been portrayed as a gradual climbing out of darkness, and neo-Darwinian theory has steadfastly assumed that we are at the pinnacle of man's habitation on Earth. Could we be mistaken? Could true knowledge of the past, and our resolve to learn from it, be our only hope of avoiding catastrophes in the near future?

We cannot emphasize enough—Man's true history is written in his *knowledge* of the sky, revealed in the names he has given to the stars and to their constellations, and demonstrated in their physical reconstruction on Earth.

An earlier culture, for millenniums peaceful in nature, in tune with the stars, trading ideas and concepts, without rancor, not only existed, but flourished and retained celestial knowledge recorded from civilizations whose existence had disappeared many millenniums past. The civilization of Atlantis flourished under the stars, inseparable from the heavens above. All over the world, when night fell, and the stars appeared, the motives and motions of the gods were made apparent to men! So too were the pathways adventurous men would follow across the seas, pathways mapped in the sky above them.

There is magic in the world. We all feel it on special nights, summer nights spent, in part, with the stars, and in part with ourselves as we remove ourselves from the trappings of the mechanized, televised, computerized world. If we find ourselves in the presence of a pyramid or a megalith it doesn't matter if we are in Belize, England or Egypt, we cannot help to feel the magic of a civilization from long ago, and a state of mind that was our past but, hopefully, may also be our future realm. We are *star matter,* and as such, we are children of the gods. And they have not gone away. On these special occasions when we wander out under a star-filled sky, whether near Stonehenge, in the outback of Australia, or on a Maya beach facing the Caribbean, we can feel our own essential beings under the stars. We tend to call such experiences "vacations." In the experience we have "vacated" ourselves of the worried and wrenching cares that have dominated us. It is an easy and greatly rewarding step backwards. Temporarily, it brings us into balance. We must find a permanence to this sense of balance, even if it means stepping backward and embracing a philosophy contrary to our present social and economic expectations. It is a step that man, if he can prove himself intelligent, must take.

Neither History nor Evolution will repeat itself, exactly. Man, either in the aftermath of another cataclysm, or in the grips of another Ice-Age, will again be confined mostly to the coastal regions of tropical shores. Will any resemblance of past civilizations exist among a people too few in numbers to remember any part of his dominant past? Will man return to aggressive primitive behavior triggering a new age of warfare. Will he achieve a new and fruitful evolution, or will he meekly die out. Balance is difficult to achieve, and almost impossible to regain, once it is lost. It is therefore all the more important to appreciate and understand that it did exist, on this planet, among our people, for thousands and thousands of years in a lost civilization called Atlantis.

•

A Lancandon Indian watched as the last tourist bus left. Only when it was out of sight did he dare to do what none of his people would any longer want to do. He climbed up the rocks of the pyramid at Chichen Itza. He didn't know exactly why he was making the climb. The pyramids were no longer considered part of the Lancondon lives. His people had deserted them over a thousand years before and now that a distant government had recreated them for tourists, they no longer held any interest for the Lancondons. It was late in the day and he had his family to return to. He had gathered sparse wood needed for that evening's fire. But he had dropped it at the foot the pyramid and he had began climbing, just as so many of his ancestors, millennia before, had done. It had been a hot afternoon and he had to continually wipe the sweat from his brow as he reached the pyramid's crown. At sunset the jungle was beautiful, transcendent green! This date might someday have been recorded as 12,012, if peoples still used the Atlantean calendar. It was December 23, 2,012 A.D. by the Christian calendar, the end of an age that had begun on the Maya date of August 13, 3113 B.C. But actually it was about to become 1 Reed of a new age. The Lancondon quickly climbed down the steep pyramid and crossed the manicured grounds to the observatory. He was now moving purposefully, as if remembering something long forgotten. As night fell he ascended the observatory. He looked out through the sightlines of the stones, just as if he understood what they meant. And he did understand, just as his people had long understood. He saw that the setting sun, moon and Venus had found perfect correlation along the sightlines. He did not need to know any skills in astronomy. There was no question. Something was about to happen. Something terrible, something vast, and something wonderful—something that would very soon change the world. The Lancondon, named Three Rabbit, waited. There was nothing else to do.

References

Introduction
1. *Natural History Magazine,* July, 1996, Vol. 105, Num. 7, p. 18.
2. *Discover Magazine,* August 1997, Vol. 18, Num. 10. p. 83.

Chapter 1
1. Tomas, Andrew, *Atlantis, From Legend to Discovery,* Robert Hale & Co. London, 1972, p.72.
2. Gardner, Joseph L., ed., *Mysteries of The Ancient Americas,* The Reader's Digest General Books, Pleasantville, NY, 1986, p.15.
3. *National Geographic Magazine,* July 1982, Vol. 162, Num. 1, p.22.
4. Ferrero, Luis, *Costa Rica Precolumbia,* Editorial Costa Rica, San Jose, 1987. p.385.
5. Tompkins, Peter, *Mysteries of The Mexican Pyramids,* Harper & Row, New York. 1976. p.164.
6. Heyerdahl, Thor, *Early Man and the Ocean,* Doubleday, New York, 1979. p.206.
7. Velentini, Felipe J., *Cuarto Viaje de Colon,* Imprenta Leharzum, San Jose, Costa Rica, 1943.
8. Lewis, David. *We, The Navigators,* University of Hawaii Press, Honolulu. 1972. p.6.
9. Ibid., p.316.
10. Gordon, Cyrus H., *Before Columbus,* Turnstone Press, London, 1972. p.128.
11. Plato, *Timeaus and Critias,* Desmond Lee (trans.), Penguin Books, New York, Rev. ed. 1977, p.37.
12. Fleming, Carrol, *Adventuring In The Caribbean,* Sierra Club Books, San Francisco, 1989. p. 10.

Chapter 2
1. *Mysteries of The Mexican Pyramids,* p. 34,35.
2. Hope, Murry, *Atlantis—Myth Or Reality,* Arkana, New York, 1991. p.247.
3. *Mysteries of The Mexican Pyramids,* p. 57.

4 Ibid., p.11.

5. Ibid., p.21.

6. Ibid., p.25.

7. Ibid., p.53.

8. Ibid., p.40.

9. Ibid., p.41.

10. Fiedel, Stuart J., *Prehistory of the Americas*, 2nd Ed., Cambridge University Press, Cambridge, UK. 1992. p.2.

11. Huyghe, Patrick, *Columbus Was Last*, Hyperion, New York, 1992. p.15.

12. Lamb, Dana, *Enchanted Vagabonds*, Harper & Row, New York. (out of print).

13. *Early Man and the Ocean, (front.)*

14. Ibid., p.215

15. Hicks, Alvah, (unpublished paper).

16. Bailey, Jim. *Sailing To Paradise*, Simon & Schuster, New York, 1994, p.70.

17. *Mysteries of The Ancient Americas*, p.28.

18. *Mysteries of The Mexican Pyramids*, p.346.

19. Sitchin, Zecharia, *Lost Realms*, Avon Books, New York, p.44.

20. Ibid., p.44.

21. Pellegrino, Charles, *Unearthing Atlantis, p.106.*

22. Nicholson, Irene, *Mexican and Central American Mythology,* Peter Bedrick Books, New York, 1985.

23. Velikovsky, Immanuel, *Mankind In Amnesia*. Doubleday, New York, 1982. p.183.

24. *Lost Realms*, p.89

25. Davies, Nigel, *Voyagers To The New World*, Macmillan. London. 1979. p.101.

26. Ibid., p.179.

27. *Lost Realms*, p.224.

28. *Voyagers To The New World*, p.101.

29. *Mankind In Amnesia, p.75.*

30. *Ibid., p.91.*

31. *Ibid., p.91.*

32. *Lost Realms*, p.220.

33. *Mysteries of The Mexican Pyramids*, p.11.

Chapter 3

1. *Prehistory of the Americas,* p.18.

2. Ibid., p.5.

3. Ibid., p.351.

4. Ibid., p.352.

5. Ibid., p.49.

6. Ibid., p.57.

7. *Mysteries of The Ancient Americas*, p.82.

8. *Natural History Magazine,* July, 1996, p.18.

9. *The New Encyclopedia Britanica,* Vol. 26, Macropaedia—Knowledge in Depth, Chicago, 1993. p.3.

10. *Prehistory of the Americas,* p.30.

11. *Natural History Magazine,* July, 1996, p.71.

12. *Science, Roosevelt, A.C., et al, "Paleoindian Cave Dwellers in the Amazon," Vol. 272, Num. 5260, April 19, 1996. pp. 373-384.*

13. *Time Magazine,* October, 14, 1996. p.81.

14. *Prehistory of the Americas,* p.6.

15. Ibid., p.41.

16. Feuerstein, Georg, Kak, Subhash, and Frawley, David, *In Search of the Cradle of Civilization,* Quest Books, Wheaton, IL, 1995. p.45.

17. *Sailing To Paradise,* p.83.

18. *Archaeology,* March/April, 1997. Vol. 50, Num. 2, p.62.

19. Dixon, E. James, *Quest For The Origins of The First Americans,* University of New Mexico Press, Albuquerque, 1993, p.104.

20. Childress, David Hatcher, *Lost Cities of North America,* Adventures Unlimited Press, Kempton, IL, 1986. p.137.

Chapter 4

1. *Newsweek,* Nov. 23, 1992, p.40.

2. *National Geographic,* June, 1989, Vol. 175, Num. 6. pp. 691-692.

3. Ibid. p.673.

4. Darwin, Charles, *The Origin of Species,* Mentor Books, New York, 1958. p.317.

5. Ibid. p.319.

6. *National Geographic,* June, 1989, p.688.

7. Ibid. p.687.

8. *Newsweek,* Nov. 23, 1992, p.40.

9. *New York Times,* May, 14, 1996.

10. Hall, Nina,(ed.), *Exploring Chaos,* W.W. Norton, New York, 1994. p.71

11. Menzel, D. H. and Pasachoff, J. M., *Stars and Planets.* Houghton Mifflin, Boston, 1983.

12. *Lost Cities of North America,* p.575.

13. *Discover Magazine,* May, 1997, p. 26.

14. *Discover Magazine,* Nov. 1995.

15. Hawking, Stephen, *A Brief History of Time,* Bantam Books, New York, 1988. p. 39.

Chapter 5

1. *Discovery,* October, 1996.

2. *Full House,* p.4.

3. *Early Man and the Ocean,* p.73.

4. *Los Angeles Times,* June 13, 1997.

5. *Prehistory of the Americas,* p.14.

6. Ibid., p.12,13.
7. Ibid., p.14.
8 Mathematical Objections to
9. Gould, Stephen Jay, *The Flamingo's Smile*, W.W. Norton, New York, 1985. p. 419.
10. *Discovery*, January, 1997, p. 34.
11. Gleick, James. *Chaos—Making A New Science,* Viking Penguin, New York, 1987. p.8.
12. *Scientific American*, August, 1986.
13. Renfrew, Colin, and Bahn, Paul. *Archaeology: Theories, Methods and Practice.* Thames and Hudson, Ltd., London, 1991. p.30.

Chapter 6
1. *Timeaus and Critias*, p.37.
2. Ibid., pp. 36-38.
3. *Atlantis—Myth Or Reality*, p.16.
4. Hapgood, Charles, *Maps Of The Ancient Sea Kings,* Turnstone Press, London, 1979. Reprinted by Adventures Unlimited Press, Kempton, IL, 1996. p.196.
5. Sitchin, Zecharia, *When Time Began,* Avon Books, New York, 1993. p.289.
6. *Atlantis, From Legend to Discovery,* p.97.
7. Ibid., p.113.
8. *Maps Of The Ancient Sea Kings,* p.197.
9. Tompkins, Peter, *Secrets of the Great Pyramid*, Galahad Books, New York, 1997, pp 3,4.
10. *Before Columbus*, p.44.
11. *Lost Realms*, p.235.
12. *Unearthing Atlantis*, p.32.
13. *Atlantis—Myth Or Reality*, p.34.
14. *Before Columbus*, p.39.
15. *Atlantis—Myth Or Reality*, p.6.
16. *Timeaus and Critias*, p.131.
17. *Atlantis, From Legend to Discovery,* p. 38.
18. Ibid., p.37.
19. Ibid., p.39.
20. Ibid., p.24.
21. *Timeaus and Critias*, p.131.
22. Ibid., p.137.
23. Ibid., p.154.
24. *Mysteries of The Mexican Pyramids*, p.76.
25. Ibid., p.327.
26. *Los Angeles Times*, October 10, 1996.
27. Gebhard, David, *Robert Stacy-Judd,* Capra Press, Santa Barbara, 1993, p.114.

Chapter 7

1. Jaffe, Aniela, *The Myth of Meaning*, Penguin, New York, 1975. p.139.
2. Campbell, Joseph, *Myths to Live By*, Viking Press, New York, 1972. p.21.
3. *Discovery*, October 1996, p.50.
4. *National Geographic*, October, 1988, pp. 482-489.
5. *The New Encyclopedia Britanica*, Vol. 26, p.49.
6. *Natural History Magazine*, July, 1996, p.17.
7. *Archaeology*, March/April, 1997. Vol. 50, Num. 2, p.62.
8. Dixon, E. James, *Quest For The Origins of The First Americans*, University of New Mexico Press, Albuquerque, 1993. p.101.
9. *National Geographic*, October, 1988, p.481.
10. Ibid., p.449.
11. *Popol Vuh*, trans. by Dennis Tedlock, Touchstone, New York, 1986. p.150.
12. *Before Columbus*, p.53.
13. *Atlantis—Myth Or Reality*, p.224.
14. *When Time Began*, p.261.
15. Goodrich, Norma Lorre, *The Ancient Myths*, New American Library, New York, 1960. p.61.
16. *Popol Vuh*, p.84.
17. *Scientific American*, November, 1996. Vol. 275, Num. 5. p.111.
18. *Atlantis, From Legend to Discovery*, p.134.
19. *Before Columbus*, p.107.
20. *Early Man and the Ocean*, p.112.
21. Vogt, Doug and Gary Sultan, *Reality Revealed*, Vector Associates, San Jose, CA, 1978. p.339.
22. *Mysteries of The Mexican Pyramids*, p.57.
23. *Reality Revealed*, p.330.
24. *Lost Realms*, p.118.
25. *Mysteries of The Mexican Pyramids*, p.292.
26. *Reality Revealed*, p.334.
27. Santillana Giorgio de and Dechend, Hertha von, *Hamlet's Mill*, David R. Godine, Boston, 1977. p.57.
28. *Reality Revealed*, pp. 334,396.
29. Ibid., p.334.
30. Ibid., p.335.
31. *Before Columbus*, p.156.
32. *Mysteries of The Mexican Pyramids*, pp. 118,119.
33. *Reality Revealed*, p.346.
34. *Atlantis, From Legend to Discovery*, p.28.
35. *Reality Revealed*, p.362.
36. Ibid., p.365.
37. Ibid., p.369.
38. Ibid., p.374.
39. Ibid., p.389.

40. Ibid., p.404.
41. *Atlantis—Myth Or Reality*, p.222.
42. Ibid., p.100.
43. Ibid., p.223.
44. *Atlantis, From Legend to Discovery*, p.105.
45. Ibid., p.28.
46. Ibid., p.33.
47. *Early Man and the Ocean*, p.21.
48. *Lost Realms*, p.33.
49. *Mysteries of The Mexican Pyramids*, p.383.
50. Ibid., p.115.
51. Ibid., p.115.
52. *Hamlet's Mill*, p.79.
53. *Reality Revealed*, p.329.
54. Ibid., p.333.
55. Ibid., p.339.
56. Ibid., p.394.
57. *Sailing To Paradise*, p.53.
58. *Los Angeles Times*, November, 20, 1995.
59. *Hamlet's Mill*, pp. 57,323.
60. *Atlantis, From Legend to Discovery*, p.59.
61. Arguelles, Jose, *The Mayan Factor*, Bear & Co., Santa Fe, NM, 1987. p.16.

Chapter 8

1. *Mysteries of The Mexican Pyramids*, p.24.
2. *Mysteries of The Ancient Americas*, p.289.
3. Thompson, Gunnar. *Nu Sun, Asian Voyages 500 B.C.*, Pioneer Press, Fresno, CA, 1989 p.98. *Columbus Was Last*, p.84.
4. *Mysteries of The Ancient Americas*, p.141.
5. *Mexican and Central American Mythology*, p.104.
6. *Mysteries of The Mexican Pyramids*, p.57.
7. *Lost Realms*, p.55.
8. *Mysteries of The Ancient Americas*, p.105.
9. *The Mayan Factor*, p.29.
10. *Mysteries of The Mexican Pyramids*, p.57.
11. Ibid., p.13.
12. *Hamlet's Mill*, p.78.
13. *Lost Realms*, p.41.
14. *Hamlet's Mill*, p.40.
15. Ibid., p.77.
16. *In Search of the Cradle of Civilization*, p.64.
17. Brandon, S. G. F. (ed.), *Ancient Empires*, Newsweek Books, New York, 1973. pp. 43-45.
18. *Mysteries of The Mexican Pyramids*, p.20.

19. Ibid., p.21.
20. Ibid., p.179
21. Ibid., p.15-16.
22. Ibid., p.160.
23. *Unearthing Atlantis*, p.107.
24. *Mysteries of The Mexican Pyramids,* p.400.

Chapter 9
 1. *Hamlet's Mill*, p. ix.
 2. *Mysteries of The Mexican Pyramids*, p.382.
 3. Scheffler, Lilian, *Chichen Itza*, Panorama Editorial, Mexico, DF, 1992. p.67.
 4. Mallan, Chicki, *Cancun Handbook*, Moon Publications, Chico, CA, 1993. p.27.
 5. *Mexican and Central American Mythology*, p.122.
 6. *Prehistory of the Americas*, p.305.
 7. *When Time Began*, pp. 240,302.
 8. *Cancun Handbook*, p.27.
 9. *Timeaus and Critias*, p.138-142.
10. Michell, John, *City of Revelation*, Sphere Books, London, 1973. p.80.
11. *Mysteries of The Mexican Pyramids,* p.256.
12. *The Mayan Factor*, p.76.
13. *Mysteries of The Mexican Pyramids*, p.247.
14. *Reality Revealed*, p.288-9.
15. *Mysteries of The Mexican Pyramids*, p.268.
16. *Reality Revealed*, p.286.
17. *Mysteries of The Mexican Pyramids*, p. 241.
18. Ibid., p.279.
19. *Reality Revealed*, p.289.
20. Ruthford, Adam, *Pyramidology*, The Institute of Pyramidology, London, 1957.
21. *Atlantis, From Legend to Discovery*, p.93.
22. *Mysteries of The Mexican Pyramids,* p.257.
23. *City of Revelation*, p.51.
24. Ibid., p.20.
25. *Hamlet's Mill*, p.230.
26. *The Mayan Factor*, p.52.
27. *Hamlet's Mill*, p.340.
28. *When Time Began*, p.196.
29. *City of Revelation*, p.62.
30. *Timeaus and Critias*, p.155.
31. *Atlantis, From Legend to Discovery*, p.135.
32. *Timeaus and Critias*, p.154.
33. *Lost Cities of North America*, p.125.
34. *Mysteries of The Mexican Pyramids*, p.53.

35. Zapata Alonzo, Gualberto. *An Overview of The Mayan World.* Editorial Dante, Merida, 1985. p.95.
36. *The Mayan Factor*, p.74.
37. *Hamlet's Mill*, p. 67-68.
38. *Stars and Planets.* p.415.
39. *Serpent In The Sky*, p. 203.
40. Hancock, Graham, and Bauval, Robert, *The Message of The Sphinx*, Crown, New York, 1996. p.74.
41. *Lost Realms*, p.159,160.
42. *Before Columbus*, p.174.
43. *Prehistory of the Americas*, p.291.
44. Ibid., p.292.
45. *Mexico City News*, April 15, 1996.
46. *Lost Cities of North America*, p.160.
47. Ibid., p.44.
48. *When Time Began*, p.79.
49. *Mysteries of The Mexican Pyramids*, p.352.
50. *The Mayan Factor*, p.77.
51. *City of Revelation*, p. 9.

Chapter 10
1. Childress, David Hatcher, *Lost Cities Of South America*, Adventures Unlimited Press, Kempton, IL, 1986. p.70.
2. *Mysteries of The Mexican Pyramids*, p.356.
3. Ibid., p.355.
4. *When Time Began*, p.66.
5. *The New Encyclopedia Britanica*, Vol. 26, p.4.
6. *Archaeology*, March/April, 1997. Vol. 50, Num. 2, p.11.
7. *Lost Cities Of South America*, p.62.
8. *Prehistory of the Americas*, p.345.
9. *Lost Cities Of South America, p.69.*
10. Ibid., p.69.
11. *Prehistory of the Americas*, p.346.
12. *Lost Cities Of South America*, p.69.
13. Ibid., p.72.
14. *Atlantis, From Legend to Discovery*, p.97.
15. *Lost Cities Of South America*, p.75.
16. Ibid., p.76.
17. *Prehistory of the Americas*, p.347.
18. *Lost Cities Of South America*, p. 145.
19. *Lost Realms*, p.227.
20. *Lost Cities Of South America*, p.153.
21. Ibid., p.137.
22. *Lost Cities of North America*, p. 255.

23. *Lost Realms*, p.222.
24. Ibid., p.224.
25. *National Geographic*, March, 1995, pp. 68-89.
26. Arriaza, Bernardo T., *Beyond Death*, Smithsonian Institution Press, Washington, 1995, pp. XI, 85.
27. *National Geographic*, March, 1995, pp. 68-89.
28. Malta, p.9.
29. Ibid., pp. 19,20.
30. *Before Columbus*, p.81.
31. Ibid., p.81.
32. Riley, Carroll L., et al, eds., *Man Across the Sea*, University of Texas Press, Austin, 1971, p.269.
33. *National Geographic*, June, 1989, p.713.
34. Malta, p. 14.
35. *City of Revelation*, p. 18.
36. *USA Today*, July 28, 1995.
37. *Mysteries of The Mexican Pyramids*, p.55.
38. West, John, A., *Serpent In The Sky*, Julian Press, New York, 1987 p.190.
39. Ibid., p.200.
40. Ibid., p.217.
41. *Atlantis—Myth Or Reality*, p.153.
42. Frazer, Sir James George, *The Golden Bough*, Abridged Ed. Collier Books, New York, 1963, p.421.
43. Ibid., p.426.
44. *Mysteries of The Mexican Pyramids*, p.44.
45. *Popol Vuh*, p.342.
46. *The Golden Bough*, p.427.
47. *The Message of The Sphinx*, p.150.
48. Ibid., p.77-81.
49. *Prehistory of the Americas*, p.310.
50. Ibid., p.278.
51. *Lost Cities of North America*, p.262,3.
52. *Prehistory of the Americas*, p.272.
53. Berkeley Students in association with the ASUC, *Mexico on the Loose*, Fodors, New York, 1994, p.280.
54. *Prehistory of the Americas*, p.274.
55. *Before Columbus*, p.174.
56. Ibid., p.171.
57. *Mysteries of The Mexican Pyramids*, p.295.
58. *Atlantis—Myth Or Reality*, p.143.
59. Calvin, William H., *How the Shaman Stole the Moon*, Bantam, New York, 1992, p.24.

Chapter 11

1. *Man Across the Sea,* p.278.
2. Fell, Barry, *America B.C.,* Demeter Press, New York, 1977, p.112.
3. Marx, Robert F., *In Quest Of The Great White Gods,* Crown, New York, 1992, p.315.
4. *Unearthing Atlantis,* p.111.
5. *National Geographic,* July, 1982, pp. 2-41.
6. Ibid., p.6.
7. *Columbus Was Last,* p.124.
8. *Mysteries of The Mexican Pyramids,* p.353.
9. *Columbus Was Last,* p.91.
10. *Before Columbus,* p.39.
11. *Mysteries of The Mexican Pyramids,* p.352.
12. *Voyagers To The New World,* p.151.
13. *Before Columbus,* p.125.
14. *America B.C.,* p.316.
15. Ibid., p.114.
16. *Before Columbus,* p.30.
17. *Early Man and the Ocean,* p.99.
18. Ibid., p.101.
19. *Sailing To Paradise,* p.36.
20. *Man Across the Sea,* p.133.
21. *Early Man and the Ocean,* p.205.
22. Ibid., p.206.
23. Ibid., p.188.
24. Ibid., p.191.
25. Ibid., p.217.
26. *Mysteries of The Mexican Pyramids,* p.169.
27. *Sailing To Paradise,* p.145.
28. *Voyagers To The New World,* p.148.
29. *Sailing To Paradise,* p.81.
30. *Atlantis—Myth Or Reality,* p.44.
31. *Man Across the Sea,* p.133.
32. *Atlantis—Myth Or Reality,* p.45.
33. *Before Columbus,* p.173.
34. Ibid., p.61.
35. Ibid., p.116.
36. Ibid., p.54.
37. *Unearthing Atlantis,* p.39.
38. *Before Columbus,* p.43.
39. *Early Man and the Ocean,* p.13.
40. Ibid., p.350.
41. Ibid., pp. 21,369.
42. *Before Columbus,* p.54.

43. *Sailing To Paradise*, pp. 31,203.
44. *Columbus Was Last*, p.64.
45. *Early Man and the Ocean*, pp. 5,6.
46. *Columbus Was Last*, p.50.
47. Ibid., pp. 47,52.
48. *We, The Navigators*, p.266.
49. Ibid., p.279.
50. Ibid., p.51.
51. *When Time Began*, p.124.
52. *We, The Navigators*, p.238.
53. Ibid., p.234.
54. Ibid., p.239.
55. Ibid., p.246.
56. Ibid., pp. 18,19.
57. *Lost Realms*, p.247.
58. *Los Angeles Times,* June 20, 1996.
59. *Science,* June, 1995.
60. *Time*, March 14, 1994, p.85.
61. *Quest For The Origins of The First Americans*, p.127.
62. *Sailing To Paradise*, p.90.
63. *Discover*, August, 1997, p.83.

Chapter 12
1. *An Overview of The Mayan World*, p.75.
2. Ibid., p.62.
3. Childress, David Hatcher, *Ancient Tonga & the Lost City Mu'A,* Adventures Unlimited Press, Kempton, IL, 1996.
4. *Columbus Was Last*, p.126.
5. *Early Man and the Ocean*, p.122.
6. *Cancun Handbook*, p.209.
7. *National Geographic*, February, 1995, pp. 50-68.
8. *Early Man and the Ocean*, p.229.
9. Ibid., p.78.
10. Ibid., p.235.
11. Spence, Lewis, *The History of Atlantis,* reprinted by Adventures Unlimited Press, Kempton, IL, 1996, p.47.
12. *Sailing To Paradise*, p.96.
13. Ibid., pp. 59,97.
14. *Early Man and the Ocean*, p.76.
15. *Sailing To Paradise*, p.95.
16. *In Quest Of The Great White Gods*, p.51.
17. Cyr, Donald L., *The Diffusion Issue*, Santa Barbara, 1991, p.26.
18. Ibid., p.105.
19. *Prehistory of the Americas,* p.67.

20. *Discover,* August, 1997, p.83.
21. *Before Columbus,* p.159.
22. *Sailing To Paradise,* p.107.
23. Ibid., p.94.
24. *Prehistory of the Americas,* p.362.
25. *Man Across the Sea,* p.108.
26. *Mysteries of The Ancient Americas,* p.24.
27. *The Diffusion Issue,* p.25.
28. *Before Columbus,* p.142.
29. *Columbus Was Last,* p.31.
30. *Mysteries of The Ancient Americas,* p.24.
31. *Scientific American,* August, 1989, p.76.
32. *The Diffusion Issue,* p.28.
33. *Voyagers To The New World,* p.65.
34. *Before Columbus,* p.18.
35. *Discover,* May, 1997, p.95.
36. *Columbus Was Last,* p.64.
37. *National Geographic,* December, 1987.

Chapter 13

1. *Scientific American,* March, 1996, p.13.
2. *Prehistory of the Americas,* p.269.
3. Ibid., 268.
4. *National Geographic,* "New Light on the Olmecs" Nov., 1993, pp. 94-110.
5. Moseley, Michael, *Maritime Foundations Of Andean Civilization,* Cummings, Menlo Park, CA, 1975, p.99.
6. *Prehistory of the Americas,* p.321.
7. Van Sertima, Ivan, *Journal of African Civilization,* 1984, p.14.
8. Roosevelt, A.C., et al, *Science,* "Paleoindian Cave Dwellers in the Amazon," Vol. 272, Num. 5260, April 19, 1996. pp. 373-384.
9. *Prehistory of the Americas,* p.292.
10. *Lost Cities of North America,* p.115.
11. *Prehistory of the Americas,* p.289.
12. *Lost Kingdoms of The Maya,* p.193.
13. Ibid., p.194.
14. *Lost Cities of North America,* p.48.
15. *Prehistory of the Americas,* p.292.
16. *The Atlas of Mysterious Places,* ed. by Marshall Productions Ltd., Weidenfeld & Nicolson, New York, 1987, p.202.
17. *Lost Cities of North America,* p.48.
18. *Atlantis, From Legend to Discovery,* p.129.
19. *The Atlas of Mysterious Places,* p.202.
20. *When Time Began,* p.285.
21. *Sailing To Paradise,* p.49.

22. *Los Angeles Times*, March 8, 1997, p.19.
23. *Sailing To Paradise*, p.57.
24. *Atlantis—Myth Or Reality*, p.43.
25. *Early Man and the Ocean*, p.67.
26. *Atlantis, From Legend to Discovery*, p.16.
27. *Early Man and the Ocean*, p.377.
28. *Atlantis, From Legend to Discovery*, p.60.
29. Ibid., p.19.
30. *Sailing To Paradise*, p.258.
31. *Ancient Tonga*, p.159.
32. *City of Revelation*, p.82.

Chapter 14
1. The Carnegie Library of Pittsburgh, *The Handy Science Answer Book,* Visible Ink Press, Detroit, 1994, 161.

Selected Bibliography

Aebi, Tania, *Maiden Voyage*, Simon & Schuster, New York, 1989.

Archaeology, March/April, 1997, Vol. 50, Num. 2.

Arguelles, Jose, The Mayan Factor, Bear & Co., Santa Fe, NM, 1987.

Arriaza, Bernardo T., *Beyond Death*, Smithsonian Institution Press, Washington, 1995.

The Atlas of Mysterious Places, ed. by Marshall Productions Ltd., Weidenfeld & Nicolson, New York, 1987.

Aveni, Anthony, *Stairways To The Stars*, Wiley, New York, 1997.

Bailey, Jim, *Sailing To Paradise*, Simon & Schuster, New York, 1994.

Berkeley Students in association with the ASUC, *Mexico on the Loose,* Fodors, New York, 1994.

Brandon, S.G.F. (ed.), *Ancient Empires*, Newsweek Books, New York, 1973.

Bunson, Margaret R. and Stephen M., *Encyclopedia Of Ancient Mesoamerica,* Facts On File, New York, 1996.

Burenhult, Goran, ed., *New World And Pacific Civilizations*, HarperCollins, New York, 1994.

Calvin, William H., *How the Shaman Stole the Moon,* Bantam, New York, 1992.

Campbell, Joseph, *Myths to Live By*, Viking Press, New York, 1972.

The Carnegie Library of Pittsburgh, *The Handy Science Answer Book,* Visible Ink Press, Detroit, 1994.

Chauvet, Jean-Marie, Descamps, Eliette B., Hillaire, Christiane. *Dawn Of Art: The Chauvet Cave,* Abrams, New York, 1996.

Childress, David Hatcher, *Ancient Tonga & the Lost City Mu'A,* Adventures Unlimited Press, Kempton, IL, 1996.

Childress, David Hatcher, *Lost Cities Of North America*, Adventures Unlimited Press, Kempton, IL, 1986.

Childress, David Hatcher, *Lost Cities Of South America*, Adventures Unlimited Press, Kempton, IL, 1986.

Clottes, Jean & Courtin, Jean, *The Cave Beneath The Sea*: Paleolithic Images at Cosquer, Abrams, New York, 1996.

Coe, Michael D., *The Maya*, Thames & Hudson, London, 1966.

Cotterell, Arthur, ed. *The Penguin Encyclopedia of Ancient Civilizations*, Penguin Books, London, 1980.

Cyr, Donald, ed., *Stonehenge Viewpoint* "Chinese 'Ice Blink' Survey Maps." Santa Barbara, 1989.

Cyr, Donald L., *The Diffusion Issue*, Santa Barbara, 1991.

Darwin, Charles, *The Origin of Species*, Mentor Books, New York. 1958.

David, K. C., *Don't Know Much About Geography*, Avon Books, New York, 1992.

Davies, Nigel, *Voyagers To The New World*, Macmillan, London, 1979.

de Tariffi, Natalia Rosi, *America, Quatro Dimension,* Monte Avila Editores, Caracas, 1969.

Discover Magazine, October 1996, Vol. 17, Num. 10.

Discover Magazine. January, 1997. Vol. 18. Num. 1.

Discover Magazine, May, 1997, Vol. 18.

Discover Magazine, August, 1997, Vol. 18. Num. 8.

Dixon, E. James, *Quest For The Origins of The First Americans*, University of New Mexico Press, Albuquerque, 1993.

Donnelly, Ignatius, *Atlantis—The Antediluvian World*, Sampson, Low, Marston & Co. Ltd, London, 1882.

Duarte, Ignacio Magalani, *Educadores Del Mundo*, B. Costa-Amic, Mexico, DF, 1969.

Fell, Barry, *America B.C.*, Demeter Press, New York, 1977.

Ferrero, Luis, *Costa Rica Precolumbia*, Editorial Costa Rica, San Jose, 1987.

Feuerstein, Georg, Kak, Subhash, and Frawley, David, *In Search of the Cradle of Civilization*, Quest Books, Wheaton, IL, 1995.

Fiedel, Stuart J., *Prehistory Of The Americas*, 2nd Ed., Cambridge University Press, Cambridge, UK. 1992.

Fleming, Carrol. *Adventuring In The Caribbean*, Sierra Club Books, San Francisco, 1989.

Flohr, Terry, Series Editor, *Focus On Earth Science,* Merrill Publishing, Columbus, 1984.

Frankfort, Henri, *The Birth of Civilization in the Near East,* Anchor Books, New York, 1956.

Frazer, Sir James George, *The Golden Bough*, Abridged Ed., Collier Books, New York, 1963.

Gardner, Joseph L., ed., *Mysteries Of The Ancient Americas,* The Reader's Digest General Books, Pleasantville, NY. 1986.

Gebhard, David, *Robert Stacy-Judd*, Capra Press, Santa Barbara, 1993.

Gleick, James. *Chaos—Making A New Science*, Viking Penguin, New York, 1987.

Goodman, Jeffrey, *American Genesis*, Summit Books, New York. 1981.

Goodrich, Norma Lorre, *The Ancient Myths*, New American Library, New York, 1960.

Gordon, Cyrus H., *Before Columbus*, Turnstone Press, London, 1972.

Gould, Stephen Jay, *Bully For Brontosaurus*, W.W. Norton, New York, 1992.

Gould, Stephen Jay, *The Flamingo's Smile*, W.W. Norton, New York, 1985.

Gould, Stephen Jay, *Full House*, Harmony House, New York, 1996.

Gould, Stephen Jay, *Wonderful Life*. W.W. Norton, New York, 1989.

Hancock, Graham, and Bauval, Robert, *The Message Of The Sphinx*, Crown, New York, 1996.

Hapgood, Charles, *Maps Of The Ancient Sea Kings*, Turnstone Press, London, 1979. Reprinted by Adventures Unlimited Press, Kempton, IL, 1996.

Hall, Nina,(ed.), *Exploring Chaos*, W.W. Norton, New York, 1994.

Hawking, Stephen, *A Brief History of Time*, Bantam Books, New York, 1988.

Heyerdahl, Thor, *Early Man and the Ocean,* Doubleday, New York, 1979.

Heyerdahl, Thor, *The Ra Expeditions,* Doubleday, New York, 1971.

Hope, Murry, *Atlantis—Myth Or Reality*, Arkana, New York, 1991.

Hunter, Bruce. *A Guide To Ancient Maya Ruins*, University of Oklahoma Press, Norman, 1986.

Huyghe, Patrick, *Columbus Was Last*, Hyperion, New York, 1992.

Jaffe, Aniela, *The Myth of Meaning,* Penguin, New York, 1975.

Jairazbhoy R.A., *Ancient Egyptians And Chinese In America,* George Prior, London, 1974.

Lamb, Dana and Ginger, *Quest for the Lost City*, Santa Barbara Press, PO Box 1431, Summerland, CA, 93067.

Lang, Andrew, *Myth, Ritual & Religion*, Longmans, Green & Co., London, 1913.

Leakey, Richard, and Roger Lewin, *The Sixth Extinction*, Doubleday, New York, 1995.

Lewis, David, *We, The Navigators*, University of Hawaii Press, Honolulu, 1972.

Lockyer, Joseph N. The Dawn of Astronomy, Macmillan, London. 1894.

Los Angeles Times, Aug. 15, 1995.

Los Angeles Times, June 20, 1996.

Los Angeles Times, October 10, 1996.

Los Angeles Times, March 8, 1997.

Mallan, Chicki, *Cancun Handbook*, Moon Publications, Chico, CA, 1993.

McKibben, Bill, *Hope, Human And Wild*: True Stories of Living Lightly on the Earth, Little Brown, 1995.

Michell, John, *City of Revelation,* Sphere Books, London, 1973.

Marx, Robert F., *In Quest Of The Great White Gods*, Crown, New York, 1992.

Menzel, D. H., and Pasachoff, J. M., *Stars And Planets*, Houghton Mifflin, Boston, 1983.

Mexico City News, April 15, 1996.

Michell, John. *Megalithomania*, Thames & Hudson. London, 1982.

Michell, John, *Secrets of The Stones*, Penguin Books, New York, 1977.

Michell, John, *The View Over Atlantis*, Ballantine, New York, 1972.

Moorehead, Paul S., and Kaplan, Martin M., eds., *Mathematical Challenges to the Neo-Darwinian Interpretation of Evolution*, The Wistar Institute Press, Philadelphia, 1967.

Moseley, Michael, *Maritime Foundations Of Andean Civilization,* Cummings, Menlo Park, CA, 1975.

National Geographic Magazine, July, 1982, "In the Wake of Sinbad." pp. 2-41.

National Geographic Magazine, December, 1987 "Oldest Known Shipwreck" pp. 693-734.

National Geographic Magazine, September, 1987 "El Mirador: An Early Maya Metropolis Uncovered" pp. 317-339.

National Geographic Magazine, June 1988, "The Eternal Etruscans" pp. 96, 743.

National Geographic Magazine June, 1989 "The March Toward Extinction" pp. 662-699. "Malta Changes Again," pp. 700-716.

National Geographic Magazine, September, 1991 "Maya Artistry Unearthed" pp. 94-105.

National Geographic Magazine, Feb., 1993, "Violent Saga of a Maya Kingdom."

National Geographic Magazine, November, 1993, "New Light on the Olmecs" pp. 88-115.

National Geographic Magazine, July, 1996. Vol. 105, Num. 7.

Natural History Magazine, July, 1996, Vol. 105, Num. 7. "Up Against a Wall."

The New Encyclopedia Britanica, Vol. 26, Macropaedia—Knowledge in Depth, Chicago, 1993.

Nicholson, Irene, *Mexican And Central American Mythology,* Peter Bedrick Books, New York, 1985.

Norman, Howard A., *The Wishing Bone Cycle*, Ross-Erikson, Santa Barbara, 1982.

Pellegrino, Charles, *Unearthing Atlantis,* Random House, New York, 1991.

Plato, *Timeaus and Critias*, Desmond Lee (trans.), Penguin Books, New York. Rev. ed. 1977.

Popol Vuh, trans. by Dennis Tedlock, Touchstone, New York, 1986. p.150.

Popular Science, December, 1994.

Prescott, William H., *History of The Conquest of Mexico*, Harper & Row, New York, 1843.

Renfrew, Colin, and Bahn, Paul. *Archaeology: Theories, Methods and Practice,* Thames and Hudson, Ltd. London, 1991.

Riley, Carroll L., et al, eds., *Man Across the Sea,* University of Texas Press, Austin, 1971.

Rothenberg, Jerome, *Shaking The Pumpkin,* University of New Mexico Press. Albuquerque, 1991.

Ruthford, Adam, *Pyramidology*, London, The Institute of Pyramidology, 1957.

Santillana, Giorgio de and Dechend, Hertha von, *Hamlet's Mill*, David R. Godine, Boston, 1977.

Scheffler, Lilian, *Chichen Itza*, Panorama Editorial, Mexico, DF, 1992.

Science, Estrada, Emilio, Betty J. Meggers, and Clifford Evans. "Possible Transpacific Contact on the Coast of Ecuador." Vol. 135, February 2, 1962.

Science, Roosevelt, A.C., et al, "Paleoindian Cave Dwellers in the Amazon," Vol. 272, Num. 5260, April 19, 1996. pp. 373-384.

Scientific American, November, 1996. Vol. 275, Num. 5. "Rock Art in Southern Africa."

Scientific American, August, 1989.

Scientific American, March, 1996, "Collisions with Comets and Asteroids."

Sitchin, Zecharia, *Lost Realms*, Avon Books, New York.

Sitchin, Zecharia, *When Time Began,* Avon Books, New York, 1993.

Spence, Lewis, *The History of Atlantis,* reprinted by Adventures Unlimited Press, Kempton, IL, 1996.

Stephens, John L. *Incidents of Travel In Yucatán.* Dover Edition, New York, 1963.

Thompson, Gunnar. *Nu Sun, Asian Voyages 500 B.C.,* Pioneer Press, Fresno, CA, 1989.

Time, March 14, 1994.

Tompkins, Peter, *Mysteries of The Mexican Pyramids,* Harper & Row, New York. 1976.

Tompkins, Peter, *Secrets of the Great Pyramid*, Galahad Books, New York, 1997.

Tomas, Andrew, *Atlantis, From Legend To Discovery,* Robert Hale & Co. London. 1972.

USA Today, July 28, 1995.

Van Sertima, Ivan, *Journal of African Civilization*, 1984.

Van Sertima, Ivan, ed., *They Came Before Columbus*, Random House, New York, 1976.

Velentini, Felipe J., *Cuarto Viaje de Colon*, Imprenta Leharzum, San Jose, Costa Rica, 1943.

Velikovsky, Immanuel, *Mankind In Amnesia*, Doubleday, New York, 1982.

Vogt, Doug and Gary Sultan, *Reality Revealed,* Vector Associates, San Jose, CA. 1978.

Watts, Alan, *The Tao of Philosophy*, Charles E. Tuttle Co., Rutland, Vermont, 1995.

West, John, A. *Serpent In The Sky*, Julian Press, New York, 1987.

Zapata, Alonzo, Gualberto, *An Overview of the Mayan World*, Editorial Dante, Merida, Mexico, 1985.

Index

The Unusual Tour

The rediscovery of Atlantis is a ongoing effort to find traces of great naviga-tional cultures in the reconstructed temples and ruins of Mesoamerica. Erikson Expeditions invites your participation in this continuing adventure. The sites of the spheres of Costa Rica, the Atlanteans of Lake Nicaragua, and the "cities without walls" of Mesoamerica will be focal points in our author-escorted adventures. Traditional sites such as Copán (Honduras), Tikal (Guatemala), Tulum, Uxmal, Chichen Itza (Yucatán, and the Sun and Moon Pyramids of Teotihuacan, and the great Atlanteans at Tula (Valley of Mexico) will be revisited from a navigational point of view.

- Selected itineraries will also include the lesser known sites of Lubaantun, Cerros Maya, and Caracol in Belize; El Ceibal, El Mirador, and Uaxactun, in the Peten jungle; Muyil and Coba in the Yucatán; and other sites not yet identified.
- 7- to 12-day trips will begin December 19, 1998, and run through April, 1999. Prices will start at $1,195 including accommodations, transportation, all meals, and airfare within Latin America.

For more information on the tours and expeditions contact:

Toll Free: 1-888-684-3161 or
Contact George Erikson directly at:
1-760-251-9342
or visit the website at:
www.atlantisinamerica.com

CONSPIRACY & HISTORY

TECHNOLOGY OF THE GODS
The Incredible Sciences of the Ancients
by David Hatcher Childress

Popular *Lost Cities* author David Hatcher Childress takes us into the amazing world of ancient technology, from computers in antiquity to t "flying machines of the gods." Childress looks at the technology that was allegedly used in Atlantis and the theory that the Great Pyramid Egypt was originally a gigantic power station. He examines tales of ancient flight and the technology that it involved; how the ancients use electricity; megalithic building techniques; the use of crystal lenses and the fire from the gods; evidence of various high tech weapons in the pas including atomic weapons; ancient metallurgy and heavy machinery; the role of modern inventors such as Nikola Tesla in bringing ancie technology back into modern use; impossible artifacts; and more.

356 PAGES. 6x9 PAPERBACK. ILLUSTRATED. BIBLIOGRAPHY. $16.95. CODE: TGOD.

THE ORION PROPHECY
Egyptian & Mayan Prophecies on the Cataclysm of 2012
by Patrick Geryl and Gino Ratinckx

In the year 2012 the Earth awaits a super catastrophe: its magnetic field reverse in one go. Phenomenal earthquakes and tidal waves will completely destroy ou civilization. Europe and North America will shift thousands of kilometers northwards into polar climes. Nearly everyone will perish in the apocalyptic happen ings. These dire predictions stem from the Mayans and Egyptians—descendants of the legendary Atlantis. The Atlanteans had highly evolved astronomica knowledge and were able to exactly predict the previous world-wide flood in 9792 BC. Orion and several others stars will take the same 'code-positions' as i 9792 BC! For thousands of years historical sources have told of a forgotten time capsule of ancient wisdom located in a mythical labyrinth of secret chamber filled with artifacts and documents from the previous flood. We desperately need this information now—and this book gives one possible location.

324 PAGES. 6x9 PAPERBACK. ILLUSTRATED. BIBLIOGRAPHY. $16.95. CODE: ORP

THE HISTORY OF THE KNIGHTS TEMPLARS
by Charles G. Addison, introduction by David Hatcher Childress

Chapters on the origin of the Templars, their popularity in Europe and their rivalry with the Knights of St. John, later to be known as the Knights of Malta Detailed information on the activities of the Templars in the Holy Land, and the 1312 AD suppression of the Templars in France and other countrie which culminated in the execution of Jacques de Molay and the continuation of the Knights Templars in England and Scotland; the formation of the society of Knights Templars in London; and the rebuilding of the Temple in 1816. Plus a lengthy intro about the lost Templar fleet and its connection to the ancient North American sea routes.

395 PAGES. 6x9 PAPERBACK. ILLUSTRATED. $16.95. CODE: HKT

SAUNIER'S MODEL AND THE SECRET OF RENNES-LE-CHATEAU
The Priest's Final Legacy
by André Douzet

Berenger Saunière, the enigmatic priest of the French village of Rennes-le-Château, is rumored to have found the legendary treasure of the Cathars. But what became of it? In 1916, Sauniere created his ultimate clue: he went to great expense to create a model of a region said to be the Calvary Mount, indicating the "Tomb of Jesus." But the region on the model does not resemble the region of Jerusalem. Did Sauniere leave a clue as to the true location of his treasure? And what is that treasure? After years of research, André Douzet discovered this model— the only real clue Saunière left behind as to the nature and location of his treasure—and the possible tomb of Jesus.

116 PAGES. 6x9 PAPERBACK. ILLUSTRATED. BIBLIOGRAPHY. $12.00. CODE: SMOD

DARK MOON
Apollo and the Whistleblowers
by Mary Bennett and David Percy

•Was Neil Armstrong really the first man on the Moon?
•Did you know that 'live' color TV from the Moon was not actually live at all?
•Did you know that the Lunar Surface Camera had no viewfinder?
•Do you know that lighting was used in the Apollo photographs—yet no lighting equipment was taken to the Moon?
All these questions, and more, are discussed in great detail by British researchers Bennett and Percy in *Dark Moon*, the definitive book (nearly 600 pages) on the possible faking of the Apollo Moon missions. Bennett and Percy delve into every possible aspect of this beguiling theory, one that rocks the very foundation of our beliefs concerning NASA and the space program. Tons of NASA photos analyzed for possible deceptions.

568 PAGES. 6x9 PAPERBACK. ILLUSTRATED. BIBLIOGRAPHY. INDEX. $25.00. CODE: DMO

WAKE UP DOWN THERE!
The Excluded Middle Anthology
by Greg Bishop

The great American tradition of dropout culture makes it over the millennium mark with a collection of the best from *The Excluded Middle*, the critically acclaimed underground zine of UFOs, the paranormal, conspiracies, psychedelia, and spirit. Contributions from Robert Anton Wilson, Ivan Stang, Martin Kottmeyer, John Shirley, Scott Corrales, Adam Gorightly and Robert Sterling; and interviews with James Moseley, Karla Turner, Bill Moore, Kenn Thomas, Richard Boylan, Dean Radin, Joe McMoneagle, and the mysterious Ira Einhorn (an *Excluded Middle* exclusive). Includes full versions of interviews and extra material not found in the newsstand versions.

420 PAGES. 8x11 PAPERBACK. ILLUSTRATED. $25.00. CODE: WUDT

ARKTOS
The Myth of the Pole in Science, Symbolism, and Nazi Survival
by Joscelyn Godwin

A scholarly treatment of catastrophes, ancient myths and the Nazi Occult beliefs. Explored are the many tales of an ancient race said to have lived in the Arctic regions, such as Thule and Hyperborea. Progressing onward, the book looks at modern polar legends including the survival of Hitler, German bases in Antarctica, UFOs, the hollow earth, Agartha and Shambala, more.

220 PAGES. 6x9 PAPERBACK. ILLUSTRATED. $16.95. CODE: ARK

24 hour credit card orders—call: 815-253-6390 fax: 815-253-6300
email: auphq@frontiernet.net   www.adventuresunlimitedpress.com   www.wexclub.com

ATLANTIS: MOTHER OF EMPIRES
Atlantis Reprint Series
by Robert Stacy-Judd
Robert Stacy-Judd's classic 1939 book on Atlantis is back in print in this large-format paperback edition. Stacy-Judd was a California architect and an expert on the Mayas and their relationship to Atlantis. He was an excellent artist and his work is lavishly illustrated. The eighteen comprehensive chapters in the book are: The Mayas and the Lost Atlantis; Conjectures and Opinions; The Atlantean Theory; Cro-Magnon Man; East is West; And West is East; The Mormons and the Mayas; Astrology in Two Hemispheres; The Language of Architecture; The American Indian; Pre-Panamanians and Pre-Incas; Columns and City Planning; Comparisons and Mayan Art; The Iberian Link; The Maya Tongue; Quetzalcoatl; Summing Up the Evidence; The Mayas in Yucatan.
340 PAGES. 8X11 PAPERBACK. ILLUSTRATED. INDEX. $19.95. CODE: AMOE

SECRET CITIES OF OLD SOUTH AMERICA
Atlantis Reprint Series
by Harold T. Wilkins
The reprint of Wilkins' classic book, first published in 1952, claiming that South America was Atlantis. Chapters include Mysteries of a Lost World; Atlantis Unveiled; Red Riddles on the Rocks; South America's Amazons Existed!; The Mystery of El Dorado and Gran Payatiti—the Final Refuge of the Incas; Monstrous Beasts of the Unexplored Swamps & Wilds; Weird Denizens of Antediluvian Forests; New Light on Atlantis from the World's Oldest Book; The Mystery of Old Man Noah and the Arks; and more.
438 PAGES. 6X9 PAPERBACK. ILLUSTRATED. BIBLIOGRAPHY & INDEX. $16.95. CODE: SCOS

THE SHADOW OF ATLANTIS
The Echoes of Atlantean Civilization Tracked through Space & Time
by Colonel Alexander Braghine
First published in 1940, *The Shadow of Atlantis* is one of the great classics of Atlantis research. The book amasses a great deal of archaeological, anthropological, historical and scientific evidence in support of a lost continent in the Atlantic Ocean. Braghine covers such diverse topics as Egyptians in Central America, the myth of Quetzalcoatl, the Basque language and its connection with Atlantis, the connections with the ancient pyramids of Mexico, Egypt and Atlantis, the sudden demise of mammoths, legends of giants and much more. Braghine was a linguist and spends part of the book tracing ancient languages to Atlantis and studying little-known inscriptions in Brazil, deluge myths and the connections between ancient languages. Braghine takes us on a fascinating journey through space and time in search of the lost continent.
288 PAGES. 6X9 PAPERBACK. ILLUSTRATED. $16.95. CODE: SOA

RIDDLE OF THE PACIFIC
by John Macmillan Brown
Oxford scholar Brown's classic work on lost civilizations of the Pacific is now back in print! John Macmillan Brown was an historian and New Zealand's premier scientist when he wrote about the origins of the Maoris. After many years of travel thoughout the Pacific studying the people and customs of the south seas islands, he wrote *Riddle of the Pacific* in 1924. The book is packed with rare turn-of-the-century illustrations. Don't miss Brown's classic study of Easter Island, ancient scripts, megalithic roads and cities, more. Brown was an early believer in a lost continent in the Pacific.
460 PAGES. 6X9 PAPERBACK. ILLUSTRATED. $16.95. CODE: ROP

THE HISTORY OF ATLANTIS
by Lewis Spence
Lewis Spence's classic book on Atlantis is now back in print! Spence was a Scottish historian (1874-1955) who is best known for his volumes on world mythology and his five Atlantis books. *The History of Atlantis* (1926) is considered his finest. Spence does his scholarly best in chapters on the Sources of Atlantean History, the Geography of Atlantis, the Races of Atlantis, the Kings of Atlantis, the Religion of Atlantis, the Colonies of Atlantis, more. Sixteen chapters in all.
240 PAGES. 6X9 PAPERBACK. ILLUSTRATED WITH MAPS, PHOTOS & DIAGRAMS. $16.95. CODE: HOA

ATLANTIS IN SPAIN
A Study of the Ancient Sun Kingdoms of Spain
by E.M. Whishaw
First published by Rider & Co. of London in 1928, this classic book is a study of the megaliths of Spain, ancient writing, cyclopean walls, sun worshipping empires, hydraulic engineering, and sunken cities. An extremely rare book, it was out of print for 60 years. Learn about the Biblical Tartessus; an Atlantean city at Niebla; the Temple of Hercules and the Sun Temple of Seville; Libyans and the Copper Age; more. Profusely illustrated with photos, maps and drawings.
284 PAGES. 6X9 PAPERBACK. ILLUSTRATED. TABLES OF ANCIENT SCRIPTS. $15.95. CODE: AIS

ATLANTIS STUDIES

MAPS OF THE ANCIENT SEA KINGS
Evidence of Advanced Civilization in the Ice Age
by Charles H. Hapgood
Charles Hapgood's classic 1966 book on ancient maps produces concrete evidence of an advanced world-wide civilization existing many thousands of years before ancient Egypt. He has found the evidence in the Piri Reis Map that shows Antarctica, the Hadji Ahmed map, the Oronteus Finaeus and other amazing maps. Hapgood concluded that these maps were made from more ancient maps from the various ancient archives around the world, now lost. Not only were these unknown people more advanced in mapmaking than any people prior to the 18th century, it appears they mapped all the continents. The Americas were mapped thousands of years before Columbus. Antarctica was mapped when its coasts were free of ice.
316 PAGES. 7X10 PAPERBACK. ILLUSTRATED. BIBLIOGRAPHY & INDEX. $19.95. CODE: MASK

PATH OF THE POLE
Cataclysmic Pole Shift Geology
by Charles Hapgood
Maps of the Ancient Sea Kings author Hapgood's classic book *Path of the Pole* is back in print! Hapgood researched Antarctica, ancient maps and the geological record to conclude that the Earth's crust has slipped in the inner core many times in the past, changing the position of the pole. *Path of the Pole* discusses the various "pole shifts" in Earth's past, giving evidence for each one, and moves on to possible future pole shifts. Packed with illustrations, this is the sourcebook for many other books on cataclysms and pole shifts.
356 PAGES. 6X9 PAPERBACK. ILLUSTRATED. $16.95. CODE: POP.

ATLANTIS: THE ANDES SOLUTION
The Theory and the Evidence
by J.M. Allen, forward by John Blashford-Snell
Imported from Britain, this deluxe hardback is J.M. Allen's fascinating research into the lost world that exists on the Bolivian Plateau and his theory that it is Atlantis. Allen looks into Lake Titicaca, the ruins of Tiahuanaco and the mysterious Lake PooPoo. The high plateau of Bolivia must contain the remains of Atlantis, claims Allen. Lots of fascinating stuff here with Allen discovering the remains of huge ancient canals that once crisscrossed the vast plain southwest of Tiahuanaco. A must-read for all researchers into South America, Atlantis and mysteries of the past. With lots of illustrations, some in color.
196 PAGES. 6X9 HARDBACK. ILLUSTRATED. BIBLIOGRAPHY. $25.99. CODE: ATAS

ATLANTIS IN AMERICA
Navigators of the Ancient World
by Ivar Zapp and George Erikson
This book is an intensive examination of the archeological sites of the Americas, an examination that reveals civilization has existed here for tens of thousands of years. Zapp is an expert on the enigmatic giant stone spheres of Costa Rica, and maintains that they were sighting stones similar to those found throughout the Pacific as well as in Egypt and the Middle East. They were used to teach star-paths and sea navigation to the world-wide navigators of the ancient world. While the Mediterranean and European regions "forgot" world-wide navigation and fought wars, the Mesoamericans of diverse races were building vast interconnected cities without walls. This Golden Age of ancient America was merely a myth of suppressed history—until now. Profusely illustrated, chapters are on Navigators of the Ancient World; Pyramids & Megaliths: Older Than You Think; Ancient Ports and Colonies; Cataclysms of the Past; Atlantis: From Myth to Reality; The Serpent and the Cross: The Loss of the City States; Calendars and Star Temples; and more.
360 PAGES. 6X9 PAPERBACK. ILLUSTRATED. BIBLIOGRAPHY & INDEX. $17.95. CODE: AIA

FAR-OUT ADVENTURES   REVISED EDITION
The Best of World Explorer Magazine
This is a compilation of the first nine issues of *World Explorer* in a large-format paperback. Authors include: David Hatcher Childress, Joseph Jochmans, John Major Jenkins, Deanna Emerson, Katherine Routledge, Alexander Horvat, Greg Deyermenjian, Dr. Marc Miller, and others. Articles in this book include Smithsonian Gate, Dinosaur Hunting in the Congo, Secret Writings of the Incas, On the Trail of the Yeti, Secrets of the Sphinx, Living Pterodactyls, Quest for Atlantis, What Happened to the Great Library of Alexandria?, In Search of Seamonsters in the Pacific, Lost Megaliths of Guatemala, the Mystery of Easter Island, Comacalco: Mayan City of Mystery, Professor Wexler and plenty more.
580 PAGES. 8X11 PAPERBACK. ILLUSTRATED. REVISED EDITION. $25.00. CODE: FOA

RETURN OF THE SERPENTS OF WISDOM
by Mark Amaru Pinkham
According to ancient records, the patriarchs and founders of the early civilizations in Egypt, India, China, Peru, Mesopotamia, Britain, and the Americas were the Serpents of Wisdom—spiritual masters associated with the serpent—who arrived in these lands after abandoning their beloved homelands and crossing great seas. While bearing names denoting snake or dragon (such as Naga, Lung, Djedhi, Amaru, Quetzalcoatl, Adder, etc.), these Serpents of Wisdom oversaw the construction of magnificent civilizations within which they and their descendants served as the priest kings and as the enlightened heads of mystery school traditions. The *Return of the Serpents of Wisdom* recounts the history of these "Serpents"—where they came from, why they came, the secret wisdom they disseminated, and why they are returning now.
400 PAGES. 6X9 PAPERBACK. ILLUSTRATED. REFERENCES. $16.95. CODE: RSW

LOST CITIES OF ATLANTIS, ANCIENT EUROPE & THE MEDITERRANEAN
by David Hatcher Childress

Atlantis! The legendary lost continent comes under the close scrutiny of maverick archaeologist David Hatcher Childress in this sixth book in the internationally popular *Lost Cities* series. Childress takes the reader in search of sunken cities in the Mediterranean; across the Atlas Mountains in search of Atlantean ruins; to remote islands in search of megalithic ruins; to meet living legends and secret societies. From Ireland to Turkey, Morocco to Eastern Europe, and around the remote islands of the Mediterranean and Atlantic, Childress takes the reader on an astonishing quest for mankind's past. Ancient technology, cataclysms, megalithic construction, lost civilizations and devastating wars of the past are all explored in this book. Childress challenges the skeptics and proves that great civilizations not only existed in the past, but the modern world and its problems are reflections of the ancient world of Atlantis.
524 PAGES. 6x9 PAPERBACK. ILLUSTRATED WITH 100S OF MAPS, PHOTOS AND DIAGRAMS. BIBLIOGRAPHY & INDEX. $16.95. CODE: MED

LOST CITIES OF CHINA, CENTRAL INDIA & ASIA
by David Hatcher Childress

Like a real life "Indiana Jones," maverick archaeologist David Childress takes the reader on an incredible adventure across some of the world's oldest and most remote countries in search of lost cities and ancient mysteries. Discover ancient cities in the Gobi Desert; hear fantastic tales of lost continents, vanished civilizations and secret societies bent on ruling the world; visit forgotten monasteries in forbidding snow-capped mountains with strange tunnels to mysterious subterranean cities!
A unique combination of far-out exploration and practical travel advice, it will astound and delight the experienced traveler or the armchair voyager.
429 PAGES. 6x9 PAPERBACK. ILLUSTRATED. FOOTNOTES & BIBLIOGRAPHY. $14.95. CODE: CHI

LOST CITIES OF ANCIENT LEMURIA & THE PACIFIC
by David Hatcher Childress

Was there once a continent in the Pacific? Called Lemuria or Pacifica by geologists, Mu or Pan by the mystics, there is now ample mythological, geological and archaeological evidence to "prove" that an advanced and ancient civilization once lived in the central Pacific. Maverick archaeologist and explorer David Hatcher Childress combs the Indian Ocean, Australia and the Pacific in search of the surprising truth about mankind's past. Contains photos of the underwater city on Pohnpei; explanations on how the statues were levitated around Easter Island in a clockwise vortex movement; tales of disappearing islands; Egyptians in Australia; and more.
379 PAGES. 6x9 PAPERBACK. ILLUSTRATED. FOOTNOTES & BIBLIOGRAPHY. $14.95. CODE: LEM

ANCIENT TONGA
& the Lost City of Mu'a
by David Hatcher Childress

Lost Cities series author Childress takes us to the south sea islands of Tonga, Rarotonga, Samoa and Fiji to investigate the megalithic ruins on these beautiful islands. The great empire of the Polynesians, centered on Tonga and the ancient city of Mu'a, is revealed with old photos, drawings and maps. Chapters in this book are on the Lost City of Mu'a and its many megalithic pyramids, the Ha'amonga Trilithon and ancient Polynesian astronomy, Samoa and the search for the lost land of Havai'iki, Fiji and its wars with Tonga, Rarotonga's megalithic road, and Polynesian cosmology. Material on Egyptians in the Pacific, earth changes, the fortified moat around Mu'a, lost roads, more.
218 PAGES. 6x9 PAPERBACK. ILLUSTRATED. COLOR PHOTOS. BIBLIOGRAPHY. $15.95. CODE: TONG

ANCIENT MICRONESIA
& the Lost City of Nan Madol
by David Hatcher Childress

Micronesia, a vast archipelago of islands west of Hawaii and south of Japan, contains some of the most amazing megalithic ruins in the world. Part of our *Lost Cities* series, this volume explores the incredible conformations on various Micronesian islands, especially the fantastic and little-known ruins of Nan Madol on Pohnpei Island. The huge canal city of Nan Madol contains over 250 million tons of basalt columns over an 11 square-mile area of artificial islands. Much of the huge city is submerged, and underwater structures can be found to an estimated 80 feet. Islanders' legends claim that the basalt rocks, weighing up to 50 tons, were magically levitated into place by the powerful forefathers. Other ruins in Micronesia that are profiled include the Latte Stones of the Marianas, the menhirs of Palau, the megalithic canal city on Kosrae Island, megaliths on Guam, and more.
256 PAGES. 6x9 PAPERBACK. ILLUSTRATED. INCLUDES A COLOR PHOTO SECTION. BIBLIOGRAPHY. $16.95. CODE: AMIC

VIMANA AIRCRAFT OF ANCIENT INDIA & ATLANTIS
by David Hatcher Childress
introduction by Ivan T. Sanderson

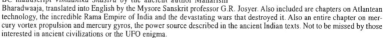

Did the ancients have the technology of flight? In this incredible volume on ancient India, authentic Indian texts such as the *Ramayana* and the *Mahabharata* are used to prove that ancient aircraft were in use more than four thousand years ago. Included in this book is the entire Fourth Century BC manuscript *Vimaanika Shastra* by the ancient author Maharishi Bharadwaaja, translated into English by the Mysore Sanskrit professor G.R. Josyer. Also included are chapters on Atlantean technology, the incredible Rama Empire of India and the devastating wars that destroyed it. Also an entire chapter on mercury vortex propulsion and mercury gyros, the power source described in the ancient Indian texts. Not to be missed by those interested in ancient civilizations or the UFO enigma.
334 PAGES. 6x9 PAPERBACK. RARE PHOTOGRAPHS, MAPS AND DRAWINGS. $15.95. CODE: VAA

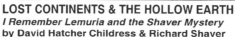

LOST CONTINENTS & THE HOLLOW EARTH
I Remember Lemuria and the Shaver Mystery
by David Hatcher Childress & Richard Shaver

Lost Continents & the Hollow Earth is Childress' thorough examination of the early hollow earth stories of Richard Shaver and the fascination that fringe fantasy subjects such as lost continents and the hollow earth have had for the American public. Shaver's rare 1948 book *I Remember Lemuria* is reprinted in its entirety, and the book is packed with illustrations from Ray Palmer's *Amazing Stories* magazine of the 1940s. Palmer and Shaver told of tunnels running through the earth—tunnels inhabited by the Deros and Teros, humanoids from an ancient spacefaring race that had inhabited the earth, eventually going underground, hundreds of thousands of years ago. Childress discusses the famous hollow earth books and delves deep into whatever reality may be behind the stories of tunnels in the earth. Operation High Jump to Antarctica in 1947 and Admiral Byrd's bizarre statements, tunnel systems in South America and Tibet, the underground world of Agartha, the belief of UFOs coming from the South Pole, more.
344 PAGES. 6x9 PAPERBACK. ILLUSTRATED. $16.95. CODE: LCHE

LOST CITIES OF NORTH & CENTRAL AMERICA
by David Hatcher Childress
Down the back roads from coast to coast, maverick archaeologist and adventurer David Hatcher Childress goes deep into unknown America. With this incredible book, you will search for lost Mayan cities and books of gold, discover an ancient canal system in Arizona, climb gigantic pyramids in the Midwest, explore megalithic monuments in New England, and join the astonishing quest for lost cities throughout North America. From the war-torn jungles of Guatemala, Nicaragua and Honduras to the deserts, mountains and fields of Mexico, Canada, and the U.S.A., Childress takes the reader in search of sunken ruins, Viking forts, strange tunnel systems, living dinosaurs, early Chinese explorers, and fantastic lost treasure. Packed with both early and current maps, photos and illustrations.
590 PAGES. 6x9 PAPERBACK. PHOTOS, MAPS, AND ILLUSTRATIONS. FOOTNOTES & BIBLIOGRAPHY. $14.95. CODE: NCA

LOST CITIES & ANCIENT MYSTERIES OF SOUTH AMERICA
by David Hatcher Childress
Rogue adventurer and maverick archaeologist David Hatcher Childress takes the reader on unforgettable journeys deep into deadly jungles, high up on windswept mountains and across scorching deserts in search of lost civilizations and ancient mysteries. Travel with David and explore stone cities high in mountain forests and hear fantastic tales of Inca treasure, living dinosaurs, and a mysterious tunnel system. Whether he is hopping freight trains, searching for secret cities, or just dealing with the daily problems of food, money, and romance, the author keeps the reader spellbound. Includes both early and current maps, photos, and illustrations, and plenty of advice for the explorer planning his or her own journey of discovery.
381 PAGES. 6x9 PAPERBACK. PHOTOS, MAPS, AND ILLUSTRATIONS. FOOTNOTES & BIBLIOGRAPHY. $14.95. CODE: SAM

LOST CITIES & ANCIENT MYSTERIES OF AFRICA & ARABIA
by David Hatcher Childress
Across ancient deserts, dusty plains and steaming jungles, maverick archaeologist David Childress continues his world-wide quest for lost cities and ancient mysteries. Join him as he discovers forbidden cities in the Empty Quarter of Arabia; "Atlantean" ruins in Egypt and the Kalahari desert; a mysterious, ancient empire in the Sahara; and more. This is the tale of an extraordinary life on the road: across war-torn countries, Childress searches for King Solomon's Mines, living dinosaurs, the Ark of the Covenant and the solutions to some of the fantastic mysteries of the past.
423 PAGES. 6x9 PAPERBACK. PHOTOS, MAPS, AND ILLUSTRATIONS. FOOTNOTES & BIBLIOGRAPHY. $14.95. CODE: AFA

THE MYSTERY OF EASTER ISLAND

by Katherine Routledge

The reprint of Katherine Routledge's classic archaeology book which was first published in London in 1919. The book details her journey by yacht from England to South America, around Patagonia to Chile and on to Easter Island. Routledge explored the amazing island and produced one of the first-ever accounts of the life, history and legends of this strange and remote place. Routledge discusses the statues, pyramid-platforms, Rongo Rongo script, the Bird Cult, the war between the Short Ears and the Long Ears, the secret caves, ancient roads on the island, and more. This rare book serves as a sourcebook on the early discoveries and theories on Easter Island.

432 PAGES. 6x9 PAPERBACK. ILLUSTRATED. $16.95. CODE: MEI

MYSTERY CITIES
OF THE MAYA
by Thomas Gann

Mystic Travellers Series

MYSTERY CITIES OF THE MAYA

Exploration and Adventure in Lubaantun & Belize
by Thomas Gann

First published in 1925, *Mystery Cities of the Maya* is a classic in Central American archaeology-adventure. Gann was close friends with Mike Mitchell-Hedges, the British adventurer who discovered the famous crystal skull with his adopted daughter Sammy and Lady Richmond Brown, their benefactress. Gann battles pirates along Belize's coast and goes upriver with Mitchell-Hedges to the site of Lubaantun where they excavate a strange lost city where the crystal skull was discovered. Lubaantun is a unique city in the Mayan world as it is built out of precisely carved blocks of stone without the usual plaster-cement facing. Lubaantun contained several large pyramids partially destroyed by earthquakes and a large amount of artifacts. Gann shared Mitchell-Hedges belief in Atlantis and lost civilizations (pre-Mayan) in Central America and the Caribbean. Lots of good photos, maps and diagrams.

252 PAGES. 6x9 PAPERBACK. ILLUSTRATED. $16.95. CODE: MCOM

IN SECRET TIBET

by Theodore Illion

Reprint of a rare 30s adventure travel book. Illion was a German wayfarer who not only spoke fluent Tibetan, but travelled in disguise as a native through forbidden Tibet when it was off-limits to all outsiders. His incredible adventures make this one of the most exciting travel books ever published. Includes illustrations of Tibetan monks levitating stones by acoustics.

210 PAGES. 6x9 PAPERBACK. ILLUSTRATED. $15.95. CODE: IST

Danger My Ally

DARKNESS OVER TIBET

by Theodore Illion

In this second reprint of Illion's rare books, the German traveller continues his journey through Tibet and is given directions to a strange underground city. As the original publisher's remarks said, "this is a rare account of an underground city in Tibet by the only Westerner ever to enter it and escape alive! "

210 PAGES. 6x9 PAPERBACK. ILLUSTRATED. $15.95. CODE: DOT

DANGER MY ALLY

The Amazing Life Story of the Discoverer of the Crystal Skull
by "Mike" Mitchell-Hedges

The incredible life story of "Mike" Mitchell-Hedges, the British adventurer who discovered the Crystal Skull in the lost Mayan city of Lubaantun in Belize. Mitchell-Hedges has lived an exciting life: gambling everything on a trip to the Americas as a young man, riding with Pancho Villa, questing for Atlantis, fighting bandits in the Caribbean and discovering the famous Crystal Skull.

374 PAGES. 6x9 PAPERBACK. ILLUSTRATED. BIBLIOGRAPHY & INDEX. $16.95. CODE: DMA

The true life adventure of
F.A. Mitchell-Hedges

IN SECRET
MONGOLIA
Henning Haslund

Mystic Traveller Series

IN SECRET MONGOLIA

by Henning Haslund

Danish-Swedish explorer Haslund's first book on his exciting explorations in Mongolia and Central Asia. Haslund takes us via camel caravan to the medieval world of Mongolia, a country still barely known today. First published by Kegan Paul of London in 1934, this rare travel adventure is back in print after 50 years. Haslund and his camel caravan journey across the Gobi Desert. He meets with renegade generals and warlords, god-kings and shamans. Haslund is captured, held for ransom, thrown into prison, battles black magic and portrays in vivid detail the birth of a new nation.

374 PAGES. 6x9 PAPERBACK. ILLUSTRATED. BIBLIOGRAPHY & INDEX. $16.95. CODE: ISM

MEN and GODS
IN MONGOLIA
Henning Haslund

This rare 1935 book is back in print!
Mystic Traveller Series

MEN & GODS IN MONGOLIA

by Henning Haslund

First published in 1935 by Kegan Paul of London, Haslund takes us to the lost city of Karakota in the Gobi desert. We meet the Bodgo Gegen, a god-king in Mongolia similar to the Dalai Lama of Tibet. We meet Dambin Jansang, the dreaded warlord of the "Black Gobi." There is even material in this incredible book on the Hi-mori, an "airhorse" that flies through the sky (similar to a Vimana) and carries with it the sacred stone of Chintamani. Aside from the esoteric and mystical material, there is plenty of just plain adventure: Haslund and companions journey across the Gobi desert by camel caravan; are kidnapped and held for ransom; witness initiation into Shamanic societies; meet reincarnated warlords; and experience the violent birth of "modern" Mongolia.

358 PAGES. 6x9 PAPERBACK. 57 PHOTOS, ILLUSTRATIONS AND MAPS. $15.95. CODE: MGM

THE FREE-ENERGY DEVICE HANDBOOK

A Compilation of Patents and Reports
by David Hatcher Childress

A large-format compilation of various patents, papers, descriptions and diagrams concerning free-energy devices and systems. *The Free-Energy Device Handbook* is a visual tool for experimenters and researchers into magnetic motors and other "overunity" devices. With chapters on the Adams Motor, the Hans Coler Generator, cold fusion, superconductors, "N" machines, space-energy generators, Nikola Tesla, T. Townsend Brown, and the latest in free-energy devices. Packed with photos, technical diagrams, patents and fascinating information, this book belongs on every science shelf. With energy and profit being a major political reason for fighting various wars, free-energy devices, if ever allowed to be mass distributed to consumers, could change the world! Get your copy now before the Department of Energy bans this book!
292 PAGES. 8X10 PAPERBACK. ILLUSTRATED. BIBLIOGRAPHY. $16.95. CODE: FEH

THE ANTI-GRAVITY HANDBOOK

edited by David Hatcher Childress, with Nikola Tesla, T.B. Paulicki,
Bruce Cathie, Albert Einstein and others

The new expanded compilation of material on Anti-Gravity, Free Energy, Flying Saucer Propulsion, UFOs, Suppressed Technology, NASA Cover-ups and more. Highly illustrated with patents, technical illustrations and photos. This revised and expanded edition has more material, including photos of Area 51, Nevada, the government's secret testing facility. This classic on weird science is back in a 90s format!

- How to build a flying saucer.
- Arthur C. Clarke on Anti-Gravity.
- Crystals and their role in levitation.
- Secret government research and development.
- Nikola Tesla on how anti-gravity airships could draw power from the atmosphere.
- Bruce Cathie's Anti-Gravity Equation.
- NASA, the Moon and Anti-Gravity.

230 PAGES. 7X10 PAPERBACK. BIBLIOGRAPHY/INDEX/APPENDIX. HIGHLY ILLUSTRATED. $14.95. CODE: AGH

ANTI-GRAVITY & THE WORLD GRID

Is the earth surrounded by an intricate electromagnetic grid network offering free energy? This compilation of material on ley lines and world power points contains chapters on the geography, mathematics, and light harmonics of the earth grid. Learn the purpose of ley lines and ancient megalithic structures located on the grid. Discover how the grid made the Philadelphia Experiment possible. Explore the Coral Castle and many other mysteries, including acoustic levitation, Tesla Shields and scalar wave weaponry. Browse through the section on anti-gravity patents, and research resources.
274 PAGES. 7X10 PAPERBACK. ILLUSTRATED. $14.95. CODE: AGW

ANTI-GRAVITY & THE UNIFIED FIELD

edited by David Hatcher Childress

Is Einstein's Unified Field Theory the answer to all of our energy problems? Explored in this compilation of material is how gravity, electricity and magnetism manifest from a unified field around us. Why artificial gravity is possible; secrets of UFO propulsion; free energy; Nikola Tesla and anti-gravity airships of the 20s and 30s; flying saucers as superconducting whirls of plasma; anti-mass generators; vortex propulsion; suppressed technology; government cover-ups; gravitational pulse drive; spacecraft & more.
240 PAGES. 7X10 PAPERBACK. ILLUSTRATED. $14.95. CODE: AGU

ETHER TECHNOLOGY

A Rational Approach to Gravity Control
by Rho Sigma

This classic book on anti-gravity and free energy is back in print and back in stock. Written by a well-known American scientist under the pseudonym of "Rho Sigma," this book delves into international efforts at gravity control and discoid craft propulsion. Before the Quantum Field, there was "Ether." This small, but informative book has chapters on John Searle and "Searle discs;" T. Townsend Brown and his work on antigravity and ether-vortex turbines. Includes a forward by former NASA astronaut Edgar Mitchell.
108 PAGES. 6X9 PAPERBACK. ILLUSTRATED. $12.95. CODE: ETT

One Adventure Place
P.O. Box 74
Kempton, Illinois 60946
United States of America
Tel.: 815-253-6390 • Fax: 815-253-6300
Email: auphq@frontiernet.net
http://www.adventuresunlimitedpress.com
or www.adventuresunlimited.nl

ORDERING INSTRUCTIONS

✓ Remit by USD$ Check, Money Order or Credit Card

✓ Visa, Master Card, Discover & AmEx Accepted

✓ Prices May Change Without Notice

✓ 10% Discount for 3 or more Items

SHIPPING CHARGES

United States

✓ Postal Book Rate { $3.00 First Item
50¢ Each Additional Item

✓ Priority Mail { $4.00 First Item
$2.00 Each Additional Item

✓ UPS { $5.00 First Item
$1.50 Each Additional Item

NOTE: UPS Delivery Available to Mainland USA Only

Canada

✓ Postal Book Rate { $6.00 First Item
$2.00 Each Additional Item

✓ Postal Air Mail { $8.00 First Item
$2.50 Each Additional Item

✓ Personal Checks or Bank Drafts MUST BE

USD$ and Drawn on a US Bank
✓ Canadian Postal Money Orders OK

✓ Payment MUST BE USD$

All Other Countries

✓ Surface Delivery { $10.00 First Item
$4.00 Each Additional Item

✓ Postal Air Mail { $14.00 First Item
$5.00 Each Additional Item

✓ Payment MUST BE USD$

✓ Checks and Money Orders MUST BE USD$
and Drawn on a US Bank or branch.

✓ Add $5.00 for Air Mail Subscription to
Future *Adventures Unlimited* Catalogs

SPECIAL NOTES

✓ RETAILERS: Standard Discounts Available
✓ BACKORDERS: We Backorder all Out-of-

Stock Items Unless Otherwise Requested
✓ PRO FORMA INVOICES: Available on Request
✓ VIDEOS: NTSC Mode Only. Replacement only.

✓ For PAL mode videos contact our other offices:

Please check: ☑

☐ This is my first order ☐ I have ordered before

Name

Address

City

State/Province   Postal Code

Country

Phone day   Evening

Fax

Item Code	Item Description	Qty	Total

Please check: ☑

☐ Postal-Surface

☐ Postal-Air Mail
(Priority in USA)

☐ UPS
(Mainland USA only)

Subtotal ➡

Less Discount-10% for 3 or more items ➡

Balance ➡

Illinois Residents 6.25% Sales Tax ➡

Previous Credit ➡

Shipping ➡

Total (check/MO in USD$ only) ➡

☐ Visa/MasterCard/Discover/Amex

Card Number

Expiration Date

10% Discount When You Order 3 or More Items!